C-GNBX

DASH 7

The de Havilland
Canada Story

The de Havilland Canada Story

Fred W. Hotson

CANAV Books

To Charles Donald Long, 1911-1972,
DH Canada engineer and historian
whose work is reflected in much of
this book.

Canadian Cataloguing in Publication Data

Hotson, Fred W., 1913-
   The De Havilland Canada story

Bibliography: p.
Includes index.
ISBN 0-9690703-2-2

1. De Havilland Aircraft of Canada, Limited -
History. I. Title.

HD9711.C34D45   338.7'62913'009713541   C83-098231-0

Designed and edited by Robin Brass
Typesetting by Arlene Weber, Second
   Story Graphics
Photo retouching by Stephen Ng,
   SNG Retouching Studio;
   and Colin Clark
Repro assembly by Rob Devine and
   Betty Mason, Printart
Additional proofreading by Ralph Clint
   and N.K. Found

Printed in Canada by the Bryant Press
   Limited, Toronto

Published by
CANAV Books,
Larry Milberry, publisher
51 Balsam Avenue
Toronto M4E 3B6
Canada

Front endpaper
Dash 7 demonstrator in brilliant colour
scheme cruises over Lake Ontario in this
famous Ron Nunney photo. (DHC)

Title page
Striking view of de Havilland Canada's
DHC-5D Buffalo demonstrator. (DHC 44189)

Below
Australia still operates a large fleet of
Caribous which continue to prove their value
in rugged, short-field situations. (Australian
Department of Defence)

Opposite page
Photographic Surveys' Fox Moth in a typical
Canadian setting. (Northway Survey Corp.)

Overleaf
A Beaver floatplane takes off in this typical
Canadian bush scene. (DHC 3905)

Back endpaper
The L-20 Beaver was the backbone of US
Army air liaison operations for many years.
Dave Fairbanks is at the controls in this
superb L-20 portrait. (DHC 8936)

Contents

Foreword

When I was a youngster building model aircraft from boxwood in Edmonton, de Havilland was a familiar name to aviation enthusiasts like myself. I used to dream of flying one of their Moths and, sure enough, a few years later, I took my training in a Royal Canadian Air Force de Havilland "Tigerschmitt."

Of the many aircraft types available for commercial service immediately after World War 2, the only one in its class that could serve the Canadian north economically on wheels, skis and floats was the dependable old de Havilland Fox Moth. I bought one of these aircraft in 1946 and, as de Havilland built more advanced utility aircraft through the years, Wardair progressed by buying and operating them commercially.

The people at de Havilland did more than build flying machines — they designed into their aircraft a certain capability to serve safely and economically in underdeveloped areas. This specialty which they demonstrated in Canada was soon put to use throughout the world.

I look back with nostalgia to those wonderful, exciting visits to Downsview when we would sit around Phil Garratt's big round table discussing the merits of flying machines with him and his creative people. I am also proud to have been in some small way a part of the story. When the world needed sound, dependable aircraft to transport passengers and freight into underdeveloped areas, de Havilland Canada provided them. I look forward to their aircraft of the future.

A lot of important history occurred at de Havilland in the years before I knew them and much went on behind the scenes to bring them success over 50 years. I am pleased to see the history of this distinguished aircraft manufacturing company recorded at such length and to read the fascinating stories of the people who lay behind its success.

Maxwell W. Ward

Preface

You might say this book began with a letter dated January 6, 1932, which I received from the de Havilland Aircraft of Canada Ltd. It was a reply to my request for employment at their new location in Downsview and was signed by the chief engineer, V.O. Levick. Mr. Levick was very polite in telling me that he had no position to offer. He noted my enthusiasm and promised to get in touch if the company were ever to increase their staff.

Fifty years later, it is my privilege to record the history of de Havilland Canada and to understand why Mr. Levick could not offer anyone a job in 1932. It was only through research that I found out how difficult that year was for the small plant on Sheppard Avenue.

The wheel of fate turned in my direction in 1935 when some Moth overhaul work for the RCAF brought an improvement in the affairs of DHC. I happened to be one of two chosen that year from a Toronto school to join the de Havilland work force.

The next five years provided exhilarating experience as we worked on everything from the small Moths to the big Rapides, but we learned our trade well under tough discipline and long hours. Lee Murray was managing director, chief engineer and test pilot when I joined. Bill Calder was in charge of the shops while Bruce Douglas and Don Long shared the engineering office. George Blanchard, John Slaughter, Harry Proctor, Frank Warren, Russ Borrett, Harry Beffort and Walter Rinaldo were all regulars at that time and there were the girls in the fabric shop—Hilda Currell, the McNichol sisters, Rhoda and Betty, Lou Thorpe and Ethel Almond. The period was not noted for big pay cheques but what we lacked on the financial side was made up with the knowledge that we were part of the growing aviation scene.

With the outbreak of war I moved to active flying which took me far from the time clock at de Havilland. I left with the blessings of Phil Garratt, but by the time I returned to the company in 1967 he had retired. I was not returning as a stranger, however, for I had visited Downsview regularly during the intervening years and always kept in touch with my friends at DH Canada. My return provided new associations as I joined in flying the Twin Otter and generally making myself useful until retirement.

All of this provided the background for a booklet on the 50-year company history which I prepared during my final year at DHC. It set the scene for a talk one day in 1980 with the new president, John W. Sandford, who encouraged me to continue my research. Cooperation came from every quarter and it was collectively agreed that the story behind de Havilland Canada should be recorded in greater depth.

No effort has been made to duplicate the existing good works on either the DH England years or the production details of their extensive product line. These can be obtained in books by Martin Sharp, A.J. Jackson, K.M. Molson, H.A. Taylor, and Sir Geoffrey de Havilland himself in *Sky Fever*. This is mainly a story of people — the thousands who carried the original de Havilland tradition through more than 50 years, made it grow with new designs of their own and brought it into the 1980s. I have also tried to relate the impact of these aircraft on world transport and touch briefly on some of the 6940 aircraft that have emerged from the production lines since 1939. A volume could be written on each of the DH Canada designs — the Twin Otter, for example, is adding daily to its astounding history. Some day they will all have a book of their own.

The historian, of necessity, becomes an analyst of his subject and sees it all in the light of hindsight. Any views presented here are, therefore, the result of research and do not reflect company policy, either past or present. Every effort has been made to obtain accuracy and, as the history of DH Canada will continue to be recorded in the years to come, I welcome any corrections or additions.

The production of this book could not have taken place without the effort and cooperation of many people. John Sandford sparked the idea and provided company cooperation, but my friends in all areas of aviation, including the Canadian Aviation Historical Society, assisted in a number of ways. The research goes back to the years when I collaborated with the late Don Long in gathering material on de Havilland history. He left his writings and photographs in my custody and I have used them to advantage. The old-timers at British Aerospace still remember the big DH on the building at Hatfield and were most cooperative. During the last hectic months before publication the de Havilland Canada photographic department, under Ron Nunney, and the publications department, under Dennis Field, provided major assistance with photographs and illustrations. In a refreshing display of enterprise, Larry Milberry and his associates at Canav Books did the impossible with deadlines while editor Robin Brass kept us all on track. I have talked and corresponded with hundreds of people about DH Canada and my thanks go out to the following who helped in many ways with pictures and information:

Peter Adams, Gary Aldred, Len Appleyard, Tom Appleton, C.J. Austin, Ernest Ball, Rusty Blakey, Russ Bannock, R.W. "Dick" Becker, Harry Beffort, Sheldon Benner, L.B. Best, Philip J. Birtles, George Blanchard, W.B. Boggs, Lou Thorpe Borrett, Russ Borrett, W. "Bill" Bozanin, R.W. "Bob" Bradford, Doug Bromley, D.L. "Buck"

8

Buchanan, Fred H. Buller, W.C. "Bill" Burlison, Alan S. Butler, Jack C. Charleson, Ralph Clint, Reg E. Corlett, Peter Crampton, George A. Cull, John Cunningham, W. Czerwinski, M.C.W. "Mike" Davy, Norm H. Davis, Fred deJersey, C.H. "Punch" Dickins, Alex Downey, John Drummond, W. "Bill" Duck, Brian Eggleston, John Ellis, Bill Etherington, Betty Ewens, W. Dennis Field, W.P.I. "Pat" Fillingham, Colin Fisher, N.K. Found, R.H. "Bob" Fowler, Ronald J. Fox, Joe Fugere, Paddy Gardiner, Jessie Garratt, John Garratt, Andre Gaudet, Geoff Goodall, Bartlett Gould, Robert S. Grant, V. Gregg, John A. Griffin, Phil E. Halsey, W.T. "Bill" Heaslip, R.D. "Dick" Hiscocks, Tony Honeywood, Marg Hotson, W.J. "Bill" Houston, George Hurren, G. "Ron" Jackson, F.A. "Ted" Johnson, Mike Kasiuba, Peter R. Keating, Enid Koyl, Z. Lewis Leigh, John Loader, Ron Lowry, George W. Luesby, Nick MacDonald-Wolochatiuk, Jim Maitre, Peter S. Martin, Shirley Matthews, W. Matthews, R.B. "Bob" McIntyre, Betty McNichol, Rhoda McNichol, Jack McNulty, David Menard, Norm Merrin, George J. Mickleborough, Larry Milberry, R.J. Moffett, K.M. "Ken" Molson, Sab Morita, Peter Mossman, W. "Don" Murray, Kay Neal, John F. Neal, George A. Neal, Ron Nunney, Cathy Parsons, Harry E. Proctor, Bob Prout, G.B. Rayner, George W. Robinson, Frank Russell, Terry Rawlins, A. Saunders, John E. Scott, C. Martin Sharp, John F.B. Shaw, W.F. Shaylor, Fred Shortt, Rae R. Simpson, John Slaughter, Richard K. Smith, C.M. Smith, Walter A. Smook, Frank A. Stanley, Jan Stroomenbergh, John W.R. Taylor, A. Toplis, Len T. Trotter, Gerry Turner, Harry C. Umphrey, Tony Verrico, Maxwell W. Ward, Frank Warren, Ab Warren, Alex Watson, Don C. Whittley, Gordon S. Williams, Gerry R. Wooll, Bob Arnold, Jean-Marie Arseneault, Charles Bryant, R. "Gobi" Gobalian, S.R. "Robbie" Robinson, Terry Shwetz, W.D. "Bill" Somerville, R.G. Halford, F.T. Smye.

Fred W. Hotson

Gipsy Moth G-CAJU prepares for a flight from Hamilton in this early Fred Hotson photograph.

9

In the Beginning . . .

Count Jacques de Lesseps about to take off from Trethewey farm in Mount Dennis. The occasion was the Toronto air meet in July, 1910. (Dr. Jewell)

Count de Lesseps in front of his Anzani-powered Bleriot XI. (James Collection, City of Toronto Archives)

The Early Days

The enthusiast who seeks to walk the "hallowed ground" of Toronto history need go no farther than Trethewey Drive in the suburb of North York. No monument marks this level plot of ground, once known as the Trethewey farm, but the present housing development forms a historic link with the city's aviation past. A quiet walk around Hearst Circle will cover the centre-field of Toronto's earliest flying display, the first ever held in Ontario.

A group of touring aviators with Wright and Bleriot machines arrived at the farm on July 8, 1910, under the auspices of the Ontario Motor League to stage a nine-day show. Count Jacques de Lesseps from France was the star performer in Bleriot XI monoplanes, while the Wright Company team of Ralph Johnstone, D. Chapelle and F.T. Coffyn flew a Wright biplane. Not every flight was a success. On July 12 de Lesseps made the only successful flight of the day and John Stratton crashed attempting to fly a Bleriot owned by William Carruthers of Montreal.

The highlight of the week-long event came on July 13 when Count de Lesseps took off in his special Bleriot XI*bis* monoplane *Le Scarabée* for the first flight of a heavier-than-air machine over the heart of Toronto. Everyone realized the historical importance of his flight and he returned to resounding cheers from the crowd in the special grandstand erected for the show. The meet also provided the first occasion when two aircraft were in the air at once over Toronto.

Another walk in the same neighbourhood, down the present Westchester Street (where it meets Parkchester), will enable the visitor to stand on another site of historic interest. Admittedly it was only a wooden hangar during the years 1928-29, but it provided employment for 30 of the local inhabitants and launched the industry that would be known for the next half century as The de Havilland Aircraft of Canada Limited.

The name of de Havilland was well known in Canada long before the company established a branch in the Toronto area. Canadian pilots returning from the sky battles of World War 1 had a deep respect for the sturdy line of de Havilland warplanes they flew in France, particularly the D.H.4 which was produced in great quantity. The '4 was built under licence in the United States and was to play a part in Canadian aviation history.

As early as 1917 a sample D.H.4 was imported to Canada for use by the University of Toronto in the ground school training of mechanics. In July of that same year Canadian Aeroplanes Limited, Toronto, built an all-Canadian version of a D.H.6 trainer at their plant on Strachan Avenue. Canadian Aeroplanes were in the midst of producing a huge order of Curtiss JN-4 Canucks for training purposes and built this one for the RFC (Canada) as a possible backup. The machine was test flown at the Leaside airfield on the outskirts of Toronto by Brig. Gen. C.G. Hoare, Commanding Officer RFC (Canada). It was of very simple construction and flew well but never went into production. Over 2000 of the type were built in England, but the Curtiss program in Canada was so solidly launched that the need for a new type never developed. The D.H.4 and the D.H.6

were Toronto's first contact with the de Havilland name and the '6 was the first British designed aircraft to be built under licence in Canada.

Like many prominent designers of World War 1 aircraft, Major Geoffrey de Havilland spent the postwar years trying to stay in business by modifying military planes for civil use. During this difficult period, in a world still talking of war, the 37-year-old de Havilland directed his thoughts along peaceful lines. Gone were the Ministry orders for weapons of destruction; it was time to turn his ambitions and those of his associates along new paths. This small group, who had continued to work under the name of Aircraft Manufacturing Co. (Airco) since the end of hostilities, banded together on September 25, 1920, to form the de Havilland Aircraft Company Limited. They established an "aerodrome" and "sheds" in Stag Lane in the quiet little London suburb of Edgware, Middlesex.

The early exploits of Geoffrey de Havilland and his close associate, Frank T. Hearle, show foresight mixed with practical application and determination. Hearle became manager, and those who joined the two pioneers in the formation of the DH company, displayed similar qualities of character and drive. The financial planning of the firm was securely in the hands of secretary W.E. Nixon, while C.C. Walker, as chief engineer, directed his genius for science toward aeronautics. A businessman turned salesman, F.E.N. St. Barbe, rounded out one of the most talented aviation teams of any era. Another wartime associate,

A.E. Hagg, joined the group as assistant designer.

No task seemed too difficult for the men of Stag Lane in the '20s as they turned mainly to the production of single-engine planes. Their method of construction and design style became as distinctive a trademark as the company logo itself: wire-braced biplanes with a tail section as graceful as a butterfly's wing. One contract they undertook in 1924 to build a private touring aircraft proved highly beneficial for it brought Alan S. Butler into the organization.

The story of Alan Butler and how he came to join de Havilland is a company legend. His contact with Canada is also important in view of his later role as the first president of de Havilland in Canada. Butler was the son of a wealthy British family and had learned to fly at the end of

The first de Havilland aircraft in Canada, a D.H.4 imported in 1917, is shown on the grounds of the University of Toronto, where it was used for ground school training during World War 1. (CAF via K.M. Molson)

World War 1. He bought a surplus Bristol Fighter which he had converted to civil use. The experience he gained as one of the first air tourists in Europe fired his spirit of adventure. In 1920-21 he joined with V.S. Bennett and Sydney Cotton to open the first air service in Newfoundland, using Martinsyde biplanes. On his return to England in 1921 he sought a sturdy touring aircraft and was referred to Geoffrey de Havilland through C.G. Grey, editor of the *Aeroplane*. The people at Stag Lane were pleased to discuss such a project with Butler but were a little sceptical that he would want to pay the cost involved. Their new customer not only signed the contract, but, as he was leaving that day, offered to invest in the company. The coincidence was heaven-sent because the directors were being forced to buy their aerodrome property at the time and were desperately in need of financing. The loan was accepted, the new aircraft started and Alan Butler became a member of the board of directors. He was made chairman

in 1924 and served with distinction and wisdom through 28 years.

Working on Butler's machine, the D.H.37, rekindled Geoffrey de Havilland's own interest in planes for air touring. Most of the available aircraft were too big or too complex for the sport pilot. He designed the D.H.51, which was in the private owner class, but it was handicapped by a heavy war-surplus engine. It did clear up many design points for de Havilland but the lack of a proper engine in the 60 hp class was proving to be a major handicap. The next two designs were at the other end of the scale, a glider (the D.H.52) and a truly light airplane (the D.H.53 Humming Bird). They were both built for competitions and did much to provide the catalyst for the ultimate sportplane.

The next two designs involved a 12-passenger airliner and a military two-seater but these never went into production. Meanwhile de Havilland had come to a decision on his engine problem and sought the advice of his long-time colleague Major Frank B. Halford. Their careers had run parallel as far back as the D.H.3 and Halford was now one of Britain's leading aircraft engine designers. He had joined the Aircraft Disposal Company following the war and, although still associated with the company, had been out on his own in a design capacity since 1923.

The ADC specialty was upgrading a large stock of war-surplus engines for the struggling civil market. In one typical case they had boosted an old Renault engine of 80 hp to 140 hp with such improvements as aluminum heads and overhead valves. They called it the Airdisco. The eight-cylinder, V-type, air-cooled engine was giving reliable service and provided Geoffrey de Havilland with the answer he was seeking for a small powerplant of reasonable weight.

"Why don't you take half an Airdisco," asked de Havilland, "mount it on a new crankcase and give me an engine of about 60 hp?" Halford agreed to take on the task while de Havilland went back to work designing a new airplane around this novel engine concept. With the D.H.60 design, the magic combination was

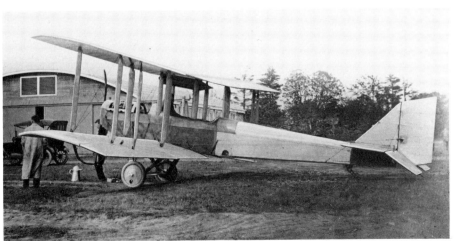

The first British-designed aircraft manufactured under licence in Canada, a D.H.6 built in Toronto during World War 1 by Canadian Aeroplanes Limited. (via K.M. Molson)

achieved. De Havilland called the new creation the Moth because of his long interest in entomology. The ADC engine that Halford produced from the Airdisco was called the Cirrus I, was rated at 60 hp, and weighed 290 pounds.

The Moth

The D.H.60 was a scaled-down D.H.51, still with two seats, but combining all the things Geoffrey de Havilland had been planning for years: low fuel consumption, folding wings for economical storage, simple construction and moderate price. Even the name "Moth" caught on in the unexpected sales rush that followed. As with his other models, de Havilland tested it himself on February 22, 1925. His new Moth performed flawlessly and was an instant commercial success. One of Britain's aviation visionaries, Sir Sefton Brancher, saw it as the answer to Britain's sagging air strength and came up with a national flying club program. His efforts resulted in the formation of five Air Ministry-subsidized, Moth-equipped flying clubs.

As in many a success story, when the product is just right for the market, the development of the Moth turned the tide for the de Havilland organization. Not only did the little airplane catch the public imagination, but it started the flying club movement throughout the world. Additional interest was sparked by the generosity of Sir Charles Wakefield, CBE, head of the huge Castrol empire, who extended his philanthropy to a number of clubs by donating Moth trainers. The Moth began to gain world recognition on May 29, 1925, when Sir Allan J. Cobham flew from Croydon to Zurich and back in one day. Its transition to seaplane status was also easy for Short Brothers had a set of floats designed for their Mussel which tested perfectly on the Moth in November 1926.

Australians had long been involved with de Havilland designs: the Moth looked like the answer to their great distances. Private flyers in the United States became interested enough to talk of manufacturing the Moth in that country—and then there was the growing need in Canada.

The honour of being the first of the Moth line in Canada fell to aircraft G-CAHK, which arrived in Halifax in 1927, crated, on board a ship from

Squadron Leader T.A. Lawrence stands on the float of the first Moth in Canada, *Spirit of the Valley of the Moon*, during its short life with the Hudson Strait Expedition in 1927. (PAC)

England. It had been purchased by the Canadian Department of Marine Fisheries and was intended as a reconnaissance seaplane for the upcoming Hudson Strait Expedition. The purpose was to study ice patterns in the shipping lanes between the proposed grain port of Churchill, on the western shore of Hudson Bay, and Europe. The high-sounding name of the Moth, *Spirit of the Valley of the Moon*, was not in keeping with the inhospitable north, but it left Halifax on July 27 on the icebreaker *Stanley*, ready for work. It served well but had a rather short career, which was recounted 44 years later to a meeting of the Canadian Aviation Historical Society by the pilot, A/V/M Thomas A. Lawrence, who flew it during that period.

"By the time the expedition reached Wakeham Bay on August 22, 1927," said Lawrence, "the Moth had made five survey flights in four different areas along the Hudson Strait. In 14 hours of flying, we had three base sites selected, which would have taken weeks if done by land or water.

"The Moth could not be taken ashore until a strip of beach was cleared of stones, which would only have been a matter of a day's work. Despite my protests, the captain of the icebreaker ordered the Moth removed from his vessel. It had to be placed at a mooring already set out for the ship's boats.

"In a few hours a wind storm of gale force blew up, making all traffic between the ship, the Moth or the shore impossible. 'HK weathered the storm for some time, up to the point where it was literally flying at the mooring, when one wing went down into the water and the craft turned upside down. In a few minutes only the floats and a mass of twisted wreckage remained. The storm lasted for about four hours. Instead of being able to take a serviceable seaplane ashore by nightfall, we salvaged only the floats and engine—all because of a non-cooperative ship's captain."

Another pilot who had a good reason to investigate the Moth was Captain Roy Maxwell, colourful head of the Ontario Provincial Air Service. Maxwell's prestige in Canadian aviation stemmed from his role in protecting Ontario's valuable forest wealth. He had pioneered in forestry flying with the Laurentide Company of Grand Mère, Quebec, and moved to Ontario as head of the new Ontario Air Service. The aircraft being used at the time for water operations were war-surplus Curtiss HS-2L flying boats, long past their prime. The aging equipment and the complexity of the task brought about a complicated organization which Maxwell managed with all the flair of a circus ringmaster —in everything from high boots and leather jacket to a blue Cadillac roadster. He saw the Moth as a new way to patrol Ontario's forests and travelled to England to investigate its potential firsthand. His visit resulted in the purchase of four Moths on float undercarriages, which did much to whet de Havilland's appetite for export markets and convince Francis St. Barbe of the potential in Canada. This first sizable shipment of Moths to Canada arrived at Sault Ste. Marie

The D.H.60 Moth which A.J. Cobham demonstrated throughout the United States and which later became G-CAIL of Western Canada Airways. *(Flight)*

in crates during July 1927 and they were put into service immediately as G-CAOU, 'OV, 'OW, and 'OX. With their ability to dart from base to base carrying fire spotters and even pumps when needed, they proved a pleasant change from the big boats. The Moths flew 700 hours during their first four months of operation to the satisfaction of all concerned. Another six were ordered for delivery in 1928.

An interesting Moth arrived in Canada during 1927 as the result of a demonstration flight by the famous British pilot Sir Allan Cobham. Cobham had done considerable testing and delivery work in England and was chosen to demonstrate the Moth in the United States. Arrangements were even then under way with a group in New York for the manufacturing rights in the US, so it was to be a

demonstration of considerable importance. Serial number 273, which had been used in the original float tests at Short's, was delivered by ship to New York.

In an appropriate display of showmanship, Cobham had the Moth offloaded at Sandy Hook and flew the remaining miles to New York. The sight of the tiny Moth cruising along the Hudson River waterfront and landing gracefully in the harbour caused plenty of excitement. It was later fitted with wheels for a demonstration to members of Congress before it went on tour. When number 273 finished its demonstration in the US it became Canadian. J.H. Holley picked it up at Buffalo, New York, and flew it to Winnipeg, where he had it registered as G-CAIL.

Two examples of the Cirrus II Moth, designated the 60X (with a split axle instead of the single cross bar), were shipped directly to Dominion Airways, Vancouver, and Western Canada Airways, Winnipeg. By the end of 1927

the total number of Moths registered in Canada had grown to eight and the Canadian government was taking an active interest.

Back in 1920

Aircraft manufactured by the de Havilland Company first appeared in Canadian government records in 1920. The British government sought to promote a strong air force within the Commonwealth and sent 12 D.H.9As to Canada as Imperial Gifts. They even allocated a block of registrations from their own civil listing, starting with G-CY. Eleven of these sturdy 9As were registered and, in a decision of great merit, one machine was reserved for spare parts. Three aircraft, G-CYAN, G-CYAJ and G-CYBF, took part in the first trans-Canada flight in 1920 from Halifax, Nova Scotia, to Vancouver, British Columbia. During the same year four US Army D.H.4s built in the USA, with American Liberty engines, flew from New York through Canada to Alaska.

In 1921 another batch of 12 aircraft arrived in Canada under the Imperial Gifts Act; this time they were D.H.4s, which were converted into '4Bs and used for transport duties and forestry patrol at High River, Alberta. They were also given the G-CY-- series of registrations and were not phased out of service until 1928. It has often been noted that, from the beginning of aircraft records in Canada to the present, there has never been a day without a de Havilland aircraft of one type or another in the Canadian military.

The first de Havilland machine to appear under civil registration in Canada was a D.H.9. It was bought from the Royal Air Force by a Major W.T. Blake, who registered it as G-EBDF, for an ambitious round-the-world trip in 1922. He planned to fly it from Vancouver to Montreal but, when the first stage of the flight, using another D.H.9, came to grief in Calcutta, the project was cancelled and the aircraft became surplus. It was sold to Laurentide Air Service of Montreal, Quebec, in 1925 and based

The D.H.9A G-CYAN at Winnipeg during the western section of the trans-Canada flight. In the front cockpit, Capt. J.H. Home-Hay; in the rear cockpit, Sgt. W. Young. (Left to right) Capt. G.H. Pitt, Sgt. J. Crowe, Capt. C.W. Cudamore, Sgt. J. McLaughlin, Lt. Col. A.K. Tylee. (CAF via K.M. Molson)

13

The Canadian Air Board D.H.9A with Capt. C.W. Cudamore, who flew the Regina-Medicine Hat section of the first trans-Canada air mail flight October 11, 1920. (CAF via K.M. Molson)

A good example of a D.H.4 with a Rolls-Royce Eagle VIII engine at High River, Alberta. It shows the early style of registration allotted from the British series for use in Canada. The lettering was applied to the aircraft according to Air Regulations 1920. (CAF via K.M. Molson)

The ski-equipped D.H.9A, G-CYBF, which was used during the last leg of the trans-Canada air mail flight in 1920, shown with a later style of marking used by military aircraft. (CAF via K.M. Molson)

after it joined the company. The pilot, C.S. Caldwell, was unhurt.

The first contact between de Havilland Aircraft Limited in England and Canada's Department of National Defence began August 5, 1927, when a telegram was sent to England asking for information on the D.H.60 Moth. Cables went back and forth that summer on the merits of the ADC Cirrus engine and one of slightly less horsepower, the Armstrong Siddeley Genet. The correspondence was typical of government mail order shopping from 3000 miles away and quotes were asked on quantities of three, five and seven.

On November 10, 1927, J.A. Wilson, Controller of Civil Aviation in Canada, announced the purchase of the first ten Moths for the flying clubs and wrote de Havilland in England for their policy on spare parts and service. R.A. "Bob" Loader, assistant business manager at Stag Lane, wrote back promptly that the company was "fully alive to the need for after-purchase service on these machines," and stated that, "F.E.N. St. Barbe is on his way to Canada at the time of

at Larder Lake. It was given the Canadian registration G-CAEU and converted to a modified '9C but had a very short life as a bushplane. It was written off on a flight from Larder Lake to Rouyn, Quebec, only 12 days

the planes in and out. Like the works shed it had the company name (spelled correctly) along the side and once again MOTH AEROPLANES. Two more Moths arrived on the railway siding on April 16; it was time to start the flying.

To handle the flying duties, Loader had hired an RCAF flying instructor, F/L Erskine Leigh Capreol. Leigh Capreol was born and educated in Ottawa, where he joined the Canadian Army after graduation. He served in France with the 77th, 73rd and 85th Battalions of the Canadian Expeditionary Force until seconded to the Royal Flying Corps in 1917. He joined the Central Flying School at

Upavon Downs as a flight lieutenant and while there was seriously injured in a training accident. He spent the rest of the war in hospital and did not return to Canada until 1920. He spent six years with the American Bank Note Company in Ottawa but by 1927 was back with the RCAF at Camp Borden, Ontario. He served 14 months as a flying instructor before joining de Havilland.

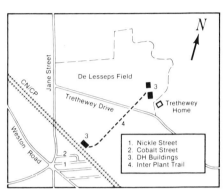

The historic first flight from the new hangar occurred on April 18 when Capreol flew G-CAJU, the *Sir Charles Wakefield,* destined to the Toronto Flying Club. The same day he tested G-CAJW and followed with the new company demonstrator, G-CAJV, two days later. On another historic date, April 27, the Toronto

The interior of the old canning shed across the tracks from Cobalt Street, Mount Dennis. Cirrus Moths from England are being assembled by (left to right) Ernie Hedger, Arthur Robins and Frank Warren. (DHC10708)

17

Noted aviation artist R.W. "Bob" Bradford, who produced many Beaver, Otter and Caribou paintings during his years with de Havilland, also produced this impression of the flight by Leigh Capreol that launched de Havilland Canada. (DHC46765)

Flying Club and Leigh Sheppard received the first two flyaway deliveries from the new Canadian company.

During the spring months George Mickleborough was busy organizing his responsibilities at the mining office so he could take over his promised job with de Havilland. He had his eye on a capable young man in the bank below the Brett-Trethewey office and, when the time was right, asked Len Appleyard if he would consider leaving the bank. Appleyard took over the business management of Trethewey's mining interests on July 26, which allowed Mickleborough to join Loader in his crowded Bay Street office. The office had room for only one large table and three chairs, enough for the two men and Mrs. E. Coates, who handled the correspondence duties. Whenever a guest arrived to discuss Moth airplanes, someone had to move into the hall.

As the business grew, one door on the works shed had to be enlarged to accommodate loading from the flatcars, but there was still a problem. The long crates had to be turned at right angles on the flatcars and inched into the building with crowbars and rollers. Accurate timing was required and a certain amount of speed so that half the crate was not projecting over the active set of tracks when a train went by. Moths began arriving on the siding in ever-increasing numbers during May and June and were built up as quickly as possible to avoid congestion in the small work area. The fuselages were assembled on their undercarriages and towed, without wings, across a prepared path to the airfield. The wings followed by truck to the hangar where they were assembled and rigged for flight.

On May 2 the first commercial Moth, G-CANS, was delivered by rail to Dominion Airways in Vancouver. Early in the month a second shipment of Moths was delivered to the Ontario Provincial Air Service at Sault Ste. Marie for assembly and they were officially entered in the Canadian register on the 11th. The first flying club Moth allotted by the government was registered to the Montreal

The first Flying Report of the new Canadian company, when Leigh Capreol tested G-CAJU and 'JW on April 18, 1928. (via Alex Downey)

Light Aeroplane Club on May 12. Only a small proportion of the first flood of orders went through the newly established shops at Mount Dennis. Since the Moths from England had already been test flown there, most were shipped directly to the clubs and companies outside the Toronto area.

As the number of Moths grew, so did the repair business. The small assembly hangar, which was always crowded with stored aircraft, was inadequate for the doping of fabric and, when a crisis arose in the overcrowded workshop, repaired components were hauled to the unfinished Trethewey billiard room for doping operations.

18

Larger components, such as fuselages, had to be carried in and out of the window, somewhat like coffins. This became a regular procedure until the eventual move to new quarters.

June was exceptionally busy. Seven Moths were received on the 4th, including one allotted to Frank Trethewey. Four days later his G-CANA was tested and delivered to him the same afternoon. He began taking instruction immediately, including a few "circuits and bumps" with his friend Philip C. Garratt of Allerdice & Garratt Chemicals Limited. The list of clubs, firms and private operators grew throughout the year at an even pace; by August 3 the RCAF had their first D.H.60X (with a Cirrus II engine) delivered to Camp Borden. It did not hurt the company's financial position that first year when they received $2000.00 for a flying display by Leigh Capreol at the annual Canadian National Exhibition.

The first fatality connected with company operations occurred during the first year on the tracks that ran by the assembly shed. Nels Farrance, who had only been with the company for two weeks to do moving between the two buildings, died as the result of a crossing accident when a train demolished the company truck.

As the output of Moths grew steadily through 1928, so did the need for working space. Even the Trethewey farm, which looked adequate during the early months, was becoming overcrowded. With Skyways Limited operating a flying training school at the west end of the field, it became obvious to management that not only a new hangar but a new airfield would soon be necessary.

The staff had grown from 3 to 30, sales were over the 50 mark and a substantial backlog of orders was on

Some of those who had much to do with the start of DH Canada in 1927-28. At left is R.A. Loader, first general manager, who came from England to start the operation. Preparing for a trial flight is Hon. W. Finlayson, Minister of Lands and Forests for Ontario, who approved the purchase of the first four Moths for the Ontario Provincial Air Service. Beside him is the man who brought them all together, Roy Maxwell, head of the OPAS. In the cockpit of Cirrus Moth G-CAPH is Leigh Capreol, first DH Canada test pilot. (DHC9649)

Three early Cirrus Moths of 1928: G-CAKO, Saskatoon Aero Club; G-CANA, F.L. Trethewey; G-CAJV, DHC demonstrator. The gentlemen in the photo are: L.E. Maynard, Jack Sanderson, J.H. Reid, Frank Trethewey, Leigh Sheppard, P.C. Garratt, R.A. Loader, Leigh Capreol, A.C. Robins, Frank Warren. This view also shows the 50 by 50-foot temporary wooden hangar completed Good Friday, April 20, 1928, which served de Havilland until September 1929 and was taken over by Frank Trethewey after the company moved to Downsview. The building was destroyed by fire April 17, 1932, while the Trethewey plane, a Great Lakes Trainer, was being warmed up for flight. (DHC9642)

The first Moth assembled by the Toronto branch of the de Havilland Company was the *Sir Charles Wakefield* for the Toronto Flying Club. It is shown here at the club's first quarters, Leaside, Ontario, with instructor Carter Guest (left) and president Earl Hand. (PAC)

The first group of DH Cirrus Moths with their Short Brothers floats undergoing a seasonal overhaul in the OPAS shops at Sault Ste. Marie. The distinctive Cirrus engine installation is clearly shown. (PAC 1604)

hand. Frank Hearle was over from England discussing the situation with Loader and they found an answer to the first of these problems. They ordered a new wooden hangar designed by Mathers & Haldenby, and had it built facing the first on the southeast corner of the Trethewey field. Their specifications showed considerable foresight: a temporary building designed in sections for easy moving.

Metal Moths

When the system of combining wood in alternate glued layers was introduced, Europeans quickly adapted this new technique to aircraft construction. The de Havilland company had always made wide use of plywood in their fuselages and used this accumulated experience to produce the Moth. Its fuselage was a plywood box, built around spruce longerons and supporting cross members. Casein

The second wooden hangar erected at Mount Dennis was built in sections and later moved to the plant at Downsview in 1929. It was moved a second time during World War 2 and still exists as part of the north complex at Downsview. (via G. Mickleborough)

Two examples of early Cirrus Moths engaged in bush flying operations: G-CATJ of General Airways and G-CAUP, belonging to Arthur Fecteau. (R.S. Baker, DHC)

A typical Gipsy Moth after assembly at Mount Dennis. This example in front of the temporary hangar has not received its registration but is a wooden-fuselage D.H.60G with a split type axle and a Gipsy I engine. Gipsy engines had a cooling cowl, in contrast to the exposed cylinders of a Cirrus Moth. (DHC via L.B. Best)

An assortment of Cirrus and Gipsy Moths ready for delivery at the flying field in Mount Dennis. (via W. Etherington)

The Trethewey farm (de Lesseps Field) in Mount Dennis as it appeared from 6000 feet in 1931. (The top of the photo is north.) The hangars of Skyways Limited are on the left, close to Trethewey Drive, while the Trethewey home can be seen in the ravine at lower right. The original square hangar built by DH Canada can be seen at the eastern end of the field. (via W.F. Shaylor)

glue and brass wood screws were used throughout to produce a sturdy, light-weight frame. It was protected on the inside with varnish and on the out-side by a layer of tightly doped fabric. The wings were of standard construction, spruce spars and built-up ribs, securely covered with fabric and doped.

With the export of the Moth to the world at large, these plywood box fuselages were subjected to a wide variety of temperatures and climates. Under most circumstances they proved quite adequate but in particularly damp areas suffered from what one American designer of metal aircraft termed veneerial disease. The American method of fuselage construction, by comparison, was usually of welded steel tubing, suitably faired with wooden stringers, and a fabric cover doped to drumhead tightness.

As early as October 1927 the use of wooden Moths in Canada was being questioned. The Ontario government aircraft experienced shrinking in the wooden engine bearers, while the varying western climate of High River, Alberta, played havoc with the rigging of the wings. On October 3 a letter to Stag Lane was the opening shot in a strictly Canadian campaign for the use of metal fuselages. The Canadian company continued the pressure, with considerable opposition from some in the British company, until a new type 60M or metal-fuselage Moth was introduced.*

The Canadians won their battle for metal fuselages at the end of 1928 when the first D.H.60M, G-CAVX, was sent to Canada for evaluation by the RCAF on wheels, skis and floats. Rigorous trials were conducted at London, Ontario, and the results were a major incentive for the next series of orders by the RCAF and the OPAS. Many of the original wooden Moths were later converted to the 60M, particularly in the forestry hangar at Sault Ste. Marie, where they had excellent shop facilities. As time went by it became common practice to upgrade Moths with higher-powered engines, a metal fuselage or a split type undercarriage. These changes were all covered within the licencing regulations and many a damaged Moth rose again with the use of borrowed components. The price of a metal Moth at the time was given as $4450.00 for the landplane and $6250.00 for the seaplane version.

*For a guide to the multitude of Moth types see the table of prewar DH aircraft in the appendices.

The RCAF received 17 Moth 60X aircraft which went early to the High River area of Alberta for fire patrol. Two Armstrong Siddeley Genet Moths were evaluated at Camp Borden but the remaining 72 Moths on the RCAF inventory over the years were Gipsy-powered with metal fuselages.

The growing worldwide sales of Moths in 1927-28 had made de Havilland uncomfortably dependent on Cirrus engines from the Aircraft Disposal Company, which also had other customers to supply. Major Frank Halford was once again called in for consultation and was invited to design a completely new engine of 100 hp. Halford relinquished his connection with ADC in 1927 and was soon busy developing an engine that Geoffrey de Havilland named the Gipsy. The Series I achieved the magic 100 hp at a weight of 285 pounds and was the

The historic Trethewey farm area as it appears today, bounded by Trethewey Drive on the south and Jane Street on the west. The Black Creek ravine remains relatively unchanged to the east. (Ontario Government)

forerunner of a long series of Halford engines produced under the de Havilland banner.

Mount Dennis

Life was never dull around Mount Dennis flying field in 1928-29 with DH Canada and "Freddie" Shaylor's Skyways Limited sharing the action. Skyways did a lot of flight training out of the west end so there was always some activity to enliven the average day. On one such occasion an instructor and student took off into a hazy sky for some airwork in the Toronto area. One of the de Havilland ground crew noticed a wheel fall off the Moth as it disappeared in the haze and immediately alerted the Skyways officials. According to the stories that have been written about such events, someone runs around holding a wheel in the air hoping the pilot will get the message and avert a crash. And that is just what was done this time. Every available wheel from the Moth stores was taken onto the field. When the

instructor returned to the circuit, he found a row of people across his landing path, each holding a wheel. Needless to say he circled again and completed a successful precautionary landing with no damage.

For those who joined the de Havilland staff early, the training was direct and thorough, as recalled by Harry Proctor. Proctor joined in the fall of 1928 with no previous aircraft experience but with plenty of ability and determination.

"Arthur Robins was a good boss," he recalled, "and we learned fast. I remember him giving me instructions on the hours of work when I joined the company. 'As long as you are here before I get here and leave after I do, that's all you have to remember.' That is the way he operated and if there was a special job where he worked into the night, we worked too.

"An aeronautical engineer, M.R. Waters, from England, was with us for a while and looked after things like designing skis. The first ski pedestals for the Moths were of welded steel tubing—that is, until one noon hour, after we had been skating on an ice patch behind the hangar. Mr. Waters picked up one of my skates and studied the construction where the metal cone met the boot. 'I think

I'll build a ski pedestal that shape,' he said, and from then on all de Havilland skis had welded cone-shaped pedestals. Waters left to take a job in California before we moved to Downsview.

"Most of us had our first flight with Leigh Capreol and we were always pleased to be asked to go along on a flight. I got one of these calls during the first winter while we were developing Moth skis. It wasn't until we got up in the air that Cap told me what he wanted. Through the 'Gosport' tube that connected both cockpits, he asked me to crawl out on the lower wing and see if the skis were at the proper angle. Now, I'm the kind of guy who can get dizzy on a tall ladder and here I was about to do my first wing-walking. One look over the leading edge confirmed that the skis were perfect and I hurried back into the cockpit to break the news to Cap.

"Talk about learning in a hurry! We were all given amazing jobs at one time or another. I remember one metal Moth seaplane which was in for repair after sinking. Robins' approach was that if one person took it apart and rebuilt it, there would be a minimum of supervision and less chance of error. I was given the job and, as we had no drawings, I went at it piece

23

A lineup of Moths owned by Aircraft Limited behind the de Havilland hangar. DHC shared de Lesseps Field with Aircraft Limited, which was the predecessor of Skyways Limited. (DHC7312)

by piece. By the time I was finished, I knew quite a lot about a metal Moth."

Incorporation

For the first six months DH Canada, which began under the laws of the Province of Ontario, operated as a branch of the British parent with provisional directors. It was always hoped that a Canadian company with its own identity could be formed when the business climate was right. The favourable showing of the first six months allowed a confident reorganization and a public stock offer with the English company holding majority control. The board of directors reflected a balance of British/Canadian participation. Alan S. Butler was named president, with Geoffrey de Havilland, C.C. Walker and F.E.N. St. Barbe, as the English directors. Canadians on the board were W.R.P. Parker, chairman, J. Homer Black and Frank L. Trethewey, all from Toronto. Bob Loader remained as general manager of the Canadian company with William Zimmerman as secretary.

During the month of October 1928 a new site was chosen for future operations in open farmland in Downsview, north of the city. The area north of Wilson Avenue at the corner of Sheppard Avenue and Dufferin Street provided a level field, clear of all obstructions, alongside the mainline CNR tracks. A 70-acre lot was purchased in April 1929 and architects were chosen to plan a new brick and steel building.

Everyone connected with the Canadian operation must have been elated with the sales results of 1928. A total of 62 Moths had been delivered as well as two of the new D.H.61 Giant Moths assembled by Canadian Vickers, one of which went to Western Canada Airways as G-CAJT and the other to the Provincial Air Service. The WCA machine was lost in a non-fatal accident two months later but the big eight-passenger G-CAPG of the OPAS had a long and eventful career (it was retired in 1941). A third Giant Moth was imported that year for London Air Transport

The delivery of the first D.H.61 Giant Moth to Western Canada Airways after assembly at Canadian Vickers, Montreal. Left, the Vickers pilot C.S. "Jack" Caldwell and, right, W.L. Brintnell of Western Canada Airways. (WCA Archives via K.M. Molson)

Limited but the company never took delivery (it was later re-engined and ended up as CF-OAK).

The small downtown office on Toronto's Bay Street was bursting with activity. Not only did the company have a new corporate identity and a new factory under way, but also a backlog of Moth sales that would keep them busy well into 1929. Thirty-four of these aircraft were to go to the RCAF Training Establishment and five to the Civil Aviation Branch as additional aircraft for the flying clubs.

Even though DH Canada had no connection with the Moth enthusiasm in the United States, it was encouraging to note that the "Moth Aircraft Corporation" had been formed in New York, with a factory at Lowell, Mass. The US model was advertised as "the light car of the air." Minton

M. Warren was president with Earl L. House and Frank M. Smith as vice-presidents. At the annual general meeting of de Havilland England for the year 1929, Alan Butler reported that the Wright Aeronautical Corporation had begun building the Gipsy engine under licence in the USA. He also added that the Moth Aircraft Corporation had joined with the powerful Curtiss-Wright group, production was in progress and royalties had been received.

The year 1929 is always regarded as the beginning of the Great Depression but it started out well for de Havilland Canada. The RCAF Moths began to flow in a steady stream along with

Launching the D.H.61 Giant Moth of the OPAS at Sault Ste. Marie. (National Museum of Science and Technology)

the first model of the new D.H.75 Hawk Moth for RCAF evaluation. The Hawk Moth was a promising-looking, high-wing monoplane of 3650-pound gross weight, with an Armstrong Lynx engine, and was fitted to carry four people. It had a lot of the Fairchild FC-2 look and hopes ran high that it would experience a similar success in Canada on skis and floats. The total number of all de Havilland Canada airplanes delivered in 1929 was 78, more than in the previous year; similar successes would continue for another year.

A New Home

It took very little work on the new field at Downsview to make it suitable for flying. The steel for the new factory was up by mid-July. Excitement built among the 35 employees at the

thought of new quarters. The entire operation moved over from Mount Dennis during the first week in September, including Loader's portable wooden hangar with the curved roof, which was to prove extremely useful in the years ahead. The new building of 20,000 square feet was well laid out for the state of the company's growth at the time. It faced north onto Sheppard Avenue with the Canadian National tracks along the west side. A railway spur line was connected to a loading ramp outside the stores department, paint shop and heating plant. The erection shop had 7500 square feet of unrestricted floor space and a set of typical sliding hangar doors facing the flying field. Two shops were on the ground floor at the entrance to the building, one for machining and metal work and the other for engine overhaul. The engineering and business offices were upstairs above the shops and were reached by a set of stairs inside the hangar.

The wooden hangar from Mount Dennis was placed 50 yards to the east with its main door and entrance ramp facing the open field. Two additional items rounded out the new quarters, a cement compass rose to the east of the wooden hangar and a small test house for engine runs beside the heating plant. Once again, signs played an important part because the district then was quite rural and isolated. There was nothing for miles but open fields and farm houses. An attractive sign was installed at the corner of Sheppard and Dufferin with an arrow pointing to the plant and a host of other information: address, telephone number, cable address, the

The D.H.75 Hawk Moth demonstrator at Downsview, still with its British markings. Only three came to Canada and the type had only a short career with the RCAF. (PAC)

Two views of the first Downsview plant. The aerial view shows the entire plant on Sheppard Avenue, looking west. The wooden storage hangar with the rounded roof from Mount Dennis is clearly seen, along with the round concrete pad for compass swinging. Beyond the wooden hangar can be seen the new assembly shop and offices, and beyond that are the engine test house, stores and paint shop, and heating plant. The CNR railway siding ran along the far side of the plant.

The second photo shows the front of the new building, which faced Sheppard Avenue. (via British Aerospace)

company logo and that it was ''The Home of the Moth.'' To assist aerial visitors, the word MOTH was painted in large letters on the round hangar roof with an arrow indicating north.

One of the first problems to be encountered at the new site was the establishment of a water supply. In the isolated Downsview farm area a water main was out of the question. The only alternative was to drill a well. An old-timer was found in the area who had some antique drilling equipment and boundless optimism. He did a survey near the factory and estimated he would find water after about 40 feet of drilling at a cost of something like $100.

At the end of the first week, the hole reached a depth of 50 feet without any sign of water. To make matters worse, the drill struck a layer of hard rock. The expert was still optimistic and authority was given to extend the drilling to a depth of 100 feet. At 100 feet there was still nothing but rock to report and the situation was becoming serious. Costs were going up and the only one to remain unmoved was the well-borer himself, who held steadfast in his optimism. In growing desperation, successive increases to 150, 200, 250 feet were authorized. At 250 feet the so-called well was as dry as ever and a board meeting was called.

With not much alternative, the board authorized another limit of 300 feet, even though the thump-thump of the equipment was beginning to get on everyone's nerves. As the digging got lower, so did the spirits of all concerned; even the aged expert began to show signs of strain. At exactly 298 feet water gushed forth to resounding cheers, but the drama of the well was not over.

It should have ended as a shining example of man's conquest of adversity, but it was not to be. The water was so brackish that it was completely useless for drinking—or even washing. In the end it could only be used for the factory boiler and it probably didn't do that any good either. For

An impressive lineup of RCAF Moths at Camp Borden, Ontario. (PAC6315)

The engine shop with a Cirrus engine (foreground) and two Gipsy engines. Left to right: Alf Rinaldo, Peter Loveday, Walter Rinaldo, Ed Lambie and Bill Etherington. (via H. Proctor)

years the drinking water for the staff had to be brought in and dispensed in paper cups from a cooler.

The Economy Slips

The entire de Havilland organization fared very well during 1929 but the world trade depression, signalled by the collapse of the US stock market, was not long in making its presence felt in both Canada and the UK. British export trade suffered somewhat in 1929 and by 1930 the corporate profits of de Havilland in England had declined to the point where 5 per cent dividends replaced the 10 per cent of the year before.

The comfortable new quarters at Downsview proved very efficient in spite of their distance from a residential area. Not everyone had a car and there was no bus service that far from the city. Car pools were the only answer and the street corner pick-ups provided a circuitous route for many a driver. By the time the last pick-up was made in the morning the cars would be rather crowded and the girls (being lighter) would usually end up sitting on some lucky fellow's knee. The reorganization at Sheppard Avenue also brought about staff changes.

On the flying side, Squadron Leader Geoffrey S. O'Brian, a distinguished RCAF officer, joined as sales manager after completing a period as instructor at Aircraft Limited, Mount Dennis. Arthur Robins, as works manager, returned to England, and M.R. Waters,

the aeronautical engineer, moved to California. Vernon O. Levick came out to fill both positions as he was also an aeronautical engineer. W.R. "Bill" Calder joined at that time as inspector.

Bill Calder became something of an institution at DHC in the years that followed. He had come originally

The metal-working and machine shop, with Bill Etherington at the bench, Russ Borrett welding and Bill Fuller at the drillpress. (via W. Etherington)

from Scotland and was the brother of Sir Ritchie Calder, noted mathematician and author. He had gone to the same school as Elizabeth Bowes-Lyon,

Six RCAF Gipsy Moths (and one civilian) shortly after the move from Mount Dennis. (via W. Etherington)

Major General J.H. MacBrien, president of the Aviation League of Canada, with the white CF-AAA in which he toured Canada. (via RCMP)

the present Queen Mother, and had served his apprenticeship in shipbuilding in Glasgow. He worked on Rolls-Royce engines as well as the airships R-33 and R-34, which provided his entry into aviation. When the first flying club was formed in Scotland — the Scottish Flying Club, Glasgow — he became its first air engineer. Calder came to Canada in 1928 and after a year in the Maritimes moved to Toronto and de Havilland.

Three D.H.75 Hawk Moths went to the RCAF in the spring of 1930, two new ones and the company demonstrator which had arrived the year before. This particular aircraft was given the registration CF-CCA and was allotted to civil aviation inspector D.G. Joy. The two Air Force machines, slightly heavier at 3870 pounds gross, started out as float-planes but all three began to show structural deficiencies. Landing accidents due to a nose-heavy condition provided work for the shops but did nothing to enhance the aircraft's reputation. The undercarriage proved inadequate for the pounding it took on skis; it required additional centre-

section bracing and wing-spar modifications.

The employees began to look upon the Hawks as a source of perpetual employment, and when one was seen to overrun the airport boundary and nose over in a neighbouring field, a loud cheer went up in anticipation of more work. Despite its sturdy appearance, the Hawk Moth was a disappointment to the British company and a complete failure in Canada. Only eight were built and the three in Canada only totalled 183 hours before they were declared unserviceable. The final indignity came October 8, 1935, when a request to cut up the airframes to

provide experience for RCAF welding classes was given unanimous approval.

In July 1930 the era of the D.H.80A Puss Moth began in Canada. Nine of these arrived as complete aircraft from England and were assembled and tested during 1930. (Later serial numbers were built up from basic components and given a DHC series of numbers from C201 to C225.) The eye-pleasing cabin monoplane showed such improved comfort over the open-cockpit Gipsy Moths that it held promise of duplicating the Gipsy's profitable sales record. The production model with its metal fuselage and inverted Gipsy III engine of 120 hp was an immediate success on both sides of the Atlantic, accomplishing many flight records during its career.

Canada received serial number 4 from the British production line as its demonstrator aircraft. It needed only to be assembled and was given the registration of CF-AGO on July 8, 1930. Two days later the cream-coloured Puss Moth began a cross-Canada tour which was probably the largest such sales promotion in Canada up to that time. The new pilot, Geoff O'Brian, flew the trip and

George Mickleborough, who now held the position of secretary/treasurer, was along to navigate, pay the bills and talk to the customers. Similar trips became routine in the years that followed but this was a major adventure in 1930.

Leaving Toronto on July 12, the pair touched down at Detroit, Chicago, Madison, St. Paul, Fargo and Grand Forks, to land at Winnipeg that evening after 14 hours flying time. At Winnipeg, the Puss Moth participated in the Manitoba Jubilee Air Meet and

dozens of demonstration flights were made before the tour continued on to Brandon, Regina, Moose Jaw, Medicine Hat, Calgary and High River—with more demonstrations en route.

Crossing the Rockies by way of the Crow's Nest and Coquilhalla Passes, the tourists saw Cranbrook and Grand Forks before stopping at Vancouver, their western terminus. After five days of demonstrations for British Columbia aviation enthusiasts, the Puss Moth headed homeward, crossing the Rockies at altitudes ranging from 6000 to 12,000 feet. On the return trip their route was planned to touch down at Lethbridge, Milk River, Edmonton, North Battleford, Saskatoon and South Bend. The last leg of the journey from Winnipeg to Toronto added another 12 hours to the flight log.

Aviation company heads inspect the new demonstrator Puss Moth. Left to right: Geoff O'Brian, Bob Loader and Vern Levick, DH Canada; Col. R.H. Mulock, general manager of Canadian Airways; Bob Cockeram, Prospectors Airways; H.A. "Doc" Oaks, first McKee Trophy winner. (DHC5832)

The interior of the assembly shop in the days of the Moth. Frank Warren (far left) is rigging CF-AGJ with Bill Calder in the cockpit. Walter Rinaldo and Pete Loveday install an engine. (via W. Etherington)

(Top photo) The demonstrator Puss Moth shortly after arriving in Canada in July 1930. (Pringle & Booth via Larry Milberry)

George Mickleborough (left) and DHC pilot Geoff O'Brian with the Puss Moth they flew from Toronto to Vancouver and back in 1930. (DHC)

An advertisement in the *Canadian Air Review*, August 1930, for the Puss Moth, following the Toronto-Vancouver flight. (via C.D. Long)

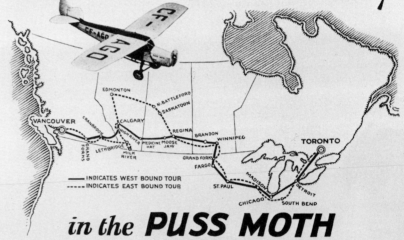

in the PUSS MOTH

Between Saturday, July 12th, and Friday, August 1st, G. S. O'Brian and George Mickleborough carried out a flying tour which demonstrated in a thoroughly practical manner the true capabilities of the Puss Moth.

Leaving Toronto at dawn they reached Winnipeg, 1400 air miles distant, the same evening, having called enroute at Detroit, Chicago, Madison, St. Paul, Fargo and cleared customs twice. Their flying time for the journey was 14 hours.

At Winnipeg the Puss Moth participated in Manitoba Jubilee Air Meet and dozens of flights were made.

The tour was then continued to Regina, Moose Jaw, Medicine Hat and Calgary, demonstrations being given at each point.

Continuing over the Rockies by way of the Crow's Nest and Coquihalla Passes, Vancouver and the western terminus of the tour was reached.

After a stay of five days, which were employed in giving flights to British Columbia aviation enthusiasts, the Puss Moth was headed homeward. The Rockies were again crossed at altitudes varying from 6,000 to 12,000 feet, and the return flight was made by way of Lethbridge, Calgary, Edmonton, Saskatoon and Winnipeg. On the last day the journey was made from Winnipeg to Toronto in 12 hours' flying.

During the whole tour, which O'Brian and Mickleborough describe as a "perfect holiday," the Gipsy III. engine ran faultlessly and no trouble of any kind was experienced.

The distance of 6,050 miles was covered in 57 flying hours—average cruising speed 104 miles per hour, and in addition the carrying of over 250 passengers accounted for 29 additional hours' flying.

The de Havilland Aircraft of Canada
LIMITED
1702 STERLING TOWER, TORONTO, CANADA

Geoff O'Brian (left), who combined purchasing, sales and assistant test pilot duties, poses with Phil Garratt, who was a regular visitor to de Havilland in 1930. (DHC5954)

tled with the farmer for another $20. We soon found the Ross Ranch—after taking off through our trail of the day before—and it is interesting to note that we sold a Puss Moth, CF-AGY, to George G. Ross, who formed Ranchers Air Line Limited two years later. [It is also interesting historically that Ross's son Stubb later built an airline, Time Air, using both the the de Havilland Twin Otter and the Dash 7.]

"When we left for a much longer flight across the Rockies, we wondered what the funny smell was in the cabin. It got worse and had the aroma of burnt coffee. It wasn't until we landed at Vancouver that we realized it was all the wheat we had taken into the heater at Lethbridge. We had to have the whole system cleaned before we took up any passengers. Here I was, back in my home town, and I couldn't let it be said I brought a bad smell to Vancouver."

DH Canada showed a net profit in 1930 of $18,020.54 with substantial assets on the books: land $29,000, buildings $90,468 and an $18,700 investment in road improvement. Eight Puss Moths were assembled and tested that year along with 50 Moths. (And the two Hawks.) The market for new airplanes declined but a welcome order of ten Puss Moths arrived at the end of the year as the result of the cross-Canada demonstration flight. DH Australia suffered a loss during 1930 and the ambitious manufacturing program in the United States faded completely in spite of the fact that 200 American Moths had been built.

Business was still strong in 1931 but the boom was beginning to taper off. The entire total of planes sold that year was only 23, compared to 67 in 1930. Twenty-two of these were Puss Moths with one new type, the D.H.60T, forerunner of the Tiger Moth. Demand for the Gipsy Moth had dried up suddenly, although improvements to satisfy the Canadian requirement were developing all the time. The main complaint with the Moth, particularly from the Air Force instructors, was the difficulty of dragging a clumsy parachute in and out of the restricted front cockpit.

Only eight pre-production Tigers

The only D.H.60T prototype Tiger in Canada, CF-APL had an inverted Gipsy III engine and a special deep door to the front cockpit. (F.W. Hotson)

The trip covered 6050 miles in 57 hours flying time, with an average cruising speed of 104 mph, which was no mean achievement considering the lack of anything resembling air routes or servicing facilities. The flight received much publicity and resulted in several sales, including 17 machines to the Canadian government.

Many years later it was suggested to George Mickleborough, long after Geoffrey O'Brian had died, that there must have been a story somewhere during those 1000 miles. "Yes, there was," said George, "and, although it wasn't exciting, it sticks out in my memory. We were in Alberta and were headed for the Ross Ranch, near Lethbridge, late in the day. All ranches out there look alike in the setting sun and we couldn't find it. Geoff decided we had better get down while we could still see. He picked a nice field but it was all wheat and we cut quite a swath in landing. By the time we had tied up to a fence, the farmer came out. He was quite pleasant but we hastened to ask how much it would cost for the damage to his crop. We settled for $20 and he drove us into town for the night.

"The next day, when we arrived back at the Puss Moth, we could hardly see it for people. They had trampled even more wheat and we set-

Experience with the D.H.61 Giant Moth in Canada favoured the Pratt & Whitney R-1690 Hornet engine instead of the original Bristol Jupiter XI. CF-OAK was fitted with a Hornet and leased to the Ontario Provincial Air Service in June 1932. It is shown here with Leigh Capreol in the cockpit. This plane was destroyed in an accident in 1935. (via L. Milberry)

were made. It was a "rearrangement" of the Gipsy Moth, rather than a new model. It had a Gipsy III inverted engine similar to the Puss Moth and an enlarged entrance to the front cockpit. The centre section and fuel tank were placed a whole bay forward to give the desired access to the front via the walkway on the lower wing. The rigging of the wings was simply adjusted until everything worked right and the Tiger Moth was born. The pre-production model shipped to Canada was registered CF-APL and the "apple," as it was called in the Toronto area, proved extremely popular. (CF-APL remained as the DHC demonstrator until 1934 when it went to the Austin brothers in Toronto as their first airplane. Walter Deisher of Ottawa had it for two years but most of its active life was spent at the Toronto Flying Club to 1942. Even after it was retired from active flying it went as a training airframe to Central Technical School in Toronto.)

By now the shop in the new plant was equipped with basic machine tools and a reputation for skilled workmanship prevailed. Overhaul and repair work was encouraged to offset the drop-off in Gipsy Moth sales and

prepare for the new models expected from England. The Moths had been in operation long enough to result in a small but steady flow of overhaul and reconditioning work. Modifications were always taking place to "Canadianize" them for the cold winter or add a new convenience. Vernon Levick took on the design of a blind flying kit for the rear seat of the Puss Moth at the request of the RCAF. He even went to the point of having the device patented.

The first serious accident at Downsview, which occurred in January 1930, resulted in injury to test pilot Leigh Capreol. That he was flying a competitor's aircraft, a Curtiss-Reid Rambler, made the circumstances all the more ironic. Like many accidents it resulted from a series of little things, but primarily the fact that the aircraft was a stranger at Downsview. It was a Rambler II, registered CF-ABS in the name of Curtiss-Reid as their demonstrator; "Cap" had been invited to fly it during a Toronto stopover. The Rambler had folding wings, somewhat like the Moth, but the locking mechanism was of different design and the early models lacked an inspection hole.

It was always policy for the pilot to supervise the folding and locking of wings, which was naturally a two-man job. When Capreol was ready to fly he called on a passing workman to give him a hand, not realizing the man was the shipper, not a mechanic. The combination of an unfamiliar locking system and a non-aviation helper resulted in the misalignment of

a locking bolt (it had happened before in a Rambler). Capreol took off and had only reached 1000 feet when one wing folded over his head and the aircraft started to spin earthward. "The ship started to swing wildly," reported Capreol later from hospital, "and the worst was I couldn't see. The lower part of the loose wing blocked my view so that I was helpless. By instinct I opened and shut the throttle to keep the nose up and break the fall."

His flying skill had kept him alive but it took nearly an hour to saw him from the wreckage. Harry Proctor was the first from the plant to reach the downed aircraft, moments after a Bell Telephone crew who had been working nearby. He noticed that a huge snowdrift had absorbed much of the fall and helped deflect the nose of the aircraft. Capreol was still conscious but jammed down almost underneath the engine. Harry made him as comfortable as possible while tools were brought to untangle the wreckage. By this time Dr. Scott, the company physician, had arrived and a Bell Telephone ladder was used to carry Capreol to the parking lot and a waiting ambulance. His worst injuries were to his right leg and ankle and it was six months before he was back in

A fine painting by Canada's leading aviation artist, R.W. Bradford, depicting the flight of Puss Moth 'AGO with Geoffrey O'Brian and George Mickleborough through the Canadian Rockies in 1930. It was presented as a retirement gift to secretary/treasurer George Mickleborough after 37 years with DH Canada. (via George Mickleborough)

the air testing again. He walked with a limp the rest of his life and needed a special boot, but completed an illustrious career of test flying. He was nominated to Canada's Aviation Hall of Fame in 1981.

Bert Hinkler

It was on a cold February morning in 1931 that a short, well-dressed man visited the company's office in downtown Toronto. He introduced himself as Bert Hinkler and general manager Loader recognized him immediately as one of the world's most successful long-distance flyers. His full name was Herbert John Louis Hinkler and he was an Australian who only a year before had established a fantastic record of 15½ days, London to Darwin, in a Cirrus-powered Avro Avian. Hinkler was called "Little Bert" because of his 5 foot 4 inch height, but he had a reputation for dogged persistence and an instinctive mechanical ability. He was admired for his competence as a navigator and had twice won the Britannia Trophy for his outstanding flights.

He had been in the United States since September 1930 unobtrusively looking over the light aircraft market there and contemplating starting charter flying in that country. He had come to Toronto to purchase a Puss Moth and part of any arrangement was that he be allowed to prepare it himself for long-distance flying. Puss Moth number 2049 was one of nine shipped from England completely equipped and ready to fly. It was assigned to Hinkler and given the Canadian registration of CF-APK on April 29. From then on, Hinkler was to be seen almost daily, dressed in overalls, working along with the men in the shop. After the test flight, the Puss Moth was moved to the wooden hangar with the round roof, where Hinkler worked day in and day out on his own designs, doing his own modifications.

Everyone helped him at one stage or another and, although he kept his intentions to himself, all developed a liking for this quiet, lonely man. Ab Warren was in charge of stores at the time and recalls seeing a lot of him during his eight months at de Havilland: "He was always very polite but never said very much. He got to know where things were kept in the tool stores and would slip back and forth borrowing what he needed." Frank

Bert Hinkler, the famous Australian flyer, poses in front of a Puss Moth (not his own) with DH officials. Left to right: V.O. Levick, works manager; R.A. Loader, general manager; S/L H.J.L. Hinkler; Charles D. Browne, manager of C.C. Wakefield & Company Limited, sponsor of the flight; and S/L Geoffrey S. O'Brian, DHC sales manager. (DHC31630)

Warren has similar recollections: "I remember him as a very fine gentleman, going about his business and never bothering anyone. He tried everything possible to save weight and even removed the navigation lights from the aircraft."

CF-APK was painted silver with the struts and registration letters in red. Fabric replaced the rear windows and all upholstery was removed to install the long-range fuel tank. The tank, which Hinkler had had manufactured in Long Island, was apparently a tight fit, taking up the rear of the cabin. He also imported a set of streamline bracing wires to modify the undercarriage. He was anxious to dispense with the weight of the standard rubber blocks in the undercarriage legs and rigged the struts into a solid unit, leaving only the tires to absorb compression. The idea didn't work. He blew both tires on his first overload test flight and had to settle for a compromise arrangement.

Harry Proctor and Frank Russell assisted Hinkler from time to time and Proctor recalls helping solve the problem of replenishing the oil from inside the cabin. "Bert wanted to keep a minimum of used oil in the engine system and regulate the flow so as to

get maximum use of the fresh oil. We were discussing this on a warm day in June and Bill Calder, Bert and I went into the shop for a drink at the cooler. I poured a cup for each of us and watched as a bubble went up in the water jug along with a resounding gurgle. 'There is your answer,' I said. 'We'll make it work like the cooler.' We built him a system to feed in new oil and all he had to do was keep a jar within easy reach, full of oil. It fed automatically, the same as the water cooler. To overcome the fact that he had to carry so many big cans in his small cockpit, we provided a pair of tin snips so he could cut the light metal into small pieces and pass them out the window."

John Slaughter was another of the employees who helped the Australian aviator, by replacing the original tail skid with a wheel. After 51 years, he still remembers the caution of Hinkler's every move. "Whenever he took the aircraft for a flight, he would taxi very slowly and check the engine a long time before he took off."

All the employees who remember Hinkler at de Havilland stress the quiet, capable efficiency that went into his preparations. George Mickleborough recalls that once the business of purchasing the aircraft was through, he was in the plant all the time: "He told us vaguely of his plans to fly down the east coast of South America but nothing more."

Three things stand out in Frank Russell's mind in recalling Bert Hinkler—his high-heeled boots, the fact that he chewed gum all the time, and

THE STAFF CHEER BERT HINKLER

For years the author wondered what occasioned the cheering pose in this photo. Some research into the Bert Hinkler story provided the answer and the search for names was renewed. Many de Havilland employees worked with Hinkler to prepare his Puss Moth and they were thrilled with his crossing of the South Atlantic in 1931. Shortly after the news was received that Hinkler had reached England, Bob Loader organized this staff photograph. Vernon Levick stands at the right giving the signal to cheer, and the resulting photo is not only a historic record but a study in human reactions. Bob Loader and George Mickleborough are missing from the picture, but after much research here are the names of most of those present:

1. Bill Calder
2. Stan Dibble
3. Tom Glasson
4. Harry Proctor
5. Bill Matthews
6. Scotty ?
7. Roy Shermerhorn
8. Bill Etherington
9. Russ Borrett
10. Ab Warren

11. Pete Loveday
12. John Neal
13. Walter Rinaldo
14. Jack Jones
15. Lou Thorpe
16. Harry Beffort
17. Hilda Currell
18. Dorothy Kirkman
19. Eric Tetsull
20. Kate Nixon

21. Esther ?
22. Jack Macintosh
23. Bert Witham
24. Edith Mitchell
25. Joe Bannigan
26, 27, 28. Three women from the downtown office
29. Unknown
30. Leigh Capreol
31. Vernon Levick

32. Bill McMillan
33. Vick Tetsull
34. George Blanchard
35. Ethel Almond
36. Frank Warren
37. Jack Dawson
38. Frank Russell
39. Bob Sheppard

his liking for the ginger beer he used to bring in from the United States. George Blanchard helped Hinkler install the big cabin tank and modify the seat. "When you worked for Bert, you were the helper—he was the boss. I did what I was told and we got along fine. I remember he was a good workman."

Bert Hinkler left Toronto quietly on October 20 with no advance publicity. He took off from Jamaica, New York, on Monday, October 26 at 2:00 p.m. with the same secrecy and headed south over the Atlantic. Because he had removed the navigation lights he was not allowed to fly the overland airways of the United States. He planned his flight so that he would spend the hours of darkness over the Atlantic coast. That night bad weather and headwinds forced him slightly off course and at 8 o'clock on the morning of the 27th he landed in Kingston, Jamaica, a distance of 1850 miles, after 18 hours in the air.

He worked his way to Natal in Brazil in easy stages and left on November 25 for a stormy crossing of the South Atlantic. He landed at Bathurst in British Gambia, a flight of 2600 miles in 22 hours. (A false report was published of his arrival at Dakar, then nothing for the waiting press for 48 hours. There was considerable concern back at Downsview until his arrival was confirmed, and it wasn't until Bill Calder received a letter a month later from Hinkler that they knew the reason. He had taken time at the tiny Bathurst airport to do a

top overhaul of the Gipsy engine while the reporters were looking for him in Dakar and St. Louis.) A further two hours took him to St. Louis, Senegal, in French West Africa, where he landed at 2:00 p.m. on November 27. The next day he continued his flight to Casablanca in Morocco and he completed his final leg of the flight to England via Paris. He landed finally at Hanworth Airport in London to a hero's welcome.

For this outstanding flight from Canada to London, he received the Seagrave Memorial Trophy, presented by the British Aeronautical Society for the most daring flying feat of 1931. Other awards he received at that time were the Britannia Challenge Trophy for the third time, the Oswald Watt Gold Plaque and the Johnston Memorial prize.

A Canadian Moth Abroad

The Moths in Canada took on a variety of roles as had been expected. Fire spotting by air was a particularly Canadian task and some early Moths were used commercially in remote areas as a forerunner of the bushplane. Most were used for training purposes and a few saw service as private aircraft for pleasure flying. In the sport of air touring few can match the record of serial number 783, a metal Moth, that started in Montreal and ended its career in Australia.

CF-ADC was delivered to Dougall Cushing of Montreal on floats in 1929 and was sold in the summer of 1932 to a Montreal businessman, Jacques

R. Hébert. He had been a co-founder of the Montreal Light Aeroplane Club, learned to fly there and had built up 100 hours of flight experience. His purpose in buying 'ADC was to make a sightseeing trip around the world combining boat and plane. He planned to ship the Moth to England, fly to Australia, return to Vancouver by boat and fly the rest of the way to Montreal.

In England Hébert had de Havilland modify CF-ADC for long-range flying and departed on his pleasure trip on October 12, 1932. He reached Cairo on October 23 where he met Tony Spooner, the former instructor of the Montreal Club. Spooner showed him around the area during the next three days, then it was off again for Amman and Baghdad. He made his way over deserts and mountains and by December 6 was ready for the dangerous over-water stretch of the Timor Sea. He took off from Koepang and reached Darwin, Australia, after eight hours in the air.

It was four days later, while making his way to Sydney, that he damaged his undercarriage substantially trying to avoid some errant goats in a field at Cloncurry. When he found out how much time it would take to make the necessary repairs, he sold the aircraft to Qantas Airlines and made his way back to Canada by boat. The Moth was repaired and, as VH-UQV, spent an interesting career in instruction, joy riding and private flying. It was stored during World War 2 and, as late as 1965, was still flying actively.

G-CAJU, the first Moth ever assembled by de Havilland Canada, seen in a scheme used by the Toronto Flying Club in the late twenties.

Illustration by Peter Mossman

Hard Times

Frank Russell stands by during engine run-up of the first Fox Moth to arrive in Canada. Demonstrator Puss Moth 'AGO is in the background. (C.D. Long)

Riding the Depression

In spite of the decline in sales during 1931, the company showed a satisfactory "liquid position" in cash and government bonds, even though a net loss of $29,555 was reported. The sudden slump was enough to bring chairman Alan Butler and director of finance W.E. Nixon out from England for the annual meeting, January 16, 1932. The report read that day stressed the need for "large economies" in the year ahead and it was not long before a series of furloughs was introduced. These furloughs became an accepted part of the employment pattern: an understanding among the workers of economic conditions and the promise of a call-back when things got better. The overall situation worsened with the report in April that the Canadian government had cut its overall appropriations for aircraft purchases from $5,000,000 to $1,700,000.

One incident to brighten the lives of the remaining workers during February 1932 was a visit by their friend Bert Hinkler. He had returned to Canada by boat after his triumphant reception in England and was making the rounds of the Toronto aviation fraternity. He went through the plant thanking everyone who had helped him and chatted with them at lunchtime about his South Atlantic trip. One story involved a small monkey he was given in Brazil

Bob Cockeram, president of Prospectors Airways Limited, in his Fox Moth *Miss Ruth 2nd,* which he flew extensively throughout Canada. (PAC A1476)

as a good luck mascot before taking off for Africa. During the long night the monkey roamed through the Puss Moth unrestricted and unnoticed until the going got rough. At one stage Hinkler had to navigate through one of the worst storms in his career, with bolts of lightning which he described as "looking like telephone poles." During the height of the lightning the monkey climbed on his shoulder and remained there, shivering and drinking the rainwater that leaked through the cabin roof.

Jim Mollison

The next Puss Moth in the growing sport of Atlantic hopping was Jim Mollison's *Heart's Content.* Mollison left Port Marnock, Ireland, on Aug-

ust 18, 1932, with his declared destination New York City. His unscheduled landing at Pennfield Ridge, New Brunswick, provided a topic of conversation at DH Canada on the morning of the 19th and immediately involved two company members. Mollison flew on to New York the next day and was met by Bill Calder and Walter Rinaldo, who arrived from Toronto to check the Puss Moth and its Gipsy engine. Mollison's original intention was to make a round-trip crossing and the two DH Canada representatives completely overhauled the engine for the return flight. The west-to-east journey got as far as New Brunswick, where it was terminated, and the Puss returned to England by boat.

The entire de Havilland organization felt the backlash of the depression in 1932. The yearly dividend was down in England to 2½ per cent with salary cuts and shorter working hours in the shops. Canadian sales dropped to three: one Puss Moth and two of the new D.H.83 Fox Moths. The Giant Moth that had come over in 1928 was re-engined with a Pratt & Whitney Hornet and leased to the Ontario Provincial Air Service as CF-OAK. Another trading loss was recorded in the annual report but the Canadian company retained its satisfactory "liquid" position.

The year 1933 started badly with the news in January that Bert Hinkler was lost on a flight to Australia. He set out from England on the 7th in his Canadian-registered Puss Moth and

York ended in a damaged undercarriage. They finally got away at midnight June 22 from the beach at Pendine Sands and battled the usual headwinds associated with a westward crossing of the Atlantic. They were six hours behind time when they reached Newfoundland and, instead of landing at New York in daylight, were faced with an emergency night landing at Bridgeport, Connecticut, when fuel ran out.

The poor wooden Dragon was severely damaged in an over-run accident at the unfamiliar airport. The newlyweds were hospitalized in Bridgeport and reached New York on July

centre of gravity. The Mollisons had taken off from a beach in England and chose the level sands of Wasaga Beach on the shores of Georgian Bay for their Canadian departure.

While the preparations were in progress, Jim and Amy were royally entertained by Toronto Flying Club members and had free use of the company demonstrator Puss Moth. Capreol acted as advisor and tested the sand conditions at the beach with the new demonstrator Fox Moth. By the morning of October 3, 1933, the *Seafarer II* was fuelled up for the attempted takeoff, but the fates frowned for the third time on the flying twosome.

The product lineup in 1932: the DH demonstrator Giant Moth 'OAK; a Fox Moth, still with the English registration G-ABUO (later CF-API); Puss Moth 'AGO; Tiger Moth 'APL; and two D.H.60M Moths, 'AGX and 'AAA. (DHC)

was reported passing over the Italian Alps. (Nothing was heard for months, then one morning in May the following year, high up in the Pratango Mountains of the Appenine range, the wreckage was found. Bert Hinkler had died in much the same way as he had lived: quietly and alone.)

The mystery of Hinkler's disappearance persisted throughout a troubled year for DH Canada. The company received considerable publicity in 1935 but it was not the kind that influenced bank managers. The Mollison name was in the news again, but even this episode was not a complete success. Jim Mollison had married the equally famous pilot Amy Johnson, and they were planning an Atlantic flight as a husband and wife team. They chose a DH twin-engined Dragon 1, G-ACCV, and had it christened the *Seafarer*. Their first attempt to leave London Airport for New

25 with mixed emotions as to their trans-Atlantic accomplishments. Their original plan was a long-distance record flight to Baghdad, but their *Seafarer* would never rise again. An enterprising department store in Bridgeport collected all of the damaged wood and fabric, ran a gigantic sale, decorated the store with the debris and gave away a sample piece with each purchase. It proved an advantage to de Havilland, as they didn't have to do all the cleaning up.

Sir Charles Wakefield came to the Mollisons' aid in early September and shipped a brand new Dragon to Canada, named *Seafarer II* this time, combining their initials in the registration G-CAJM. The publicity spotlight shifted to Dufferin Street and Sheppard Avenue, Toronto, when reporters heard the famous pair were preparing their new plane for a Canada-Baghdad flight. The hangar staff pitched in with overtime and soon the Dragon was ready for test by Leigh Capreol. George Blanchard went along on the test flight to crawl back and forth in the narrow crawl space to test the

The winds, which blow predominantly across the beach at Wasaga, severely complicated the takeoff. On the third attempt to become airborne, one wheel of the 3½-ton machine buckled under the load and the attempt was abandoned.

Russ Borrett rushed the strut to Toronto for an overnight repair but conditions the next day discouraged the intrepid aviators and the *Seafarer II* was flown to Downsview for shipment back to England. The newspaper headlines of the Mollisons' activities were not hiding the fact from the directors that it was a bad financial year. Only six new aircraft were sold during the twelve-month period: five Fox Moths and the first Dragon 4 (similar to the *Seafarer II*) to Canadian Airways.

The excellent start of the first four years coupled with current assets of $198,813 and $82,677 in cash and bonds, meant that the situation was not desperate, but the net loss of $19,952 at the end of 1933 called for drastic "further economies." This time they were to go right to the top and involve senior personnel. The

Trans-Atlantic flyer James Mollison stands beside the Puss Moth he flew solo from England to Pennfield Ridge, near Saint John, New Brunswick, August 19, 1932. (National Museum of Science and Technology)

(Far right photo) Two of the early employees at DH Canada, Frank Warren (left) and his brother Ab pose in front of the Mollison *Seafarer II* after assembly at Downsview September 1933. (DHC47048)

(Lower right) Jim Mollison makes a final inspection of the *Seafarer II* before his attempted takeoff from Wasaga Beach October 3, 1933. (via D. Williams)

parent company sent out L.C. Lee Murray to fill the multiple role of manager, aeronautical engineer and test pilot. This allowed Loader and Levick to return to England and Bill Calder to move up from inspector to works manager. Leigh Capreol left to form a charter flying company at the Toronto waterfront with Chuck and Jack Austin.

Lee Murray was a pleasant soft-spoken Australian who studied engineering in his native country and turned his attention to aviation. He began flying at Point Cook, Victoria, in 1924 when he joined the Royal Australian Air Force, and went on to a colourful flying career in India. In later years he owned a Desouter II monoplane in Australia, and when he accepted a job with de Havilland England in 1932, he chose a novel way of getting there. He had the plane shipped with him to Vancouver then flew it across Canada to Montreal. He left it to be sold there and made the rest of the trip to England by boat. Murray arrived in Toronto on December 1, 1933, during deteriorating

economic times to try to keep the company alive. Only a skeleton staff remained at Sheppard Avenue and even their work hours were drastically reduced.

The Puss Moth Mysteries

In spite of the lovely flying qualities of the Puss Moth and the thousands of record-breaking miles, the aircraft developed a Jekyll-and-Hyde tendency and a reputation for mystery that it has never shaken. An accident on October 13, 1930, in Western Australia, brought the first indication of an elusive structural problem which recurred in an unfortunate series of similar events. All accidents took on the same pattern in which one or both wings would come off in flight. Most were associated with turbulent weather and high speed; nine such accidents were recorded by the end of 1933.

DH Canada's test pilot, Leigh Capreol, had occasion to complain of rudder flutter at high speeds and a great deal of correspondence resulted in view of the growing concern. Testing was done at Downsview and the

Canadian reports provided considerable input into the investigations. The only wing separation accident in which anyone survived occurred in Ottawa on March 21, 1932, to Flying Officer Arthur L. James (later A/V/M James), who was able to make a substantial contribution with his report on the accident sequence. There were other related incidents in Canada and a recall of all Puss Moths was instigated for mandatory strengthening modifications.

On January 7, 1933, a second Canadian-registered Puss Moth was lost, Bert Hinkler's CF-APK, which everyone at Downsview knew so well. Details of the investigation were scarce for the wreckage was only found months after the event. The pattern was familiar: turbulence over the Italian mountains had evidently caused the wing to break away in the air. All modifications had been applied to Hinkler's machine in England, where it had been re-engined with a Gipsy Major and given a thorough check before his last flight. That the wing had broken away in the air was dem-

Early Moths

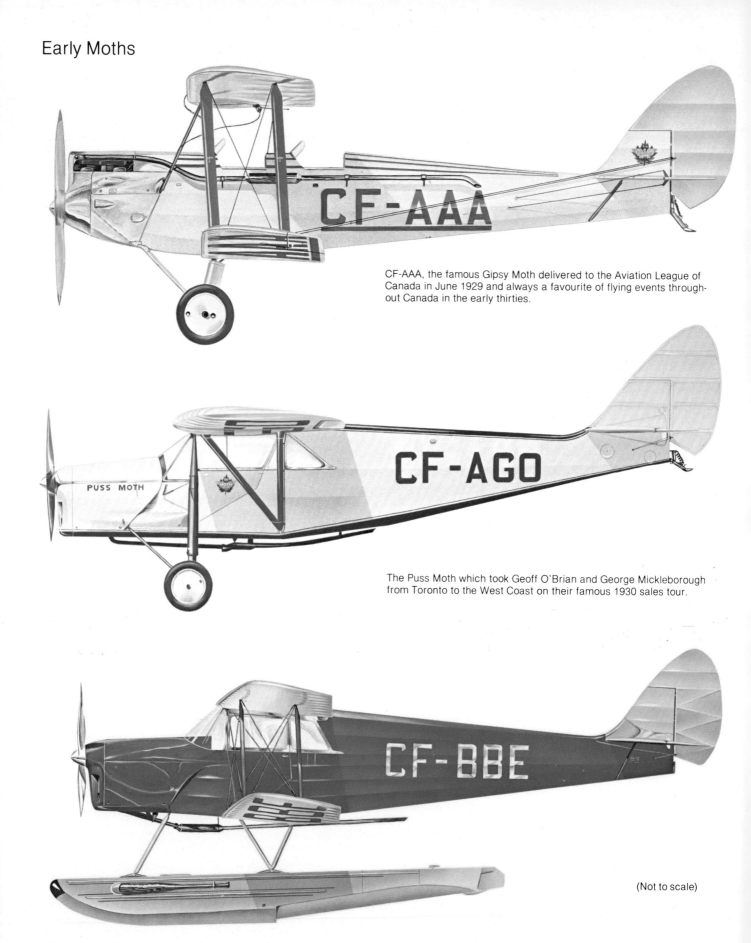

CF-AAA, the famous Gipsy Moth delivered to the Aviation League of Canada in June 1929 and always a favourite of flying events throughout Canada in the early thirties.

The Puss Moth which took Geoff O'Brian and George Mickleborough from Toronto to the West Coast on their famous 1930 sales tour.

(Not to scale)

Illustrations by Ronald E. Lowry

Hornet Moth CF-BBE which operated for over 20 years. It is shown here in the colours of Consolidated Mining and Smelting.

onstrated by the lack of splitting at the wing joint and the fact that the wing was found 270 yards from the fuselage. The Italian authorities gave their opinion that the wing broke off as a whole in the air.

The company and airworthiness officials were continually alert to the situation for the next few years, but one more case arose involving a Canadian Puss Moth. It had originally been sold to Dougall Cushing of Westmount, Quebec, and at the time of the crash was owned by Leavens Brothers Air Services, Toronto. Arthur Leavens was flying CF-AGQ from Toronto to Detroit on May 20 with two passengers when he encountered thunderstorm turbulence near St. Marys, Ontario. Eyewitness accounts told the unfortunate story: "The airplane appeared to lose a wing while still in the air."

In spite of its acceptance in Canada and around the world, the wing failures of the Puss Moth were a blot on its otherwise outstanding history.

Canadian Airways' CF-AVD was a Dragon II with two Gipsy Major engines and came to Canada in January 1935. The fuselage was the plywood box type and the outer wing panels, which could be folded, were standard Moth wings. The Canadian models had the extended dorsal fin shown here. This aircraft served in many parts of Canada on wheels, skis and floats until May 26, 1944, when it was destroyed in a takeoff accident at Baie Comeau, Quebec. (Gordon S. Williams)

The Len Reid Story

Any conversation with DHC veterans of the 1933-34 era will sooner or later turn to the story of Len Reid. Most of the tales are told with a chuckle, for Len was one of those likeable characters who never took life seriously. He was sent out from the English company yet he was not an Englishman. He had family prestige but he shunned high office. Captain Leonard Gillespie Reid was born in Montreal, Canada, the grandson of Sir Robert Reid, who had made his fortune building railway bridges in the time of John A. Mac- 'donald. He was the third son of Sir William Duff Reid of Hocliffe, Bedfordshire, England, who had been instrumental in building Newfoundland's railway. Another attribute to which he laid no claim was that he was the brother-in-law of Alan S. Butler, chairman of the board, de Havilland England.

In 1929 Len Reid joined the group at Mount Dennis in a role that Bill Calder used to refer to as "remittance man." He was made stores manager, married a Toronto girl, Phyllis Austin, and flew as a private pilot at the Toronto Flying Club. He left Toronto in 1931 but a year after the Mollison failure at Wasaga he returned to Canada as an aspiring trans-Atlantic pilot. He came with a well-known Britisher, Captain James R. Ayling, intending to try for the distance record the Mollisons had abandoned. He had

spent all his money on the long-range Dragon that had been sitting idle in England and which was shipped again to Canada, this time as the *Trail of the Caribou.*

Reid said the renaming was just a matter of sentiment, resulting from his many pleasant years in Newfoundland and his service with the Newfoundland Regiment during World War 1. The attempt was to be sponsored by Alan Butler and the pattern of the Mollison flight plan was to be duplicated—including the takeoff at Wasaga Beach. During assembly and testing at Downsview, Len Reid had some innovations of his own to add, involving an idea to overcome carburetor icing in the Gipsy Major engines.

The regular Gipsy engine drew warm air from the crankcase automatically at low throttle settings to overcome the icing problem in a glide, but took cold air at full throttle. Reid reasoned that with a special control to the valve he could get crankcase heat whenever he wanted it and look after the dreaded icing. He bought two automotive push-pull controls and connected the long cables from the engines to the cockpit. (It is not known what authority or approval he got for this modification.) He also learned that the Mollisons had kept the tail of the Dragon too low on their takeoff attempt; he was determined it would not happen to him.

There was considerable delay await-

ing suitable weather for the flight. One early-morning attempt with reporters and photographers in attendance had to be called off due to strong crosswinds on the beach. Lee Murray was acting as advisor for this flight and tested the winds with a circuit in a Gipsy Moth. On August 8 they tried again and John Neal of the de Havilland staff described the activity that morning:

"We worked from two o'clock in the morning, filling the huge tanks with 400 gallons of special fuel imported in drums from Holland. When the sun came up the gasoline overflowed and got into the spar caps and crevices. We had to work our way into these areas on our stomachs and

The Dragon *Trail of the Caribou* on the Downsview ramp with the two pilots, Richard Ayling (left) and Len Reid, before their flight from Wasaga Beach to London in 1934. (via Larry Milberry)

mop up the excess gasoline with rags. We had to have someone standing by to pull us out by the feet in case we passed out with the fumes. Reid and Ayling got away as early in the morning as possible and, although there was a bit of crosswind, they ran the whole length of Wasaga before they inched into the air and disappeared over the treetops."

The observers noted that the tail of the aircraft rose higher than in the Mollison attempt of the year before —one of Len Reid's ideas had worked. Five hours later they were sighted over Quebec City, but during the rest of the day and night speculation ran high at Downsview. Atlantic crossings were still dangerous and Baghdad was a rather ambitious destination. The guessing game ended suddenly at noon Greenwich time, August 9, with a news flash that the *Trail of the*

Two names of the thirties: *Trail of the Caribou* and Charlie Powell. Charlie was the timekeeper/watchman in prewar days and the driving force behind the Canadian Legion branch in World War 2. The writer recalls listening to King Edward VIII's abdication speech as we all crowded around Charlie's time office radio at quitting time. (DHC9237)

Caribou had landed at Heston Airport, near London, after 30 hours and 50 minutes in the air. The pilots had abandoned their long-distance attempt for lack of fuel, but had completed 3700 miles and the first non-stop flight from the Canadian mainland to England.

The story of that historic flight might have been lost in the shuffle of unconfirmed reports if Len Reid had not returned to a job at Downsview. He rejoined his friends, in the shops this time, and bit by bit the story of that long Atlantic flight came out. Icing had indeed played a major part in the crossing and provided their greatest concern. "But, what of the heater controls?" his friend asked. "Didn't they work?" The answer was apparently, "No," for they stuck when needed and forced the engines to take in unheated air at all times. When the conditions were right for carburetor ice, the engines simply lost power until the aircraft descended into warmer air, often with the waves only feet away. Bumping the throttles to clear the ice only resulted in bending one of the controls and further complicating their situation. And so it went, up/down, ice/de-ice, throughout the long night with a considerable waste of fuel. They still had 200 gallons when they reached London, but decided not to press on to Baghdad.

Once the story of the flight satisfied the boys in the shop, the next question was, "What happened to the Dragon, *Trail of the Caribou*?" In keeping with the bad luck story, Reid explained that, once the flight was over, he had spent all his money and there was not much coming in. He tried taking the aircraft around the British Isles, selling rides, but ended up writing it off in a field at Hamble where he clipped a hedge on landing. "Even that didn't go off well," explained Reid. "I had a lady on board at the time and her husband was quite prominent in the neighbourhood."

Len Reid was killed some years later in an automobile accident in London, England, but his name and that of his companion, Jim Ayling, live on. The Historic Sites and Monuments Board of Canada erected a cairn in memory of the flight near the spot where they took off at Wasaga Beach. It was fittingly unveiled August 24, 1954, in front of a large crowd who still thrilled to the memory of those early flights of daring.

Taste of the Headlines
During the excitement of preparing the *Trail of the Caribou* for its Atlantic flight, a new era was descending on Ontario. The election that year had unseated the long-standing Conservative government of George S. Henry and replaced it with a Liberal regime under the dictatorial Mitchell Frederick Hepburn. The mercurial onion farmer from the Elgin West riding won the greatest Liberal victory in the province's history on the promise of cutting costs, and he went at the task with all the ruthless abandon of a fox in a chicken house. He began by cutting his own salary and those of his ministers the moment he was sworn in on July 10, 1934. He closed the Lieutenant Governor's official residence, and followed up with mass firings at Ontario Hydro and the Liquor Board. Every warden in the provincial Department of Game and Fisheries was summarily fired.

With the newspapers warming up to this unprecedented political bloodletting, he chose the extensive government automobile fleet for his most spectacular showmanship. He spurned the chauffeur-driven government car of his predecessor, George Henry, and bought his own in a well-publicized stunt. He organized a ceremony in which he was to present his cheque and receive the keys. He was a master of the quips and when asked to smile for the assembled photographers, his retort was, "How can you smile when you hand over a cheque for $1700?"

His next grandstand manoeuvre was to herd 47 automobiles used by the former government into Varsity Stadium in Toronto and auction them off to the tune of $34,000. By July 27 he had started six inquiries, including one into the affairs and operations of the Ontario Provincial Air Service.

Meetings were convened in Sault Ste. Marie and Toronto under Commissioner D.W. Lang, K.C. Questions were asked about everything from the original purchase of flying boats in 1924 to the making of non-aircraft andirons in the shops. The cost and supervision of a $1100 pigeon loft was also severely questioned. It wasn't long until the purchase of DH Moths came up and it was noted that American Edo floats had been ordered to replace those made by the British Short Bros. These evidently added 30 pounds extra weight so that new, higher power Gipsy II engines had been installed. As in all such inquiries, there were shop specialists who disagreed with Roy Maxwell's flamboyance and were pleased to inform the judge that they had also arranged for one of the mechanics to work on the superintendent's big blue Cadillac.

Things were going badly for Maxwell, whose own unorthodox way of developing an air service did not sit well with either the legal mind or the accountant's fine pencil. Ontario's taxpayers were treated to a first rate sideshow with daily reports in the newspapers. The headlines flamed anew when it was revealed that Maxwell held shares in de Havilland Aircraft of Canada Ltd., which during 10 years had sold the OPAS $197,924.42 of aircraft and equipment (including the disputed Gipsy II engines). Needless to say, by the time Commissioner Lang published the report of his findings, Roy Maxwell had resigned from the Air Service. It is possibly not by coincidence that he was replaced by a pilot friend of Hepburn's, George Ponsford, who had been his personal driver at election time.

Bruce West, in his book on the Ontario firefighting services, *The Firebirds*, covers the subject in detail and puts an accurate appraisal on the de Havilland purchases in his summary of the event: "In the matter of Maxwell holding some shares in de Havilland Aircraft of Canada, this was clearly a case of creating a direct conflict of interest. Nevertheless, there seems to be no question whatever about the fact that—as events later proved beyond doubt—the DH Moth was one of the most useful and economical pieces of flying equipment ever acquired and operated by the O.P.A.S. . . . There was nothing to indicate that Roy Maxwell allowed his stock in de Havilland to influence him in the purchase of machines inferior to others of the same type which might have then been available on the market."

The Low Point
The parent company in England had weathered the storm of 1934 but the Canadian plant came closer to closing than at any other time in its history. It was definitely the worst year up to that time, with a total net loss of $41,000. Some progress was made developing a set of floats for the Dragon in conjunction with Fairchild Aircraft Limited, but at this point there was only one Dragon in the country. The only bright spot during the year was the introduction of the D.H.89 Dragon Rapide and a sale to the leading operator of the day, Canadian Airways. Two Puss Moths were the only other aircraft sold during 1934. The board of directors was bolstered that year with three proven businessmen: A.H.K. Russell, W.M. Archibald and R.A. Laidlaw.

The pattern of furloughs that had been introduced in 1933 became even more prevalent as time went on because there was a great need to keep the well-trained staff. "We all took turns sharing duties with the regular watchman," recalls John Neal, "and it was arranged around the type of work to be done. I remember getting a call to be watchman one day because there was a Bellanca rudder to repair. I had the place all to myself and before I was finished, I had done metal work, woodwork, fabric work, doping and painting. When it was all finished I even crated it up ready for shipping. We had to be able to do a lot of things in those days."

Frank and Ab Warren, who had been on the staff since the Mount Dennis days, also shared in the watchman duties, coming and going whenever there was a job to be done. Ab Warren, as head of the stores depart-

The de Havilland employees of 1935 gather for a photo at the annual picnic in Port Dalhousie August 16. Left to right, front row: G. Blanchard, G. Otter, J. McNamee. Second row: B. McNichol, H. Currell, G. Mickleborough, L. Thorpe, Lee Murray, L. Granger, W. Calder, E. Almond, M. Currell. Third row: D. Long, B. Witham, J. Slaughter, T. Glasson, M. Borczak, R. Barber, W. Rinaldo, H. Proctor, R. Borrett, A. Nixon, F. Warren. Back row: H. Beffort, G. Gilmour, P. Loveday, J. Neal, R. Ruse, A. Warren, D. Murray. Within ten years the number of staff would be multiplied by more than 200! (via C.D. Long)

ment, probably experienced more employment than most throughout the crisis. "I had to go in on the weekends," he said, "look after any parts orders and keep heat on the boilers. The boiler wasn't a difficult job. I only had to keep it at 15 pounds pressure."

About mid-summer the overhaul work improved considerably and the year ended on a happy note. A steady trend continued through 1935 with RCAF Moths to overhaul and an influx of new machines from England. The overhaul work resulted in a small financial comeback in 1935 and accounted for a net profit of $4077 at the year's end. Even the sales were up to seven, the highest they had been in four years. The first D.H.87A Hornet Moth arrived that year, along with the first D.H.82A Tiger Moth. There were one each of the Puss, the Fox and the Rapide and two twin-engine Dragons sold.

The Dragon Line

If ever there was an aircraft that proved the point of designing to economic conditions, it was the D.H.84 Dragon, the poor man's airliner. A.E. Hagg and his British design staff had done well with their development of the original Moth until it evolved into the Fox Moth at 17 ton miles per gallon. With the advent of difficult times, DH England came up with the Dragon 4 that gave 19 gross ton miles per gallon. It became known as the first multi-engine transport that could pay its way without subsidy. It flew like a big kite and, although the payload was not great on Canadian Fairchild floats, it did get into the air and the economy was right. It had folding wings outboard of the engines and could accommodate six people or be modified for eight on short hops. Only three D.H.84 Dragons came to Canada: CF-APJ and CF-AVD served with Canadian Airways from 1933 to 1944; CF-AVI started out with Consolidated Mining and Smelting but ended up with Howard Watt and North Shore Airways Limited competing with Quebec Airways and their Rapides on the winter St. Lawrence.

The Dragon was the first twin-engine aircraft used by Canadian Airways and set the scene for the D.H.89 Dragon Rapide, which followed in fair numbers. In appearance the Rapide closely resembled the Dragon as it used the same fuselage shape. It had finely tapered mainplanes and sleek engine nacelles combined with faired wheel pants. The larger 200 hp Gipsy Six engines gave it a much more lively performance and improved payload. It also carried six to eight people, and although its fuselage was made of plywood like the Dragon, the wood stringers and fabric cover gave it a sleek, streamlined appearance. Sixteen eventually came to Canada. Three were in active use from 1936 to 1951, while seven were used regularly from 1939 to 1946.

In retrospect it can be said that the Rapide was a success in Canada, for it not only carried the budding airline industry from the single-engine to the twin-engine stage but proved to be one of the first real money-making aircraft in the business. Its size and economy proved just right for the period and, although it was never designed with tough Canadian flying in mind, it converted well to skis and floats. Canadian Airways Limited made wide use of Rapides on the west coast, but it was with their Quebec affiliate, Quebec Airways, that the Rapide was best known.

The entire North Shore of the Lower St. Lawrence River became ice-bound and isolated during the winter months. Quebec Airways and a number of private operators had always spent busy winters keeping communications open and the mail flowing. Quebec pilot Romeo Vachon had pioneered the first air mail to Sept Iles as long ago as 1927 while chief pilot for Canadian Transcontinental Airways. With the arrival of the Rapides he was the logical person to inaugurate an improved winter service along the North Shore.

The added seat capacity of the Rapides, compared to the earlier single-engine ski-planes, made them popular. The distances involved were short and special winter landing strips were prepared by the local communities to im-prove the service. The success of the operation was reflected in 1937 with the presentation of the Trans Canada (McKee) Trophy that year to Romeo Vachon. He left Quebec Airways in 1938 but the Rapides continued the winter runs well into the postwar per-iod when Canadian Pacific Airlines and, later, Quebecair modernized the air service.

Skis and Floats

In January 1936 de Havilland Canada were asked by the National Research Council to build a set of experimental skis for a Rapide. They were to have a number of novel features and be self-aligning in the air due to their stream-lined shape. The objective was to do away with the complex fore and aft cables associated with standard skis and eliminate much of the drag. Engineer J. Bruce Douglas was res-ponsible for overseeing the NRC dir-ectives while George Blanchard was assigned to build the skis. They were to be 15 feet long with spruce plank-ing over a series of bulkheads to pro-duce the streamlined form.

After the spruce structure was built, it was varnished on the inside and covered with doped fabric on the out-side. The snow bottoms were ash planks rivetted to the shell and pro-tected with metal sheathing. A standard streamlined ski pedestal was used and the only check cables used were almost entirely contained within the cowling.

The skis were ready by the middle of March but it was doubtful if there would be enough snow for a test. A heavy spring snowfall on March 17 permitted a test with Rapide CF-AYE on the 18th. It was heavy, wet snow, and although the skis looked perfect in their shining silver, they cracked and groaned as Lee Murray taxied out. Professor Tom Loudon of the

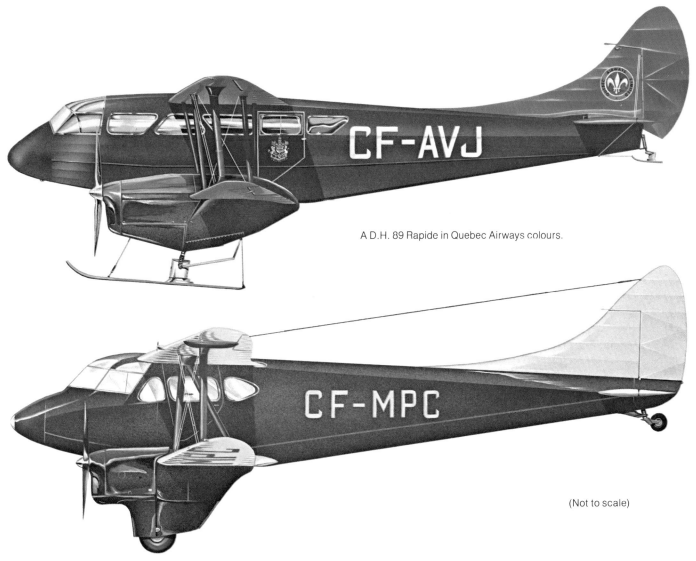

A D.H. 89 Rapide in Quebec Airways colours.

(Not to scale)

Illustrations by Ronald E. Lowry

One of the RCMP's D.H. 90 Dragonfly coastal patrol aircraft.

Dragon 'AVI started its career with Consolidated Mining and Smelting in 1935 and was returned to de Havilland in 1937 as a down payment on a Rapide. Bought by Howard Watt, it served on the Quebec North Shore until January 13, 1941 when it was destroyed at its mooring during a windstorm at Godbout, Quebec. It is seen here on Fairchild floats lifting off from Ramsey Lake in Sudbury. (Rusty Blakey)

Canadian Airways Dragon 'APJ after overhaul at Downsview in 1937. The flap on the trailing edge allowed the outer wing panels to fold back for storage. (F.W. Hotson)

University of Toronto was on the flight along with DHC engineer Pete Loveday. They headed for Camp Borden, where there was more snow, and completed a number of landings there. When it started to rain they headed back, knowing that the little snow at Downsview would soon disappear. There were open grass patches but the skis rode over the slippery grass as easily as snow. The skis performed well aerodynamically but were too weak structurally to have been placed in regular service.

Canadian modifications to the British de Havilland line of aircraft proved a distinct challenge for the small DHC staff. Through the critical years, from the Fox Moths to the Rapides, the design work was shared by J. Bruce Douglas and C. Don Long, both graduates of the University of Toronto. Most of the designs during that period involved improvements for winter conditions. Keeping the engines and pilots at operating temperatures had a high priority but the design of ski undercarriages became a specialty.

From the days of the Cirrus Moth, DHC had built their own ski pedestals and the art had improved through the period of the Fox, Hornet and Tiger.

Laminated wooden skis with copper rivets and brass bottoms, made by Elliot Brothers of Sioux Lookout, proved the most suitable. They were installed with a standard set of rubber bungee cords and check cables to hold the skis in proper flying position. The

The wooden streamlined skis built by de Havilland Canada at the request of the National Research Council in 1938. They were only flown once. (F.W. Hotson)

46

A typical winter scene along the St. Lawrence River when a Quebec Airways Rapide drops the daily bag of mail for a North Shore community. (via F.W. Hotson)

The postwar colour scheme of Canadian Pacific Airlines Rapides on the Quebec North Shore service. Shown at Mont Joli, Quebec, CF-BND crashed on Digby Island, B.C. on July 29, 1949 after running out of fuel. (F.W. Hotson)

bigger Rapide and Dragonfly presented additional torque problems due to the greater track and the use of differential power, but these were overcome with the aid of struts and braces.

The streamlined wheel pants on the Rapide and Dragonfly were not practical for skis and floats, so a new, lower cowl, looking somewhat like half a bath tub, was devised to replace the original. It allowed for the torque strut positioning on skis and for the float struts, with all their bracing wires, in the summer configuration. Seaplane installations were handled by Fairchild Aircraft Limited of Longueil, near Montreal, first with floats of their own design and later with the American Edos.

Another feature of the winter Rapide was the quick-drain facility for removing the hot oil. It protruded below the cowling for easy access and was covered with a quick-release fairing. Another modification to the Rapides in Canada was the installation of an additional door on the starboard side for seaplane use. Probably the most distinctive feature of the Canadian Rapide was the extended dorsal fin tapering down the back of the fuselage. It provided the lateral control needed to offset the forward bulk of the seaplane floats.

In Quebec Airways' North Shore Rapides, a special mail chute was built into the floor in the rear of the cabin for dropping mail bags. The mechanic on the flight had to open the trap door at the appropriate time and throw out the bags as quickly as possible when the pilot signalled with a buzzer.

De Havilland air engineer Don Murray spent a winter with Quebec Airways in 1937 and participated in the mail drop. "I learned in a hurry not to let the mail bag get into the slipstream before the buzzer went," said Don. "On my first drop, the wind began taking the bag, making it more and more difficult to hold. By the time the pilot signalled to drop, I was starting to slide out of the hole."

During the summer float season in the 1930s there was always a lot of traffic between Downsview and the Toronto air harbour at the foot of Yonge Street. Repair and modification work was always in progress and sometimes the workers would be down there for weeks on end. At changeover time there was always the task of moving the aircraft through the city traffic; nobody liked that assignment. The bigger machines required a motorcycle policeman in front and a car behind for protection. Most of the difficult towing was planned for the very early hours of the morning.

Harry Beffort's first such trip took place back in the Moth days when he was in charge of the company truck. It was fall and a Moth had been removed from floats at the waterfront. The early Moths were designed for towing behind a car with their biplane wings folded and locked. Even though he was alone, Beffort regarded it as an easy assignment as he headed for the centre of the city.

He had just entered University Avenue, northbound, when a policeman stopped him with, "Where do you think you are going?" Beffort explained his mission and got the reply, "Not with that thing, you're not!" It was the day of the Santa Claus Parade and by now he was in no position either to back up or to turn around. The police helpfully ushered him up a narrow lane and he sat through the parade wondering how he would get the Moth back onto the street again. Fortunately there were plenty of police, once the parade was over, who enjoyed solving their first aircraft traffic problem.

Then there was the story of George Otter and the Hornet Moth oil tank. George was a young engineering student who, because he had a motorcycle, was assigned the job of taking a repaired oil tank down to the waterfront. He padded it up, tied it securely and set off from Sheppard

Avenue about mid-afternoon. He made the trip down in good time but on arrival could find nothing but some rope and bits of packing tied to his carrier. It must have been a traumatic moment as he visualized the expensive aluminum tank lying on the road somewhere, flattened beyond recognition.

Slowly he retraced his route, looking back and forth at every curb. He passed the other employees leaving work and arrived at last back at the de Havilland parking lot, wondering what excuse he would use first. Most of the cars were gone but he was pleased to note that Russ Borrett was still there. At that moment Russ came out with a parcel under his arm, and said, ''Looking for this, George?'' Evidently the tank had been found beside the road, half a mile from the plant, returned to have a few scuff marks removed, and repainted ready for a second trip to the lake — this time successfully.

Drama at Moose River
A news drama of some impact broke in Eastern Canada during the early months of 1936. The Moose River gold mine, near Halifax, Nova Scotia, suffered a collapse in its lower levels, trapping a prominent Toronto doctor and his two companions, who were down on an inspection trip. The event

affected DH Canada and emphasized dramatically the value of aircraft in emergencies. The affair took a serious turn when one of the men died and the Toronto medical profession made an all-out effort to assist in the rescue of Dr. D.E. Robertson and Alfred Scadding. At the mine site a hole had been drilled into the area where the men were trapped and contact established. Back in Toronto it was decided that help could be administered through that hole and two projects got under way involving de Havilland machines.

George Phillips of the Ontario Provincial Air Service was detailed by Ontario Premier Mitchell F. Hepburn to fly bales of woollen strips to the mine head on the theory that they could be forced through the hole and would provide warmth for the trapped men. He used the large D.H.61 Giant Moth and, in keeping with the news value of the trip, carried reporters Ken McTaggert of the *Mail and Empire* and Ron Williams of the *Globe.*

The second project involved the DH Rapide demonstrator aircraft, CF-AYE, and DH general manager Lee Murray. The radiology department of the Toronto General Hospital reasoned that if a radium capsule was lowered to the men, it could give the rescue crews better direction in their

digging operations. The plan received immediate approval at Queen's Park and they contracted with de Havilland for the use of their new twin-engined Rapide. Excitement grew at Sheppard Avenue as government officials and reporters phoned back and forth. The Rapide was still receiving its finishing touches as it was pushed from the hangar to load the radium container and board the experts who were to accompany the flight. DH air engineer Peter Loveday and Lee Murray climbed on board, but 'AYE had only taxied 100 yards when it became stuck in the mud. Everyone on the field joined in a great pushing exercise and, with the engines running full blast, managed to get the aircraft to higher ground. At 2:00 p.m. on April 21 the plane took off and made a successful trip to Halifax, with a stop at St. Hubert Airport near Montreal. The trapped men were eventually rescued but there were never any reports of them wrapping themselves in wool strips.

Philip Clarke Garratt
Through the hiatus of the thirties the Tiger Moth made its faltering start in Canada. When the first genuine D.H.82A Tiger, CF-AVG, arrived on August 24, 1935, the RCAF was in a state of ''hold'' and, although the training officers loved its improved

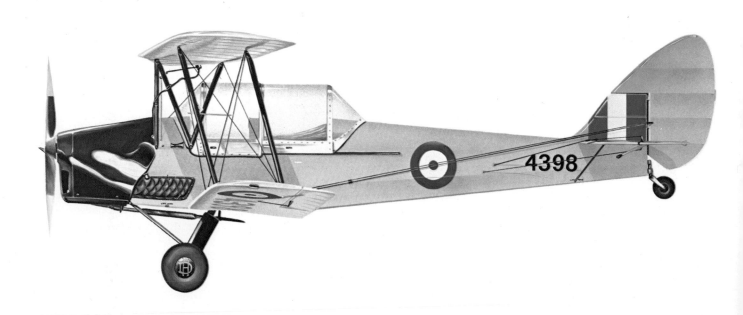

A typical RCAF Tiger Moth in British Commonwealth Air Training Plan colours.

Illustration by Ronald E. Lowry

48

Two Rapide wings are assembled while a number of RCAF Moths are stripped awaiting overhaul. The Rapide fuselage has just received its fabric cover. (via British Aerospace)

flying features, there simply was no budget to purchase it. CF-AVG was fitted with a coupe top, inverted flying equipment and everything the Air Force thought important. Lee Murray took it to Ottawa, Camp Borden and every flying club within a reasonable distance of Toronto. The effort resulted in four sales to the flying clubs but the aircraft spent most of its time as a "hack" for local flying around Downsview.

The complete overhaul of RCAF Moths continued into 1936 but it was sporadic. Lee Murray applied his diplomacy with two tactful letters to Ottawa. On January 2 he wrote, "We have completed the RCAF aircraft allotted and there is very little work from other sources. If it is convenient for you to issue two or three aircraft requiring overhaul, it would be most appreciated." When nothing happened, he wrote again on February 14 inquiring if the RCAF was likely to have any overhaul work in the next few months. "This particular part of the year is always rather slack," wrote Murray, "and any government work would be most helpful."

His letters brought results but the staff had hardly begun reconditioning Moth 60s than a rush of civil work plus the arrival of four Tiger Moths cut into the RCAF overhaul contracts. As so often happens in this cyclical industry, Murray had to write again to Ottawa but this time with apologies for delays. He explained the situation, saying that the staff were working overtime "to within the limits of Provincial labour laws" and that they were trying desperately to "apportion the work."

On May 8, 1936, a quiet little event occurred in the DH Canada family atmosphere when manager Lee Murray brought a tall, smiling man around to each employee and introduced him personally. Some on the shop floor did not know Philip Clarke Garratt, but he had been part of the de Havilland scene since the days of the first Moth tests. He was manager of his own chemical company in Toronto but had been indulging his great love of flying by helping with the testing duties in his spare time. He became a director of de Havilland Canada in 1935 and on May 8 was preparing to take over from Murray as general manager. (The official "signing in" took place May 10). A farewell party was held at the St. Regis Hotel later in the month for Mr. and Mrs. Murray, who were returning to life in England where he was to become DH general manager. They were to see Canada again during the war years.

P.C. Garratt was born in Toronto and educated at Jarvis Collegiate and University of Toronto Schools. He was studying medicine at the Univer-

An excellent view of the D.H.89A Rapide on Edo floats at Vancouver while serving with Canadian Airways Limited. Imported in 1937, CF-BBH spent most of its life on the West Coast. It ended its career at Pentecost, Quebec, March 19, 1947 in a takeoff accident. (Gordon S. Williams)

sity of Toronto when World War 1 broke out and began taking flying lessons at the Curtiss Aviation School at Toronto in 1915 as a means of getting into the Royal Flying Corps. He joined the RFC the following year as a second lieutenant, saw service as a fighter pilot in France and was posted as captain to flying instruction in England. In 1920 he became associated with Bishop-Barker Aeroplanes and he served for a while as instructor in the RCAF at Camp Borden. He settled into the chemical business in 1928 and later managed his own company but he kept close to aviation by assisting with the test flying at Mount Dennis and Downsview.

One small incident on Phil Garratt's arrival as manager was typical of his direct approach to all problems. He never did like the sign at Sheppard and Dufferin. It was an awkward corner and the ditches were high. More than one car had come to grief and he reasoned that the sign, with all its information, was a bit of a distraction. In a matter of days the sign was painted black, with large letters reading only DE HAVILLAND AIRCRAFT.

When Phil Garratt assumed the reins of DH Canada and took stock of the situation, he was faced with "What to do with the demonstrator Tiger Moth?" The four club machines

were being picked up by Moose Jaw, Hamilton, Kingston and Calgary and it was time to try a new tack with W/C E.W. Stedman and the men who made the decisions in Ottawa. An interesting series of letters followed which indicated one of a number of possibilities. Either the Air Force training budget was extremely small, or the thinking of the decision makers was.

Garratt opened the correspondence July 25, 1936, offering the demonstrator Tiger, CF-AVG, at $5000 (plus tax). He stressed that the aircraft was imported to interest the department, adding that an expenditure of over $6000 had already been made and "that it wasn't being used to advan-

The British-built Tiger Moth CF-AVG showing the early design of coupe top. This aircraft was dismantled and used as a model for production jigs and fixtures. It was later rebuilt, modified and delivered to the RCAF as No. 238. (C.D. Long)

tage." W/C Stedman agreed that it would provide an opportunity for the RCAF to test the type, particularly as they had a spare Puss Moth engine in stock. He evidently did not comprehend that the Tiger had the new Gipsy Major for he asked a quote on the machine less engine. The general manager wrote back that he would greatly regret selling the airframe alone as the Gipsy III, of less horsepower, would not show the aircraft to its best advantage. Another letter from George Mickleborough repeated the point, adding that all the inverted flying gear would have to be removed in such a case and emphasizing the extra work involved.

During the long summer months, the correspondence went back and forth. Garratt offered to take the Gipsy III in exchange for $300 and revised his quote to $4700. W/C Alan Ferrier then got into the act, asking about their policy on spares and the

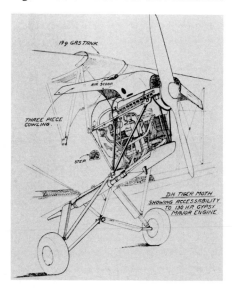

19 g. GAS TANK

AIR SCOOP

THREE PIECE COWLING.

STEP.

DH TIGER MOTH SHOWING ACCESSABILITY TO 130 H.P. GIPSY MAJOR ENGINE

This photograph taken by the author, December 21, 1937, shows P.C. Garratt in a proud moment taxiing out to fly the first DH aircraft wholly manufactured in Canada since World War 1. (F.W. Hotson)

exchange of Gipsy IIIs. In his next letter Garratt regretted that the issue was not clear, explained the difference in engines and repeated his offer. When the fact that the Major was an upgraded Gipsy III finally sank in, Stedman replied that they would be dealing with "a lone engine of a new type" and suggested that the idea of the sale be dropped. Finally, with the arrival of fall, a letter was received on September 24 from the director of contracts that "His Majesty's Government had decided not to take up de Havilland's offer for one Tiger Moth."

The All-Canadian Tiger Moth

As suppliers of elementary trainers to the RCAF, de Havilland's supremacy came to an abrupt end in 1930 when Gipsy Moth orders ceased. Thirteen Puss Moths were delivered in 1931 but they were intended for advanced instruction and instrument training in Ottawa and Camp Borden. Fleet Aircraft of Canada under Jack Sanderson had done an excellent job of promoting the robust Fleet Fawn and sold a total of 20 to the RCAF in 1931. Even while Phil Garratt was trying to sell the lone Tiger demonstrator in 1936, ten more Fleet Fawn IIs went to Canada's military airmen.

These facts did not deter Garratt, who continued to prepare for a made-in-Canada Tiger Moth incorporating

all the improvements the RCAF kept requesting. By 1937 there were 35 Fleets on RCAF strength and a strong case was developing for a second primary trainer in the service. Early in March a load of assorted angle iron was dropped off at Sheppard Avenue and the "buzz" on the shop floor was that it was for Tiger Moth jigs. On the 12th the speculation was over; an order was confirmed for 26 machines (the much discussed demonstrator and 25 others). These were to be the basic British A model with designed-in-Canada modifications: wide walkways on the lower wings, mass-balanced ailerons, metal interplane struts, a new perspex canopy, heavier axles, single hinged cowlings and a host of smaller things based on eight years of experience with the Moths.

From the moment the order was confirmed, things moved quickly. CF-AVG was dismantled and stripped to bare components for use in building jigs and fixtures. Two new "tin hangars" were built, backing onto the spur line, beside the heating plant. The closest was fitted as a paint shop while the other looked after aircraft storage. The much-used wooden hangar was transformed into a woodworking shop and an experienced specialist, W. "Bill" Houston, joined to take on the manufacture of ribs and formers. "Marm" Borczak checked out on the new router to become the expert on wing spars. New people were hired to round out the existing departments and the Tiger work soon blended with the coming and going of the Rapides, Dragonflies and Hornet Moths. The year 1937 was busy: by fall, Tiger produc-

tion was in full swing — enough to have serial number C301 (RCAF 239) ready for testing a few days before Christmas.

Phil Garratt came down from his second-floor office on the cold noon-hour of December 21, 1937, climbed into 239 and took it for its first test flight. A few workers braved the outside cold to watch the proceedings, while those inside jockeyed for position and ate their lunch beside the nearest windowsill. It was rather an historic occasion since it was the first Canadian-made de Havilland airplane since the World War 1 D.H.6 and the first completely manufactured in Toronto since Canadian Aeroplanes Limited closed in 1918. It tested perfectly and was delivered to the RCAF 28 days later, starting a pattern that continued at regular intervals throughout the rest of the year.

The first D.H.82A (Can) Tiger Moth had been delivered in ten months from receipt of order, and throughout this period a trickle of RCAF Moth 60Ms had been in for overhaul. There had always been a cry of not enough equipment in the RCAF so it was rather a surprise when a letter arrived from Ottawa dated February 10, 1938, announcing headquarters' decision that there would be no more Moth 60 aircraft rebuilt, nor would any more Gipsy I and II engines be overhauled when they were "time expired." Now that the Tigers had been ordered, the policy was to slowly withdraw the Moths from service.

The D.H.90 Dragonfly

Years after the era of the Dragon and Rapide, Don Long prepared an article for the Canadian Aviation Historical Society Journal describing the D.H.90 Dragonfly. He called it a milestone in the career of de Havilland Canada and the end of a decade as importers and modifiers of British airplanes.

"The builders of fifteen thousand biplanes made their last contribution to this configuration with the most beautiful of all, the D.H.90 Dragonfly. The final stage in the evolution of the de Havilland biplanes started in 1932 with the D.H.84 Dragon. It proved that an ugly airplane could be effective, but its immediate descendants, the D.H.86 Express Airliner and the D.H.89 Dragon Rapide, put style back with the functional high aspect ratio wing.

"By this time the men at Hatfield realized that future airliners would have to be monoplanes with monocoque stuctures, but in 1935 they distilled all of their biplane experience into one last fling, a twin-engined airplane too small for an airline, but suited to the well-heeled private owner and the business executive. It wasn't strictly the last; in 1937 a D.H.92 Dolphin was built — Dragonfly format with Rapide dimensions — but it was too late; the Albatross and Flamingo had already taken the stage. There was only the one Dolphin, but 67 Dragonflies were built in 1935-38.

"One could say that they went too far in quest of beauty, but with the materials used it wasn't that expensive, and it was worth it! The wings

Phil Garratt (left) welcomes his fellow director William Archibald to Downsview to take delivery of the Dragonfly CF-AYF, seen at right, landing at Vancouver. (C.D. Long and Gordon S. Williams)

were long and tapered, with unequal spans and unequal chords, and with less exposed bracing than any biplane since the Fokker D VII. In going from the Dragon to the Rapide to the Dragonfly, the count of external struts was reduced from 20 to 12 to 6, and of wires (or pairs of wires) from 30 to 18 to 4.

"The lower centre section was a cantilever, running through the fuselage from one landing gear to the other, carrying the engine nacelles and two 30-gallon fuel tanks; this provided bending and torsional stiffness without external bracing, and a platform on each side of the cabin that you could walk all over without fear of breaking through or of scalping yourself with wires. All the controls and services to the nacelles were carried through the leading edges of the wings which were hinged at the front spar. The main gear was assisted by side stays and torque linkages when skis were used.

"The fuselage was plywood-skinned, nearly elliptical in section, with flat sides tapering to nothing at the nose and tail: a true monocoque construction. A cabin door on the left side led to the wide rear seat, to a single seat on the right side, or forward through a wide space to the pilots' seats and dual controls. There was a large luggage space in a compartment behind the cabin.

"The powerplants were Gipsy Majors with Schwarz-finished wooden propellers, in cowlings which were split and hinged on their centrelines so that they could be very easily opened. There was electric engine starting plus navigation and landing lights, direc-

tional gyro, artificial horizon, an airlog, as well as the customary instruments of the time.

"The performance was quite snappy, with a cruising speed of 125 mph on 12 gallons of fuel per hour and an ultimate range of 625 miles. The takeoff ground roll was 900 feet in a 5 mph wind and the landing distance from 50 feet was 1020 feet. Nowadays this would be regarded as nearly STOL! Two short split trailing-edge flaps on the lower centre section steepened the glide about 25 per cent. The early price tag was $8000.

"The first Dragonfly flew at Hatfield on August 12, 1935. The sixth machine was shipped to Toronto by sea and was flown by P.C. Garratt at Downsview, Ontario, on June 26, 1936. It was registered CF-AYF and delivered to Consolidated Mining and Smelting company of Trail, British Columbia."

William M. Archibald, manager of Consolidated Mining and Smelting Ltd. of Trail, B.C., is generally considered the father of business aviation in Canada. He earned his flying licence at the age of 53 and began applying his new-found skills in the operation of Consolidated. He was also a long-time supporter of de Havilland and, according to the records, must have spent much time at Downsview signing aircraft purchase documents. As early as May 8, 1929, he bought his first private Cirrus Moth and later that month ordered two Moths for company operations. He began a training school within the company for pilots and ground crew, which was rather a novelty at the time and proved highly successful. When

the Puss Moth came on the scene, Archibald acquired one of the first and extended his business trips to include the whole of Canada.

Two more Puss Moths went to C.M.&S. in 1930 and 1934, followed by a new Dragon on floats in 1935. It was in 1935 that his work was recognized in his use of aircraft for business and he was awarded the Trans Canada (McKee) Trophy. In 1936 Consolidated bought a new Hornet Moth, and the boss moved to two engines when he and the company chief pilot, Page McPhee, arrived in Downsview to take delivery of the Dragonfly on July 16, the first twin-engined executive aircraft in Canada. Three Hornet Moths followed in 1937 and the company turned its Dragon in on a Rapide in 1938. It also rounded out its DH stable of aircraft that same year with a Fox Moth.

It was obvious from the start that Archibald was a good customer. His involvement with aviation and his reputation in the business world had earned him a place on the DHC board of directors on January 29, 1934. His only leave was a short period in the war years when the Canadian Government managed the plant, but he continued as a director until November 11, 1949.

The Flying Newsroom
A short-lived venture into the corporate aviation field began in June 1937 with an impressive christening

The *Globe and Mail* ''Flying Newsroom'' after the installation of Edo floats shown on the seaplane ramp at the Toronto Air Harbour. (C.D. Long)

ceremony at de Havilland's Toronto plant on Sheppard Avenue. The man behind it all was a self-made financial genius who had learned his trade in the mining fields of northern Ontario. George McCullagh had arrived on the Toronto scene earlier in the year as publisher of the newly formed *Globe and Mail*. His partner in the venture was another wealthy mining man, William Wright, and it was clear the new paper would take a special interest in mining. Wright remained silently in the background, but the outgoing McCullagh planned to keep in close personal touch with the north by air.

On June 10 he purchased a new twin-engined D.H.89 Dragon Rapide, CF-BBG, and had it outfitted at Downsview for northern travel deluxe. It was named the ''Flying Newsroom'' and Toronto pilot Jim Crang was hired to fly mining reporters and analysts anywhere in Canada on wheels, skis and floats. De Havilland representative Don Murray was given leave to accompany the plane and act as air engineer. The ceremony in Toronto included speeches from DH manager Phil Garratt, the district inspector of the DOT, Col. Douglas Joy, and pilot Jim Crang in full uniform. McCullagh told of his ambitions for the airplane and invited his wife to formally christen the Rapide. As soon as all flight tests were completed, the ''Newsroom'' went on floats and headed for the mines of northern Ontario.

CF-BBG returned to the Toronto waterfront Air Harbour at the foot of Yonge Street, August 21, amid great

publicity. Other trips were planned for the next day and refuelling operations began at 6 o'clock in the evening. One tank was successfully filled but as the hose was moved to the other side, a spark from the nozzle ignited the gas fumes from the empty tank into a ball of flame. The wood and fabric plane did not last long and all that could be done was to float it away from the dock and let it burn. It was a severe setback to George McCullagh's enthusiasm and foresight, but he returned with a second private aircraft after the war, a Grumman Mallard, CF-EIZ.

RCAF overhaul work tapered off in 1936 but Phil Garratt was launching a drive to obtain civilian repairs. When he received a call from Roy Brown, head of General Airways, that their Fox Moth CF-API had gone through the ice and sunk in the Ottawa River, Garratt's reply was prompt: "Salvage all you can and get it to us on a truck. I'll guarantee to sell it for more than the repair costs." It was a sorry looking load of parts that arrived some time later but, API was reborn in 1937 looking like new. Recalling the incident years later, Garratt said, "George Blanchard was our woodworking expert in those days and he practically lived in that Fox Moth fuselage."

Once again from General Airways came a call that their Bellanca CH-300, CF-AEC, had been severely damaged. It looked like a writeoff but "What could de Havilland do?" Garratt's reply was the same: "Send it down. We'll repair it at cost; it will keep the plant busy." When the wreck arrived in a boxcar on February 26, 1935, it was in bad shape. The sternpost was gone and the sturdy Bellanca undercarriage, looking somewhat like a bridge, was pushed high into the cabin. The wings and assorted controls were in reasonable shape and were soon spread around the shop for repair. Russ Borrett, the welding specialist, and a helper worked steadily until the fuselage again took shape. By summer, AEC was back together again and, according to the test pilot, flew better than ever.

Wings for the Mounties
One of the early visitors to the new plant on Sheppard Avenue was the distinguished Major General Sir James Howden MacBrien. He later became head of the Royal Canadian Mounted

The RCMP's Dragonflies were very modern aircraft during their period, with electric starters, radio, a landing light and plush seating. CF-MPA later served with the RCAF as 7626. (C.D. Long)

Police and will go down in history as the man who gave wings to the Mounties. Sir James was one of the most energetic aviation enthusiasts of the era, a lifetime soldier and an accomplished private pilot. His full and exciting career went back to the South African war, followed by a tour in the Royal Canadian Dragoons and Australian Light Horse. In World War 1 he was made a brigadier general of the 12th Infantry C.E.F. and was mentioned in dispatches six times. Promoted to major general, he became Chief of General Staff Overseas Military Forces of Canada, 1919-20; Chief of the General Staff Military H.Q. Ottawa, 1920-23; and Chief of Staff, Department of National Defence, 1923-28. He had at one time been general manager of Canadian Airways Limited and he became Commissioner of the RCMP in 1931.

His position as president of the Aviation League of Canada and first president of the Canadian Flying Clubs Association brought his name to the attention of Sir Charles Wakefield in England. Sir Charles had earlier made a gift of a Moth to the Toronto Flying Club and he now sought to recognize MacBrien and the Aviation League in a similar way for the work he was doing. A new metal-fuselage 60M Moth arrived in Canada for General MacBrien's personal use as a gift from Sir Charles Wakefield and was registered CF-AAA on June 15, 1929, to the Aviation League of Canada (a group of air-minded enthusiasts). The general made good use of the aircraft during the next five years for he loved to travel. The all-white Gipsy Moth was seen regularly at aviation functions from coast to coast. Phil Garratt used to tell the story of one such flight when the general was asked to attend a flying meet to mark the opening of the new Moncton airport. In view of General MacBrien's position in the RCMP, the episode can only be labelled "The Case of the Unluckiest Smuggler."

On the day in question, military promptness and a good tailwind brought the RCMP Commissioner and his Moth to Moncton much earlier than expected. His arrival was to be

The only "casualty" during RCMP training at Toronto Flying Club happened when Staff Sgt. Michelson veered into a taxiing Puss Moth. (via C.D. Long)

part of the program so the committee asked him to leave for a while and arrange his return as part of the opening ceremony. This posed no problem for the general and soon he had landed in an out-of-the-way field with nothing to do but wait out the clock. MacBrien made good use of the time by conducting a detailed inspection of the ground in preparation for takeoff. As he strolled across the grass he came upon a few old boards covering an irregular depression. His curiosity got the better of him, and when he probed the situation further, he discovered a cache of illegal rum.

It was the illicit liquor traffic in eastern Canada that helped put the Mounties in the flying business. The need for air mobility had been felt for many years and patrols in conjunction with the RCAF had been going on in British Columbia and New Brunswick since 1928. Better mobility was badly needed in northern Canada, where weeks of travel by surface methods did little to speed law enforcement. In 1932 the incident of the "Mad

Trapper of Rat River" drew worldwide publicity and emphasized the value of the airplane in police work, especially in remote areas. The 29-day manhunt in the Arctic for the man who had killed one Mountie and wounded another was one of the first cases in which an aircraft was called in to assist overland patrols.

During the same year the RCAF was asked to organize air patrols with single-engined Fairchild 71s on both coasts, using RCMP observers. Prohibition in the US had brought a rash of rum-running in the eastern provinces. Drug traffic along the British Columbia coast was a problem, even in those days. As the need for aircraft patrols increased, the hard-pressed RCAF found their involvement increasingly burdensome. Only 154 aircraft were on strength with the RCAF at the end of March 1936. This was reduced to 135 aircraft one year later, with 8 of these unserviceable. Ian Mackenzie, defence minister in the new Liberal government of 1936, was under pressure to decrease RCAF participation in the civil operations of mapping and patrol. The military won their point and, although it was a timely break for the RCAF, it meant that the RCMP had to shift for themselves.

Commissioner MacBrien was a firm believer in close headquarters contact with all outlying areas of the RCMP network. In 1936 he completed a historic, four-week, 11,000-mile inspection trip of Canada by air, using a float-equipped Fairchild 71 on loan from the RCAF and piloted by Flight Lieutenant R.C. Gordon. Later that year he was one of the first to investigate the new de Havilland D.H.90 Dragonfly which arrived from England in the summer of 1936. Its size was ideal for patrol operations and the two engines seemed more appropriate for the long over-water flights. Four Dragonflies were promptly ordered for the RCMP.

The plan for the new Air Division went forward quickly with the signing of the order and the small DH staff soon found itself involved in this interesting project. An RCMP detachment moved into North Toronto, April 1, 1937, and took up quarters in the second storey of the Post Office Building on Montgomery Avenue. A flight refresher course was started at the Toronto Flying Club under chief flying instructor R.W. "Ray" Goodwin weeks before the large boxes of aircraft parts began arriving at the Downsview siding. The eight pilots allotted to the new wing had a variety of previous flying experience—four from the RCAF and four with flying club backgrounds.

Excitement grew at de Havilland as they began assembling the Dragonfly wings and building up the engine nacelles, and they soon came to know the men who would be flying the aircraft. In overall charge of the operation was Superintendent R.E. Mercer,

Officer Commanding "O" Division in Toronto. The pilots were Staff Sergeants T.R. Michelson and M.P. Fraser; and Sergeants R.H. Baker, G.F. Hart, W. Munro, L. Dubuc, P.M. Grant and W.E. Barnes. (The last five doubled as mechanics.)

The de Havilland demonstrator Dragonfly CF-BBD had been flying since October 1936 and was used for familiarization flights and instruction. Ray Goodwin, who later became Director of Civil Aviation, Department of Transport, was given a checkout on the aircraft by de Havilland's general manager and began instructing on the new twin at the Toronto Flying Club field at Dufferin Street and Wilson Avenue. April 19 provided the only awkward incident in the whole conversion program.

Staff Sgt. Michelson was doing practice landings that day when his plane veered dangerously close to aircraft on the hangar line. Sitting in the Toronto Flying Club Puss Moth CF-CDM with the engine running was Dr. Easson Brown, prominent Toronto physician, and his daughter, waiting to go aloft for a pleasure flight. To the doctor's dismay, the Dragonfly headed straight for him. Michelson managed to brake his new charge to a halt, but not before it had straddled the nose of the Puss Moth and forced it into a distinct crouching position. The main damage resulted from all propellers turning at the moment of impact. The Puss Moth received considerable wing damage and never flew again. Its metal propeller cut through the plywood side of the Dragonfly, breaking Michelson's left leg. The accident caused considerable activity at the factory. John Slaughter was sent over to the Flying Club to put a new panel in the side of the Dragonfly and Phil Garratt flew it back to the plant for further repairs. It later emerged as CF-MPC, the third

in the series. The first Dragonfly, CF-MPA, in its dark blue fuselage and yellow wings was delivered to the Mounties on May 5, 1937. CF-MPB followed on May 29, 'MPC on July 15 and 'MPD on June 26. For simplicity and identification, each was given the name of a flower coinciding with the last letter of the registration: *Anemone, Buttercup, Crocus, Dandelion.*

At the end of the training program the planes went immediately to Moncton and took up the anti-smuggling patrol over the Gulf of St. Lawrence, the Bay of Fundy and the waters off Nova Scotia. The operation had a distinct and immediate effect on rum-running in the area. Sergeant W.E. Barnes, who later became a captain on Trans Canada Air Lines, put it down to their use of aircraft radio, a considerable innovation at the time. The easy contact between the searching planes and marine cruisers soon put a damper on coastal smuggling.

It did not take General MacBrien long to put his new aircraft to work. With Sgt. Barnes as pilot, he left Ottawa on June 19, 1937, for an inspection trip across Canada and back that included Kapuskasing, Winnipeg, Regina, Edmonton, Calgary, Lethbridge, Grand Forks and Vancouver. Barnes noted in his log book at the time: "Sir James is a damn good man but guess who was boss?"

Of the eight Dragonflies that came to Canada, six of them were taken over by the RCAF for twin-engine training at the start of the war. These were the DHC demonstrator, three from the RCMP and two new ones that had not been sold. 'AYF continued in use with Consolidated Mining and Smelting, while the fourth RCMP machine was sold to Leavens Brothers. Two Dragonflies were written off in RCAF service and four were eventually re-

This photo shows the engineering done by DHC to provide skis for the British-designed Dragonfly. The Elliot Brothers' skis on DHC pedestals required torque struts, check cables and "bungee" cords. The installation on the Rapide was similar. (C.D. Long)

turned to civilian use. They all slowly retired from service and the last to go was CF-BFF, which sank through the ice on the Ottawa River on December 21, 1949, while in service with Gold Belt Air Service of Rouyn, Quebec.

The Imperial Airways *Cambria*

August 1937 had been a busy month with the Tiger Moth production line starting to take shape on the hangar floor. In fact, it had been a good summer all around. The Mounties had departed for the east coast with their new Dragonflies and the yellow Dragonfly CF-BFF had been adapted for floats at the Fairchild company in Longueil. Now it was Canadian National Exhibition time when Toronto life quickened with programs at the waterfront, including aviation.

This year the "Ex" was to feature a visit from Imperial Airways' giant Short flying boat *Cambria*, G-ADUV, making a special side trip from its experimental Atlantic trials. Nothing that size had ever flown into Toronto before and its arrival on Lake Ontario before thousands of Exhibition visitors was to be something of a spectacle.

"It was the talk of the shop that day," recalled one of the employees, "and I remember we were all disappointed that we had to work. The arrival was scheduled for 5 o'clock in the evening and we had adjusted our minds to the fact that we would have to hear about it on the radio that night. We saw Mr. Garratt leaving with a group about 3 o'clock and commented that there were some advantages, after all, in being the boss. I was working on Tiger Moth jigs at the time and got home as quickly as possible to hear the radio news.

"It was evident that we had missed quite a show, for the *Cambria* had experienced difficulty at the lakefront and had knocked off one of its wing floats. Sure enough, in the papers the next day were pictures of the flying boat being towed to the Toronto Harbour Commission dock and the story

The Imperial Airways *Cambria* in difficulty off the Toronto waterfront, and below in a lagoon at Toronto Island undergoing repairs. (via F.W. Hotson and C.D. Long)

of what had happened. Little did we know at the time that, being the only aircraft factory in Toronto, we would be called upon to do the repairs. It turned out to be quite an exercise!''

The story in the papers made it quite clear that the *Cambria* had landed at right angles to the wind and provided spectators with an exciting few minutes. It arrived at 5 p.m. as scheduled and, after circling the Exhibition grounds, began its approach over the Dufferin Street buildings and the Exhibition flagpole. The flag on the pole indicated a westerly wind but, because the approach was to the south, old-time boat pilot Roy Maxwell was heard to exclaim: ''Good Heavens, he's in for it!'' According to the reports, the flying boat hit with a cloud of spray and, with its left wing in the water, swung slowly around facing the crowd. Captain Powell, the flying boat skipper, claimed in an interview that he had hit an object in the water, but E.L. Cousins, manager of the Harbour Commission, countered that he had two boats out sweeping the area for two days before the arrival.

Next day de Havilland was asked to repair the damaged *Cambria*, now tied near the coal piles—under guard —at the foot of Cherry Street. Frank Warren took Reg Corlett and Don Murray to begin a long stint at the Toronto waterfront. It was a case of removing all the damaged components, repairing torn sections of metal and ordering new parts. Imperial Airways sent a new float and parts via the *Queen Mary* to New York, whence they were brought to Toronto by truck. Working on such a large, all-metal airplane (now moved to a secluded bay at Toronto Island) was a new departure for DH Canada, which had been dealing almost exclusively with wooden aircraft.

''You can just imagine us,'' recalled Don Murray, ''bouncing around in a boat, trying to put metal patches on the underside of this big wing. Reg and I had just about got one piece of dural skin in position when it slipped and fell into the water. We poked around in the weeds with a stick but didn't have much luck. I spotted something shining and stripped off my shorts and dived in, scraping around in the mud until I felt it. I brought up the piece but found it had been scratched, so we had to make another. This is the way it went, often into the night. I remember I was working late

one night and couldn't stay awake. I went to Frank Warren and asked if I could have some time off to curl up and have a sleep.'' After ten hectic days of hard work the *Cambria* was airworthy again and Captain Powell and his crew made their departure. Before leaving for Montreal they said thanks to the de Havilland staff with a flight over the hangars at Downsview.

Hornets to the RAF

An interesting transaction involving D.H.87 Hornet Moths which might be classed as a ''boomerang sale'' took place in 1939. When the first Hornet arrived in Canada in 1936 it was sent to Fairchild Aircraft for the instal-

An interesting advertisement in 1936 for the Canadian Hornet Moth. (DHC)

lation of a set of seaplane floats designed by their chief engineer, Francis Hyde-Beadle. The Hornet's side-by-side cabin and two doors made it handy for float operations. Its performance on water compared favourably with that of the Fox Moth of the same period.

Four years later, in 1939, a call came from the British Air Ministry inquiring about the availability of Hornet seaplanes. They were needed for a hurry-up program training seaplane pilots, and their folding wings facilitated stowage on board ship for "special assignments." The inquiry could not have come at a more opportune time as four Hornets were at Downsview awaiting customers; three bore Canadian registrations and one was still in its crate. CF-AYI had belonged to Frank Trethewey in 1936 but was back with DHC a year later. The demonstrator CF-BFJ had sunk at its moorings in Toronto Harbour in 1937 but had been rebuilt ready for sale. CF-BFN had been tested on floats and was also up for sale. The three active aircraft went off the Canadian register in May 1939 and subsequently emerged as Ministry numbers P6788, P6785 and P6786 respectively. Hornet serial number 8134 was not yet on the Canadian registry but was fitted with floats and shipped with number P6787. They were all flown extensively at Felixstowe in England and were later restored to wheels. Two survived the war and ended up on the British civil registry. Ex-Canadian 'BFJ became G-AHBL and ex- 'BFN became G-AHBM.

There was a fair amount of secrecy surrounding the British Ministry Hornets but the program was successful enough that when war broke out, British naval officials commandeered all existing Hornet Moths in Canada to be used in "special work."

One that got caught up in the order was CF-BFK, which sported an RAF roundel and the number 5600. It served in Canada with RAF Transport Command and was stationed at North Bay, Ontario. It was returned to the civil register after the war as CF-DIP.

(Above) The prewar Hornet Moth CF-BFK taken over during the war as 5600 by the RAF Transport Command and returned to the civilian registry as CF-DIP in 1946. (J. Reed via Jack McNulty)

(Below) A Canadian Hornet Moth with the RAF in England, 1939. CF-BFJ became RAF P6785 and after the war took the British civilian registration G-AHBL. (via C.D. Long)

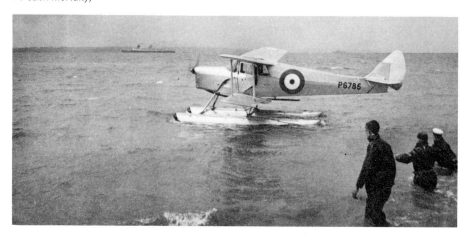

(Below) The only D.H.94 Moth Minor to come to Canada before the war is shown at Toronto Island Airport with Phil Garratt in the cockpit. The Minor was a sleek all-wood trainer designed during 1937 as a Gipsy Moth replacement. Its production was cut short at 100 in 1939 when the pressures of war descended on the British company. Another Moth Minor came to Canada via Australia after the war as CF-AOO. (via R.G. Halford)

The War Years

Some of the early '82A(Can) Tiger Moths in service on skis at Camp Borden, Ontario in the early days of World War 2. (RCAF via Jack McNulty)

The fabric shop girls apply tapes along the ribs of Tiger Moth wings during the busy days of 1940. (National Museum of Science and Technology)

When war broke out in 1939 de Havilland Canada was one of the smallest aircraft companies in the country. Although employment fluctuated considerably during the years leading up to the war, the numbers at Downsview always remained small compared with other aircraft manufacturers. If old photos of company picnics are any guide, DHC had 30 employees in 1935 and 52 in 1936. The Tiger Moth contract boosted the total to 195 by the end of 1939, still well below close competitor Fleet Aircraft Limited at 519. Montreal consistently led the Canadian aircraft scene in manpower and continued to do so during that critical year of 1939. Canadian Vickers Limited employed 450 and Fairchild Aircraft Limited totalled nearly 1000. Canadian Car and Foundry of Fort William employed 700, while Noorduyn Aviation Limited of Cartierville, near Montreal, had a rather small group of 140 people. The National Steel Car Corporation Limited opened its new factory at Malton, northwest of Toronto, in 1938 to build Lysanders and from the very beginning had more employees than its neighbour at Downsview. Throughout the build-up of military business, de Havilland Canada continued to serve its civilian customers and no move was made to join in the building of any other company's airplane.

Most Canadian manufacturers were building aircraft under licence and in 1938 a new organization emerged to supply Handley Page Hampdens for the Royal Air Force. This came about as the result of a British air mission to Canada investigating Canada's potential in their own air armament program. A central company was formed, known as Canadian Associated Aircraft Limited, to contract directly with the British government. Assembly factories were built in Montreal and Toronto, with six companies supplying components. De Havilland Canada was too busy with its own expansion at the time to join the Hampden plan and Phil Garratt preferred to stick with the DH family of aircraft. The six subcontractors—Fleet, Canadian Car, Fairchild, Ottawa Car, Canadian Vickers and National Steel Car—already had orders involving Hawker Hurricanes, Bolingbrokes, Stranraer flying boats, Northrop Deltas and Lysanders. In Vancouver, Boeing Aircraft of Canada Limited was also busily engaged in building the Blackburn Shark.

With all this activity, the RCAF order in 1937 for 26 Tiger Moths was

D.H.82C fusealges nearing completion while completed models near the door are prepared for flight. (A.W. Gifford)

a rather small piece of the business in a country verging on war, but everyone at Downsview believed an additional contract would follow in due course. As a production program, construction of the Tiger Moths went well, but by the time the last Tiger was delivered on April 12, 1939, no new order had appeared. While de Havilland was delivering their first 26 Tiger Moths to the Department of National Defence, Fleet added another ten Fawn IIs to the RCAF inventory.

Shutting down the production line came as a distinct shock for de Havilland after such a promising start in the manufacturing business. Some modest help came in the form of repair work, for in spite of the earlier letter from Ottawa that no more Gipsy Moths would be overhauled, 12 arrived at the plant for reconditioning. The contract specified that after overhaul the Moths were to be turned over to the flying clubs ''under a new RCAF training scheme.'' Fortunately de Havilland England came through with an order for 200 Tiger fuselages to supplement their own production;

otherwise lay-offs would have been considered.

Engineering work went ahead, improving the Tiger Moth (now called the 82C) with wheel brakes and a fully castering tail wheel instead of a skid. Elevator trim tabs were introduced, similar to those on the Hornet Moth, along with numerous refinements suggested by the RCAF. The last overhauled Gipsy Moth in the government order was turned over to the Regina Flying Club in August 1939—then, suddenly, Canada was at war.

The Tiger Moth jigs were beefed up in anticipation of further orders, but the only delivery during that historic September was a Dragon Rapide to Quebec Airways. It was a unique experience, to have a war in progress with management considering temporary furloughs. Admittedly Ottawa had a hectic program on their hands as they put the country on a wartime footing, but it was a frustrating period for the DHC board of directors. The most likely prospect for work seemed to be the British Commonwealth Air Training Plan, which was announced December 10, 1939, and went into force seven days later.

Both Fleet and de Havilland Canada were primarily producers of train-

ing aircraft in the 1930s and were therefore very dependent on government orders for survival. Each had its civil types to sell, but the impetus to start manufacturing on a large scale did not come to either company until the war was into its fourth month. Light trainer orders were balanced between the two companies but in the light of hindsight could hardly be called industrial mobilization.

When the trainer contracts were finally placed, Fleet Aircraft received a contract for 404 of their Finch model in January 1940, while in an obvious move of fair play, DHC received an order for an equal number of Tigers in February. After a ten-month lapse, the Tiger production line started again with the improved 82C model, powered with the DH Gipsy 1-C engine of 140 hp, built in England and supplied by the British Ministry of Aircraft Production. Propellers were made in Canada by the Laidlaw Lumber Company, Toronto, and S and S Propellers Ltd., Winnipeg.

By April 1940 Tiger Moths from Frank Warren's production line were rolling again into an enlarged flight department. One of Canada's veteran pilots, G. Ralph Spradbrow, joined the company as chief test pilot. He had been a career officer in the RCAF, a bush pilot with Dominion Skyways Limited, and more recently the private pilot for John David Eaton, head of the T. Eaton Company's chain of department stores. Soon the plant was in full swing again, moving slowly into overtime work and eventually round-the-clock operation. This sudden reversal of affairs raised the need for considerable expansion in land and housing.

Garratt's executive assistant for the past year had been W. John McDonough, and it became his task to develop 96 acres of newly acquired property into a full-scale airport complete with paved runways. A section bordered by Dufferin Street on the east and Wilson Avenue on the south was bulldozed into oblivion. Houses were demolished and trees felled in the name of the war effort. The need for additional hangar space before winter produced two new brick and steel assembly bays directly south of the original plant.

The Anson

Another decision by the Commonwealth experts meeting in Ottawa to set up the training plan was the choice of a twin-engine trainer. The aircraft selected was the Avro Anson, made in England by the A.V. Roe Company. It had been used in the early days of the war and found completely inadequate as a fighting machine. Ansons were to be supplied first from

surplus British stock and later from components manufactured in England. The first of the used Ansons to reach Canada arrived on the de Havilland Canada siding on Saturday, February 25, 1940, ready for assembly. An eager group of employees, working through the weekend, got them into the air by Sunday afternoon and delivered to the RCAF on Monday morning. A steady flow of British Ansons continued to stations across Canada, bringing a certain war urgency with their gun turrets and camouflage paint. Some even had bullet holes, testifying to their hasty withdrawal from action over the English Channel. DH Canada assembled a total of 264 British Mk. Is but they hadn't seen the last of the Avro Anson.

Under the training plan Anson components were to be supplied from the UK, except for wings, which were to be made in Canada because of their wood content and size. Even the metal fittings for the wings were to come from England. With the spring 1940 crisis in Europe and the sudden evacuation of Dunkirk, the supply of British Ansons to Canada was suspended. This turn of events presented an immediate supply crisis for Commonwealth training; Ansons must now be manufactured entirely in Canada —and quickly.

A number of plans were considered at the highest level that would involve a large portion of the Canadian manufacturing industry. A crown corporation, Federal Aircraft Ltd., was formed almost overnight, headed by Nova Scotia businessman Ralph P. Bell, to organize and manage this huge undertaking. Bell was president of Pickford and Black Ltd., a shipping company on the east coast with interests in fishing and lumber. He was drafted to his post as a "dollar-a-year" man in the

executive committee of the Minister of Munitions and Supply, Hon. C.D. Howe. Bell became the first president of Federal, charged with administering the Anson program. The new organization was formed June 24, 1940, with its headquarters office in the Insurance Exchange Building on St. James Street, Montreal.

The first task was to find an American-made engine to replace the English Cheetah, but the major US companies were already overextended. Finally the Jacobs L6MB of less horsepower (330 hp for the L6MB against 335 hp for the Cheetah IX) was adopted for the Canadian model, which would be called the Anson II. Canadian Vickers

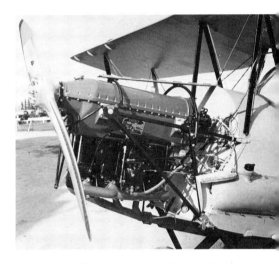

The Menasco Pirate 4 engine was fitted to the Tiger in case the flow of Gipsy Major engines from England was curtailed. It was heavier than the Gipsy with less horsepower. As it had a generator attachment 10 of the 136 built were used as wireless trainers. They were designated D.H.82C2 by de Havilland but called Menasco Moths by the RCAF (C.D. Long)

The first British Avro Anson to be assembled for training in Canada (N9913) was test flown on Sunday, February 25, 1940 by Ralph Spradbrow and Bruce Douglas. (G.A. Neal)

Phil Garratt joins former general managers of DH Canada on the steps of head office in Hatfield in 1939. Left to right: Bob Loader, who opened the first operation at Mount Dennis and supervised the move to Downsview; Phil Garratt, who was manager from 1936 to 1965; and Lee Murray, whose term began December 1933 and ended in 1936 when he handed over the reins to Garratt. (DHC)

was given the assignment to engineer the Jacobs conversion and the task of doing the first installation fell to de Havilland Canada. While this was going on, Federal Aircraft put together a huge subcontracting program composed of five final assembly and manufacturing companies along with four supporting companies.

Final assembly and manufacture
Canadian Car and Foundry Company Limited, Amherst, N.S.
The de Havilland Aircraft of Canada Limited, Toronto, Ont.
MacDonald Brothers Aircraft Limited, Winnipeg, Man.
National Steel Car Corporation Limited, Malton, Ont.
Ottawa Car & Aircraft Limited, Ottawa, Ont.

Supporting companies
Canadian Car and Foundry Company Limited, Montreal, Que.
Boeing Aircraft of Canada Limited, Vancouver, B.C.
Cockshutt Plow Company Limited, Brantford, Ont.
Massey-Harris Company Limited, Weston, Ont.

Canada's aircraft manufacturing industry, which before the war was struggling to survive, was now struggling to cope with its unprecedented growth. There was much movement from company to company of men with experience, who found themselves in a world that lumped airplanes with land vehicles and farm equipment. One such transfer worked decidedly in de Havilland's favour because it brought the eminent Francis P. Hyde-Beadle to Downsview along with the Burlison brothers, George and Bill. Hyde-Beadle was one of the most respected aeronautical engineers in the country with a professional background that went back to the first days of flight in England. He began his career at the famous S.E. Saunders company, where he built racing motor boats. He was one of the first six technical people to join the old Army Balloon Factory at Farnborough, the name of which was changed in 1911 to the Royal Aircraft Factory.

The first test pilot at the time was none other than Geoffrey de Havilland, who was developing his first designs for the government. This was about the time de Havilland and Hearle's first aeroplane had been designated the F.E.1 and "DH" took "H-B" for his very first flight in the machine. With a background of high-speed boat hulls it was only natural that Hyde-Beadle would move to flying boats, which became his design specialty. He designed a complete amphibian for Saunders in 1921 and Schneider Cup seaplane floats for Gloster. In 1928 he moved to Fairchild in the USA and later to the newly organized Fairchild plant in Longueuil, near Montreal. He held an associate fellowship in the Royal Aeronautical Society and was a member of the US Institute of Aeronautical Sciences.

Dick Moffett in a postwar photo while associated with Canada's Atomic Energy Board. He served two and a half years as production manager during the Tiger Moth and Anson period. (via R.J. Moffett)

When National Steel Car established their plant at Malton to build Hampdens and Lysanders, Francis Hyde-Beadle left Fairchild to become chief engineer. He brought with him a number of Fairchild experts but it was a strange "non-aircraft-oriented" world he encountered. In the language of a later day, he became "disenchanted" with management at Malton and was welcomed with open arms by de Havilland. By a stroke of good fortune (for DHC) he persuaded his two top men to join him in his move to Downsview. The Burlison brothers were both veterans of the Canadian Vickers and Fairchild companies. George Burlison moved into production while Bill took a leading part in the growing inspection department under Bill Rouse.

A similar story involved Richard J. "Dick" Moffett, a highly qualified aeronautical engineer of English background, who became disenchanted with Federal Aircraft and was welcomed at de Havilland Canada.

Moffett had come over from Britain to Canadian Vickers in early 1928 as a stress engineer during the successful period when they designed and built six Vancouver flying boats. He became manager in 1930 and held that position throughout the depression years when the staff went down to four. In 1935 he brought the company to life again with RCAF contracts for the large, all-metal Northrop Deltas and Supermarine Stranraers (they built 20 of each).

As war threatened, Vickers joined Canadian Associated Aircraft in the building of Hampdens and the company became involved in the Anson program at the declaration of war. When the crisis in Anson supply forced the formation of Federal Aircraft, Dick Moffett was invited to become its general manager and promptly resigned from Vickers to assume this important post on July 22, 1940. The story is best told by D.A. Newey, who was Moffett's assistant through the depression years and who left Vickers to accompany him to Federal. "It quickly became apparent that Federal Aircraft was by no means a 'happy ship'," wrote Newey in a later history of the period. "Unfortunately it turned out that Moffett was not satisfied with arrangements at Federal and was very soon in a small war, particularly with Ray Lawson, who had been appointed by the government as President of Federal after Ralph Bell went to Ottawa as Director General of Aircraft Production.

"Mr. Lawson, while undoubtedly a very successful businessman, knew nothing about aircraft and quickly succeeded in antagonizing the entire aircraft industry, which reciprocated with the idea that the infant, Federal Aircraft, should be strangled and mercifully put out of the way before it got its eyes open. Moffett endeavoured to resign August 7th but was not allowed to do so. He resigned again on September 18th and finally compromised by undertaking to build the prototype Anson at de Havilland, where he had already secured employment as Production Manager — as soon as he could become released from Federal Aircraft.

"Fortunately, someone in Ottawa saw the light and succeeded in securing the services of Mr. A.W. Newman, at the time chief mechanical engineer of Canadian Pacific

Railway, as director of engineering and production. From that day, Federal Aircraft proceeded to go into business and set about building the Anson without more than the normal mistakes that can be expected from such an ambitious project under war conditions. One of the first things Mr. Newman did was to accept the resignation of Dick Moffett, therefore releasing him to take over his duties with de Havilland and clearing the air for all concerned."

Moffett left Federal in November and settled in Toronto on Christmas Day, ready for his new job. He brought with him a well seasoned veteran, Ed Forrest, and suddenly DHC had a formidable factory management team — their own old-timers plus the cream of the Vickers/Fairchild experience. On his arrival at Downsview Moffett saw that the existing machine shop was completely inadequate and he had a new one set up and furnished with the very latest equipment. He delegated clear-cut responsibilities on both the Tiger and Anson lines, with Frank Warren in charge of the Tigers and George Burlison steering the Ansons through. In a search for talent within the existing plant, he put Bill Houston in charge of all woodwork, Reg Robinson in charge of machine shop and elevated George Blanchard to the new position of production control.

The first Jacobs engine conversion

A line of '82C Tiger Moths prepared for delivery by the author in the spring of 1941.
(F.W. Hotson)

was carried out by de Havilland to Vickers drawings, using an Anson Mk.I airframe. It was completed quickly at Downsview and test flown by Ralph Spradbrow on January 9, 1941. By this time de Havilland had been allotted their share of the Anson work. The DHC contract called for the production of fuselages, engine nacelles and wing root fairings, together with the assembly of Ansons from other subcontracted components. All test flying and preparation of the 375 units would be done at Downsview.

A massive hiring program was begun under Garratt's brother-in-law, Edgar H. Featherstonhaugh; almost everyone who applied received a try, from musicians to carpenters, piano tuners and school teachers. There had always been a number of girls in the fabric shop, but as time went by more and more women were asked to join the work force. Since 1934 Toronto's Central Technical School had started many a student on a successful career at de Havilland. The war quickly boosted Central's output, with most of the graduates headed for Downsview and a set of DH overalls. In spite of the heavy influx of new workers, the transition to aviation skills went quickly.

A solid base had been established during production of the first batch of Tiger Moths, along with strict discipline and high standards. Bill Calder as works manager ran a tight ship during that first program and had much to do with the high quality of workmanship that prevailed. Bill

Rouse and Bill Burlison added new men to the inspection team and were joined by L.A. Taylor and John MacDonald as AID (Air Inspection Detachment) watchdogs. A training section under former Central Technical School instructor D.D. Flett was established for the upgrading of employee skills. New brick buildings smelling of concrete and fresh paint were ready by the fall of 1940 to accommodate this growing activity.

Because of the work done by de Havilland in converting the first Anson to Jacobs power, a batch of 75 Mk.I Ansons arrived (less engines) for similar treatment. They were promptly converted and went out as Anson Mk.IIIs. Along with the Anson bombers from Britain were 38 Fairey Battles needing assembly. The plant was now on a full wartime footing and coping successfully with the month-by-month expansion. The production of Anson fuselages got so far ahead at one time that they were hauled up into the ceiling for storage. The shop poet laureate even put the subject into verse:

The ships come pouring off the line
At such a dizzy pace,
And then go soaring for a time
Until they take their place
Beside the incompletes,
That hang from up above,
Awaiting wings and other things
That all good airmen love.
For without motors, wings and tails,
They cannot turn and dive;
Let's hope that they can hit the trail
By Nineteen Forty-Five.

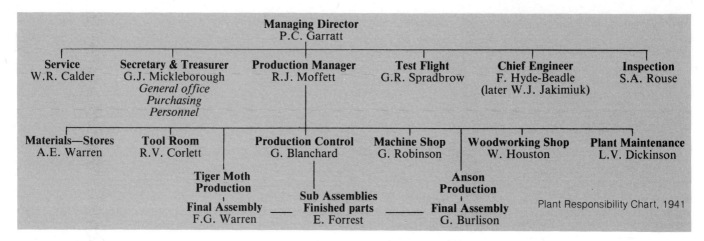

Plant Responsibility Chart, 1941

		Managing Director P.C. Garratt				
Service W.R. Calder	**Secretary & Treasurer** G.J. Mickleborough *General office* *Purchasing* *Personnel*	**Production Manager** R.J. Moffett	**Test Flight** G.R. Spradbrow	**Chief Engineer** F. Hyde-Beadle (later W.J. Jakimiuk)		**Inspection** S.A. Rouse
Materials—Stores A.E. Warren	**Tool Room** R.V. Corlett	**Production Control** G. Blanchard	**Machine Shop** G. Robinson	**Woodworking Shop** W. Houston		**Plant Maintenance** L.V. Dickinson

Tiger Moth Production
Final Assembly
F.G. Warren

Sub Assemblies Finished parts
E. Forrest

Anson Production
Final Assembly
G. Burlison

By the end of 1941 Ansons and Tigers were rolling in quantity from the production lines for delivery to the Department of Munitions and Supply. A quarterly report to end the year mentions a Tiger production rate of 60 per month and an additional order for 200 machines.

The Polish Connection

Another name entered the DH Canada scene in the summer of 1940, one that was to have considerable impact on the company for the next ten years. Wsiewolod J. Jakimiuk was the first of many who made their way to Downsview when Poland fell to the Nazi onslaught. He had been chief engineer at the National Aircraft Factory in Warsaw and was the designer of Polish PZL fighters and a successful commercial transport. He was well known to the parent company in England and during the prewar days of their all-metal D.H. 95 Flamingo they had journeyed to Poland to consult with Jakimiuk. He was an engineer's engineer, totally European by culture and upbringing, proud and serious, and exuding confidence based on experience.

An agreement between the Canadian government and the Polish government-in-exile opened the way for the transfer to Canada of dozens of Polish aeronautical engineers who were either in active service with or at the disposition of the Polish Air Force. The arrangement looked ideal on the surface but because governments cannot function even in wartime without red tape, entanglements developed over payments for transportation and other trivial matters. At this point DH England cut through the red tape by guaranteeing the cost of transportation of the Polish war guests to Canada. The

Anson Mk. IIs and Tiger Moths fill the field during the summer of 1942. (DHC)

cost of some $200,000 was quite a sum at the time but was all later repaid by the engineers. W.Z. Stepniewski, writing of the incident years later, said, "I believe that de Havilland's guarantee was largely due to the confidence they held in Jakimiuk and his professional reputation."

Stepniewski and Waclaw Czerwinski were the first to join Jakimiuk out of an eventual total of 40. Both were senior engineers with aircraft designs to their credit and were to make substantial contributions to the Canadian effort.

"When we arrived," continues Stepniewski, "Jakimiuk was already well established, both technically and socially. He had become a member of the prestigious Granite Club — an exceptional feat for a newcomer in the ultra-conservative, very English Toronto of those days. In addition to all his technical qualifications, Jaki spoke English well and could, in an almost opera-quality bass-baritone, sing a vast repertoire of songs from

operatic arias to folk melodies. He had a charming, good-natured French-English wife, Mary, whose memory can never be erased from the hearts and minds of all Polish engineers and their wives who were fortunate enough to have met her socially."

Waclaw Czerwinski had been one of the leading designers of gliders and high performance sailplanes in Poland (as well as an advanced twin-engined trainer called the Wyzel). After working a few months at de Havilland he suggested forming a gliding club within the engineering department to design and fly their own glider. His idea was enthusiastically accepted by members of the design office and the management, including Phil Garratt who took a special interest in the project. The members of the club spent two nights a week on their own time for six months completing the drawings for what was later to become the Sparrow. The glider was built in the experimental shop under Bill Burlison and the first flight was completed by Czerwinski in the spring of 1942. It was a utility type glider of

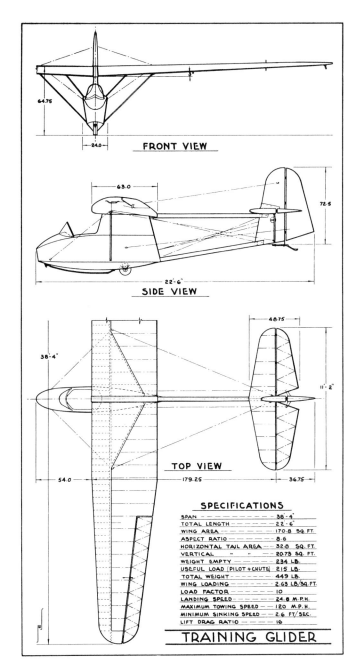

FRONT VIEW

64.75

24.0

SIDE VIEW

63.0

72.5

22'-6"

TOP VIEW

38'-4"

48.75

11'-2"

54.0   179.25   36.75

SPECIFICATIONS

SPAN	38·4"
TOTAL LENGTH	22·6'
WING AREA	170.8 SQ. FT.
ASPECT RATIO	8·6
HORIZONTAL TAIL AREA	32·8 SQ. FT.
VERTICAL "	20.73 SQ. FT.
WEIGHT EMPTY	234 LB.
USEFUL LOAD (PILOT +CHUTE)	215 LB.
TOTAL WEIGHT	449 LB.
WING LOADING	2.63 LB/SQ. FT.
LOAD FACTOR	10
LANDING SPEED	24.8 M.P.H.
MAXIMUM TOWING SPEED	120 M.P.H.
MINIMUM SINKING SPEED	2.6 FT/SEC.
LIFT DRAG RATIO	16

TRAINING GLIDER

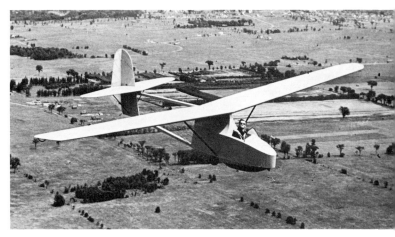

The DH Sparrow training glider was designed and flown by DHC employees in their off hours. The direction and design assistance came from the Polish gliding expert and war guest W. Czerwinski. (DHC)

(Below) A group of Polish engineers formed Canadian Wooden Aircraft Limited to manufacture aircraft components. Here they complete a complex moulded plywood wing tank for a Mosquito. (via W. Czerwinski)

simple construction with a wingspan of 38 feet 4 inches and a length of 22 feet 6 inches. Many who were in the club look back on the project as an educational challenge, a diversion from the pressure of the war effort and a complete success. It led to the later collaboration of Bev Shenstone and Professor Tom Loudon in producing the Wren and Robin gliders and Harbinger sailplanes, a distinct contribution to the development of the gliding movement in Canada.

Czerwinski brought another specialty to the North American aircraft industry, the expertise to form plywood sheets in a variety of complex curves. He had developed the science in his wooden trainer design and looked over the Canadian Anson, then under construction, to see what could be made simpler and less costly with formed plywood. He started with wing fairings and engine cowlings and it was not long before his efforts caught the eye of the National Research Council in Ottawa. They were conducting a drive to save metal of all kinds and to turn wherever possible to wood.

He soon found himself working on a project for the National Aeronautical Establishment to build a North American Harvard wing entirely of wood while NRC concentrated on a wooden fuselage for the same aircraft. DH Canada had too much work at the time to get into the manufacture of small wooden parts, so a new company was formed in the fall of 1942 to concentrate on this specialty. Canadian Wooden Aircraft Limited was organized and financed by a Polish lawyer, H. Stykold, with Czerwinski as technical manager. They set up their first shop in the small Mason and Risch piano factory and later moved to a larger plant on Sorauren Avenue. Many of the Polish experts joined the new company, whose products were almost entirely for the de Havilland war effort. First it was the Ansons, saving thousands of pounds of precious aluminum with their wooden components. When the Mosquito came along the shop was invaluable for the fabrication of nacelle side panels, pitot masts and even hydraulic tanks.

When the need for extra long-range

The Anson Mk. II production line at DH Canada. (DHC JH17)

Four of the DHC test pilots during the Anson period. Left to right: Ralph Spradbrow, Jim Follett, Frank Fisher and Mike de Blicquy. (DHC JH502)

tanks arose for the Mossie, Canadian Wooden Aircraft took on their most difficult but rewarding task. They devised a smoothly streamlined slipper tank from veneer panels cut to size and shaped to the necessary compound curves in hot steam pressurized tanks (autoclaves). The process was unique in Canada and delegations from Britain and the United States came to observe it. A report from the Ministry of Aircraft Production and the United Kingdom Wood Mission paid glowing compliments to Czerwinski's process: "All our members were impressed by the methods you have adopted for producing the Mosquito drop tank, as we have not seen, previously, anything of a similar nature on such a scale. We admired the artistry by which you made difficult problems look simple, and thought that your war effort was an excellent one."

Central Aircraft

De Havilland had always worked closely in prewar days with Ottawa's National Research Council on experimental projects — the building of streamline skis for the Rapide was a typical case — but when the war came such projects only complicated factory planning and interfered with production. This situation confronted Phil Garratt about the time of the major plant expansion and he talked it over with his assistant, W. John McDonough.

McDonough had been in and out of Canadian aviation for years — as a mail pilot, and prospecting and bush flying in northern Canada. He had test flown the first Noorduyn Norseman and since early 1939 had been assisting Garratt in a number of jobs,

most recently the new airport layout. When the company was confronted with these new requests for highly specialized projects, the answer became obvious: the work should be organized under a separate company banner away from the manufacturing problems yet in a close working relationship with de Havilland. A subsidiary company, Central Aircraft Limited, was formed with headquarters in London, Ontario. McDonough would act as manager, and the challenge of highly specialized engineering assignments attracted Francis Hyde-Beadle immediately. Polish designer W.J. Jakimiuk had just arrived at the company and could certainly look after engineering at Downsview. A former Trans Canada Air Lines captain, Harry C. Umphrey, had recently applied for work in the test flight department and accepted the role of chief pilot in the new company.

These three people and a few hand-picked specialists made their way to London and were soon involved in experimental war projects both large and small. What started as an overflow operation for de Havilland soon became involved in projects of its own. One was the design of a set of special skis for a Lockheed Ventura intended for liaison with the underground in Norway. There would be many more special assignments when the Mosquito came to Canada.

The Birth of the Mosquito

While expansion was the order of the day at Downsview, events were taking place in England that would affect the lives of thousands of Canadians. In great secrecy, de Havilland England was designing not only a revolutionary aircraft but a whole new concept of aerial warfare. They called it the Mosquito and its sting was to be felt by the enemy in ever-increasing fury for the balance of the war. The design work had gone on since 1939 in an old Hertfordshire mansion as a private venture, with more opposition than support from a sceptical Air Ministry.

The quickening pace at Downsview during the first year of the war was commendable on all counts, but nothing could compare with the feverish development of the Mosquito back in England. None of the workers on the Canadian Tiger Moth line on November 3, 1940, had even heard of the Mosquito, let alone that it was leaving Salisbury Hall that day on the back of a lorry heavily wrapped in tarpaulins. They had no idea of the excitement at Hatfield 22 days later as the new plywood bomber took to the air under the guiding hands of the founder's son. It was not until Geoffrey de Havilland Jr. began demonstrating the sleek new prototype that the Ministry brass were convinced enough to start placing orders. The manoeuvrability on one

The British D.H.98 Mosquito flies for the first time at Hatfield with Geoffrey de Havilland Jr. at the controls. (DH492B)

engine was spectacular, as was its speed of 425 mph at 30,000 feet. Its design intent was speed instead of defensive armament, and from the moment it first flew until 1944 it was the fastest plane in the war. It was originally planned as a light bomber but soon proved itself in high-level photography and every phase of intruder operations. Enthusiasm intensified at Hatfield as the Mosquito advanced through the testing stage, but there was still much convincing to be done. It was a closely guarded secret to most, but Canada's Minister of Munitions and Supply, C.D. Howe, was one of the first Canadians to witness a demonstration of the new aircraft. The demonstration took place on December 29, 1940, only 15 days after the dynamic minister had been rescued in mid-Atlantic from the torpedoed *Western Prince*.

About the time the Sheppard Avenue plant was beginning its production of Jacobs-powered Anson trainers, a key event took place in England that was to decide the future of the controversial wooden bomber. The date was April 20, 1941, when a top-level demonstration was convened at Hatfield for Air Ministry officials and Chiefs of Staff. Geoffrey de Havilland Jr. flew the Mosquito superbly that day and sent a new wave of enthusiasm through the hard-pressed British High Command. One of the most enthusiastic guests in the audience was America's General Henry Arnold, who in those days of strained US neutrality was an extremely concerned observer of events in Europe. This veteran airman sized up the Mosquito's potential immediately and received top-level co-

operation from the British. He was given data on the machine for US evaluation but his enthusiasm met a wave of resistance from the military and manufacturers on his return home.

Five American companies were asked to evaluate possible manufacture in the USA — Fleetwings, Beech, Hughes, Fairchild and Curtiss-Wright. They were unanimously opposed to the aircraft and a blunt appraisal at the time by the respected Beech organization summed up their collective views:

"It appears as though this airplane has sacrificed serviceability, structural strength, ease of construction and flying characteristics in an attempt to use construction material which is not suitable for the manufacture of efficient airplanes."

Prejudice toward wooden construction was a severe handicap to any production in the United States. Even the growing operational successes of the RAF did little to change the American stand on its manufacture. Plans to build the Rolls-Royce Merlin in the US, on the other hand, went forward without a hitch, for it was needed in their own North American P-51 Mustang.

Fortunately the debate on the merits of plywood airplanes was not allowed to continue. Even while the Americans deliberated, plans were finalized for mass production of the Mosquito in England, Canada and Australia. It was almost with a sigh of relief that the US investigation died, and was replaced with a healthier "back the Canadians" approach — particularly with the supply of Packard Merlin engines.

Canada to Build the Mosquito

By late 1941 Canada's contribution was figuring heavily in the North American "Arsenal of Democracy." The British Commonwealth Air Training Plan was shipping trained flight crews to the sky battles over Europe. Canadian Pacific Airlines had quickly put together a trans-Atlantic ferrying organization under C.H. "Punch" Dickins which was now fully operational as the RAF Ferry Command. The decision to build the Mosquito in Canada brought an immediate response from the parent company. A mound of drawings and vital parts for 25 aircraft were to be dispatched in a series of shipments to Canada along with a completed Mk.IV model as a production sample. The urgency of the situation was realized in Downsview when Hatfield's general manager Lee Murray arrived from England on July 30 to examine every detail of the Canadian potential. Murray was well known to the seniors in the staff, for he had been their general manager from 1933 to 1936. He spent a busy month in both Downsview and Ottawa, which culminated in the British Ministry of Aircraft Production order of 400 Canadian-built Mosquitos. These were to be the bomber version powered by the Packard Merlin 31 engine.

The announcement of a British order was followed ten days later by the arrival in Canada of W.D. "Doug" Hunter and Harry Povey with bundles of drawings and micro-film. The two were quite impressed with their first trans-Atlantic flight, which allowed them to leave England on Thursday and begin work in Toronto on Saturday. Povey was a jovial dynamo of a man who had been deeply involved with the Mosquito from the beginning. He had joined the company in 1924 and was described as "an aircraft production engineer without peer." Hunter had started his career as a draftsman with the Graham White Aviation Company in England and had been chief

An early meeting on the Canadian Mosquito brought together (left to right) Ralph P. Bell, Director General of Aircraft Production; Harry Povey, Doug Hunter and Phil Garratt. (DHC JH50)

technical engineer at de Havilland since 1925. He was always immaculately dressed, spoke quietly and punctuated every conversation with "quite!"

Both were to figure heavily in the trials and tribulations at DH Canada during the next three challenging years. Their arrival coincided with a new threat to the program — shipping losses in the battle of the Atlantic. In the very first shipment, a 2 per cent loss in vital drawings was experienced, but it was only a sample of what was to come later. On September 13, a flyable Mk.IV, DK 287, was shipped from Liverpool for Halifax, but arrived after a series of delays with such shipping damage that it required extensive repair. Vital castings suffered from serious salt corrosion and

many irreplaceable assemblies ended up at the bottom of the Atlantic.

Povey's first move on arrival was to press for a separate plant to build Mosquito fuselages. Bill Houston was selected to head the group and given a vacant building at 888 Dupont Street, formerly occupied by Baldwin-Beehive woollen mills. He took one look at the pile of microfilm and asked for an assistant to translate them into full-size profiles. Lofting was a new departure for DH Canada but a young draftsman, G.M. "Bill" Kelley, tackled the project on October 14 with considerable success, translating the curves from drawings to huge sheets of plywood on the floor. During the same month the Massey-Harris Company in Weston contracted to build the wings. An English fuselage jig arrived at Dupont Street on December 9, permitting the first fuselage shell and a Canadian jig to be completed two and a half months later.

It was during this period that R.B.

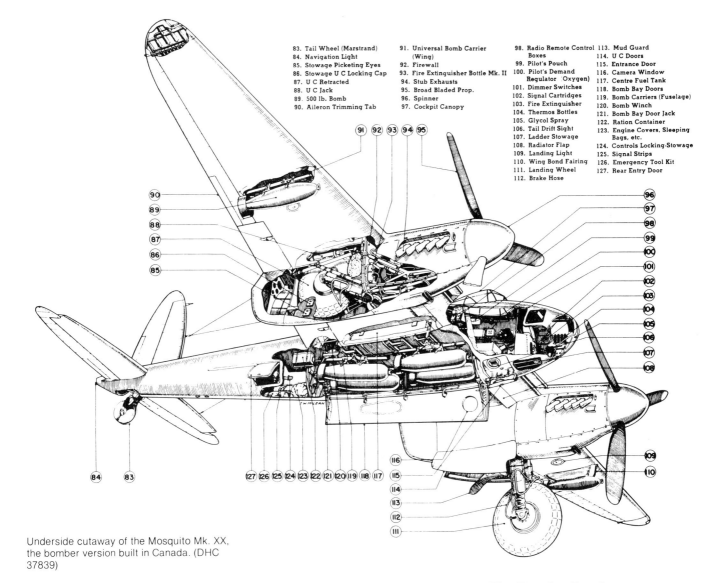

83. Tail Wheel (Marstrand)
84. Navigation Light
85. Stowage Picketing Eyes
86. Stowage U C Locking Cap
87. U C Retracted
88. U C Jack
89. 500 lb. Bomb
90. Aileron Trimming Tab
91. Universal Bomb Carrier (Wing)
92. Firewall
93. Fire Extinguisher Bottle Mk. II
94. Stub Exhausts
95. Broad Bladed Prop.
96. Spinner
97. Cockpit Canopy
98. Radio Remote Control Boxes
99. Pilot's Pouch
100. Pilot's Demand Regulator (Oxygen)
101. Dimmer Switches
102. Signal Cartridges
103. Fire Extinguisher
104. Thermos Bottles
105. Glycol Spray
106. Tail Drift Sight
107. Ladder Stowage
108. Radiator Flap
109. Landing Light
110. Wing Bond Fairing
111. Landing Wheel
112. Brake Hose
113. Mud Guard
114. U C Doors
115. Entrance Door
116. Camera Window
117. Centre Fuel Tank
118. Bomb Bay Doors
119. Bomb Carriers (Fuselage)
120. Bomb Winch
121. Bomb Bay Door Jack
122. Ration Container
123. Engine Covers, Sleeping Bags, etc.
124. Controls Locking-Stowage
125. Signal Strips
126. Emergency Tool Kit
127. Rear Entry Door

Underside cutaway of the Mosquito Mk. XX, the bomber version built in Canada. (DHC 37839)

"Bob" McIntyre began his long association with de Havilland through the newly formed Aircraft Division of Massey-Harris. McIntyre had grown up in Toronto and, after graduating from the University of Toronto in 1936, went to Cambridge University on a Massey Fellowship. In 1938 he lectured at the University of Toronto and two years later joined Massey-Harris.

James S. Duncan, head of the giant Massey farm machinery company, had responded to Canada's call to arms by steering the entire organization into war work. First it was the 1940 need for Anson wings which transformed their Weston Road plant within weeks into a huge wood-working establishment. The new aircraft division was headed by Morley Lazier. Bob McIntyre was chief engineer and Harry Proctor, who had been on loan from DHC to Fleet Aircraft and later National Steel Car, was given the post of chief inspector. Other de Havilland specialists moved

over to broaden the aeronautical experience: Bob Blanchard, George Lawrence and, later, Harry Beffort.

The Massey group built up a formidable production record of Anson wings and were the first invited to build Mosquito wings. "Depending on how you look at it," recalls Bob, McIntyre, "we got off to a good start with Harry Povey. On his first visit to Weston Road he began telling us we should build our jigs of wood, like de Havilland England. We had already started building ours of metal and made the observation that there were probably more important problems that needed his attention back at Downsview.

"We promised our first Mosquito wing by mid-May and delivered ahead of schedule. We always were ahead of schedule with Mossie wings, to the point where we had to store them until needed. The switching around from one variant to another caused us problems for it meant modifying the stored wings before delivery."

The Wooden Bomber

Volumes have been written about the birth of the DH Mosquito bomber and its struggle for acceptance by the High Command, and even more about its unique construction. The use of wood for medium-to-large aircraft was not uncommon but de Havilland led the world in this type of construction — an art that was slowly giving way to metal. The Mosquito was to be the last fling by DH in entirely wooden monocoque design after the racing Comet, the Dragonfly and the Albatross. Decades later the wisdom of combining these special skills with non-strategic materials and trades, under the pressure of war, has been applauded in the light of hindsight.

The Mosquito, as many were to find, was no ordinary aircraft. The Canadian model was to be predominantly the Mk.XXVI and the only information coming through to Downsview at the time was that it was an all-wood, mid-wing monoplane, for a crew of two and powered with twin Packard Merlin engines built in the United States under the famous Rolls-Royce patent. The general optimism as they started into the project was well founded for DH Canada had boosted its staff 140 per cent in one year, building Ansons and Tiger Moths. They were a cohesive, production-oriented group, but this Mossie was not the orthodox construction they had learned. Everything about it would be new.

The fuselage was of an oval, tapering cross section, built in two halves and joined along the top and bottom centre lines. A stiff monocoque construction was obtained by using two layers of plywood sheeting glued together with a balsa wood filler. Whenever concentrated loads occurred spruce or birch inserts were glued between the plywood skins. Occasional wooden bulkheads provided reinforcing and stiffening. The total thickness of the fuselage shell was 7/16 inch and was constant throughout. Birch 3-ply was used in the heavily stressed sections while the nose was 2-ply spruce.

The wing being built by Massey-Harris was a one-piece cantilever structure consisting of two box spars extending over the full span. The covering was of stressed plywood skin, reinforced by span-wise wooden stringers. Ten self-sealing fuel tanks were housed within the wing and were accessible through detachable panels on the underside. The flanges around these openings were of spruce with 3-ply birch. The top and bottom skins were also of 3-ply birch while the stringers were of Douglas fir, with ash wherever additional strength was required. Wood screws were used throughout the entire structure and were driven while the glue between the joints was still wet. The finished wings were attached to the fuselage by four main bolts after being fitted with hydraulically operated ply-covered flaps and metal-covered ailerons.

Like the wing, the tail plane and fin obtained their strength through a box structure and stressed plywood skins. The elevators and rudder were of "Alclad" metal with fabric covering on the rudder and metal sheeting on the elevators. The two nacelles housing the 1525-horsepower Packard Merlin 31 or 24 engines were finely streamlined and completely enclosed the main wheels in flight. The tail

wheel also retracted, making the Mosquito the most streamlined of any wartime aircraft — fighter or bomber.

Everything about the Mosquito was unique, from the two big spinners in front to the distinctive de Havilland rudder in the back, and even the coolant radiators, which were housed within the forward section of the wing profile between each engine nacelle and the fuselage. Armament varied as the war progressed, but the Canadian Mk.XXVIs mounted four 20mm guns in the underside of the fuselage, four 303 machine guns and a camera gun in the nose. Space was provided for two 500-pound bombs. Two more 500-pound bombs could also be carried under the wings.

The crew operated behind a bullet-proof windscreen in a tubular cockpit entirely covered in Plexiglas. Their working space was minimal to provide overall streamlining — the only major complaint from the operational crews.

By March of 1942 the parking lots at Downsview were expanding to accommodate 2400 employees, and a new cafeteria had replaced the early circus tent. There are stories told of that tent cafeteria, but none to compare with its successful transition to an airborne vehicle one summer night in 1940. The event took place during a violent storm which had three of the boys on duty fighting desperately with the tie-down ropes. One was actually carried aloft before he bailed out and let the elements take over. Next day the sun shone down on a novel open-air luncheon.

These three photos show stages in the construction of the Mosquito fuselage. First plywood sheets are pressed over a concrete form, glued into position and dried with infrared light. (National Film Board)

The two half-shells of the fuselage have interior equipment added before being glued together along the top and bottom centrelines. (National Museum of Science and Technology)

The finished fuselage with components has been assembled. (National Film Board)

On May 5, 1942, Phil Garratt left for meetings in England on one of the early RAF Ferry Command flights. It was a cold, dreary trip from Dorval in a dim, windowless Liberator but he was warmed by the thought that he carried with him a contract for an additional 1100 Canadian Mossies, financed by United States Lend-Lease. With the total order now 1500 and the test model nearing completion, Garratt's nine days in England were filled with enthusiastic planning. By that time, high-level priority battles between the services were beginning to plague the parent company, where demand was running ahead of production. Garratt received a first-hand briefing close to the drama of war and a forewarning of similar problems ahead for the Canadian company. It was during this meeting that special mark numbers were set aside for the designation of Canadian variants, beginning with XX and ending with XXIX. A production schedule was set, calling for eight aircraft in 1942 and passing through the 50 per month mark in June 1943.

Back in Canada, Harry Povey was conducting a frantic search for new plant equipment, particularly in the forming and pressing of metal. Negotiations with subcontractors were in high gear, requiring constant compromises between British and North American machine standards. The drive to build the first test aircraft proceeded as planned with a typical demonstration of wartime urgency. When the Boeing company was unable to meet the schedule for tailplanes, John Slaughter built a couple of sets at Downsview to keep the project on time. The first Massey-Harris wing arrived on May 9, 1942. In just 11 months the Canadian prototype, KB 300, was ready for flight, the second not far behind.

Canadian Mossie Airborne

The high secrecy surrounding the Mosquito provided increasing problems as the day neared for the test flight. Such an occasion called for a celebration and the hard work of the past year deserved formal recognition. Phil Garratt sent a query to the ministry asking if they wished to publicize the coming first flight of the prototype, adding a cautious note that he "wouldn't be hurt or annoyed" if there was to be no ceremony to mark the occasion. The reply from Munitions and Supply was an enthusiastic approval, for they felt it would be "a milestone in aircraft production in this country" to have the flight recognized. The date was set for the afternoon of September 23, 1942, with invitations sent to high ranking officials and military leaders. From the beginning it was planned that Geoffrey de Havilland Jr. would come over to do the flying; after all, he had conducted the early type testing and his spectacular flying displays had been a major factor in promoting the aircraft. He would be the star of the show!

Very little thought was given to British weather during the early planning for the event, but it proved a major factor when the day arrived. The September weather was ideal in Toronto for a celebration, but completely foul in England where Geoffrey Jr. was preparing to leave on an RAF Transport Command flight. When the news reached Downsview that he would be delayed, there was no turning back. "The show must go on." Attention shifted im-

The test crew of the first Canadian Mosquito: Peppy Burrell (left), engineer from DH England flight department, and Ralph Spradbrow, chief test pilot for DH Canada. They first flew the aircraft, shown in the photograph at right, on September 23, 1942. (DHC JH324, JH462)

mediately to DH Canada's chief test pilot Ralph Spradbrow, who up to this point had been kept busy with Tiger and Anson testing. Fortunately, F.H. "Peppy" Burrell of Hatfield's test department was serving as liaison engineer at Downsview for some time and had "Sprad" well briefed on the Mossie. At the appropriate time the two took their places in the cockpit of KB 300 and taxied the aircraft to the end of the runway. When the Mosquito took to the air it was not the rolling climbing display that had become the trademark of the younger de Havilland, but it brought grins of satisfaction from all who saw the event as a red-letter day in the company's history. The fact that a Canadian was at the controls seemed all the more appropriate.

Public relations headaches increased astronomically with this momentous event for, although most publications adhered to the government request for "no publicity," others tried to get around the ruling. In the words of one participant, "all hell broke loose" when a station newspaper at No. 5 SFTS, Brantford, reported the Mosquito's first flight in detail. Other magazines demanded the same privileges and reams of futile correspondence resulted. An official world press announcement on September 26 of a Mosquito raid on Oslo relieved the pressure and soon a

notice went out admitting that the Allies *did* have a new high performance airplane and it *was* being produced in Canada.

When Geoffrey de Havilland Jr. arrived at Downsview six days after the first flight, he put on his own brand of demonstration, wringing out the Canadian model. The employees, who were given time off to witness the event, had never seen such a display. First it was a steep climb off the runway until he was lost from view, then a low-level pass over the hangars, followed by a series of well executed rolls. Many citizens of downtown Toronto saw the Mosquito for the first time that day and the people back at Downsview witnessed Geoffrey's specialty — climbing rolls with one engine feathered. After 15 minutes of flying he came down to be welcomed by Air Marshall Breadner, Phil Garratt, John McCurdy (the first man to fly a heavier-than-air flying machine in Canada) and 4000 employees.

One month after the first Canadian Mosquito flight, Geoffrey demonstrated KB 300 to the doubting Americans at Wright Field, Ohio. He returned to Bolling Field, Washington, and National Air Station, San Diego, in December, where he remained until the end of the year. A novel plan was devised to move the Mosquito around the country as Geoffrey was unfamiliar with the North American airway system. The countryside was all new to him but he was quite used to flying formation. Captain Jim Follett of Trans Canada Air Lines had just joined Test Flight and, as he was thoroughly current on the airways, flew the support team in a Lockheed Hudson. Geoffrey de

Havilland, with Peppy Burrell as crew, simply flew in formation.

Convincing the Americans

It took more than young de Havilland's spectacular flying to sell the doubters south of the border, but more and more American officers became enthusiastic after flying the aircraft themselves. In another combined Canadian/British effort to convince the Americans, an English-built Mosquito was put at their disposal for an all-out evaluation. This was the original Mk.IV, DK 287, that had come to Canada aboard ship as a model for Canadian production. It was sent to Wright Field in March 1943 but was lost shortly thereafter due to an engine fire at 14,000 feet. The crew bailed out successfully, but the accident only reinforced the arguments of the anti-Mosquito group. They complained about the cramped cockpit and the small escape hatch and clung to their dislike of plywood construction. In spite of the opposition, the US Navy and the Marines wanted the type badly. The Mossie range was beginning to impress the strategists and the speed advantage over their own P-38 had been firmly demonstrated.

Perhaps the greatest support for the Mosquito came from a new source that brought weight from the very top of the high command. Col. Elliot Roosevelt, son of the US President, began flying a British Mk.IV early in the African campaign with the 5th Reconnaisance Group with outstanding success. His reports provided the operational back-up needed to convince the test and development boys back home. The advantages of a twin-engined fighter were also catching on among the hardened proponents of the single-engine school. Suddenly, as had happened in England, the Mosquito was in demand. Unfortunately at this critical time Canadian production was badly behind target and causing much concern in Ottawa.

Pilot Ralph Spradbrow had done an excellent job of filling in on the first flight of the Mosquito, but the time had come for him to broaden his experience and learn the testing techniques of Hatfield. He left for England in late 1942 but was almost immediately confined to hospital for a serious ulcer operation. To fill the gap at Downsview, DH England prepared to send out Pat Fillingham for test flight duties in Canada. The year ended on an encouraging note with a cheery Christmas letter to all from manager Phil Garratt. Addressing what he always termed the ''DH Family'' in a year-end letter of 1942, Garratt expressed great confidence in his team, as he outlined the challenges of the coming year. ''In the past 11 months,'' he said, ''we have produced 362 Ansons, 550 Tiger Moths, overhauled 119 aircraft and 178 engines, including modifications to 209 Jacobs engines; all of this on top of the development work on the Mosquito.'' He could have added that the first flight of the Mosquito had also been on time.

The cold January of 1943 augured a bad year for both Garratt and DH Canada. The war was in its most critical phase; the demand for Mos-

quitos grew daily. Even as the first Canadian machine flew, the British shadow factories had delivered 450 to the hard-pressed RAF squadrons. On the Canadian side Harry Povey was struggling with the inevitable production compromises while trying to cope with the erratic flow of material from England. On two occasions batches of valuable drawings covering variant changes were lost at sea; vital hydraulic assemblies never reached their destination at Downsview. More parts were coming from England than most people in the plant realized, for some of the subcontractors were still not ready with their components. Even without the losses at sea, the experts could tell there would be a gap in production after the first 25 aircraft. These snags were compounded by yet another penalty of war — the battle among the commands for priorities. Original MAP contracts called for Canada to produce the bomber version, but this was later changed to include the fighter-bomber, FB Mk.XXI. Almost as an afterthought, Canada was asked to produce its own dual-control trainer while in the midst of converting to the two-staged Packard Merlin. It was quite obvious that pressures were building up at Downsview.

By now Ralph Bell had moved from Federal Aircraft to the position of Director-General of Aircraft Production, reporting to the minister, C.D. Howe. Back in 1941 Bell had pushed for the production of the

fighter Mosquito instead of the unarmed bomber. The about-face by the British Ministry of Aircraft Production in ordering the fighter-bomber brought out his natural reaction, ''I told you so!'' He saw it as a major production problem and expressed his views in a letter to Deputy Minister Charles Banks in England. ''I am sorry that we ever touched the thing, for it never would have been done without my very enthusiastic support. So far as I am concerned, it is the last time I will have a thing to do with English aircraft in Canada.'' He sent a similar long memo to C.D. Howe, April 13, 1943, with assorted correspondence so that his boss would ''have all the facts.'' By mid-April only 12 Mosquitos had been produced with 14 more on the production line. Only seven had been officially accepted.

There is no doubt that relations between the Department of Munitions and Supply and de Havilland Canada were becoming severely strained. Garratt went to England for meetings in February, followed in March by Povey and Hunter. The Director-General of Aircraft Production was becoming increasingly impatient. Hatfield responded by sending out their general manager, Lee Murray, on a full-time basis in November 1942. His prestige and knowledge of the Canadian scene had a stabilizing influence but the underlying problems continued. Once again in April, another variant problem arose — the conversion of machines for USAAF reconnaissance.

The Allied war effort was at the stage where all the countries were working closely on matters of supply.

P.C. Garratt introduces Geoffrey de Havilland Jr. to the DHC employees after he flew the first Canadian Mosquito. Also on the stage is A/M L.S. Breadner of the RCAF. (DHC JH372)

A reconnaissance Mosquito in US markings. A moulded plywood slipper tank can be seen under the wing. (DHC 1501)

The RAF and the RCAF were juggling their own drastic needs to release reconnaissance Mosquitos to the USA. Weighty exchange points were to be gained in a share of the heavy bomber production that was growing south of the border. US Air Force personnel began to appear on the flight line at Downsview, where a new brand of Mossie emerged from the paint shop bearing the "star and bar" instead of the usual roundel. These American F-8s began to find their way into the US photo reconnaisance pool, but never in the quantities requested. Only 40 F-8s were delivered from Downsview.

While all these changes were taking place, the plant bulletin faithfully recorded activities around the company with everything from softball tourna-

Air hero Buzz Beurling poses with a group of "the girls" during his visit to the Mosquito production line. (DHC M19)

ments to weddings. The *De Havilland Mosquito* had been launched in 1941 by personnel manager "Feather" Featherstonhaugh, assisted by Ivan Kirkhouse, Doug Higgins and Joe Holliday. In the summer of 1942 it recorded the visit of an RCAF bomber pilot, P/O Johnny Highman, DFC, of Saskatchewan, who did a morale-building tour of the plant. On February 22, 1943, Canada's number one ace, F/O George "Buzz" Beurling, DSO, DFC, DFM and bar, was given an official welcome. He toured all the departments, posed for pictures with the ladies and was given a Mosquito flight by test pilot Fillingham.

All the drama that Hollywood attaches to test flying descended on the flight operations office during the late afternoon of April 26. A terse radio message from F/L Gerald R. Wooll at 4:30 p.m. informed operations that they were returning from a routine test at 20,000 feet over the east end of the city and that smoke was coming from behind the starboard nacelle. Moments later another message explained that while feathering the propeller a fire had broken out and that he and his observer/mechanic, T.J. "Tim" Stone, were taking to their parachutes at 17,000 feet. Their position near the lakeshore caused some concern and, while chief pilot Spradbrow alerted the harbour police, pilot Jim Follett rushed to prepare the Grumman Wigeon in case the two

should land in the lake.

Stone released the emergency door and jumped first with no problem. Wooll trimmed the machine and eased himself through the same opening and soon he too was falling free under a canopy of silk. Both had fears of drifting into the lake but were able to speed their descent enough to remain over land.

Tim Stone touched down near the Don Ravine without any trouble at Research Enterprises and was approached by a guard who thought it was a Victory Bond stunt. When he learned that the unheralded arrival was the real thing, he took Stone to the cafeteria for a cup of tea. Wooll, on the other hand, had the bad luck to land in the middle of a set of railway tracks near Dawes Road and found it difficult to get his footing.

F/L Gerry Wooll was one of the first to fly the Mosquito in Europe and had completed 85 operations before force landing in Switzerland. He was unable to go back on active operations following his exchange as an internee and spent the rest of the war on coastal command and test flying at DH Canada. (DHC M150)

He was dragged a few feet before he could spill the 'chute, damaged his wrist and picked up a cinder in his chin but was otherwise unscathed.

The flaming Mosquito, scattering debris for miles, plunged into the farm of Arthur W. Mason. Two local farmers took Wooll to the de Havilland first aid office. While he was getting his cuts and bruises wrapped up, a big arm appeared around his shoulder. It was Phil Garratt coming to ask how he felt after the harrowing escape. "I've been wanting to meet you, Mr. Garratt," said Wooll. "Sorry I had to pick this way to do it." Wooll spent the next day in Christie Street Military Hospital but was soon ready to test more Mosquitos. The trouble was traced to a faulty exhaust manifold leaking flames to a propeller feathering line. When the prop was feathered the ruptured line acted like an oil burner and the flames took over.

Pat Fillingham left Downsview shortly after the Wooll incident to take up testing duties for the Australian company, which was now getting into production. Jim Follett was appointed chief pilot and Spradbrow became flight liaison officer to Doug Hunter.

C.D. Howe Takes Over

The underlying stresses and strains at the management level were unknown to most of the workers in the DHC wartime production program and unappreciated by those who were more concerned with their own advancement. Throughout the first two years, Plant One had produced Tiger Moths very successfully under Bill Calder and later under Frank Warren. Plant Two operated as a completely separate unit, turning out Ansons under George Burlison, with Dick Moffett as overall production manager. Both lines had produced ahead of schedule, but now that all were required to unite in one single project, a new set of responsibility problems arose: who would share the honours of command? Harry Povey's weight as the British production expert, plus the fact he had been sent out by the English company, put him in charge of "all production departments." Garratt asked Moffett and Burlison to work under Povey, but both stoutly disapproved of his production methods, particularly in the construction of jigs. George Blanchard adroitly summed up the differences some 40 years later in one sentence. "Dick and George were used to the North American way of doing things, Harry Povey the British." Management changes were tried in a frantic effort to cope with sagging production and keep up with the daily directives. It was no longer a case of a small plant grown bigger, for Canadian government investment in everything from buildings to equipment had now become a dominant factor. Little of the prewar plant remained. The same owner/government also held responsibility for the British order for Mosquitos under the Department of Munitions and Supply. Aircraft production was solidly in the hands of the Director-General, Ralph P. Bell, who in the final analysis was the undisputed boss.

Through the spring of 1943 government production officers at Downsview sent such pessimistic reports to Ottawa that Bell's executive assistant, Fred T. Smye, visited the plant to size up the situation for his superior. He was given cooperation by everyone from Phil Garratt down and freedom to contact anyone. "Things were a real mess," recalled Smye years later, "and as an illustration, I found three different officers who told me that they were responsible for produc-

tion." Smye wrote a complete report of his findings, which were reviewed in a tension-packed meeting at Downsview presided over by Director-General Ralph Bell. The de Havilland board rejected the report, claiming complete confidence in the plant management, but Bell took a very tough stand. He and the government were holding the board personally responsible, he said, and called for a prompt reply to the findings.

It was time for the board to do some investigating on their own and it was agreed that there was a production problem at Downsview. Garratt remained steadfast in his view that the existing management could provide the answer and that was that! The spotlight then fell on director J.

At the signing of the first labour agreement, June 7, 1943, (left to right) C.V. Coulson, president of local 112, UAW; P.C. Garratt, managing director DHC; J.C. Adams, secretary, Industrial Relations Institute; Frank Irvine, chairman of the office committee, local 112; Richard T. Frankensteen, international vice president of UAW; and Morris Jackson, chairman of the bargaining committee, local 112. (DHC M469)

Grant Glassco, who had been on the board since February 2, 1940. Glassco was a prominent Toronto lawyer and member of the firm Clarkson, Gordon, Dilworth and Nash. He was a government appointee and serving as a "dollar-a-year" man for the Munitions Department.

Two weeks after the critical meeting in Downsview, Ralph Bell got a call from Glassco seeking an appointment. The request was immediately granted

and Glassco made his way to Ottawa carrying a divided opinion of the DH Canada board. The two went immediately to see the Minister, the Hon. C.D. Howe, for a decision.

There is no doubt that C.D. Howe was the most powerful man in Canada at the time, whose authority on matters of war supply was supreme. He reacted in his typical abrupt style to rearrange management at Downsview in a number of areas. The first step was to have an Order in Council (PC 4668) passed appointing J. Grant Glassco as controller of de Havilland Canada, to act as head of an advisory committee and administer the company. An extraordinary meeting of the board of directors was called by Director-General Ralph Bell, who attended as the head of aircraft

production, Department of Munitions and Supply. Others in attendance were R.A. Laidlaw, P.C. Garratt, L.C.L. Murray, J.G. Glassco, W.M. Archibald, J.D. Woods and G.J. Mickleborough. Laidlaw chaired the meeting and Mickleborough acted as secretary.

Ralph Bell stated the purpose of the meeting and read the wires and cables on the subject of Mosquito production. Copies of the Order in Council were tabled, explaining the action the Minister had taken. Bell was careful to stress the fact that these drastic steps were taken solely by the Department of Munitions and Supply and were not made on the recommendation of anyone connected with the company. P.C. Garratt would remain de Havilland representative in Canada and members of the existing directorate, R.A. Laidlaw (chairman), Bethune L. Smith and J. Douglas Woods, would serve with Glassco on the committee. Bell asked that extreme care be used in announcing the management change to employees.

An announcement by the parent company backed Garratt's authority by naming him a director of de Havilland England and appointing him their official representative in Canada. This letter was read to the directors' meeting of July 29, 1943. Instructions from Ottawa forbade any liaison between de Havilland Canada and the former general manager, who set up a new office in the Bank of Commerce building on King Street in Toronto, staffed by his secretary of long standing, Ann O'Neil.

The New Broom

In another significant move from Ottawa, C.D. Howe brought in W. "Bill" Stewardson from the minister's home riding of Fort William to act as the new works manager. Stewardson was a tall, lean man, described as hard-hitting and production-wise. He had been six years with Canadian Car and Foundry, four and a half of them as shop superintendent on the Hawker Hurricane being manufactured under licence at Fort William. He was received with mixed reactions at DHC for, although he was a friendly person, he swore a lot and, according to one report, "scared the hell out of everybody." He was brought in under pressure of war and tackled the project as he saw it.

"Stewardson was what we needed in the shop at the time," says John Slaughter, who worked as his assistant for the rest of the war. "He had this rough approach, but he knew what he was talking about. He had been all over North America learning production techniques to build the Hurricane, whereas we had never been outside Downsview. In spite of his profanity, he was not a drinking man. He was well read, didn't socialize and just lived, ate and slept aircraft production. He had a three-point philosophy on the subject: good tooling, good processing and good parts control. He wouldn't let anything stand in the way of these objectives. He spent the first two weeks in Downsview just walking around observing before he went into action. I remember his comment during one

Bill Stewardson, who took over as works manager in 1944, came from Canada Car, Fort William, where he had been involved in the manufacture of Hawker Hurricanes. (DHC206)

problem when he exploded, 'There's still too many bosses around here — we've got to get it down to one.'"

Former plant manager Dick Moffett and his assistant George Burlison and Ed Forrest, who had achieved such a fine record with the Anson production at the end of 1942, resigned to accept other positions in the aviation war effort.

In July a new man was appointed as assistant to controller Glassco. George A.C. Bear had been a member of RAF ground crew during the 1914-18 war and worked his way up in the automobile trade to become manager of Ontario Automobile Company. He was moved to de Havilland by Ralph Bell from Clyde Aircraft Limited of Collingwood, where he had been serving as president. The director described him as decisive, dynamic and straight-speaking. He had a knack of dealing with people in large groups or small and "hit it off" right away with Stewardson.

In December 1942, six months before the Canadian government stepped in, only four Mosquitos had taken to the air at de Havilland Canada. By December 1943, the output hit 20 per month for the first time and this put the total over 100. In keeping with Stewardson's plan to "get the bosses down to one," Harry Povey had been asked to return to England in October 1943, with the announcement that George Bear would assume the role of general production manager. The war was

into its fourth year and few of the original DH Canada staff remained. Phil Garratt was sitting out the war in downtown Toronto. Bill Calder, Frank Warren and the "old guard" were now in secondary positions — or other wartime work. Don Murray, Fred Hotson and George Neal left to fly at the Air Observer Schools. Francis Hyde-Beadle, George Burlison, Dick Moffett, Ed Forrest and Harry Povey had all come and gone since 1941. Perhaps the only member of the Anson period still in any position of authority was Bill Burlison, who managed the experimental department. For some time the major de Havilland presence

J. Grant Glassco and Vincent Massey during the latter's visit to de Havilland Canada. (DHC M1260)

in this purely government environment was Lee Murray, assistant to the controller, who stood like the Rock of Gibraltar throughout the whole troubled period. Doug Hunter and W.J. Jakimiuk along with their engineering personnel were able to remain outside production's political battles.

The parts problem began to ease somewhat by the fall of 1943 as the North American suppliers came to grips with their assignments, but the last quarterly report for that year showed little improvement in production. "Although the controllership installed at de Havilland Aircraft has materially improved the management of the company," it read, "this improvement has not yet resulted in the production of Mosquitos." There were troubled times for everyone in the plant as promotions and demotions took place,

76

without pattern or precedent. Employee morale was at a new low and was further complicated by a dispute over union participation. From 1941 to 1942 de Havilland was in the favourable position of operating their own internal union headed by Tom Caskie. In 1943 a series of elections put in UAW-CIO representation after a long, sometimes bitter struggle. C. Vince Coulson was made president of the new Local 112; Frank Irvine was named chairman of the office committee.

Considerable care was used in breaking the news of the management change to the employees as requested by Ralph Bell; it was dispensed in small doses. The gentle approach was evident in the subsequent issues of the *De Havilland Mosquito*. The June 1943 issue welcomed Bill Stewardson as works manager and at the same time offered best wishes to R.J. Moffett, "who leaves to assume the post of Chief Engineer with Canadian Propellers, Limited, Montreal." Nothing was mentioned of George Burlison, who had resigned some time earlier. Page seven showed a photo of

Phil Garratt on June 7 after signing a labour agreement, but no mention that he vacated his position three days later. The only word of top management change came in the July/August issue announcing that George Bear had joined and, again in March 1944, that Harry Povey had returned to England. Finally in the May/June issue of 1944 (ten months later) a message on the second last page announced "CHANGE IN MANAGEMENT. In June 1943 P.C. Garratt left and became a Director of the English company. J. Grant Glassco became the executive directing head of DHC. In October 1943 Harry Povey returned to England and G.A.C. Bear became General Production Manager. Since that time top management had been: Glassco, Bear, W.D. Hunter, L.C.L. Murray and T.G. Dalglish.''

Deliveries Begin
Once Mosquitos began flying regularly at Downsview it became clear that the east-west runway was too short for safe operations. The approach areas across Dufferin Street were cleared to permit maximum use of the runway and, as a temporary measure, stoplights were placed north and south of the approach path. The lights were activated to halt road traffic whenever an aircraft was on final approach but this arrangement was far from satisfactory. Meetings were held with the City of Toronto

for permission to enlarge the airport boundary eastward.

A report in the *Toronto Star*, August 22, 1944, stated that an alternate road 2000 feet to the east of Dufferin Street would be built at the responsibility of the Federal government. A stipulation was made at the meeting that Dufferin be returned to its original status north of Wilson unless a civic airport was continued on the property. Controller Bob Saunders — later Mayor of Toronto and Hydro Chairman — offered the opinion that the old Dufferin Street would never be reopened to highway traffic. On November 24, 1944, the last house on Dufferin Street between Wilson and Sheppard was moved to make room for the airport.

The first few deliveries of aircraft went to No. 36 Operational Training Unit, RCAF, in Greenwood, N.S., but the time had come to test the Canadian-made Mosquitos in action. The long flight over 2000 miles of ocean required the design of long-range fuel tanks. The task was taken in hand by W.J. Jakimiuk and his group of engineers, who soon designed a 200-gallon tank to fit snugly into the Mosquito bomb bay. In a major effort of cooperation by the shop specialists, the first tank was ready for installation 21 days after the drawings were received. Five such tanks were prepared for the first series of trans-Atlantic deliveries.

As part of the public relations efforts of the day, delivery of the first overseas machines was coordinated with the drive for Victory Bonds. In July a number of government officials, including Ralph Bell, came down from Ottawa for a unique ceremony — the christening of the first five Mosquitos for the Royal Air Force. The aircraft were named after the Canadian cities with the best sales records in the recent loan drive. The *Acton*, KB 328; the *New Glasgow*, KB 162; the *Moose Jaw*, KB329; the *Saskatoon*, KB160; and the *Vancouver*, KB161 (all Mk.XXs) were lined up in front of the assembled employees for a formal unveiling. In a fitting ceremony including people from all the cities involved, the aircraft were turned over to the Dorval-based RAF Transport Command.

The *Acton* was the first to reach Hatfield, piloted by P/O J.G. Uren with navigator F/O R.C. Bevington. It arrived August 12, 1943, closely

Senior engineering personnel in the Mosquito program. Left to right, back row: C.D. Long, W. Burlison, W.K. Aykroyd, W. Jackson, R.B. McIntyre, J.B. Houston. Front row: W.J. Jakimiuk, W.D. Hunter, F.H. Burrell. (DHC8237)

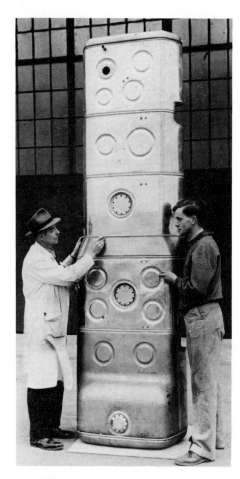

The *Acton*, the first Canadian manufactured Mosquito to be delivered to England August 12, 1943, flown by P/O Uren (right) and F/O R.C. Bevington. (DHC)

(Left) Arnold Gorman and Fred Holterman of the tanks section stand beside special trans-Atlantic fuel tank produced within 21 days after receipt of the drawings. (British Aerospace 21273)

(Below) An interesting aerial view of Downsview airport during the expansion in 1944. The original Dufferin Street runs north from the corner of Wilson Avenue (lower left) and a new east-west runway is in preparation. The Toronto Flying Club buildings can be seen off Wilson Avenue (lower right) where the TTC subway terminal now stands. (DHC690)

followed by the *New Glasgow,* ferried by an American civilian crew. Both aircraft used the Newfoundland-Greenland-Iceland route under ideal summer conditions. By November the remainder of the five aircraft were safely in Britain, but further problems arose: the RAF would not accept the Canadian solid windshields. They were all sent to No. 13 Maintenance Unit RAF, Henlow, for installation of shatterproof glass. It was not until December 2, 1943, that the first of the Canadian group went into action. The *Vancouver* earned this distinction with a raid on Berlin which was completed successfully by Canadian pilot F/L G.W. Salter in spite of engine troubles and frozen controls. The *New Glasgow, Moose Jaw* and *Vancouver* all served well with 139 Squadron before being written off in operations.

Up to now, Downsview visitors had been mostly war heroes in support of the bond drives. The fall of 1943 brought a new group whose interest in

the Mosquito was to have considerable bearing a few years later. A delegation from the Nationalist Chinese Air Force was given a cordial welcome to Downsview and a plant tour under the direction of Lee Murray.

The five successful trans-Atlantic deliveries ended 1943 on an encouraging note, with total Canadian production inching upward. Now that preliminary details had been worked out with RAF Transport Command, the stage was set for a wholesale movement of Mosquitos. Regular deliveries began in the summer of 1944, with weather being the major difficulty. Pat Fillingham returned to Downsview from Australia in April of the new year on his way home to England. His instructions were to assist with the ferry planning and deliver a Mosquito himself in the process. It was June before he finally departed Dorval and, as with so many of the northern deliveries, he took 11 days en route. Mosquitos began mixing with the Mitchells and Dakotas along the northern staging route and, although there were snags along the way, they were all lumped together as a matter of routine. There

were no major incidents, but if the planners thought they were in for clear sailing from then on, they were greatly misled. This relatively easy summer on the Atlantic was later described as ''living in a fool's paradise.'' The next series of headaches for de Havilland Canada came from a completely unexpected source — long-range deliveries.

Trouble on the Atlantic

As the weather became colder over the northern route, reports of low operating oil temperatures were received, along with increasing instances of oil cooler failures. One complete engine failure occurred to KB 452, October 18, 1944, and another to KB 489 on the 25th. These incidents resulted in wild rumours among the ferry crews, who on more than one occasion shut down an engine unnecessarily when oil gauges gave false readings. The starboard engine failure on KB 489 was of a major nature with a push rod through the crankcase. This presented a new concern for the right-hand engine was the only source of generator power. All radio was lost when the battery was exhausted during the

Mosquitos on the tarmac at Downsview. A lone Tiger Moth occupies a clearing of its own. (DHC1505)

A study in Mosquito cockpits: the British model (top) with the P6 compass and the turn and slip needles, and (bottom) as made in Canada with US-style instruments. (DHC980 & DHC1241)

ween Goose Bay and Greenland without even an SOS. To add to the pilots' jitters, one of the OTU training Mosquitos crashed near Summerside, P.E.I., in a snowstorm. The situation called for drastic action.

The problem of unexplained disappearances, coupled with the engine failures, was compounded by the unreliability of the oil temperature gauges. The possibility that a starboard engine shut-down would also exhaust the battery helped to bring about a major decision. Deliveries over the northern route would cease for the time being and be replaced by the longer, warmer South Atlantic route. Arrangements were made for de Havilland service engineers to be stationed along the key points of the route. Jerry Irvine went to Nassau in the Bahamas, Ed Jack to Natal in Brazil and Bill Duck to Rabat-Sale in Morocco. On the morning of December 15, 1944, 22 Mosquitos were dispatched by RAFTC through the well-used southern bases.

The very next day two of the machines, KB 626 and KB 620, disappeared without trace within 40 minutes flying time of Belem. These flights involved seasoned ferry crews under good weather conditions. A sudden explosion which prevented even the sending of an SOS was suspected. It set the experts thinking that the previous disappearances might not have been weather-related after all. The next day KB 634 landed at Zanderry Field with one engine failed; KB 378 set down at Caicos under similar conditions. These incidents, combined with the previous losses, presented an unprecedented crisis within Transport Command — particularly for the crews still on the route. An order went out grounding all Mosquitos in the system until further notice. Rumours were as widespread as they were unreliable and feelings ran high.

The problem took on a new urgency, calling for drastic action. A high priority meeting was convened under the direction of Air Commodore G.J. Powell, Administration Officer RAFTC, on Tuesday, December 19, at Dorval Headquarters of "45 Group." Representatives from de Havilland Canada were Doug

feathering operation but the aircraft was fortunate in reaching its destination at Narssarssuaq, Greenland. The pilot, T.L. Clark, ended his report on the incident with, "As the result of my experiences, I suffered from nervous shock and was taken to hospital at BW-1."

A delegation from Dorval, including a Packard Merlin representa-

tive and the chief RAFTC maintenance foreman, was sent over the northern route to give special instructions to the maintenance people but the troubles did not improve. Suddenly, on November 12 KB 504 was lost on a flight from Gander to Greenland. An SOS was received but no details of the trouble emerged. On November 30 KB 535 disappeared bet-

Hunter, Peppy Burrell and chief pilot Jim Follett. Thirty-two people joined in the tension-packed discussions in Dorval, which ranged from the very serious disappearances to minor snags. Known facts were explored in a step-by-step process, with action delegated wherever applicable.

Even though cold weather conditions on the North Atlantic were first blamed, it became obvious that other possibilities should be investigated. The pilots were now paying much more attention to their snag sheets and even the smallest problem was suspect. The oil coolers were given special attention, as were the reports of gasoline fumes in the fuselage. A series of monitored tests were flown to record the explosive potential of gasoline fumes in the cockpit. It was found that an explosive mixture could be brought about following a dive and steep climb and the blame was traced to a poorly positioned venting tube. The snag was quickly corrected but not all the ferry pilots were convinced this was the answer.

Oil temperature and pressure gauges in waiting aircraft were to be removed and bench tested for accuracy. Reports of toppling gyros and bottoming instrument panels were to be checked on a high priority basis. Damaged engines, removed after failure, were to be sent back to the Packard Company for a complete post-mortem. Stainless steel exhaust stacks that were burning out on long flights were to be replaced by the much more exotic inconel. On top of it all, the weather-related incidents were explored in detail. Every flight henceforth must be conducted in visual flight conditions whenever possible.

Even with this multitude of directives, five hours of additional flight testing was ordered prior to every delivery. This obvious effort to establish pilot confidence in the aircraft would be undertaken by Central Aircraft Limited of London, Ontario. Central was the de Havilland subsidiary under W. John McDonough and Francis Hyde-Beadle, with Harry Umphrey as chief pilot. Transport Command pilots from Dorval were immediately detailed to assist in this sudden workload, shuttling aircraft between Toronto, London and Montreal. Frank Baillie of RAF Transport Command had been working liaison with Downsview Test

Hereward de Havilland (right) brother of the founder, visited de Havilland Canada in 1944 and is shown here in discussion with Lee Murray, advisor to controller Glassco. (DHC57)

Flight Department for some time and supervised this phase. The London organization expanded overnight to become the finishing depot for Mosquitos. This arrangement continued well into the final days of the war and proved to be a wise one.

The ferry problems brought another senior officer of the parent company to Canada for consultation — Major Hereward de Havilland, brother of the founder and one-time manager of the Australian branch. Hereward had provided engineering liaison between the company and the operating squadrons since the birth of the Mosquito; his quiet, thorough manner earned him the reputation of a true diplomat and trouble-shooter. He arrived in Toronto February 26, 1944. Major Hereward concentrated on the operational problems and took more than the average interest in the move to mechanize the entire production line.

Production Increases

The new production line was to be the ultimate in production engineering, making use of all the latest volume manufacturing techniques. It was planned around a system introduced at the Hurricane plant in Fort William in which sophisticated carriages moved along a conveyor track. Each carriage acted as a "jig" to mate components and move them through the assembly bays. Each had platforms to give access to every possible work area on the aircraft and was completely self contained, with racks for components and small parts storage. Transfer tracks moved semi-completed aircraft between the bays and returned the empty cradles to the start of the line. At the first station,

the wing, complete with engines, was placed in position and the fuselage was lowered onto its mounting brackets. From there the whole assembly inched its way around 2400 feet of track as the work shifts came and went. At the final station an overhead crane lifted the finished Mosquito for movement on its own wheels to the paint shop. Production bosses Stewardson and Bear were behind the mechanization planning but putting it into operation was the responsibility of L.V. "Dick" Dickinson, head of plant engineering. The carriages were called corvettes, which soon gave the system the unofficial title of "Dickinson's Navy."

By March, Hereward de Havilland was to see all three bays full — even before the start of the sophisticated mechanization — with 80 aircraft produced that month. The movement became so good at one point that a veritable log jam resulted at the testing facility.

As far as Transport Command was concerned, Mosquito movements slowly returned to normal, even though pilots tried to steer clear of the type. Captain Don McVicar, who was an RAFTC training pilot at the time, recalled the period. "Any of the crews I met in the hall would literally disappear before my eyes," he said. "I'd turn my head and they would be gone."

On September 17, 1944, a message from C.D. Howe announced the resignation of Grant Glassco, who was returning to private business. Howe praised him as an outstanding administrator who had served without remuneration for the duration of the war. "Mr. Glassco has given all his time and talents to the problems of the Mosquito production. He has encountered and surmounted many difficulties and problems and it is only with regret that I have accepted his resignation." In the same notice, George Bear was named general manager of the plant to serve with the existing directors in what would now be known as the "Control Committee."

The celebration of the new year 1945 brought a much more relaxed feeling to management and workers, for the flow of parts from 200 contracting plants had now become routine. The production of fuselages that had been so well launched by Bill Houston at Dupont Street at one time

MOSQUITO'S-EYE VIEW OF MECHANIZED ASSEMBLY LINE

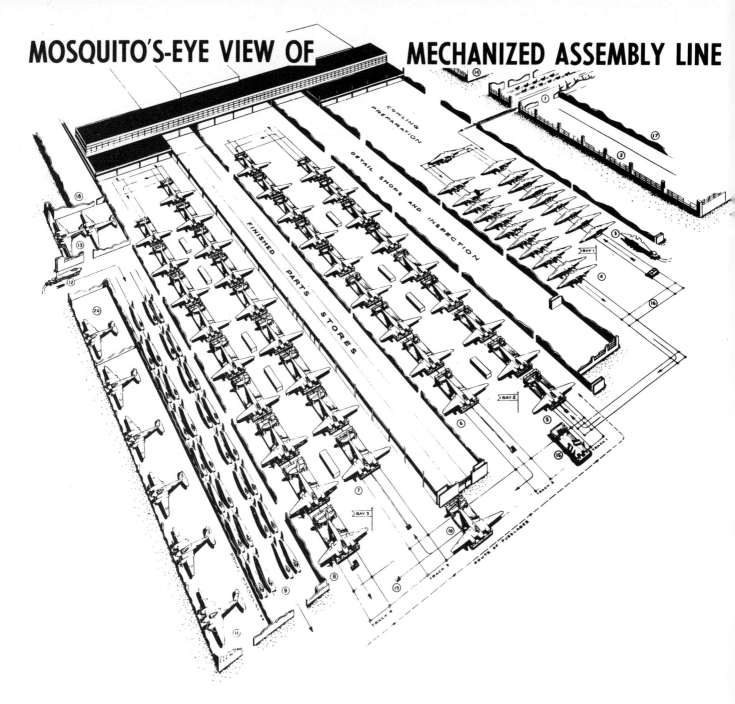

A mechanized final assembly line was started for the Canadian Mosquitos in June 1944. It occupied the two large assembly bays (2 and 3), each approximately 600 feet long and 130 feet wide. The line made a "U" circuit in Bay 2 and another in Bay 3 to give a total length of 2400 feet from the starting point at which the wing and fuselage were mated. Transfer tracks located outside the building handled the movement of semi-completed aircraft between Bays 2 and 3 and also the return of empty cradles or "carriages" to the start of the line.

The line carried 39 carriages in active moving positions. Assembly and installation work, functional tests and inspections were divided into stations providing necessary man-hour distribution along the line. Carriages were equipped with multiple electric and compressed air outlets, compartments for larger components and parts kits. The plat-forms gave full access to all working areas.

1. Engine and propeller assembly shop.
2. Receiving room for engines and propellers.
3. Point at which wing is transferred from truck to wing buggy.
4. Wing, now complete with engines and radiator assemblies, is trans-ferred to first position of main assembly line.
5. Wing meets fuselage on carriage at start of main assembly line.
6. Carriage, after chain-driven "U" circuit through Bay 2, moves via transfer track to first position of Bay 3 assembly line.
7. Carriage entering assembly line in Bay 3 for its final "U" circuit.
8. Final position of assembly line at which complete aircraft is hoisted from carriage, ready for paint shop and test flight.

9. Fuselage assembly lines and travel route to position No. 5 (see above).
10. Carriage (with plane) en route to Bay 3 on transfer track located outside of building.
11. Trainer assembly bay.
12. Fuselage on truck entering fuselage assembly lines.
13. Experimental hangar.
14. Plant No. 2—Fitting, welding and small assemblies.
15. Empty carriage en route to position No. 5.
16. Return track for empty wing buggies.
17. Paint shop.
18. Experimental shop.
19. Air winch for drawing carriage (with plane) up incline from Bay 2 to Bay 3.
20. Experimental hangar No. 2.

This sequence of photographs can be related to the diagram on the facing page. The completed Mosquito wings arrive by truck from Massey-Harris (above) and are mounted on carriages where engines, undercarriages and auxiliary wing tanks are installed. The photo below shows the conveyor track in action with the carriages or "corvettes" moving the Mosquitos along. (DHC)

exceeded demand. They were stacked side by side in a remote corner of the hangar until needed and provided an excellent opportunity for one enterprising young lady. She sought the seclusion of one of the compact fuselages to set up a temporary branch of the world's oldest profession. From all reports business became quite brisk when word got out that it was "the second fuselage from the end." But this show of private enterprise was short-lived. It is

Dick Dickinson, head of plant engineering, who was responsible for making the conveyor system (called "Dickinson's Navy") work. DHC M259)

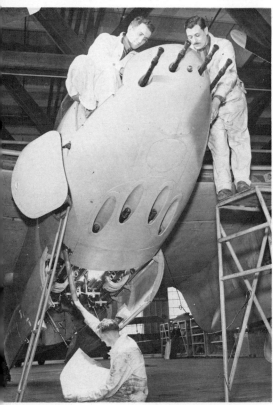

The two major variants of the Mosquito manufactured in Canada were the KB or bomber series and the KA fighters. Here the machine gun and cannon arrangement of the fighter is clearly shown along with the repositioned door. (DHC196)

not known whether one of the patrons talked too much or an alert guard noticed the increased traffic.

Bill Houston cut back on his production of fuselages at Dupont Street to balance the flow but maintained control of all wood fabrication techniques among the subcontractors, particularly the gluing and testing. Downsview had now become a huge assembly centre, putting together the labours of 15,000 Canadians from coast to coast. Production quotas became assured once "Dickinson's Navy" began operating and the problem areas became testing and delivery. With the steady flow of Mosquitos from the production line, Central Aircraft at London became a busy modification centre. Most of the work involved hours of testing and re-testing so that the pilot group, under Harry Umphrey, eventually grew to 14. Delivery incidents were considerably reduced as a result but they were not completely eliminated. De Havilland Canada had taken a major part in the cleanup program but was also on the receiving end of a lot of criticism and innuendo. The pressures of war overshadowed the fact that the Mosquito was not designed for the vagaries of Atlantic weather and that the art of ocean flying was still relatively new. The significance of the whole Mosquito ferry saga can be seen in the fact that by Victory in Europe day RAFTC had delivered 646 of these specialized aircraft to England.

By early 1945 many Canadian Mosquitos were credited with 50 or more sorties over Europe. Canadian Mosquito bombers played a major role in the night offensives that characterized the latter months of the war. They took part in 31 consecutive night raids on Berlin while serving with 139, 162, 163 and 608 Squadrons. Other squadrons with which they served in action were 109, 128, 142, 578, 627 and 692. Some went to the Admiralty for special duties while others were dispatched to the Middle East. Closer to home Canadian Mosquitos served with No. 133 RCAF at Patricia Bay, British Columbia, No. 7 OTU at

Debert, Nova Scotia, and No. 8 OTU at Greenwood, Nova Scotia. No. 133 Squadron was a home defence unit whose duty it was to patrol the B.C. coast for Japanese fire balloons.

Mosquitos lost on trans-Atlantic delivery flights: KA 100, 153, 197, 237, 259, 260, 316, 317, 968 and KB 119, 196, 230, 296, 313, 340, 370, 457, 504, 506, 535, 536, 562, 575, 589, 591, 593, 620 and 626.

"Shop" Lifting

Every wartime factory has to establish security practices, particularly with anything involving aircraft. To most employees war work becomes a respected pattern of employment, while others look upon it as a challenge to "beat the system" and try a little petty larceny. The sport becomes even more attractive when the government is involved and everything movable seems "fair game." A book could probably be written about the illegal "expropriations" that go on, both during and after all wars, wherever human nature and authority mix. De Havilland Canada in World War 2 was no exception.

A company vise seemed to be the ultimate challenge; but few who tried for this prize outdid the ingenuity of the "turkey raffle caper." As the story goes, an enterprising worker made his way through the security gates at quitting time with a parcel from which dangled two turkey legs. He made a great play of his luck that day in winning the department raffle and might have won his acting debut if the package hadn't come apart just at that moment and deposited a ten-pound vise at the guard's feet.

On another occasion a railway serviceman came into the guard house carrying a de Havilland vise he had found beside the railway tracks. The culprit was never identified but when management heard of the find they felt that anyone who could throw a vise 15 feet from the boundary fence should win some kind of prize — even if he didn't get to keep the vise.

Then there was the employee who worked in the moulding shop making the forming dies. They used a metal called "kirksite" that had a low melting point and was quite valuable. An alert guard noticed that this chap carried his lunch box differently each night. Sometimes it would swing light and easy, while at other times it looked heavy with no swing at all. On one of the "heavy" nights he was asked to "open up" and, sure enough, inside was a neat block of kirksite, just made to fit. A search of his home revealed quite a number of these carefully made bricks awaiting a buyer.

Celebrities and Ceremonies

From the beginning of the war effort, de Havilland Canada welcomed many celebrities who visited the plant to mingle with the workers on the production line. The Duke of Kent dropped by during the early stages of the Tiger Moth program and a number of flying aces came in for a tour of the plant. They all did their part to publicize the sale of Victory Bonds, but none could match the glamour of the visitor who was driven up to the front door on May 14, 1944. All eyes strained that day to catch a glimpse of the beautiful movie star Joan Fontaine, who had come to christen a Mosquito in her honour. She was given a royal welcome, not only for donating her time to the bond drive, but because she was a member of the famous de Havilland

family and cousin of the founder. Managing director Grant Glassco led a huge crowd as their guest unveiled Mosquito KB 273, named *Joan,* followed by a tour of the factory that rivalled any Hollywood production.

By fall 1944 the staff was approaching the 7000 mark, and many of the early problems were only a memory. The Victory Loan drives were still

Movie actress Joan Fontaine unveils a Mosquito named in her honour during a visit to the plant on May 14, 1944. (DHC239)

One of the first five Mosquitos to leave Canada, the *New Glasgow,* shown loading up for another bombing run over Europe. (DHC642)

A typical morning on the flight test line at Downsview with completed Mosquitos being prepared for delivery to London, Ontario, and Montreal, Quebec. (National Film Board)

active and pressure mounted for a full-scale family day at the factory. One of the prime movers was the active World War 1 veterans group under longtime employee Charlie Powell. Charlie led the company ex-servicemen in forming their own branch of the Canadian Legion, whose project during the past year had been the preparation of a de Havilland memorial to record the names of employees who lost their lives in the war. The six-foot stone cairn topped with a bronze Mosquito over a world globe was erected in a garden area outside Plant 1. An aluminum faceplate bore the names of the DHC honour roll.

The unveiling took place on Family Day, October 8, 1944. Thousands of cars jammed the narrow roads leading to the plant. It was the first such large event and the organizers soon found themselves parking cars in open fields and sideroads. The tour of the factory and the dedication of the memorial cairn were carried off in fine style. Padre Sidney Lambert of Christie Street Military Hospital officiated at the solemn wreath-laying ceremony. Charlie Powell read the honours list, followed by "taps" and a moment of silence. The flag-draped memorial was uncovered by Mr. and Mrs. G.H. Baker, whose two sons had once worked for de Havilland and had lost their lives serving with the RCAF.

A special ramp had been constructed, allowing guests to mount a few steps and look inside the cockpit of a Mosquito bomber. The long line-up proved the aircraft's popularity and acted as a prelude to the flying display to follow. Three Mosquitos performed to perfection, but a sudden rain forced many to take cover, including the announcer, Woody Walden, who continued his commentary under a flatbed truck. Scheduled addresses by general manager Bear and the president of Union Local 112 were cancelled, but a display of the de Havilland glider by B. Baronowski was completed as planned. A rain-soaked RCAF band brought the day to a close with the National Anthem.

Two other occasions were found during that month to show the de Havilland flag, starting with a sub-contractors' preview day October 6 and a salute to the Air Cadets on the 15th. The latter activities were conducted under sunny skies and totalled 4500 officers, NCOs and air cadets.

Guests that day included Air Marshall W.A. "Billy" Bishop, senior officers of the RCNVR and Toronto Mayor Fred Conboy. The events started with a march-past with Air Vice-Marshall A.T.N. "Tom" Cowley taking the salute at the reviewing stand. A conducted tour of the plant was followed by a drumhead service and the highlight of the afternoon, a flying display featuring three Mosquitos and the DHC glider. As the glider landed from its display, the cadets were bussed to their form-up area, where a round of doughnuts and milk ended their action-packed day.

Another opportunity to get acquainted with the subcontractors was arranged for Sunday, January 21, 1945, when 1200 members of the Massey-Harris company of Weston came over to see what was being done with all the Mosquito wings they had been building. This time it was overcoat weather, but they were treated to another flying display and tour of the plant. On April 19, 1945, movie actor Pat O'Brien visited Downsview to help launch the 7th Victory Loan Campaign. Once again there was a plant tour with a hangar ceremony and flying display. O'Brien removed a large Union Jack from the nose of RCAF KB 171, serial number 750.

The Final Year
By the end of 1944 the Allies were finding stubborn resistance in Europe, though it was obvious that victory was

Charlie Powell of woodshop inspection and president of DH Branch 339, Canadian Legion, displays the Mosquito ornament, cast in bronze to top the DH Canada War Memorial cairn. (DHC851)

only a matter of time. A long, nasty battle was forecast in the Pacific even after the expected European surrender. As it happened, 1945 proved to be the final year for DH Canada's war effort, but instead of a glorious ending, the year was marked by a number of fatalities that hit very close to home.

Actually the year began in the wake of the first test flight fatality since the opening of the plant in 1928. Two days before Christmas, Jack Rogers and his observer, Arthur Copp, found themselves with a jammed aileron on a routine flight, which started a dramatic exchange with the control tower on what procedure to take. The crew was given permission to jump but the final decision was left to the captain, who felt he could get his crippled craft down safely. The wheels-up approach seemed to be proceeding well but at the last moment the Mosquito nosed over in a nearby field and crashed, killing both occupants. The investigation revealed the dreaded spectre that always haunts the aircraft manufacturer — faulty workmanship, compounded by an inspection slip-up. A circular wooden plug covering an inspection opening was lacking a simple retaining screw. The plug vibrated out of position, jamming the aileron. Quality control had waged an on-going battle from the beginning, but this glaring incident brought forth a new drive with explicit photographs posted throughout the plant telling everyone exactly why the aircraft crashed.

In spite of the gloom and remorse that started the year, production was on schedule, even if the ferry flights were still giving trouble. The company was making a determined effort to resolve every snag that cropped up in this touchy area. One step was a round-trip visit by chief aeronautical engineer Jakimiuk to one of the more difficult staging points, Bluie-West-One (BW 1), Greenland (now Narssarssuaq). Every problem tended to revive the ferry rumour mill, particularly the Mosquito's lack of de-icing equipment.

In the summer of 1944, during the delivery clean-up program, a young Torontonian had joined the company as assistant to Lee Murray. The 30-year-old Woodrow "Woody" Walden had been circulation manager for *Canadian Aviation,* and when he joined Murray in a liaison capacity had just completed two years as an Anson pilot flying navigation students. He received a check-out on the Mosquito and became involved with the ferry problems at Dorval. The company backed his request to do a delivery himself, which was agreed to by Transport Command. He was allotted aircraft KB 593 and briefed with radio/navigator Tom Scotland for a flight via Gander and the Azores.

The weather on their arrival at Gander presented one of those nasty frontal situations over the Atlantic which had a number of Mossie crews nervously holding over, waiting for a break. At the first sign of clearing, the Air Force crews were ordered to go and had no alternative, but most of the civil crews balked, considering the weather still unsuitable. Walden, carrying the DH banner, found himself in an extremely touchy position, particularly as it was his first Atlantic crossing.

The atmosphere in the Met. office that March 6, 1945, grew as chilly as the outside air when Walden decided to go despite considerable opposition. He teamed with Jim Henderson, who was on his sixth Mosquito delivery, and they planned to go over together in radio contact. "There were about 23 crews in Gander at the time," recalled Henderson, "and we had been holding ten days for weather. Woody asked if he could go with me so we taxied out together. He went back with an engine temperature problem and got off ten minutes later than I. We never did make radio contact. It was clear weather when we left but after an hour or so we were in haze at 15,000. A weather alert came from Gander when we were 2 hours and 40 minutes out and I climbed to 23,000 without finding a top. I noticed the shiny glint of ice on the wing so I figured it was about time I headed back to Gander. I was just starting a slow turn when the old girl stalled from under me and it took a dive to 10,000 feet before I could regain control. Six crews went out that day; some got through and some went back. All were accounted for but Walden, and I imagine he got into the same conditions we did. I was asked to be on the court of inquiry." This tragedy less than a month before VE day further damaged the Mosquito's Atlantic reputation and did nothing to solve the ferry problems.

Canadian Mosquito Record Flights
During 1943, chief pilot J.R. "Jim" Follett completed a number of point-to-point Mosquito flights in North America, all of them records at that time:
Toronto-New York 55 minutes
Ft. William-Toronto 83 minutes
Toronto-Kansas City 2 hr. 45 min.
Toronto-Burbank, Calif. 7 hr. 20 min. (with stops)

When meteorological conditions were right (with tail winds), direct Atlantic crossings by Mosquitos provided a series of interesting record flights:
May 1944-W/C J.D. Wooldridge DSO, DFC and Bar, with F/O C.J. Burns, Goose Bay to Prestwick in Mosquito KB 233, 6 hr. 46 min.
The same day, Capt. Kirk Kerkorian and F/O L.J. Stuart, Goose Bay to Prestwick in Mosquito KB 263, 7 hr. 9 min.
October 1944-Capt. E.M. Gill and R/N W.E. Francis RAFTC, Gander to Prestwick, 6 hr. 44 min.
Capt. Gill with R/N J.P. Lagadec later in the month flew KB 534 from Goose Bay to Prestwick, 6 hr. 8 min.
May 1945-F/L H.C. Graham and F/O F.C. Seindenkranz in KB 649, from Gander to Prestwick, 5 hr. 38 min.
The same day, Capt. J.G. Naz and R/N F.G. Paxton RAFTC, Gander to Prestwick in KB 683, 5 hr. 37 min.

In a spectacular near-fatal incident, April 17, an air bottle exploded in KA 970 as it approached Scotland, tearing a seven-foot hole in the side of the fuselage. An exciting wheels-up landing ended the episode successfully, but the aircraft never flew again. It did not console anyone that the fault was traced to a pressure regulator which froze at altitude and "let go" as the crew descended into the warmer air of Prestwick.

From the early spring of 1944, a celebrated British Mosquito had been touring Canada in support of the huge Victory Loan drive. "F for Freddie" had been featured in a movie, had survived 213 operational missions over Germany and was accompanied by its crew: F/L Maurice Briggs, DSO, DFC, DFM, and F/O John Baker, DFC and Bar. Ed Jack of de Havilland, who had been seconded to Transport Command, acted as their service engineer. The aircraft's schedule brought it to Downsview on May 6, where Bill Burlison's experimental test crew touched up its ruffled paint and primped it for a western tour. "F for Freddie" arrived in Calgary with a superb demonstration, May 9, and was scheduled to repeat it the next day as a wind-up to their tour. Eddie Jack was to ride right seat on the 10th but felt a strange nausea after climbing into the cockpit. The regular crewman, Johnnie Baker, promptly replaced him for takeoff, on what the service pilots used to call a "legalized beat-up." The spectators were thrilled again, but tragedy struck, when

"Freddie" ticked a wing on the control tower and went hurtling to the ground. Jack had watched the performance from the control tower and was just going downstairs when the crash occurred. It was two close calls in one day for the colourful Eddie Jack.

In April 1945 tragedy struck the flight department again with the loss of two pilots. Both had only recently joined the testing staff and were delivering a Mosquito from Toronto to Washington. Flight Lieutenant T. Murray Mitchell, DFC, came to DHC as an experimental test pilot after an

The crew of "F for Freddie," F.L. Maurice Briggs and F/O John Baker, taken at Downsview May 6 before their western bond tour which ended fatally in Calgary four days later. (DHC2104)

Jim Follett flies Mosquito 1000 from the production line, July 19, 1945. (DHC2451)

operational tour on Mossies. W.G. "Gord" Hiltz had been a civilian pilot at No. 1 Air Observers' School at nearby Malton. Their aircraft was cleared from Malton in the late snowy afternoon and crashed 20 minutes later on a 1700-foot hill between Attica and Varysburg, in New York state. Weather was blamed.

There was great rejoicing with Victory in Europe day May 8, 1945, but the effort to finish off the war in the Pacific continued. How this would come about was of little concern to the factory workers, but it was conceded by most that their years of war employment were coming to an end. Some gave the matter little thought as long as the war with Japan continued, for they had adapted to the comfortable routine of daily challenges and regular pay cheques.

At the start of 1945 a total of 1700 had been laid off due to the improving efficiency of the production line, but when the main lay-offs came they were swift and devastating. On August 28 the balance of the Mosquito contract was cancelled and a decision taken that only 18 on the existing line would be completed. A notice went out the same night that 3000 workers would be laid off immediately on a seniority basis. The suddenness caught everyone by surprise, particularly the union heads, who sent a delegation to Ottawa and petitions outlining their

The top men at DHC when the war ended were (left to right) Doug Hunter, George Bear and Bill Stewardson. Here they proudly claim their last Mosquito as 1134, yet official records show only 1133 completed and flown. It is felt this KA model was a completed machine but untested at the time of the photo. (DHC737)

Canadian Subcontractors for the Mosquito

Aircraft Hydraulic Company - *jacks*
Aluminum Company - *aluminum alloy castings*
Boeing Aircraft Company (Canada) - *tailplanes*
S.F. Bowser Company - *parts and assemblies*
Canadian Power Boat - *fuselages and flaps*
Canadian Pratt & Whitney - *propellers*
Canadian Westinghouse - *metal elevators*
Cockshutt Plow Company - *undercarriages, rudders and elevators*
Delaney & Pettit - *casein glue and adhesives*
Dominion Chair Company - *control fittings*
Dominion Oilcloth & Linoleum Company - *sheet metal parts*
Dominion Screw - *bolts and bushings*
Duplate Glass Company - *canopy tops and windshields*
General Motors Canada - *fuselages*
Gutta Percha - *parts and assemblies*
Hoover Company - *propeller pitch mechanisms*
Humber Engineering - *tail fins*
Kelsey Company - *wheels*
Lysaught Dominion - *propeller spinners*

Massey-Harris - *wings*
McCord Company - *radiators*
Robert Mitchell - *aluminum alloy castings*
Moffats - *fuel tanks*
O'Donnell Mackie - *torque tubes*
Otaco Company - *tailwheel assemblies*
George W. Reed & Company - *hydraulics and fuel tanks*
Research Enterprises - *parts and assemblies*
Sparton of Canada - *instruments and indicators*
Stone Franklin - *bomb winches*
Toronto Metal Spinning - *small parts*
Universal Cooler - *tanks*
York Button - *small parts*

Tooling by: Myers Engineering, Otis Fensom, Aurora Engineering, Duplate Tool, Canada Cycle and Motor, Precision Tool.
From Packard Motor Company in the USA — *Packard-Merlin engines.*

suggestions to the Minister of Munitions and Supply, C.D. Howe. They demanded that Ottawa begin immediate conversion to civil work and that the employees receive one month's severance pay for each year of service.

The workers at de Havilland were not alone, for similar notices were going out in all the plants building aircraft: 4000 at Noorduyn, Montreal, 2000 at Victory Aircraft, Malton, 1200 at Massey-Harris, Weston, 825 at Central Aircraft, London. There was talk of mass protest meetings and the employees of Clyde Aircraft in Collingwood even threatened to remain in the plant until Howe stated his plans for their company. The rows of unfinished Mosquito bombers made for dramatic articles in the daily papers, with photos of Downsview housewives discussing their future —

and their mortgages. It was an emotional time, which was punctuated by the surrender of the Japanese in September. C.D. Howe issued a typical government statement that "all existing war plants will be converted to civilian production at the earliest possible date." Most soon realized it would be a long time before there would be many jobs at DHC and busied themselves looking for other work.

The transition was not without a little drama here and there, for many were reluctant to leave. One particular workman in the fitting shop insisted that he was still needed and should go on a little longer. He used every ruse possible to stay on the job, until a search of his orderly work area revealed the reason. Most of the parts he was making had nothing to do with aircraft. Under his bench was a neat

production line of fixtures for table lamps. When confronted with the evidence, his excuse was that he could not quit yet for he still had orders for 200 sets.

By August the company made an agreement with the government to do commercial work and there was the obvious overlap of new planning and finishing the Mosquito line. The biggest job would be putting the Mossies into storage. By September the long ordeal of war was over; the workmen packed their tool boxes one last time for employment in other fields. Test pilots Jim Follett and Gerry Wooll combined to test the last Mosquito, KA 534, on October 13 and by the end of the month the once-full parking lots were deserted. The noise of Packard Merlins in the circuit seldom broke the silence that descended over Downsview.

A de Havilland Canada-built Anson II delivered to the RCAF March 6, 1942. It is seen wearing No. 9 Bombing and Gunnery School (Mt. Joli) nose art. 7126 was sold to the USAAF later in 1942.

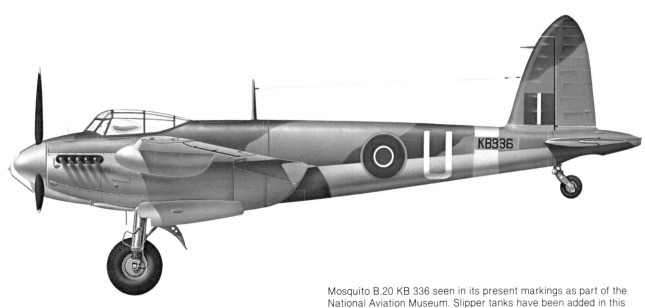

Illustrations by Peter Mossman

Mosquito B.20 KB 336 seen in its present markings as part of the National Aviation Museum. Slipper tanks have been added in this profile.

Recovery

Throughout the days of turmoil that surrounded the Mosquito in Canada, engineering and experimental work went on almost unnoticed in the background at Downsview. To the casual observer, de Havilland's 98th design seemed simply a British aircraft under manufacture in Canada with decisions made in England, but the complex Mossie, with its thousands of components and its ever-changing variants, did not conform to any such concept: a skilled engineering capacity, backed by an equally competent experimental department, was needed from the very beginning. While all eyes were on production at Downsview and the glamour of operational reports of this outstanding aircraft, DH Canada slowly built an engineering capability that was to prove a key factor in the competitive years ahead.

Every new Mosquito problem, be it the type of glue or the fitting of a US bomb sight, was turned over to engineering. Rocket projectile fittings, revised bonding and trans-Atlantic fuel tanks, all had to be designed, tested and applied to production. Every new mark of Packard Merlin engine added hundreds of engineering man-hours, what with rocker box breathers, tropical air intakes and carburetor de-icing. The use of North American hardware on a British design provided a constant challenge which involved everything from ball races to nuts and bolts. The fact that the subcontractors did not have aeronautical engineering experience only added to the responsibility of the experts at Downsview.

The men who headed these departments were seasoned professionals in their respective fields and ideally suited to their tasks. The bulk of the work fell on the shoulders of "Jaki" Jakimiuk, whose background of experience in Poland had already been well proven. His presence at Downsview had attracted many of his expatriate countrymen who were respected for their design skills, drive and enthusiasm. To head this group on the experimental side was Bill Burlison. His years in Montreal when that city led the country in aircraft manufacture provided an ideal background for the position. Hovering over it all, like a maestro in an orchestra, was Doug Hunter, an engineering administrator

W.J. Jakimiuk, the Polish aeronautical engineer who played a major role in wartime design at DH Canada and who stayed on after the war to take part in the Chipmunk and Beaver programs. (DHC1317)

steeped in the parent de Havilland tradition.

These were all creative people whose daily conversations revolved around new methods and new projects, and as early as 1943 part-time study began in a quiet corner of the plant on a boxy-looking, high-wing passenger plane with an in-line Gipsy engine. A couple of plywood cockpit mock-ups were even built to form a basis for their discussions. A low-wing trainer was also in their talks and a model of their collective ideas graced the desk of their boss Jakimiuk. This was the situation as the balance of war swung slowly in favour of the Allies. It was also the time that DHC began thinking of the future in terms of design capability.

Fred Buller Joins

If pragmatism is the "philosophy which tests the validity of all concepts by their practical results," then Fred Buller was pragmatic. He was educated in western Canada and his roots in aviation began with W. Leigh Brintnell at the Edmonton-based Mackenzie Air Service Limited. He had great admiration for Brintnell but by 1943 the time had come for a change. Buller left the west for Ottawa, where he offered his services to the war effort. This began a series of moves that brought him into the de Havilland sphere of operations.

He went first to Central Aircraft of

London, Ontario, where Francis Hyde-Beadle was resident aeronautical engineer. As part of the war program, Central was now becoming involved in the production of Mosquito fuselages, as well as the shakedown flying of these aircraft before delivery. At the age of 53 Hyde-Beadle was suffering from a recurrent heart condition and his doctors advised him to cut down his activities. This was easier said than done for an engineer of his stature, and Ottawa agreed that he should have assistance. Buller was asked to go to London, which involved him immediately with de Havilland engineering staff, the ferry problems and bringing the Mosquitos up to delivery status.

On December 14, 1943, Francis Hyde-Beadle died in London, ending an outstanding career in aeronautical engineering. Fred Buller took over responsibility and, in doing so, impressed his counterparts at Downsview. During the final weeks of the war Bill Jackson offered Buller a position at de Havilland. He moved to Toronto and "hit it off" immediately with de Havilland's Jakimiuk because of their similar views on metal aircraft construction. The two began experimenting with metal laminates and before long Buller began taking part in discussions of both a trainer aircraft and the proposed cabin utility plane.

Doug Hunter clearly understood the mandate as chief engineer Phil Garratt had given him and was quietly pleased with the staff that was developing under his command. Besides Jakimiuk and Buller, he had Bill Jackson, with DH Canada since Tiger Moth days, Bob McIntyre, who had moved over from Massey-Harris midway through the war, Bob Klein, another University of Toronto graduate serving as chief stress engineer, and Jim Houston, whose entire career had involved engines and propellers. Jim travelled with his father a great deal in the years between the wars and found himself in England about the time the de Havilland Technical School was organized. He became one of the first graduates of this prestigious institution and began specializing in the new art of controllable pitch propellers. When the war came he took a major role in modifying the

A postwar gathering in front of the Sheppard Avenue office. Left to right: A.F. MacDonald, R. Bannock, G.J. Mickleborough, W.D. Hunter, G.C. Ross (of DH South Africa), P.C. Garratt and H.R. Smyth. (DHC C50)

early British fighter aircraft with the latest propeller techniques to keep ahead of similar German technology. He came to Canada during the Mosquito program as propulsion expert and remained in this capacity — through seven Canadian designs — until his retirement in 1976.

A New Primary Trainer
It was not until three months after VE Day that government permission was received to do commercial work again at Downsview. Mosquito production was being phased out rapidly as attention went more and more to postwar projects. Francis St. Barbe was over in Canada visiting Phil Garratt to discuss this very subject and could not take his eyes off the trainer model on Jakimiuk's desk. He saw it as an ideal Canadian project, based on his seasoned view of the world market. He took a very positive approach, as reported by Martin Sharp in his book *DH, An Outline of de Havilland History,* with the comment, "If you make a good trainer I'll sell it." Everyone paid attention to St. Barbe's words for they were based on the company's long-range strategy; the Tiger Moth was now 14 years old and no longer a strong competitor in the light trainer market. Design enthusiasm ran high at Downsview and all attention was now directed to the trainer. By October 1, 1945, Bill Burlison and Reg Corlett began laying out

the contours on large sheets of brown paper. On the 31st of the same month a go-ahead order was issued for two experimental machines.

At this stage, the design office had dropped from a wartime 700 to 30 people but the adjustment had been slow and orderly. The key men in the department made the transition from war to peace without even changing their desks. The "ball game" had changed in favour of design and it was the engineers' turn at bat. Their team had been carefully rounded out with new specialists, and experiments were started, particularly in new metal techniques.

The Fox Moth Reborn
The shutdown of the Mosquito line had a traumatic effect on the lives of thousands as they scrambled back to peacetime living. All the empire-building and jockeying for position in the name of the war effort dissolved overnight into a new quandary — how to stay in aviation at all. The coming of peace put the de Havilland originals in the spotlight again for Phil Garratt was back in command with the full support of de Havilland England. He seldom discussed the C.D. Howe-Ralph Bell edict that had sent him into isolation for 26 months of the war. The subject came up one day in England during a discussion with W.F. Shaylor, who used to fly Moths with Garratt at Mount Dennis back in 1928. Shaylor was now a fellow director of DH England and they were discussing a situation with similar political overtones. "What do you do in a case like this?" Shaylor asked, and Garratt came back with one of his

short answers that held a lot of meaning: "Just sit tight and saw wood."

Garratt wanted to steer the company back into the production of small civil aircraft and saw the Fox Moth as an ideal interim type until wholly new designs could be developed. It was a well proven design for which a market still existed, and the fact that it shared many components with the Tiger Moth meant that it could be put into production quickly using recycled Tiger parts.

The de Havilland D.H. 83 Fox Moth was described as the first aircraft to support itself financially in the air and had established itself as an economical performer in the years before the war. It used Tiger Moth mainplanes, tail unit, undercarriage and engine mounting. The only different component was a deep plywood fuselage with an enlarged cabin between the wings that held up to four people. It had adapted well to floats and skis during the 1930s and proved itself in the Canadian bush. The prewar models had the Gipsy III engine but the new D.H. 83C to be built at Downsview would have the 145 hp Gipsy Major IC.

One of Garratt's first moves was to return Bill Calder to the position of works manager, where he had been before the Mosquito shuffle. This canny Scotsman, who had always viewed the wartime staff as temporary

William A.R. Calder, who served as inspector, works manager and service manager through his 30 years with de Havilland Canada. (DHC)

The Canadian Fox Moth production line, which went back into operation quickly after the war, completed 53 aircraft before it closed in 1948. (DHC)

help, had his own ideas about how he would get things back to the way they had been. First he would remove all the stools from the benches in the fitting shop, wage scales would go back to their prewar standard and new numbers would be issued to postwar help of his choice. While top-level planning went on in the upstairs office, a whole new world was opening on the shop floor at Sheppard Avenue.

It was a dramatic period for those who received Bill Calder's nod of approval. Typical of those returning was Alex Downey, who had been in charge of Tiger engine installation in the early 1940s. He returned to DHC after a stint with the Canadian Army to take part in the final days of the Mosquito.

"Bill asked me if I wanted to join the new company," recalled Alex, "and his offer was 90 cents an hour — the amount I had been making on the Tigers. After a long haggle, we settled for $1.10 and I was given the new number five. Bill took me to the old dope shop, where he wanted to set up engine overhaul. He opened a cupboard full of Gipsy engine parts and my first job was to reclaim a thousand spark plugs that he had squirrelled away during the war years. Jack Hall joined me and we were soon rebuilding Gipsy Major engines to the latest specifications.

"It was about this time that I got involved in the Fox Moth, for John Neal had been invited back and was rebuilding a Fox that had sunk. Jack Hall and I were told to study all the Tiger Moth parts that were compatible with the Fox and get ready for a very important trip. It all seemed so secretly 'hush-hush' as we waited with our bags one cold, grey morning for a pick-up at the corner of St. Clair and Dufferin Streets. At the appointed hour, along came Bill Calder with his wife in the front seat and we dutifully took our places in the back. We had no idea where we were going but seemed to be heading in the direction of Montreal.

"Bill drove like he had never heard of a comfort stop and it didn't help our predicament to have Mrs. Calder on board. He didn't believe in restaurants either and it was fortunate that we had brought some sandwiches along. The trip was memorable for more reasons than our bladder discomfort for in Montreal we collided with a cyclist and draped a young French Canadian across the hood of the car. I was afraid the police would be involved but all Bill could say was, 'Look at the mark he put in my fender.' Our eventual destination turned out to be Cap de la Madeleine and, as we drove down one of their narrow streets, someone threw a brick on the top of Bill's car. We arrived exhausted at the hangar of the former No. 11 EFTS with about 200 Tiger Moths lined up.

"Our job, Bill told us, was to remove all components that could be used for a Fox Moth and prepare them for shipment to Toronto. After a one night stop-over, the Calders returned to Toronto but, somehow, nothing was mentioned about what we would use for money while we did the job. Jack and I worked like beavers to remove wings, tail sections and fittings according to instructions, and a couple of woodworkers came down from Toronto to pack the stuff into boxcars. All we left in the hangar was a row of Tiger fuselages stripped down to their engines and we made our way back to Toronto on the CNR with a lovely choice of washrooms.

"When the boxcars finally arrived in Downsview, Calder came storming into our shop asking, 'Where are the engines?' We had never been asked to remove the engines and no message had been sent. A phone call to Cap de la Madeleine confirmed that the demolition boys had taken a sledge hammer to everything that was left, including the engines, so there was no use going back there. The problem was overcome when Ab Warren went to a depot in Fort William and soon we had plenty of Gipsy Majors for a full scale overhaul program."

It did not take long to set a Fox Moth production line into operation. There was plenty of war surplus plywood and the woodworking skills, after the Mosquito years, were of a very high order. Design improvements to the Fox Moth included a larger cabin door, a two-part engine cowling, a bubble cockpit canopy and a reinforced cabin floor. With so many of the Cap de la Madeleine components on site, the first Fox was flying very soon. The test flight department had dwindled to one man but George Turner, who used to fly Mosquitos and spent part of his time in the engine shop, was available to take the first D.H.83C CF-BFI-X into the air on December 5, 1945.

Fox Moth Customers

The first customer for the new Canadian Fox Moth was Arthur Fecteau of Fecteau Transport Aerien Ltée. of Senneterre, Quebec. He was an old friend of de Havilland, having begun operations with his brother in 1936 using one of the early wooden Cirrus Moths. During the years 1940 to 1942 he operated a British-built Fox Moth from his base on the Bell River, near Senneterre, flying the local Indians and fur traders throughout northern Quebec. He took delivery of the first production Fox, CF-BFI, on January 12, 1946, and operated it until September 1950. He returned to DHC many times in later years when the Beaver and Otter came on the scene.

The saga of the Canadian Fox Moth cannot be told without the story of serial number 29 and its proud owner, Maxwell W. Ward. Max Ward grew up in Edmonton with aviation as his dream and an intense desire to emulate the feats of Dickins, May and Berry. He won his wings in the RCAF in 1941 and, although he tried every ruse to be posted overseas, he spent the rest of the war on training assignments across Canada. He investi-

gated aviation possibilities in the Yellowknife area after his discharge from the Air Force and was determined to go into business for himself. He made his way to de Havilland one August day in 1946 and arrived in Sandy MacDonald's office with his mind set on obtaining a Fox Moth.

He had his war bond savings, some $1500 and a loan from a friend, but his total assets fell considerably short of the amount required. The attitude and perseverence of this clean-cut young man made quite an impression in the meetings that followed and he was soon sitting down with George Mickleborough working out the details of a contract. "I remember I

made payments to the Industrial Acceptance Corporation to the tune of $515.64 a month," said Ward years later. "I'll never forget that number as I had to work so hard to get it together every time."

The story of his early hardships and eventual success is the history of the present world charter giant Wardair. When other bushplanes were built at Downsview in later years, Ward was back for Beavers, Otters and Twin Otters. The long-standing Wardair/de Havilland association was demonstrated again in 1977 when Maxwell Ward became one of the first customers to place his confidence in the Dash 7 with a substantial order. He operated two with great success in the high Arctic before withdrawing from bush flying to concentrate on his holiday charter business.

The Fox Moth program provided everything Phil Garratt had hoped for. It gave DHC a chance to renew acquaintance with its old commercial customers and make new friends in the business. It began a new pattern in

A Canadian-built Fox Moth exported to New Zealand just after the war. (Ron Killick via Peter Keating)

Max Ward's original airplane, a D.H.83C Fox Moth. This little bush-plane launched what is today one of the world's great airlines, Wardair.

Illustration by Ronald E. Lowry

the company's activities — exports. Sixteen Fox Moths were eventually exported to five countries and by the time the program closed in 1948, 53 aircraft had been built. A set of components was combined by Leavens Bros. Ltd. of Toronto in 1952 with equipment from the original CF-API to produce CF-EVK. A few Fox Moths are now in museums and some are still flying. One notable example that still flies is CF-DJB, recently rebuilt by Max Ward, who still remembers his early days with the Fox.

The Chipmunk Takes Shape
The year 1946 found both the Fox Moth production line and the experimental shop alive with action. Jakimiuk's team of draftsmen was turning out drawings for the trainer at a great rate while Bill Burlison's men were making parts and devising jigs as they went. Bob McIntyre acted as project manager, coordinating all departments and planning the eventual production. The design responsibilities were spread throughout the engineering department, with Bill Jackson doing the front fuselage, Fred Buller the rear fuselage and undercarriage, Jack Greeniaus the wing, Len Trotter the controls and John Mazur the stressing. Jim Houston managed all the power plant responsibilities, along with Jack Ball on electrics, while Jack Satterthwaite did all the sketching and layouts.

The first DHC-1 Chipmunk takes shape in Bill Burlison's experimental department during 1946. Two were built in this department while jigs and fixtures were designed for a production run. (DHC)

The team was outnumbered by the staff on overhaul work but they developed a sense of purpose with the realization that a new design era was developing at DH Canada. The growing drafting office responsibilities produced a core of personnel for the years ahead — people like Norm Bell, George Luesby, Bill Kelley, Dick Nelson, Simon Gung, Jack Anderson, Bill Somerville, Art Wynne and Doug Ward. Jakimiuk and Buller were pleased that they were winning the battle for all-metal construction. The production of detailed parts began December 21, 1945, only a few months after the go-ahead was given, and the aircraft was ready for test in May of the following year.

The DHC-1 Chipmunk reflected the widespread changeover in aircraft manufacturing to metal, stressed-skin construction. The fuselage was all-metal as were the fin and tail plane. The wing had a single spar with a stressed-skin leading edge and fabric sections. The control surfaces and flaps were of metal construction, fabric covered. The two cockpits, in tandem arrangement, were well suited to the military style of instruction and were enclosed with a built-up perspex canopy.

As the little trainer took shape everyone began calling it the Jakimiuk in deference to the chief designer and his leadership in the project. The subject of a name came up officially during lunch one day in the executive dining room. Garratt had been watching the chipmunks at his cottage the day before and felt that would be a good name. Everyone liked the idea as it sounded so much

like Jakimiuk and in a wave of enthusiasm decided they would name all their future designs after Canadian animals.

"Bread and Butter"
By April 30, 1946, the de Havilland portion of the plant was officially returned to the company from government control and Garratt was securely back in his corner office. The rest of the building complex was to be administered by DHC under a series of lease-purchase arrangements with Ottawa. The problem now was to put the hangars to active use.

Ever mindful of the struggling thirties, Phil Garratt went shopping for overhaul work and it was not long in coming. The Netherlands bought six Consolidated Mk. IVA Catalina flying boats from Garratt's friend C.R. "Peter" Troup of Aircraft Industries of St. Jean, Quebec. The extensive refurbishing could only be done at a large plant so de Havilland got the work. A complete overhaul depot was set up at the Toronto Island Airport for these big "boats" and soon quotes were being asked by many customers on Canso overhauls. Such "bread-and-butter" contracts added a new dimension to de Havilland's recovery program, broadening plant skills and building stability.

The British D.H.104 Dove came on the market in the latter part of 1945 and was considered a replacement for the prewar Rapide. Because of the Rapide's early acceptance in Canada, much hope was held for Dove sales in this country. The first aircraft from the Hatfield production line came to Canada in 1946 and was shown around the country by sales manager Sandy A.F. MacDonald as CF-BNU. It was used for some time for executive flying by Imperial Oil Limited but they never put it into regular service. Serial number 15 also came to Canada for testing on floats but proved less than satisfactory due to its rather limited power. Eventually 14 Doves came to Canada in various capacities but the aircraft's greatest success in North America was in the US, where it was marketed by the Riley Aeronautics Corporation.

Dick Hiscocks Joins
Shortly after the test flight of the all-Canadian Fox Moth, Phil Garratt had a visit from a young man who had

An ex-RCAF Consolidated Canso during overhaul for the Netherlands at Toronto Island in 1946. It was the first such contract after World War 2. George Smith and Jimmy Davidson work on the engines. (DHC M10)

The first postwar connection with the parent de Havilland was the promotion of the D.H.104 Dove in Canada. Imperial Oil operated the demonstrator 'BNU for a trial period. (Jack McNulty)

worked at the plant back in 1936. Richard D. Hiscocks was a Torontonian who had built model airplanes of such quality during his schooldays that he won numerous prizes in local competitions. One of these awards in 1928 was a flight in a Gipsy Moth at the Mount Dennis flying field with test pilot Leigh Capreol. Dick obtained summer employment at Downsview during 1936 to augment his engineering studies at the University of Toronto. He was put to work on the assembly of the *Globe & Mail* Rapide, helping with the RCMP Dragonflies and generally making himself useful. Upon graduation he broadened his studies in England and, with the help of Phil Garratt and Lee Murray, found himself in the manufacturing mainstream at DH Hatfield. The shop experience was rewarding

A deluxe Canso conversion for a South American company done as part of the postwar overhaul program. (DHC)

but his efforts to study technical reports and advanced aerodynamics fell short of his expectations. An offer from the National Aeronautical Establishment of the National Research Council in Ottawa drew him back to Canada where he soon established himself with leading scientists.

With the war the number of experimental projects doubled at NRC and Hiscocks' talents were directed to wood replacement projects in case of a metal shortage. He took a major design role in the wooden Harvard training plane which never went into production and a new wooden Anson that did. This was the Anson Mark V, with its plywood bonded fuselage and improved features for pilot training and the instruction of navigators, eventually built by MacDonald Bros. and Canadian Car and Foundry.

The highlight of Dick Hiscocks' career with the National Research Council came when he was named a member of Canada's scientific delegation to Britain at the end of hostilities. It met with similar groups from the Allied countries and not only reviewed aeronautical advancements but interrogated German scientists in

an unprecedented exchange of information. It was in this exhilarating environment that new concepts of wing design and flap arrangement excited Hiscocks. He projected them into his own personal dream of the ideal bush airplane and became even more enthusiastic. It was this enthusiasm that brought him for the third time in his career to see Phil Garratt. The meeting expanded into discussions with Hunter, Jakimiuk and Buller, who were now well into the Chipmunk design. They all listened intently to Hiscocks' reasoning and were impressed; he was asked to join the team.

The Chipmunk Flies

During the first week in May 1946 an ocean liner ploughed westward through the Atlantic bringing a new member to the expanding DH Canada family. On board was the DH veteran Fred Plumb, a factory man of de Havilland's Stag Lane days when the

company's star was rising. He had taken a major role in building the first Mosquito and, although he had no specific assignment in Canada, was hoping for a senior position in the growing Canadian staff.

Arriving about the same time by air was a new member, W/C Russell Bannock, DSO, DFC and Bar, who was reporting for duty after a distinguished career in the RCAF. He had been chosen by Francis St. Barbe to become test pilot and operations manager at Downsview. Bannock had been in the RCAF from the start of the war, and although most of his service career had been in training and administration, he built up an amazing total of 11 enemy aircraft and 19 buzz-bombs downed in only 11 months of action over Europe. He commanded the famous 418 City of Edmonton Squadron at one time and led Canadian pilots in the number of buzz-bombs destroyed.

As the time drew near for testing the new Chipmunk, arrangements were made to have Geoffrey de Havilland Jr. over from England to do the first flight — as had once been planned for the Mosquito. The first flight of a de Havilland aircraft, wholly designed in Canada, was to be a historic milestone and aroused considerable interest in England. Geoffrey was unable to spare the time away from Hatfield so delegated Pat Fillingham for the job. Two others — Bob Loader and Martin Sharp — were on board the TCA Lancaster with Fillingham as it headed for Canada on May 17, 1946. Loader had been the first general manager of the company in Canada and was now head of the advertising company, Samson Clark & Co., which handled all the de Havilland promotion. Martin Sharp had held many positions in the British company and since May 1937 had been publishing the in-house publication, the *DH Gazette*.

Pat Fillingham went to work acquainting himself with the Chipmunk and on May 22, 1946, he took it aloft for the first time on a successful 60-minute flight.

In test programs, the excitement usually takes place in the air, giving the pilot a chance to exercise his trade. With the Chipmunk, the airborne chores bordered on the routine but some excitement was generated in one of the after-flight discussions.

It became the usual procedure at the end of the day for the engineering heads to gather in Jakimiuk's office to discuss the progress of the test program. One spring evening the group was listening to test pilot Fillingham, who sat smoking his pipe and tapping his ashes nonchalantly out the open window. The problems of the day were minimal, but as everyone prepared to leave, a curl of smoke was noticed rising from below.

The awnings on the lower window were burning and provided a cause for alarm which the engineering hierarchy tackled without a moment's delay. Fred Plumb was early on the scene with a fire extinguisher, closely followed by Jakimiuk. Unfortunately Jaki turned his extinguisher upside down while tucking it under his arm as he hurried to the burning awning. By the time he reached Plumb, the nozzle was spraying foam in every direction. Most of it landed on Fred's dark suit, which provided quite a colour contrast. The fire was quickly brought under control, and although Plumb was a bit annoyed at first, he soon saw the funny side and joined in the general laughter.

A minor modification to the rudder control was the only change incorporated during the initial flight testing of the Chipmunk. The second test machine went into the air on June 30, 1946, and the program with the first two hand-built models went surprisingly well until January 19, 1947. Test pilot Charles Stockford had been

Pat Fillingham at the controls of Chipmunk No.1, during a local test flight from Downsview. (DHC)

working with Alex Downey for most of that week, completing data on a series of spin trials. They were slowly adjusting the loading for each stage and the time had come for the farthest aft condition. Because of the position of the weights, Downey did not accompany Stockford on the flight.

Stockford did his series of manoeuvres in the sky south of Highway 7 and all went well until it came time for the final spin recovery. The Chipmunk entered the spin quickly enough but it was obvious from the ground that it was taking much too long to recover. Witnesses thought it was going to plough straight into the Dufferin Street farm of Thomas Bowes but it partially levelled off at 25 feet with no chance for a normal landing. The propeller dug into the frozen ground and one undercarriage leg went through the wing. CF-DFJ bounced once and travelled 100 yards across the snow-covered field. The wing and fuselage were severely buckled and the engine dislodged. The 34-year-old, ex-RCAF pilot was taken to Toronto Western Hospital with a fractured skull and other injuries. He recovered but his injuries precluded any further test flying for the company. The loss of test aircraft number two was a blow to the program even though the criteria on spins were firmly established.

Fred Plumb's arrival in the midst of the Chipmunk program brought about a shuffling of responsibilities on the manufacturing side. His background in the shops at Stag Lane and Hatfield made him a natural choice to take over Chipmunk production because up to this time only the two machines had been built by Bill Burlison's group in the experimental department. The move relegated Bill Calder to the service department for Bill Matthews was running the Canso overhaul. Frank Warren was then moved to plant superintendent under Plumb. The responsibility charts were beginning to move again — almost like 1941.

News of the successful Chipmunk certification soon reached St. Barbe in England, whose immediate reaction was "Let's have one over here." The test machine was the logical demonstrator for Britain and CF-DIO-X was duly crated and shipped. On arrival it was quickly assembled by the eager

Two RCAF Chipmunks perform a formation loop. The Chipmunk entered RCAF service in April 1948 and served primarily at RCAF Station Centralia. It remained on strength for 20 years with the last examples retired from active use at CFB Borden in 1968. In all, 79 Chipmunks were procured for the RCAF and many remain in use today as civil sportplanes. (DHC)

The above photo of DH Chipmunks looping was taken by DHC photographer Reg Corlett. The Professional Photographers of America chose a series of four of his DHC photos for a special award in New York during a photographic conference in 1956. (DHC3145)

(Left) The first Chipmunk, CF-DIO-X, being packed for shipment to England. (DHC C69)

During the testing stage Chipmunk number 1 was evaluated with a reduced area rudder. (Jack McNulty)

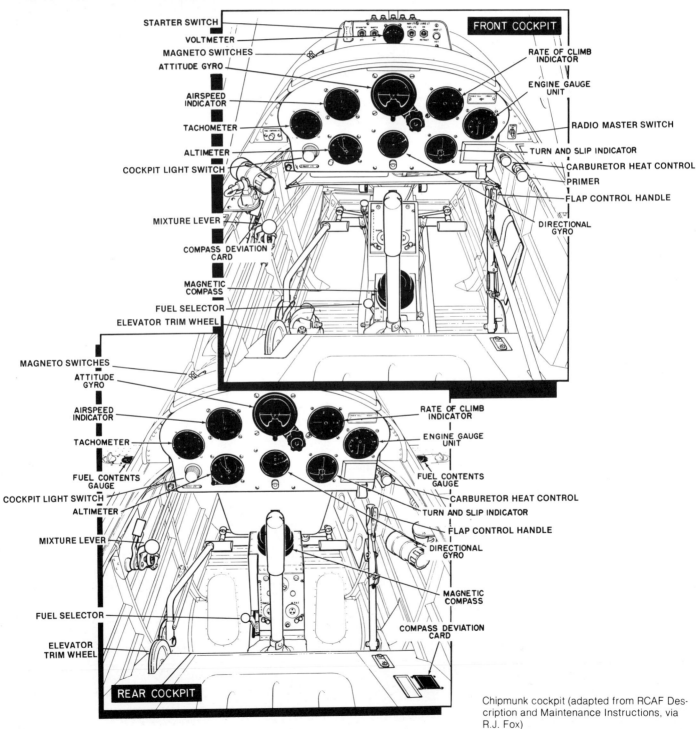

FRONT COCKPIT

STARTER SWITCH
VOLTMETER
MAGNETO SWITCHES
ATTITUDE GYRO
AIRSPEED INDICATOR
TACHOMETER
ALTIMETER
COCKPIT LIGHT SWITCH
MIXTURE LEVER
COMPASS DEVIATION CARD
MAGNETIC COMPASS
FUEL SELECTOR
ELEVATOR TRIM WHEEL

RATE OF CLIMB INDICATOR
ENGINE GAUGE UNIT
RADIO MASTER SWITCH
TURN AND SLIP INDICATOR
CARBURETOR HEAT CONTROL
PRIMER
FLAP CONTROL HANDLE
DIRECTIONAL GYRO

REAR COCKPIT

MAGNETO SWITCHES
ATTITUDE GYRO
AIRSPEED INDICATOR
TACHOMETER
FUEL CONTENTS GAUGE
COCKPIT LIGHT SWITCH
ALTIMETER
MIXTURE LEVER
FUEL SELECTOR
ELEVATOR TRIM WHEEL

RATE OF CLIMB INDICATOR
ENGINE GAUGE UNIT
FUEL CONTENTS GAUGE
CARBURETOR HEAT CONTROL
TURN AND SLIP INDICATOR
FLAP CONTROL HANDLE
DIRECTIONAL GYRO
MAGNETIC COMPASS
COMPASS DEVIATION CARD

Chipmunk cockpit (adapted from RCAF Description and Maintenance Instructions, via R.J. Fox)

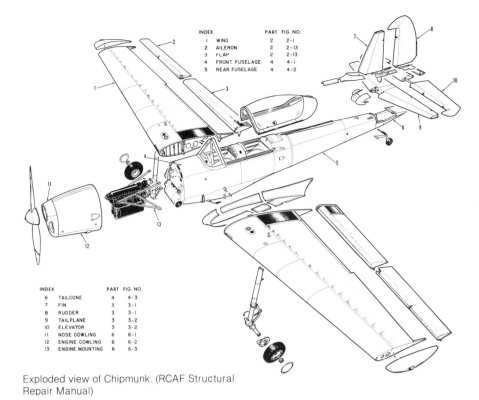

INDEX		PART	FIG. NO.
1	WING	2	2-1
2	AILERON	2	2-13
3	FLAP	2	2-13
4	FRONT FUSELAGE	4	4-1
5	REAR FUSELAGE	4	4-2

INDEX		PART	FIG. NO.
6	TAILCONE	4	4-3
7	FIN	3	3-1
8	RUDDER	3	3-1
9	TAILPLANE	3	3-2
10	ELEVATOR	3	3-2
11	NOSE COWLING	6	6-1
12	ENGINE COWLING	6	6-2
13	ENGINE MOUNTING	6	6-3

Exploded view of Chipmunk. (RCAF Structural Repair Manual)

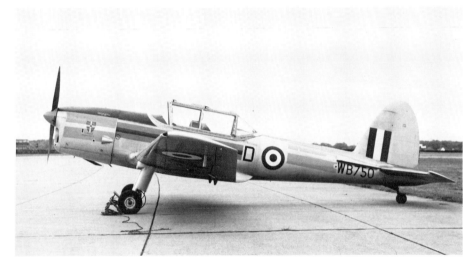

staff at Hatfield, who were anxious to pass judgement on the new Canadian product. Pat Fillingham was soon flying it over the fields of Middlesex and demonstrating it around the country as G-AKEY. The RAF began a series of tests with a view to making it their primary training machine. (It is a fitting climax to Fillingham's association with serial number 1 that he used 'KEY to win the prestigious Kings Cup race around England in 1955.)

The Chipmunk became the primary trainer of the RCAF and a number were issued to Canadian flying clubs by the Department of National Defence for refresher training. Most of the Canadian production went to the RCAF in two lots; 47 up to 1952 and a further order for 60 in 1956. Only 5 were sold in Canada outside the RCAF. Large export orders were: 43 to India, 22 to Egypt and 18 to the Royal Thai Air Force.

The RAF adopted the Chipmunk as trainer for the volunteer reserve and 1000 were eventually built in Hatfield and Broughton, England. The Duke of Edinburgh trained on one of the

The Chipmunks manufactured in England varied slightly from the Canadian model as shown: anti-spin strakes, a built-up canopy, and forward-angled undercarriage legs with landing lights in the fairings. (via K.M. Molson)

With inscription "Akash Dhara," a Canadian-built Chipmunk runs up at Safdarjung Airport, Delhi, India, on October 29, 1957. Other DHC Chipmunks went to such far-off lands as Egypt, Thailand and New Zealand. (Peter Keating)

A Lycoming 190 hp engine was tried in the experimental Chipmunk in 1951 but the larger frontal area nullified the advantage of extra power and no further work was done. (Jack McNulty)

RAF machines, WP861. Sixty additional Chipmunks were built at the Portuguese Government OGMA factory under licence. DH Canada's DHC-1 thus became the first Canadian design to be built under licence abroad. Chipmunks are still popular sport planes around the world and many have been re-engined with more horsepower for aerobatic shows.

The Great Chinese Mosquito Caper

Although official records show 1133 Mosquitos completed at Downsview, 100 of these machines had not been put up for Air Force acceptance when the war ended. They immediately took on war surplus status and in late 1945

The first Mosquito for the training of Chinese pilots is shown at Downsview in the marking of the First Bombardment Group. (Jack McNulty)

they were placed, along with 110 others still in Canada, in what was then called "storage reserve." Except for some high-level photography, there was very little Canadian need for the Mosquitos. They were spread around a number of airports and de Havilland even had some cocooning done for outside storage. These efforts were becoming more and more burdensome because of lack of space but it was not long before the War Assets Corporation had a customer. As early as 1944 a delegation from China had visited Downsview to evaluate the Mossie for their own military needs. They were back again in the summer of 1947 ready to negotiate a purchase.

Very little detail remains of the transactions that followed. One surviving official report dated July 12, 1948, mentions the agreement by War Assets to sell the surplus Mosquitos to the Chinese government for $5,000,000 "where is — as is." A total of 300 would be made available although it was noted that some were not serviceable and "reduced to spares." Four hundred spare engines

would be made available plus some operating equipment. M.L. "Mac" McIntyre, in researching the subject for the Canadian Aviation Historical Society, puts the number at 205 Mosquitos reaching China but there are many gaps in the record. DH Canada became involved immediately, particularly the new works manager, Fred Plumb. His experience with the British Mosquito in the experimental stages and the challenge of a foreign assignment drew him away from Downsview. Under a contract with the Chinese government he was to manage the transfer of aircraft to China and oversee their reassembly. DH Canada assistance was going to be necessary in both training and supervision. By mid-October, in what must be a historic record of sorts, a Mosquito "disassembly" line was established in Bay 1 to ready the aircraft for packing and crating.

An item in *Canadian Aviation* speculated that the aircraft were being purchased for $10,000 to $15,000 each and that the whole deal ran to about $12 million but it was pure conjecture. The Canadian government took great pains to avoid publicity, emphasizing that it was purely a commercial sale. No mention was made of Chiang Kai-shek and his battle with the Communist forces. The transaction between the Canadian and Chinese governments came under close scrutiny by the American advisory group in Washington that continued throughout the rest of the project.

The work of placing the wings and fuselages in protective cocoons went on unobtrusively in the hangars at Downsview but the neighbours must have become curious when they saw Mosquitos flying regularly again. The

A much modified Chipmunk. One of several conversions, this example is owned by famed Californian Art Scholl. Among other features, it has a 260 hp Lycoming engine, redesigned tail, and retractable gear. (Larry Milberry)

original plan was to have all the flight training done in Toronto by ex-RCAF Mossie pilots and it began in the cold month of February 1948. The 15 Chinese Air Force pilots were making the transition from nose-wheeled B-25 Mitchells and found not only the tail-wheeled Mosquitos but the Downsview snowbanks intimidating. The high-performance Mossie, with its tendency for a tail swing on takeoff and landing, gave the Chinese pilots a hard time. When seven aircraft had been written off, mostly in the snowbanks, the plan was changed to have all flight training done in China. Word quickly got back to their homeland that a Mossie was a "wicked" airplane and the pilots promptly named it "Lin Tai Yu," after a legendary empress who was beautiful but wicked. The 15 Toronto-trained pilots must have been travelling under a shadow; they later accounted for nine more "prangs" back in China.

As the components were prepared for rail shipment to Halifax and their long ocean voyage to Shanghai via the Atlantic and the Suez Canal, a group of technical specialists was chosen to go to China. Eddie Jack was selected as foreman of the team and was given veteran Mosquito experts in each of the trades. Jim Crowe was an RAF squadron leader with lots of Rolls-Royce engine experience, while Les

Abiss, also from the UK, was a former inspector from DH England. Bill Morgan would look after radio and electrics, while Bill Hall covered hydraulics. George Smith, a long-time member of the Mosquito test flight department, would manage the flight line and be joined in May by another veteran of the service department, Bruce Glassford.

The ground crew hired for the training operation in China comprised Don Lewis, crew chief, John Howlett, engines, Geoff Williams, hydraulics, Ernie Croydon, electrical, Bill Mann, airframes, and Ed Slater, armament. Their function was primarily to instruct the CAF personnel but it did not always work out that way.

The flight training started in Hankow on April 12, 1948, and in the first two months there were 13 accidents, including a number of fatalities. Canadian pilots had their share of thrills but managed to survive the unique training conditions and the change in environment. The Chinese attempted to set up an additional training unit of their own in Tazang and in eight days wrote off five trainers. As the accidents were still mostly in ground handling, Eddie Jack built them a taxi trainer. It had heavy steel braces from each undercarriage leg to the fuselage but even that was wrecked when it ran off the runway and bogged down in the mud.

A report reached de Havilland through Ottawa that the project was going badly on all fronts: the shipping

losses had been high, the aircraft were badly packed and so on. The author of the report also noted that during a demonstration and flypast for the military brass, one Chinese Air Force general was noted sitting in the back seat of his car practising on a mouth-organ. Numerous other problems reached Garratt's desk, prompting him to send Alex Watson over to act as supervisor and chief inspector.

There was more training than actual combat because the Mossies were not truly suited to that kind of war. Chiang Kai-shek's forces were equipping themselves with sophisticated surplus World War 2 equipment which was no match for the guerrilla tactics of the Communist forces (a lesson that was later to repeat itself in Viet Nam). The Canadians knew little of activities at the front except that the situation was getting worse. The Communists were advancing, the currency was failing and the non-Chinese were beginning to leave the country. On December 10, Peking fell and by the 17th word came for the de Havilland contingent to "get out." Some exciting scurrying took place during the next few days and most of the Canadians took the Refugee Special, a two-day train ride to Hong Kong, and eventually reached home.

Alex Watson and George Smith were asked to stay a little longer than the rest, with no idea what would come next. On one occasion they were rushed to the airport in a jeep loaded with soldiers with stern determined looks on their faces. On arrival they found a DC-4 with three engines running and one that refused to start. The two Canadians were marched to the balky engine with the simple instruction to "fix it." They managed to get the engine running and later learned that the plane was carrying the last of the gold and valuables to Formosa. Finally it was arranged through efforts at Downsview that Watson and Smith would board a special DC-6 flight out of China, but Watson got another request from the Chinese at the last minute to stay behind. It was hard to argue with all the soldiers around, the sound of gunfire in the distance and the aircraft loading for departure. With some pre-arranged help from the crew he managed to make a last-minute dash to the taxiing aircraft and disappeared into the airport confusion.

Wheels, Skis and Floats

The Ubiquitous Beaver

If ever an airplane was destined for immortality alongside the Douglas DC-3, the DHC-2 Beaver was that machine. Even after a number have been retired to museums around the world, the demand for this half-ton truck of the air remains as strong as ever. Any aircraft that boosts its original selling price of $32,000 to $125,000 after 32 years must hold something more than the secret of eternal youth. Certainly it was the right airplane at the right time, but analysts through the years credit a fine design team, a little bit of luck, and a first-class quarterback calling the signals. The fact that it was all done without government help makes the accomplishment all the more outstanding in light of later industry trends.

There is no doubt that a new Canadian bushplane came into the early postwar discussion of Garratt and St. Barbe, but to launch the project immediately would have been a little premature. It would take some time to test the design team, get a production staff together and still generate enough income to meet the weekly payroll. These objectives were tackled on the three-pronged front of overhaul, production and design.

The Fox Moth revival gave the plant a production line in a very short time and it was not long until the growing overhaul business took care of the wages. The bushplane idea was shelved for the time being with Garratt's approval. The engineers and draftsmen, under Jakimiuk, made short work of the Chipmunk design with only 7 months, 22 days from the first lofting to test flight. The study of a side-by-side fuselage for the Chipmunk was under way but a sudden order came through halting any more engineering work on the trainer. It was time to revive the bushplane studies — without delay!

To appreciate fully the background of the Beaver story it is necessary to go back to the prewar days at Downsview and tne modification of British aircraft to Canadian needs. Whereas US planes were predominantly of steel tube construction with wooden wings, the British concentrated on all-wood construction, which was never practical in the harsh Canadian

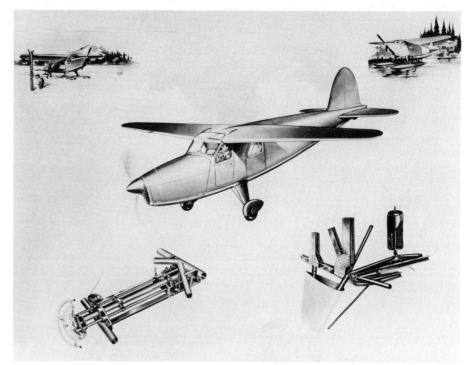

An artist's drawing of the early Beaver concept showing a cantilever wing and a tail section similar to that of the Chipmunk. (DHC)

Robert B. McIntyre of the engineering department (left) and T. Wes Hurley of sales discuss early plans for the DHC-2 Beaver in March 1945. (DHC B5)

weather. Most of the DH England designs were biplanes, which made them difficult for bush loading or manoeuvring on floats. The conversions carried out by the small Sheppard Avenue shop were successful in spite of these handicaps but the style of the ideal bushplane was firmly established with the Fokkers, Fairchilds, Bellancas and, in 1935, the Noorduyn Norseman. DH Canada had rebuilt all of these types at Downsview before 1939 so the core of the postwar staff was well acquainted with bushplane fundamentals.

One aspect of the Beaver equation that cannot be ignored is the move of general manager Phil Garratt away from the Mosquito program in 1943. The seclusion of his downtown office allowed him more time to think about the company's future. He had been through the days of Canadianizing the British Rapides and had taken on almost impossible rebuild jobs in the

late thirties to keep his men busy. He was the right man to dream of a new bush design, even though he freely admitted he was no engineer.

Competition

While DH Canada engineers were busy with their Chipmunk, Fairchild Aircraft Limited of Montreal were designing an aircraft specifically for the Canadian north. It was called the Husky and flew for the first time on June 14, 1946. The Fairchild name had been formidable in the bush trade before the war and it now looked as though they had stolen a lead on de Havilland. The F-11 Husky had a novel all-metal fuselage with rear loading and a Pratt & Whitney Junior engine. To cap it all, Fairchild had an offer of "25 machines" from Frank MacDougall, flying deputy minister of the Ontario Department of Lands and Forests, providing the aircraft met his department's requirements. MacDougall was heading a drive to replace the department's aging Stinson SR-9s. He liked the general size and performance of the Stinson, but the pounding it took in forestry work caused cracking in the wing support tubing. One Stinson bushplane had shed its wings in flight because of this problem and there had been many close calls among the department's SR-9s. They managed to live with the situation during the war when suitable replacement aircraft were not available but now they were decidedly in the market for new equipment.

Fortunately Lands and Forests had been a longtime customer of de Havilland, dating back to the first purchase of Moths in 1927. Frank MacDougall made the same verbal offer to Garratt for 25 machines, but by the time design work started on the new project at Downsview, Fairchild had 50 flying hours on their prototype Husky.

Very little paper work was exchanged during these early negotiations between DHC and the Ontario government because MacDougall was a direct man who believed in the straightforward personal approach. In recalling the period years later, he explained that he took Hunter and Jakimiuk for a flight in a forestry Stinson at Algonquin Park. "I wanted

An excellent view of the Fairchild F-11 Husky which was produced by Fairchild Aircraft Ltd. at the same time as the Beaver. It was larger than the Beaver but had the same Wasp Junior powerplant. (Arnold Warren)

to show them what to shoot for in their new airplane," he said. "I showed them the plastic covers we used to inspect the wing support fittings on the Stinson and told them, "Just design it so the wings don't come off!" " To those seasoned engineers, MacDougall's words must have represented a novel way of expressing a design definition. MacDougall elaborated on his theory that bushplanes should be built stronger than the average and have at least a 20:1 strength factor. "Doug Hunter paid attention to me," he recalled, "which was quite impressive, particularly as I knew nothing about designing airplanes. I met him on the ferry at the Toronto Island one day and he told me he had strengthened a support in the tail because of my suggestion. I always thought he was a pretty good engineer after that."

The first official act to set the Beaver in motion was a document signed September 17, 1946, authorizing preliminary engineering studies. These began on the 20th, leading to a wooden mock-up on November 20. The decision was made on December 4 to build one prototype and the appropriate internal sales order was issued that day. The project was well launched by spring but the selection of the engine became more and more of an issue. The Gipsy Queen 50, delivering 295/330 hp, was still undergoing tests in England. It had not been proven in service and the horsepower hardly fitted the "half-ton truck" the designers had in mind. If it was ready in time, would the supply of production engines be adequate. What about spare parts and product support?

Doug Hunter had been made director of engineering by Phil Garratt, who was often described as a boss "who was not one to meddle." He liked to give complete authority to his appointees and he was not going to change now. Hunter's engineering roots were decidedly British, and he had strong diplomatic contacts with the parent company. It is understandable that he favoured not only the English engine but metric hardware as had been the case with the Chipmunk. Chief engineer Jakimiuk headed the actual design team of Dick Hiscocks, aerodynamics; Fred Buller, design; and Jim Houston, propulsion, with Bob McIntyre acting as liaison between the office and the shops. They were designing to a number of new concepts and doing a good job with the in-line engine profile of the Gipsy and a proportionate fuselage. They were going for complete metal construction, which in itself was rather a new departure for a bush airplane.

Fred Buller was given a clear mandate on the type of construction while Dick Hiscocks was to replace the RAF airfoil section originally chosen with one of his own. This was the curve he had calculated as the result of his studies in England and closely resembled the NACA 4416. His other concepts, including a 15-degree droop to the ailerons when the flaps were fully down, were also to be incorporated. Buller's approach to the airframe construction was to use steel from the engine to the firewall, heavy aluminum truss frames with panels and doors throughout the front seat area, lighter trusses toward the rear and all monocoque construction aft. The method proved itself in the Beaver and was later extended to the Otter in even more complex form.

Punch Dickins Joins
The healthy sale of Fox Moths through 1946 had placed "Sandy" A.F. MacDonald firmly in the role of sales manager. As the design details of the Beaver began to take shape he sent a few letters to prominent bush pilots outlining the project and soliciting their comments. One of those receiving his letter was C.H. "Punch" Dickins, whose experience in flying the bush went back to his days with Western Canada Airways in 1928. He had conducted many pioneering flights in the north, won a McKee

This letter accompanied the questionnaire sent to bush pilots to solicit their views on the Beaver concept. (DHC)

Trophy for his efforts and was a logical choice for such a survey. Like many in the postwar period, Dickins was pondering his future about the time he received the letter. It served to rekindle his interest in northern flying and his enthusiasm for the concept of an all-Canadian bushplane grew as he prepared to answer the de Havilland letter. Punch felt strongly on a number of points, particularly the choice of engine. He could not see any future in a Gipsy engine for the bush and prepared a carefully considered list of other recommendations.

Early in 1947 he took the opportunity to deliver his answer to Phil Garratt in person, for he was not only well known at Downsview but always a welcome guest. Garratt took him to lunch, as was his custom, and the two had a long chat about many things. On January 10 it was announced that the dean of Canada's bush pilots had joined de Havilland Canada and was to become a director of the firm.

A Major Decision
The choice of engine was becoming a controversial topic. The matter came up at a luncheon meeting one day in Montreal between Phil Garratt and his friend James Young, president of Canadian Pratt & Whitney. Young announced a breakthrough in his own company, for it had recently managed the certification of war-built Wasps. Most of these engines had been made under licence, outside P &

W control. There was some doubt that the Hartford headquarters would approve them for civil use but the Canadian vice president, John Drummond, had been able to convince both his parent company and the Canadian government to approve the engines providing all parts were overhauled and certified as airworthy. The Longueuil plant was beginning to process Wasp Juniors from surplus Anson Vs across the country. At two engines per Anson, there was a good supply.

James Young argued with Garratt against the use of the Gipsy engine in any new de Havilland bushplane. He cited the difference in power between the two engines and forecast supply problems with the manufacturer so many miles away. To back his argument he offered a ready supply of the R-985 Wasp Juniors. He did not hesitate to point out that the opposition Fairchild Husky had a Junior engine. These arguments gave Garratt much food for thought as he made his way back to Toronto in his yellow Hornet Moth.

About this time rumours were circulating that all was not well with the Gipsy Queen program back in England. It was therefore reasonable that Garratt should send Hunter and Jakimiuk overseas to check the situation and make a decision. It was also not unreasonable to suggest that the two go by boat for Doug Hunter never did like those long ocean flights. Hunter knew there was opposition to his choice of engine so he issued strict instructions to his subordinates that nothing was to be done on the subject until his return. The climax to the growing drama came one morning while the two senior engineers were in mid-Atlantic and Garratt sat alone in his office pondering a new wire from

Hatfield. The prototype engine had broken down on the test stand; the problem was solving itself.

In the midst of his deliberations, Garratt looked out of the window and noticed Fred Buller going across Sheppard Avenue for an early lunch. He put the telegram in the desk and went down the stairs in the direction of the cafeteria. There were very few in the lunch room at that time and Buller was sitting at a table, all alone, staring into a bowl of hot corn chowder. He was one of the engineers unhappy with the prospect of the Gipsy Queen and was having more than a little difficulty balancing the long engine and positioning the accessories. Garratt made his way to Buller's table and the conversation

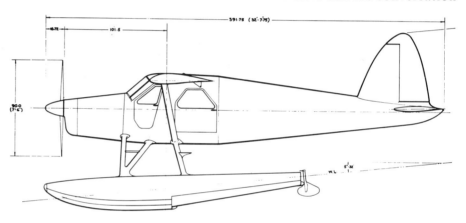

The Beaver profile as it appeared in a 1947 drawing with a streamlined nose housing an inverted Gipsy Queen engine. The prototype was two-thirds completed before it was decided to use the Pratt & Whitney 985 Junior. (DHC)

soon came around to the new plane and its engine.

No mention was made of the message from England but questions arose as to the possibility of using a Pratt & Whitney R-985 Wasp Jr. Garratt quietly reasoned that seaplanes in the past never did have enough power and that he could get plenty of these engines from Pratt & Whitney by just making a phone call to James Young. Buller was slow to reply. He was inwardly elated that the boss was taking this approach but was exceedingly cautious in view of the directive he had received from Hunter. When he was sure "PC" was serious, Fred Buller admitted that it would be practical to switch to the P & W engine and it could be accomplished even with two-thirds of the aircraft designed. He was told to

The prototype Beaver fuselage is tested under landing loads during July 1947. (DHC B35)

The prototype Beaver CF-FHB-X with Russ Bannock at the controls lifts off on its first flight, August 16, 1947. (DHC40801)

proposal and sent word to the DH general manager that they were "heading for trouble!" Both Garratt and Hunter were dubious but an agreement was reached to leave the system intact for the test program. A simple linkage between the flaps and the ailerons performed so effectively on test that nothing more was said on the subject.

The choice of a name was much easier and was once again decided at the executive dining room table. When the subject came up everyone agreed with Garratt that the DH Canada line of aircraft should be named after Canadian animals and that calling the trainer the Chipmunk had been a success. It did not take long to relate the hard-working beaver to the bushplane they had in mind and even before coffee was served the decision was made.

check out the details and report. In a meeting that followed Buller required only a few seconds to gain unanimous approval from the other engineers and the results were duly reported to Garratt that afternoon. The answer was an immediate "go ahead." The crisis was over.

New problems were to be expected under the circumstances but design changes went forward with enthusiasm —a new engine mount, a higher undercarriage to provide propeller clearance, strengthening of the wing, repositioning of the oil tank. The work was well advanced by the time the senior engineers returned from England and no further comment arose at any level regarding the choice of an engine.

The design program had other hurdles of a different nature to overcome. A small all-metal plane was a bit of a novelty in those days and much was new to the old-time bush engineer. The use of flap for take-off and the combination of droop ailerons raised more than one eyebrow in the trade. Knowledgeable people heard of the

Some of the key people behind the Beaver. Left to right: Dick Hiscocks, Doug Hunter, Russ Bannock, Jaki Jakimiuk, Jim Houston and Fred Buller. (DHC23885)

The Beaver Flies

On a hazy afternoon, August 16, 1947, the prototype Beaver, CF-FHB-X (combining the initials of F.H. Buller), was test flown by operations manager and chief test pilot Russ Bannock. After all the pressure of last-minute changes in design, the test flight was almost anti-climactic. The fuselage that had been designed for 300 hp now had 450 hp in the nose; everyone expected good performance. There were actually two flights on the day that de Havilland STOL was born, one a 20-minute hop when Bannock landed to check an oil supply problem and the other of one hour.

Test pilot Bannock completed 150 hours of development flying on the prototype then turned the float certification over to George Neal. George Neal's association with DH Canada went back to 1936 when he joined the struggling little group on Sheppard Avenue beside the CNR tracks. He had his private pilot's licence in those days and, because of his previous automobile experience, was given en-

George Neal flies Beaver number 1 over Toronto during float trials. An experiment is shown in progress to improve the airflow around the wing root and windshield. (DHC B121 via L.B. Best)

Punch Dickins, Phil Garratt, Sandy MacDonald, Pat Reid and Frank MacDougall look with confident anticipation at the prototype Beaver. (DHC39411)

gine overhaul and test stand duties. Like many who were flying actively before the outbreak of war, he went into full-time flying with the Air Observer School movement. He trained at No.1 AOS Malton and was posted to Chatham, where he became a senior member of the staff, in charge of all test flying.

With 4000 hours now in his flying log and his reputation for getting things done, George Neal was welcomed back to Downsview in 1945. Once again he specialized in engine overhaul, but this did not last long. His flying experience was called upon more and more, what with Dove flights, Chipmunk tests, Fox Moth

deliveries, a Rapide for South America and now the Beaver.

On a major design project, problems sometimes come from the most unexpected sources. Fred Buller recalled one such case that provided embarrassment for a very good customer —the Ontario Department of Lands and Forests. Shortly after the department's decision to purchase the Beaver, orders went out to start building hangars at all the district headquarters in northern Ontario. Somehow their construction people picked up the wrong dimension of the Beaver wingspan. It was only after the work was well under way that the doors were found to be four feet too small.

Buller and Hiscocks got a frantic call inquiring if the wingspan of the new aircraft could be decreased, which was unthinkable for more reasons than one. In the interests of diplomacy they referred the question to Phil Garratt, who set their minds at rest with a simple reply: ''Leave it with me.'' The problem disappeared promptly and the Beaver wing dimension remained intact.

There was a certain amount of urgency in the Beaver test program as the Fairchild Husky had already been demonstrated to Ontario's Frank MacDougall. The deputy minister was holding his judgment at the time and was soon invited for a Beaver evaluation flight at the Toronto waterfront. George Neal allowed the veteran forester to fly the plane in every configuration and gave him a convincing

demonstration of the use of flap for take-off. MacDougall came away impressed with the Beaver's performance and promptly placed an order for four of them. The Ontario forestry people never did buy a Husky. Only 12 Huskies were built and soon the proud name of Fairchild vanished from the Canadian scene.

As early as June 1947 the decision was made to go into limited production of 15 Beavers, followed by the issuing of shop drawings on August 5. The first aircraft from this batch, registered CF-OBS, was test flown February 5, 1948, and delivered to Lands and Forests on April 26.

The production model of the Beaver varied considerably from the original prototype. When 'FHB first flew it had short exhaust stacks on each side. The final configuration had a collector ring directing the exhaust to the heater underneath. For some time surplus Anson V heaters were used with much success. The original fin and rudder

unit, looking much like that of a Chipmunk, soon had an added dorsal fairing tapering gracefully to a position midway down the back of the fuselage. A very distinctive feature of 'FHB when it first flew was soon modified: the original windshield sloped back behind the leading edge of the wing which curved to meet it. A raised windshield soon replaced the original and allowed a smoother airflow around the cabin.

The Beaver that went into production had a functional rugged look with a square-sided fuselage and sturdy undercarriage legs. The strut-braced wing was of constant chord with large-span, slotted flaps. It had two doors up front and two large removable doors in the cargo/passenger area. There was accommodation for six and the pilot: three on a hammock seat across the back, two on single seats and one beside the pilot. There was room for light baggage behind the hammock seat and a suitable door for

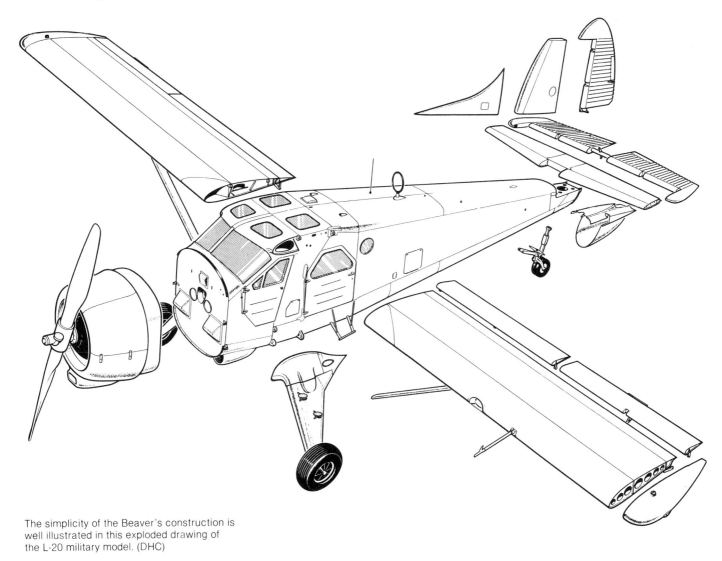

The simplicity of the Beaver's construction is well illustrated in this exploded drawing of the L-20 military model. (DHC)

The first takeoff using the float dolly went well (left photo). On the second delivery, with no wind, the dolly misbehaved. In the right photo the dolly takes to the grass while the Beaver lifts clear. (DHC)

the loading of long objects. All but the pilot's seat could be removed for carrying freight. With the bush operator in mind, the fuel was stored in easy-to-reach tanks under the floor. All controls were simple, with flaps that were operated by a hydraulic hand pump.

Beaver and Chipmunk Sales

A new aircraft type provides exciting times in any aircraft company and the birth of the Beaver was no exception. Full certification came March 10 and the four Ontario Department of Lands and Forests aircraft were delivered quickly. Further orders followed which brought their total to 16 before the year was out. Laurentian Air Service in Ottawa was the first commercial aviation company to put the Beaver to work, while the Quebec North Shore Paper Company was the first private corporation to order one. The Manitoba and Saskatchewan governments, along with the federal Department of Transport, soon followed Ontario's lead with orders in 1948.

On June 1 Punch Dickins put his prestige in western Canada to work with an extensive tour in the prototype CF-FHB. He was delivering the machine to Russ Baker of Central B.C. Airlines and touched down at all the important bases along the way to show off the new aircraft. He combined with Stan McMillan to do another demonstration flight on skis during the following winter via Sioux Lookout, Kenora, Lac du Bonnet, The Pas and all stops to Edmonton. Established veteran bush pilots such as Matt Berry, Stan McMillan and

Arthur Fecteau began operating the Beaver. Colourful contractor Harry McLean bought aircraft 42 for his personal use, flown by his pilot, Dick Preston. During the Leduc, Alberta, oil rush of 1949 Russ Bannock was sent west to try his luck in that area and ended up selling 12 aircraft.

While the Beaver was getting the lion's share of attention, Chipmunk sales were building slowly. True to St. Barbe's prediction, most of the early ones went to faraway places but many countries that might have bought the little trainer could not handle the hard currency requirements. India proved to be the best customer until 1949 and interest grew throughout the Commonwealth. Britain's Royal Air Force liked the sprightly little trainer and it was at this time that the decision was taken to build the Chipmunk under licence at Chester, England. Bill Kelley and R. McLeod from the Downsview engineering office went to England to work with the Chipmunk team at Hatfield and Chester. Their first night in England was almost their last.

Dick Hiscocks was already in Hatfield working on the project but, because his hotel was full, the lads from Canada were sent to a small hotel on the outskirts. Arrangements were made for the next day's work at the design office. When they did not show up at the appointed hour, Hiscocks became worried. By telephone he learned that the new arrivals were recovering in hospital from near asphyxiation. The gas heater in their room had malfunctioned and they were lucky to be alive.

The Wayward Dolly

Whenever de Havilland old timers talk of "dollies" they are referring to the unique system they devised to deliver Beavers (and later Twin Otters) to the waterfront on floats. In prewar

A later four-wheeled dolly provided more stability and had a brake which came on once the pressure of the aircraft was removed. (DHC via R.J. Fox)

days it was always a high insurance risk towing fragile aircraft fuselages through the Toronto traffic to the air harbour at the foot of Yonge Street. Another couple of trips with wings, floats and an assembly crew made the whole process costly and time-consuming.

With these recollections and a little experience with Fox Moths, it was decided early in the Beaver program that there had to be a better way. A three-wheeled dolly was built in the shops that would accommodate a float-equipped Beaver. It was aimed down the runway for takeoff and was designed to run in a straight line until the aircraft lifted clear. Russ Bannock made the first takeoff successfully into a stiff breeze but the test flight crew did not like the dolly's directional behaviour. They suggested a brake and other modifications but the system had already cost a lot and nothing more was done.

The story most often told about DH dollies happened one day when Phil Garratt took a couple of custom-

A typical Beaver, CF-OCP, at Ignace in northern Ontario, August 24, 1976. (Larry Milberry)

One of Max Ward's Beavers seen in a typical northern setting. It is fitted with the long-range belly tank. (DHC)

ers onto the field to witness this novel procedure. He parked his new Studebaker beside a cross runway and the three walked over to a vantage point where George Neal was preparing to deliver the second Ontario Forestry Beaver to Toronto Island. This time there was no wind and the dolly misbehaved badly at the critical point of lift-off. Neal was able to get the machine into the air but the dolly careered off the runway on a path of its own. There was no danger to the onlookers but they stood transfixed as it circled completely around toward the Studebaker and scored a direct hit. Needless to say an order for "suitable modifications" was on Harry Proctor's desk the next day.

Engine Overhaul
A major part of the postwar program in 1946 was the search for overhaul work of all kinds. It got off to a good

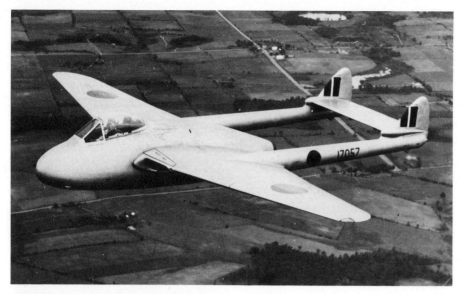

George Neal flying one of the RCAF Vampires. The Vampire was the RCAF's first operational jet, entering service in February 1948. (DND via K.M. Molson)

George Neal poses beside a Vampire with Battle of Britain ace, Douglas Bader. (DHC)

start and continued for the next ten years, averaging 33 aircraft per year. A wide variety of types went through the shops, including everything from flying boats to jets. Overhaul work had the double-barrelled advantage of providing an extremely versatile shop capability along with a stable income. It did even more, for it led naturally to the overhaul of engines and an early move into the turbine age.

De Havilland Canada had overhauled Gipsy and Cirrus engines during the prewar days and the engine shop was one of the first rehabilitated in 1945 to look after the Fox Moth program. As the volume of work grew, so did the size of the engines, but it was the arrival in Canada of the D.H.100 Vampire with its Goblin engine that brought new techniques to Downsview—jet engine overhaul.

As soon as the first Vampire jet fighter reached the RCAF, Phil Garratt saw the need for overhaul facilities for this new type of power plant. There were no shops in Canada capable of overhauling jet engines and the Air Force certainly did not have the facilities. He called in Bob McIntyre, who

was at that time in charge of Canso overhaul, and asked him to set up a new engine division. McIntyre went to England to obtain the necessary background and returned with some DH Engine Company personnel to help start up shops in Canada. Reg Corlett was delegated to establish a jet engine school and also went to England for training. By the time the Goblin engines started arriving for overhaul, the department was organized and the staff soon made the transition to the new techniques. Later, when the RCAF purchased two D.H.106 Comet airliners, the shops were in an excellent position to overhaul the larger Ghost engines.

The division's big move forward came when the Mk.5 and 6 Canadair F-86 Sabres were built with Orenda engines, replacing the General Electric J-47s. General Electric did not want to overhaul the Orendas and the Canadian government asked de Havilland to carry out the work. Bob McIntyre later recalled that busy period: "At the height of the program, 30 to 40 engines would be in process on the overhaul line during a single week. The key to the company's success was the establishment of a fixed-price contract which allowed the government to control its costs and allowed de Havilland to make a profit on the volume of work processed. The two test cells

ran 24 hours a day and consumed a tank car of kerosene each day."

With the replacement of the Canadair Sabres with Voodoos and Starfighters in the early 1960s, de Havilland's engine activity waned. When the company disposed of the last of its Gipsy engine work and spares to Standard Aero in the mid-60s, de Havilland Canada engine activities passed into history.

Beaver Superiority

One year after the Beaver had been in operation, Russ Bannock headed north to Edmonton with a demonstration aircraft on one of his regular visits. He was renewing his acquaintance with western life when he read in *Aviation Week* that the 10th Search and Rescue Squadron USAF was expanding its operation in Alaska. The "10th" was commanded by Colonel Bernt Balchen, famous Norwegian Arctic pilot, and they were currently using Cessna 195s on floats and skis. They were looking for something capable of carrying 1000 pounds, which just happened to conform to the Jakimiuk-Hiscocks-Buller design. Bannock got busy with a letter to Balchen offering a demonstration of the Beaver, and August 1 found him in Anchorage working out of Elmendorf AFB with the US Air Force.

It was a pleasant month spent with the "10th" because Balchen had a highly skilled group working in a demanding, rugged requirement. The officers were impressed with the Beaver's performance and were continually thinking up new challenges, including fishing trips.

The ultimate challenge turned out to be a greyling river some 100 miles east of Fairbanks. Up to then it had only been approached by a tortuous overland trail—"Could the Beaver go in?" Russ agreed to a flight which ended up with six people, including Brigadier General Gaffety and Balchen himself. The winding greyling river presented a formidable challenge, for although there would be no trick in setting down, the test would come in getting out again. While the officers were fishing, Russ marked out the deep-water channels with a series of sticks as he planned his takeoff. The fishing was terrific that day, which only added to the gross weight for takeoff. When the time came to leave, Russ was able to rudder through the channel onto the step for a convincing

Some of the competing aircraft in the US Army competitions held at Dayton, Ohio, and Fort Bragg, N.C. Clockwise from bottom left are the Ryan Navion, Atlas, Aero Commander, Bellanca Skyrocket, Beaver and Cessna 195. (via L.B. Best)

takeoff and return to Fairbanks.

On the strength of the month's demonstrations, Balchen placed an order for ten Beavers, along with a glowing recommendation of the aircraft for other military tasks. In due course, a request went through to Washington for the purchase of 22 aircraft which promptly ran into fierce opposition. American manufacturers were up in arms, citing everything from single-source restrictions to the "Buy American Act." As time went by the argument drew increasing Congressional fire along with considerable nationwide publicity. Any decision for orders, it was decreed, must come as the result of a competition.

Later, in 1950, the argument was compounded by a new factor south of the borders—the US Army's interest in the Beaver. Russ Bannock read, once again in *Aviation Week*, that Colonel Louis Compton, Commander of the Artillery Board, was considering larger aircraft for liaison and utility duties. Soon Russ was down at Fort Bragg, N.C., amazing everyone with the go-anywhere, carry-everything agility of the Beaver. The Army immediately wanted this rugged performer to replace the Piper Cubs they had been using but ran into the same arguments about buying outside the country. New fuel was added to the long, bitter argument and served to bring the matter to a head. Both the USAF and the US Army arranged fly-off competitions; the winning aircraft in this new single-engine class would be designated the L-20. Bannock and his crewman, Norm Davis, were looking forward to any kind of fly-off, for by now they were well versed in the US service requirements. With their experience they felt they had a considerable lead against any opposition.

A New Approach to Sales
In December 1950 a total of 13 aircraft signed in for the long-awaited competitions, with the first to be held at Wright Field, Dayton, Ohio, for the

The cockpit area of the L-20 model showing the location of the flap lever and hydraulic pump. (DHC)

In its international orange colour scheme, this US Army Beaver on wheel-skis was seen at Thule AFB in May 1958. (David W. Menard)

A production lineup of L-20s for the US Army. (DHC)

USAF and the other at Fort Bragg, N.C., for the US Army. Cessna fitted a bigger engine in their "195" and Beech put two in their Bonanza. Aero Commander had their new twin-engine prototype. Probably the most serious competition would come from the prototype Helio Courier, which was specially designed for short takeoffs. Numerous old-timers, including Bellanca and Noorduyn, showed up, along with a new contender called the Atlas. The de Havilland team of Bannock and Davis spent three months on the scene, supported on occasion by Dick Hiscocks, Fred Buller and Alex Watson. The discussions seemed endless but the action picked up during the flying displays. Every conceivable test manoeuvre was devised, including landings and takeoffs over a 50-foot barrier. The DHC-2 Beaver breezed through them all and was particularly spectacular in the latter category.

With the first round at Wright Field firmly "in the bag," the entire group of aircraft moved to Fort Bragg for the second challenge. The Army had their own series of tests but, once again, the most points were given for short takeoffs and landings. This time the Beech twin prototype, trying to match the Beaver's landing distance, might have come close if it had not pushed the landing gear through the wings in the resulting crash.

The attending crowd quickly dragged the aircraft from the test area and, although it was clearly out of the running, the question arose as to what to do with the remains. Of all the companies in the competition, Bellanca and de Havilland were the only ones with attending service personnel. George Taylor of Bellanca and Norm Davis of de Havilland looked the situation over to see what might be done. Fortunately Davis had a wheel and tire of the right size, which he loaned to the cause. They then visited the local junk yard and acquired a few pieces of rusty angle iron; a trip to the hardware store for bolts and hacksaw blades was next, then they went to work on their competitor's aircraft. They first locked the gear in the down position, then reinforced all the damaged areas with angle iron and, after installing the spare wheel, made the aircraft suitable for a ferry flight to the factory. ''We received a nice thank you letter from Beech when they returned our wheel and tire,'' Davis recalls.

The US Army manoeuvres were once again a victory for de Havilland's stubby-nosed workhorse, which opened the way to an eventual flood of orders. First of all, six production models

The L-20 Beaver at work with the US Air Force. (DHC 2123)

A standard US Army L-20A Beaver poses for a formal company portrait. After making its mark in Korea, the Beaver went on to a long career with the US military, 981 serving with Army, Navy and Air Force units. Today many of them have returned to Canada as surplus aircraft and are hard at work throughout the northland. (DHC)

were taken "off the shelf" for evaluation in every sphere of operations, including Balchen's search and rescue squadron in Alaska. Next it was a total of 100 planes for the USAF tactical force, then a series of orders for the US Army. The US military version was called the L-20, with only a few changes from the civil model—a larger pilot seat, roof windows and other minor modifications. To manage this new-found contract Russ Bannock became director, military sales.

While a lot of attention was being given to the sale of the DHC-1 and DHC-2, life on the production floor had not been neglected. Chipmunk manufacture had been solidly organ-

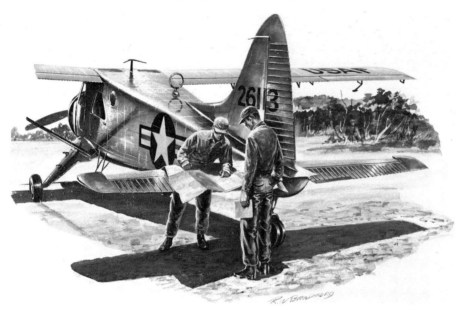

The Beaver at work with the USAF, depicted by Robert W. Bradford. (DHC)

ized by Fred Plumb, and when he left for the Chinese Mosquito contract, Bill Burlison was asked to take over. The supply of manpower from the overhaul shops allowed an orderly build-up of the new Beaver line, which averaged 30 aircraft a year for the first three years. The welcomed sales to the US military services suddenly drew everyone's attention to the manufacturing side of the company; some even doubted that the new delivery schedules could be met.

Burlison took the new challenge in his stride and immediately began farming out small components to subcontractors. The assembly line was enlarged and shop management was reorganized. George Blanchard's role of production control increased daily.

Phil Garratt had heard of Bill Stewardson's production reputation from the war days and broached the subject of his return to DHC. "Phil suggested that I needed an assistant," recalled Burlison, "and mentioned Stewardson's name. I looked on it as an order so contacted Bill, who had been working with the Ontario Department of Highways, and brought him back." John Slaughter, who had been Stewardson's assistant during the last years of the Mosquito, was invited to return and the new group soon developed into a formidable team. The delivery schedule of the US Beavers left little time for any expansion program, however; the first unit was delivered on schedule and deliveries continued throughout the entire L-20 contract until the last one on May 6, 1960.

The six YL-20 evaluation Beavers, serial numbers 98, 99, 109, 110, 114, 115, were delivered without fanfare to the USAF in the spring of 1951. Once regular deliveries started to the US Air Force, a formal hand-over ceremony was organized. The date was November 13, 1951, and the resulting press headline must have been encouraging to everyone in the plant: DE HAVILLAND CRASHES THE US AIRCRAFT MARKET, it read, and went on in a similar vein:

"For the first time in its peacetime history, the United States of America accepted delivery on November 13th of a foreign-made military aircraft. Not since the war has the United States gone outside their own boundaries for procurement of military aircraft. The purchase of Beavers from

de Havilland is a significant departure from the traditional policy and a new milestone in Canadian-American relations.

"The ceremony was at Downsview Airport Toronto where in the presence of a large gathering of high ranking Air Force officials and industrial leaders, Canada's Defence Production Minister, the Right Honourable C.D. Howe, turned over the first de Havilland L-20A to the United States government. The aircraft was accepted by Major General Mark E. Bradley, Director of Procurement and Production US Air Materiel Command. The first two aircraft lined up that day for the ceremony were serial numbers 150 and 151 bearing the USAF registrations 51-16463 and 51-16464."

The Beaver Goes to War

The Beaver entered service with the United States military while that country was going to the aid of the beleaguered South Korean forces. By June 1952 a hundred L-20s were with the US Army and it was not long until 50 per cent of them were participating in the Korean war. The L-20 was promptly dubbed the "flying jeep" and its natural environment was the battlefront. It carried out thousands of medical evacuations, hauled supplies of all kinds, and ferried generals and an endless stream of congressmen up and down the front. (When General Eisenhower became president of the USA, he too travelled Korea by L-20.) Beavers in uniform carried exterior loads under the wings, laid telephone wire from tree to tree from under-wing canisters and transported ammunition to the troops in action. The more they coped with difficult jobs, the more they were used.

As the number of L-20s grew in the Korean action the US Army asked for a DHC field representative in the area. Russ Bannock offered the position to Bruce Best, who was then chief engineer of the Toronto Flying Club. As Best was also a licenced pilot, he checked out on the Beaver and was soon on his way to Ascom City in Korea, a big US Army repair and maintenance depot.

It was a tough testing ground for any aircraft and much was learned to benefit future Beavers coming off the production line. A total of 17 modifications was recommended by Bruce Best during his year of action with the US Army. As the war progressed into

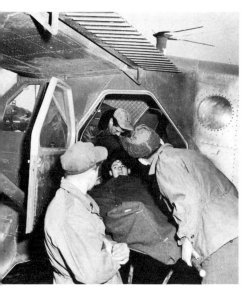

The Beaver in Korea. From the top left: a US Army L-20 carries out a medical evacuation; Beaver 64418 loaded with underwing stores; the first Beaver turned over to the Korean Air Force; 6266, "Jeep of the air," in a protective revetment; DH tech rep L.B. Best. (via L.B. Best)

Chipmunk in RCAF markings.

Pacific Western Airlines operated Beavers on the West Coast for many years.

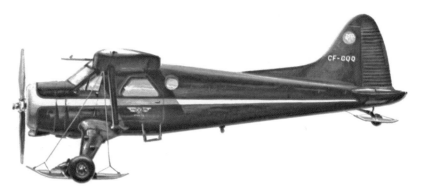

Austin Airways flew Beavers in its northern Ontario domain for over 25 years.

CF-NWX, de Havilland's long-time Otter demonstrator. It has recently been serving with Austin Airways.

Illustrations by D.P. Bromley

116

Turbo Beaver in standard OPAS colours.

Illustrations by D.P. Bromley

One of Wardair's Twin Otters which operated from the airline's
Yellowknife base.

One of de Havilland's Twin Otter demonstrators lifts off in this
Canadian winter scene. The Twin Otter's large skis trail plumes of
snow. (DHC)

1953 the damages piled up to the point where L-20s were being shipped in bulk lots back to the USA on a plan called IRAN (Inspect and Repair as Necessary).

With years of repair and overhaul experience at Downsview it was easy for de Havilland to bid on US Army requests for the overhaul of damaged L-20s. Phil Garratt spurned a cost-plus arrangement and insisted on a low, fixed-cost contract, based on volume and improving performance. The contract was no sooner signed than L-20s began arriving from the US and abroad. A few were flown in but most arrived by truck or boxcar. Those used as ammunition carriers in the front line had taken quite a beating; there was every type of damage imaginable. A veritable production line developed in Bay 4 totalling 16 aircraft a month with a tight turn-around schedule that pleased the US Army. Five hundred and sixty-three eventually went through the system and the results were so satisfactory that a similar program was arranged in later years in which US Army Caribous destined for Viet Nam came to Downsview for special military fitments.

The Beaver at home. CF-FHN gets ready for a trip somewhere along the rugged British Columbia coast in October 1956. (DHC 3875)

Royal Visitors

Early in October 1951 Princess Elizabeth and Prince Philip arrived for their first trip across Canada. They landed at Quebec City on the 9th and took part in festivities in four major centres involving rides in an open convertible through cheering crowds. The October weather was always threatening rain and a sudden shower on one occasion forced them to finish the trip in a closed car. The royal visitors were reportedly upset that the waiting crowd could not see them properly and took the matter up with their transportation officer. The Princess suggested a perspex canopy and Prince Philip even sketched a few ideas for the Army colonel.

The officer's next move was to approach the automotive industry—General Motors, Ford and Chrysler—for quotes on a canopy. The replies were not encouraging for the price ranged from $50,000 to $100,000 and the time required would be four to six weeks. When the news was relayed to Prince Philip he thought for a while and said, "Why don't we go to de Havilland? They are used to this sort of thing." It was not long before manager Phil Garratt got a personal phone call from Prince Philip, who explained the project and the preliminary sketches. Garratt ran it through his mind a couple of times, noting that it was Friday the 11th, and said, "How long do we have?" "Monday," was the prompt reply and, after a few pleasantries, the general manager suggested that the car be sent up whenever it could be spared.

Phil Garratt called in Doug Hunter, who promptly formed a team to tackle the project. By the time the car arrived at the plant after work on Friday, Fred Buller from engineering and Bill Burlison from the shops had their key personnel ready to start work. In recalling the incident years later, Russ Bannock said, "I knew the project was going on around the clock and

The special Plexiglas canopy designed and built during a weekend for the 1951 cross-Canada tour of Princess Elizabeth and Prince Philip. (DHC10251)

The prototype Otter prepares for its first flight on a cold December 21, 1951. (DHC)

went out on Sunday to see how the job was coming along. I was utterly astounded, for they had the canopy built and were fitting Chipmunk cockpit lights around the frame so it could be lit up at night." By Monday the car went out of the plant complete with canopy, ready for the rest of the royal tour. "It was an amazing accomplishment," said Bannock, "and to think that de Havilland got nothing for it except a personal 'thank you' from Prince Philip and a nice letter."

The DHC-3 Otter

With the sale of 1692 Beavers to 62 countries around the world and the large military numbers involved, the question has often been asked, "Why did Canada's RCAF never buy any?" According to all accounts, the answer is simply that they found it too small for their requirements. They still had a lot of the war-proven Norseman and it was the size of bushplane they preferred. The argument that the Beaver was too small may never be settled, but the resulting deliberations led to the next DHC model—the Otter.

It was only reasonable after the initial success of the Beaver that thoughts should turn to something a little bigger, possibly the size of the Norseman and Bellanca. Other potential customers backed the RCAF point of view, particularly the Ontario Department of Lands and Forests, who liked the size of the Beaver but

envisioned a one-ton truck as well as the half-ton variety. The RCAF was serious enough in their interest to take part in the research funding.

By 1950 the basic concept for a new type was evolved, mainly under the original Beaver design group, but this time they were missing Jaki Jakimiuk. A call had come from Hatfield during the engineering lull that followed the Beaver for design assistance with their Heron, Comet and Vampire. Jakimiuk headed the Downsview team of Charlie Bishop, Jack Greeniaus, Bill Heaslip, George Luesby, Al Marten and John Mazur that went to England to work on the night fighter version of the Vampire, the D.H.113. Jakimiuk resigned while in England to take up a position with the French company Sud Aviation. The remainder of the Canadian engineering team returned by September 1950 to take part in a challenging new design, the DHC-3.

Late in 1950, specifications were being laid down for the DHC-3, which was then called the King Beaver. In general terms it was to have the same takeoff performance as the Beaver with twice the payload. The cabin volume was to be increased two and a half times. This was a formidable challenge, considering that there was only 33.3 per cent more power to do all these wonderful things. This time, however, they would have access to a lot of new technology along with the well proven Pratt & Whitney R-1340 engine. On November 29 a factory instruction was issued for a design start with the understanding that a single prototype would be built. It was an

encouraging time for the 40 members of the engineering staff: their Chipmunk had sold 122 copies up to then and was being manufactured under licence in Britain, and Beaver sales were going well with deliveries nearing the 100 mark.

Another Major Decision

Market surveys on a bigger aircraft were in agreement with the Wasp engine and storing fuel under the floor as was done in the Beaver. Even the once-disputed linking of the aileron and flap was approved without question. Punch Dickins felt an engine/ propeller combination compatible with the Norseman would be a good sales point when talking to operators, but Dick Hiscocks insisted on the geared version of the "H" Wasp for maximum engine efficiency. Garratt approved the decision but was immediately confronted with a supply problem. Only a few of these engines had been manufactured during the war for the Australian Wirraway and they were not in regular production. A world search was conducted with the aid of Pratt & Whitney and a used aircraft entrepreneur, Charlie Babb. The search covered four continents and took on all the aspects of a detective mystery. Fifty engines were found in Sweden and, although it was not enough for a production program, it was sufficient for a start. When the details were presented for decision, Phil Garratt said, "Why don't we go ahead. I think I can talk my friend Jim Young into making the components. I know he would like to get into

119

1 Hamilton Standard constant-speed, counterweight-type propeller
2 Propeller hub and counterweight assembly
3 Pratt and Whitney 'Wasp' R-1340, nine-cylinder, air-cooled, supercharged engine rated at 600 BHP
4 Engine air exhaust pipes
5 Engine air exhaust augmentor tubes
6 Engine air intake - providing ram or filtered air to carburetor

32 Wing flap push/pull rods
33 Wing flap bellcrank - inboard
34 Wing flap bellcrank - outboard
35 Wing flap push/pull rod idler arms
36 Wing flaps - full span, double-slotted, fore and trailing flaps type. Outboard trailing edge portions operate independently as ailerons
37 Wing flap control rods
38 Wing flap hinge arms
39 Ailerons - used as conventional ailerons in flight mode - droop when flaps are selected down in landing mode
40 Wing fore flap/aileron hinge arms
41 Aileron control rod
42 Aileron control cables and pulleys
43 Wing fences - to improve lateral stability in stalls
44 Landing light - left wing only

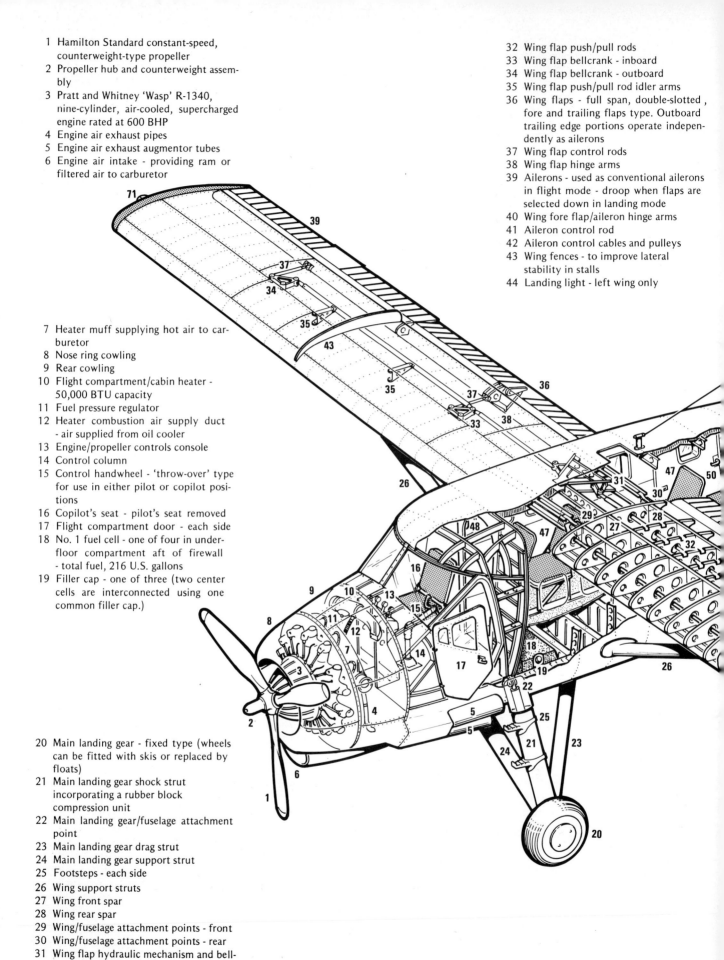

7 Heater muff supplying hot air to carburetor
8 Nose ring cowling
9 Rear cowling
10 Flight compartment/cabin heater - 50,000 BTU capacity
11 Fuel pressure regulator
12 Heater combustion air supply duct - air supplied from oil cooler
13 Engine/propeller controls console
14 Control column
15 Control handwheel - 'throw-over' type for use in either pilot or copilot positions
16 Copilot's seat - pilot's seat removed
17 Flight compartment door - each side
18 No. 1 fuel cell - one of four in underfloor compartment aft of firewall - total fuel, 216 U.S. gallons
19 Filler cap - one of three (two center cells are interconnected using one common filler cap.)

20 Main landing gear - fixed type (wheels can be fitted with skis or replaced by floats)
21 Main landing gear shock strut incorporating a rubber block compression unit
22 Main landing gear/fuselage attachment point
23 Main landing gear drag strut
24 Main landing gear support strut
25 Footsteps - each side
26 Wing support struts
27 Wing front spar
28 Wing rear spar
29 Wing/fuselage attachment points - front
30 Wing/fuselage attachment points - rear
31 Wing flap hydraulic mechanism and bellcrank installation

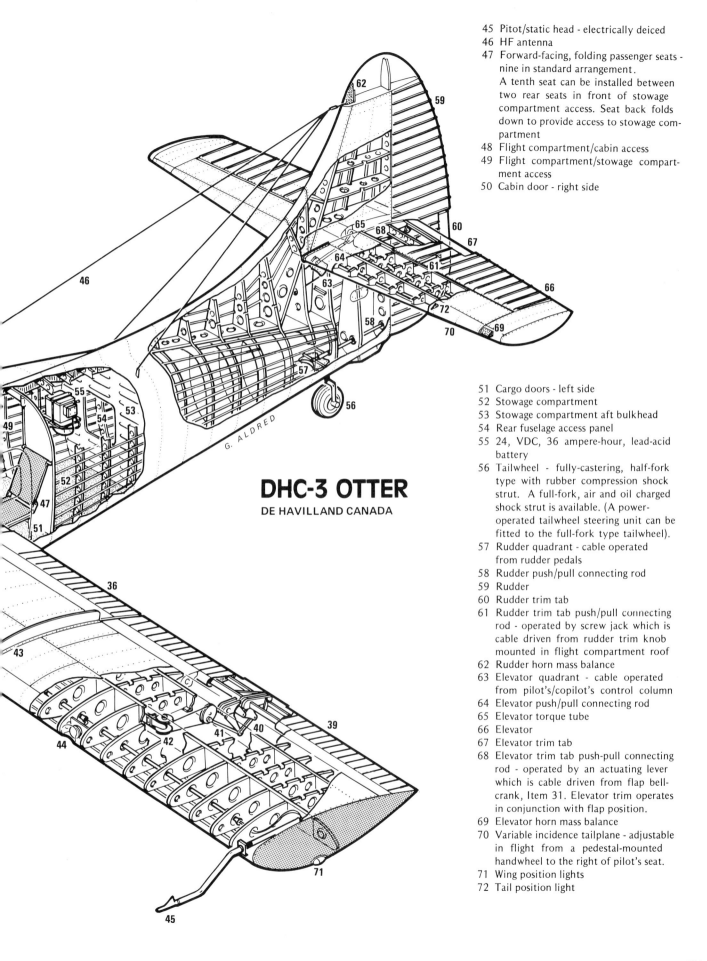

45 Pitot/static head - electrically deiced
46 HF antenna
47 Forward-facing, folding passenger seats -
   nine in standard arrangement.
   A tenth seat can be installed between
   two rear seats in front of stowage
   compartment access. Seat back folds
   down to provide access to stowage compartment
48 Flight compartment/cabin access
49 Flight compartment/stowage compartment access
50 Cabin door - right side

51 Cargo doors - left side
52 Stowage compartment
53 Stowage compartment aft bulkhead
54 Rear fuselage access panel
55 24, VDC, 36 ampere-hour, lead-acid
   battery
56 Tailwheel - fully-castering, half-fork
   type with rubber compression shock
   strut. A full-fork, air and oil charged
   shock strut is available. (A power-
   operated tailwheel steering unit can be
   fitted to the full-fork type tailwheel).
57 Rudder quadrant - cable operated
   from rudder pedals
58 Rudder push/pull connecting rod
59 Rudder
60 Rudder trim tab
61 Rudder trim tab push/pull connecting
   rod - operated by screw jack which is
   cable driven from rudder trim knob
   mounted in flight compartment roof
62 Rudder horn mass balance
63 Elevator quadrant - cable operated
   from pilot's/copilot's control column
64 Elevator push/pull connecting rod
65 Elevator torque tube
66 Elevator
67 Elevator trim tab
68 Elevator trim tab push-pull connecting
   rod - operated by an actuating lever
   which is cable driven from flap bellcrank, Item 31. Elevator trim operates
   in conjunction with flap position.
69 Elevator horn mass balance
70 Variable incidence tailplane - adjustable
   in flight from a pedestal-mounted
   handwheel to the right of pilot's seat.
71 Wing position lights
72 Tail position light

DHC-3 OTTER
DE HAVILLAND CANADA

G. ALDRED

Test pilot George Neal after testing the first DHC-3 Otter at Downsview, December 1951. (DHC)

the manufacture of engines." The "old boy" system went into operation again and another crisis was over.

While the prototype Otter took shape, a factory order for 15 machines was issued, encouraged undoubtedly by the recently announced Beaver sales to the US military. Pre-production orders were taken from the Ontario Department of Lands and Forests

The interconnected slotted flap and droop aileron of the Otter are shown in this sequence: (1) both in the normal flight position; (2) half flap with a partial droop to the ailerons; (3) the flaps fully down and maximum aileron droop. (Industrial Pictures via R.G. Halford)

along with some from a new-found market—the booming oil industry in Alberta. A push was on to get the new plane, now called the Otter, into the air in less than a year from the start of the design.

George Neal, now chief test pilot, accomplished this objective on a cold December day in 1951, which was followed by a busy year of test and development flying. The tight guidelines imposed by limited power had forced a maximum effort in all areas of design. Fred Buller's airframe design had the lowest structural gross weight of any aircraft in this class up to that time. The large fuselage was smoothly streamlined and could almost be described as a wide-bodied bushplane. A double slotted flap was introduced as an improvement over the Beaver system; and then there was the geared engine. The complicated gearing added to the overall weight but allowed the "H" Wasp to swing a larger propeller at lower rpm. It resulted in a slower air speed at altitude but gave the desired extremely short takeoff run. The rather novel ejector cooling cowls were employed to squeeze maximum efficiency from the engine along with a portion of augmented thrust. The gross weight of the Otter that Neal flew on December 12, 1951, was 7200 pounds, which grew with later models to 8000 pounds.

The most obvious difference between the prototype Otter and the production models was a larger dorsal fin area. The added torque of the large propeller on the geared engine could destabilize the aircraft in extreme yawing manoeuvres. To overcome such a tendency, an increased fin area was added which remained standard on all production models.

Certification came on November 5, 1952, with the delivery of the first production aircraft to Hudson Bay Mining & Smelting the following day. Imperial Oil was the next customer to receive an Otter, only days ahead of the Ontario Department of Lands and Forests. The Royal Canadian Air Force received its first machine on February 14, 1953, the first of an eventual 63. Maxwell Ward ordered and paid for Otter number 5 but had to await finalization of his charter before he could put the airplane to work.

By 1951 de Havilland Canada's postwar stability was firmly established. The Beaver successes with the US Army and Air Force were being widely acclaimed and it was a rewarding period for all personnel as they moved to the testing of their new Otter. It was also cause for great satisfaction on the part of vice president and managing director Philip C. Garratt when the announcement was made in Ottawa by the Honourable Brooke Claxton, Minister of National Defence, on May 21, 1952, that he had been awarded the Trans Canada (McKee) Trophy. The trophy was first presented in 1927 to the "person rendering the most meritorious service during the year in the advancement of aviation in Canada" and had been donated by the late Captain James Dalzell McKee to commemorate his first seaplane flight across Canada. Garratt's citation read: "In recognition of his outstanding contribution to the advancement of Canadian aviation in 1951." A presentation was made by chief of the air staff, Air Marshal W.A. Curtis, at a meeting in the Seignory Club, Montebello, Quebec, in November 1952.

A study of the Otter tail section (left photo) as it was first flown and (right) with the larger dorsal fin that characterized the production version. (DHC via R.J. Fox)

The Comet in Canada

One spring day in 1952 Punch Dickins was in Ottawa, making the rounds, and dropped in on his friend of bush flying days, "Lewie" Leigh. Group Captain Z. Lewis Leigh was Director of Air Operations RCAF and, like Dickins, a winner of the prestigious Trans Canada (McKee) Trophy. Punch had come to talk about de Havilland's D.H.106 Comet jetliner and the two were soon discussing the

The first D.H.106 Comet to join the RCAF 412 Transport Squadron in 1953. The RCAF thus became the first air force to operate jets in their transport service. (DHC3859)

possible role of jet transport within the RCAF. They got together with other senior officers and it became quite obvious that the RCAF took a very positive view on the future of jets.

The meetings prompted a further study of the subject and that summer Dickins and Leigh proceeded to Hatfield for a closer investigation. The RCAF interest was confirmed with the purchase of two Comet 1As, which made them the first air force in the world to operate jet transports. The honour of being the first air force crew fell to F/L C. Brown, F/L M.D. Broadfoot, S/L J.D. Dixon (Captain), F/L K.A. Wark and W/O C.W. Baine. They were trained in England by BOAC and took delivery of RCAF number 5301 on March 18, 1953. Number 5302 was accepted on April 13.

The RCAF Transport Command was the envy of their United States

counterpart and the Comets were welcomed regularly in New York and Washington. They ran into opposition at first from both airport authorities because of the jet noise factor but soon the opposition dwindled until their visits became routine. They crisscrossed Canada working closely with the DOT on the subject of jets and piston transports in the air traffic system. When all Comets were temporarily grounded in 1954 due to pressurization problems, the hours on the RCAF machines were below the critical point. Many modifications were carried out at Downsview, however, while the problem was being investigated. Both aircraft were converted to the IXB model in 1957 and served well until their retirement in 1965. During the Comet years in Canada Harry Hunter of the DHC service department acted as technical representative and RCAF liaison officer.

Otter number 411. CF-ODV was delivered to the Ontario Provincial Air Service on April 20, 1961 and has served steadily with its original owner since that time. It performs the host of tasks required by the OPAS, from fire fighting to game counts, fish stocking, photography, hydrological surveys or whatever the Ministry of Natural Resources may require. It's seen here on a trip over the Kenora region. (Robert S. Grant)

A New Beaver

During the certification stages of the Otter in 1952, discussions started on the advisability of a British version of the Beaver for European and "soft currency" countries. The British Army had expressed interest and there was talk of putting it into production in England. The English-built Alvis Leonides engine was available with 100 horsepower more than the P&W Wasp Junior; it had accumulated a good record of reliability installed in the British Provost and Prince. The physical dimensions were compatible with the Beaver and all performance estimates showed a Leonides-powered Beaver to be an attractive proposition as well as an engineering challenge.

These estimates suggested a shorter takeoff distance could be achieved, which prompted a further study to shorten the landing run. While awaiting a sample Leonides engine and three-blade, nine-foot-diameter pro-

The test flight of the Alvis Leonides engined Beaver with the large fin. (DHC and K.M. Molson)

The Leonides Beaver in England, demonstrating a spectacular takeoff. (DHC7227)

peller from England, a larger fin and rudder unit was flight-tested on a Beaver with the regular Pratt & Whitney engine. The new engine installations provided the usual problems of adapting British standard threads to American, but all these problems were overcome and George Neal took it up for its first flight on March 10, 1953.

The weight penalty worked out to 96 pounds in exchange for the added

100 horsepower, with the gross weight remaining at 5100 pounds. To shorten the landing run two simple steps were taken. The incidence was increased two degrees and Goodyear disc brakes were installed. Tests proved an increased top speed and rate of climb, and during the cooling tests the enlarged vertical tail surfaces were found more than adequate to offset destabilization. As the battle was now

A British Army Beaver doing landing trials on a carrier deck. (DHC14379)

between increased performance and weight, a second smaller rudder was built and the previous dorsal strake removed.

A Canadian certificate of airworthiness was obtained and the aircraft was shipped to England for evaluation. The high-performance Beaver aroused enthusiastic comments in England but the cold economic facts did not justify the expense of any change in the aircraft. The Hatfield demonstrator, G-ANAR, had an interesting life in England and returned to Canada

many years later as the personal plane of Charles Robson of Oshawa, Ontario, now registered CF-CNR. The British Army, who were thoroughly involved in the evaluation of the Leonides Beaver, eventually bought 46 of the standard L-20 models between 1960 and 1967.

A New Building

With Beaver sales booming, the Otter coming along and overhaul work taking up a good proportion of the hangars, lack of space was becoming a problem. By coincidence an opportunity to solve the space problem presented itself. The Crown still owned most of the buildings on the Downsview site and wished to acquire the entire north complex for a new RCAF base. The government offer was $5.5 million and a 96-acre parcel of land on the southwest corner of the airport on a 99-year lease, in exchange for the existing de Havilland buildings. Phil Garratt considered the offer satisfactory and ordered plans to begin immediately for a new factory and offices.

Another Canadian military veteran, Otter number 7 with RCAF tail number 3661. It carries skis and has a non-standard black cowling. It's seen at Trenton, Ontario, on December 27, 1960. It was sold in April 1963 to the Indian Air Force as BM-1004 and remains in service there. (Nick MacDonald-Wolochatiuk).

The original Downsview plant and wartime additions shown after the Canadian government turned it into an RCAF military base. To the right are the original DH buildings, many times extended. The large wartime complex where Mosquitos were produced can be related to the diagram on page 82. (DHC11016)

George Burlison was given overall responsibility for the new building and, after a quick look around similar factories in the United States, could see that his budget would be tight. He evolved a novel system of using squared plastic to compare existing space with that needed in the new plant. With the help of Reg Corlett he went back and forth to the managers, having them plan their own areas. There was a bit of cutting and trimming when the proposal went to management but after considerable re-arrangement of the squares the project was turned over to architects Sheppard and Powell, who took it from there.

The next few months were busy ones for Bill Burlison, who reflected in later years that they were the most rewarding in his career: "We had our problems, of course, but made many moves that proved successful over the years. We were able to install overhead mobile cranes, which we never had be-

fore, use automatic doors, and even put a door on both ends of Bay four. I received a lot of opposition to this idea but it proved very flexible as we moved to bigger aircraft. One thing that worked well was the small supply train that moved parts through the aisles to the various work areas. It is still going years later and was particularly useful in transferring Ab Warren's stores department to the south plant—from the spares bins in the old plant to their new location in only one move! We transferred one department at a time, usually overnight, and every bench, cupboard and tool box would be sitting in its new spot ready for the shift next morning. It got a bit rough in the cold weather but everyone cooperated and we only slipped production of one aircraft during the whole transition. We knew the building was too small when it was built and that additions would soon be needed, but we got maximum value for our dollar, with $6 per foot for the ground floor and $12 per foot for the upper storeys."

By the end of January 1954 most of the structure for the new building was up and the move from the north plant was in the planning stage. The flight test hangar was first, then the cafeteria,

followed by the shops and offices. DH England's Francis St. Barbe had taken great interest in the proceedings and was over at the end of February to have a look around. The cafeteria was operational and it seemed a good idea to have the first party in the new building in honour of their visitor.

The date was set for February 25. That morning Garratt and St. Barbe went over to Orenda Engines to have lunch with their old friend Frank Trethewey, who was vice president of Orenda, a part of Avro Canada. There had always been a close tie between the men since the days when Trethewey had been chairman of the DH Canada board but their paths had gone different ways during the war years. The family mining business of Brett-Trethewey Mines was closed in 1940 and Frank, who had once been flight commander of 110 City of Toronto Squadron, joined the RCAF as C/O of No.6 and No.9 Repair Depots. The arrangement worked to the advantage of de Havilland for it allowed Len Appleyard to move from the mining business and become a valued assistant to George Mickleborough for the next 30 years.

On the day of the luncheon, Trethewey welcomed his guests at Orenda and ushered them to the security desk for visitors' badges. A few jokes were made about the security risks involved but nothing more was said when they turned in their badges to leave. The whole event stirred Phil Garratt's imagination and he arranged a security pass for Trethewey, who was due to attend the de Havilland party that night.

Frank Trethewey arrived at the de Havilland entrance at the appointed hour. He was welcomed by the security chief, Sgt. Ritchie, and asked to sign in. When this was completed he was issued with the pass that Garratt had organized for him. It was large, weighed ten pounds and had a rope to put around his neck. It came complete with bells and tassels and a suitable inscription. It is not known how long he wore it at the party, which turned out to be a gala affair.

The $8,000,000 plant covering 10½ acres was connected to Wilson Avenue

during the summer of 1954 by the newly named Garratt Boulevard, as plans went forward for a formal opening. Sir Geoffrey and Lady de Havilland came over from England for the event, their only visit to Canada. The ceremony took place on September 29 before a distinguished gathering of about 800 leading industrialists and political and military leaders from Canada, the United States, the United Kingdom and South America.

After a detailed tour of the new plant and a flying display, the guests gathered in the flight test hangar for the official ceremonies. It was a proud day for vice president and general manager Phil Garratt, who introduced the guests on the speakers' platform that afternoon. From the de Havilland Aircraft Co., Ltd., England, came Sir Geoffrey de Havilland, president of DH Canada, and Francis T. Hearle, the recently retired chairman at Hatfield. Another well known member of the de Havilland enterprise was Major

Frank I. Trethewey, who owned the first DHC flying field, is presented with a special visitor's pass on arrival at Francis St. Barbe's party. (DHC V-95)

Francis E.N. St. Barbe of the parent de Havilland company. His interest in the Chipmunk had much to do with launching the company's line of successful designs. (DHC)

An impressive gathering on the front steps of the new administration building at the time of the formal opening. Left to right: Phil Garratt, managing director DHC; George J. Mickleborough, secretary treasurer; Francis T. Hearle, recently retired as chairman of DH England; Lady de Havilland; Sir Geoffrey de Havilland; W. Doug Hunter, director of engineering; Punch Dickins, director of sales; and Russ Bannock, director of military sales. (DHC839)

F.B. Halford, chairman and technical director of the de Havilland Engine Co., Ltd. Representing the Canadian government were the Hon. C.D. Howe, Minister of Defence Production, and the Hon. George Marler, Minister of Transport. On the military side were Lieutenant General G.G. Simmonds, Chief of the General Staff, Canadian Army; Air Marshal C.R. Slemon, Chief of the Air Staff, RCAF; Major General F.R. Dent Jr. of the USAF Air Materiel Command; and Vice Admiral E.R. Mainguy, Chief of the Naval Staff, RCN.

In his opening address Phil Garratt paid tribute to C.D. Howe for the untiring interest and assistance he had always given the aircraft industry. Howe, in performing the official opening ceremonies, recalled his association with "the oldest aircraft company in this country" from the time

Three of the US Navy's original Otters during a predelivery photo session. These later served with VX-6 Squadron in, among other places, the Antarctic. (DHC)

Like all postwar DHC types, the Tracker has shown real staying power and will remain in CAF service into the nineties. This one was photographed August 31, 1972. (Larry Milberry)

of the first building erected at Mount Dennis. He spoke also of the "great initiative and resourcefulness of the company management," adding that he was speaking from personal experience. He stressed the part that the company had played and continued to play in the "Canadian Century."

Sir Geoffrey de Havilland, in one of his rare public appearances, paid tribute to the progress of the Canadian company and concluded, "One gains a sense of the great future that lies before Canada, and of the stability of the country in its handling of great national resources and responsibilities."

A historic photo of three dynamic personalities: C.D. Howe, in a characteristic pose, stands between Sir Geoffrey de Havilland and P.C. Garratt in front of the company Heron during the opening of the new Downsview plant. (DHC)

A DHC-built CS2F-2 Tracker unfolds its wings as it taxis out at Oshawa, June 15, 1962. HVAR rockets are under wing. (Larry Milberry)

The Grumman Tracker

The extensive overhaul work that played such a role in DH Canada's postwar recovery required a versatile management to accommodate such a variety of projects. As contracts manager, George Neely was constantly dealing with new customers, both civil and military. The need for modifications on customer conversions moved Len Trotter from the Chipmunk design team in 1945 and for the next five years he specialized in the field of contract engineering.

Early in 1954 the Royal Canadian Navy indicated that they were prepared to order a quantity of new Grumman S2F anti-submarine aircraft to replace their aging Avengers. There was talk of a quantity order along with the fact that they might be built in Canada. Neely and Trotter discussed the possibility of de Havilland involvement but were rather sceptical in

view of Phil Garratt's reluctance to become involved in building other companies' airplanes. Meetings between the Canadian Department of Defence Production and the Aircraft Manufacturers' Association went ahead quietly during the summer of 1954 on a national manufacturing plan. Neely had been representing de Havilland's interests in the negotiations and when the news broke it was sudden and complete. Instead of being an "also ran," DH Canada was to be the prime contractor for the new "search and strike weapon," which would be assembled and test-flown at Downsview.

Len Trotter was sent immediately to Bethpage, Long Island, to act as DHC representative in the contract negotiations. Shortly after the new Downsview plant opened, the entire plan was publicized. It was to involve a wide sector of Canadian manufacturing. The wings would be built by Canadian Car and Foundry Limited of Fort William, the rear fuselage section by Canadair Limited, Montreal, and the tail section by Enamel & Heating Products Limited, Amherst, N.S. The engine nacelles were to be produced in the west by MacDonald Brothers Aircraft Limited, Winnipeg. The undercarriage shock struts were to be made under licence by Jarry Hydraulics of Montreal, the nose undercarriage and tail bumper by Dowty Equipment of Ajax, and the bomb-bay doors, hatches and covers by Fleet Manufacturing of Fort Erie. As prime contractor, de Havilland Canada would build the forward

Representing thousands of Canadians who helped produce the Tracker are some of the men who supervised its assembly. Left to right: Bill Bozanin, Bill Stewardson, Art Bradley and Charlie Cobb. (DHC5170)

A former RCN Tracker converted to a fire bomber, dropping a load of water at Downsview during certification tests. (DHC)

fuselage section and the pilot's compartment, assemble the aircraft, look after the installation of the electronic gear and test the aircraft for RCN acceptance.

The $100 million defence contract was the biggest since World War 2 and even the engines were to be manufactured in Canada. At one stage converting the aircraft from Wright to Pratt & Whitney engines was considered in order to provide work at the Longueuil plant. The Department of Defence Production instead negotiated with the Curtiss-Wright Corporation for the building of 400 Wright Cyclones under licence by Canadian Pratt & Whitney. The Canadian Navy bought one US-built S2F-1 as the test model. Those made in Canada were to be called the CS2F-1 and given the name "Tracker." The all-weather, twin-engined, high-winged, anti-submarine aircraft was to employ the most sophisticated electronic gear in

the hunter/killer role and be capable of carrying a wide variety of weapons.

Everyone at de Havilland, including Phil Garratt, became enthusiastic at the prospect of a new production line. His comment was quoted in the February 1955 issue of *Canadian Aviation:* "It is not only good business, but as the largest and most complicated aircraft DHC has yet undertaken, it is a most interesting project. Our whole organization feels quite keenly about the CS2F-1 and looks forward to the first model off the line."

Representing the company on the business side in all contacts with Grumman, the Canadian Navy and Government was George Neely. Bill Burlison was to manage production and Len Trotter was to be project engineering coordinator. Promotions and new employment followed hand-in-hand as everyone tackled the new challenge. The first strike in the company's history put a dent in the schedule but in May 1956 the first Tracker was tested. George Neal and Tony Verrico took it into the air on the 31st. RCN number 1502 was delivered in a ceremony on October 12.

The basic aircraft from the point of view of structure and flying qualities resembled the US-built Grumman model. The electronic gear, including the tail boom and special radar, was of Canadian design and manufacture. Production went well in the new plant and deliveries continued at a regular rate. From serial number 43 on, a number of RCN modifications were incorporated. Later 17 of these aircraft were passed on to No.1 Squadron of the Royal Dutch Navy.

Although records show 100 Tracker aircraft delivered from the de Havilland production line, only 99 were fully manufactured in Canada (S/N 1502-1600). The extra aircraft was a Grumman-built machine used in the development program and rebuilt later as RCN number 1501.

A few Grumman Trackers still patrol coastal waters for the Canadian Forces. From all accounts these sturdy aircraft have served the navy well and even when some were declared surplus, they found a new role as forest fire bombers. The Ontario government, in conjunction with Field Aviation Limited, worked to incorporate a chemical retardant tank and release system. The test model returned to de Havilland in 1976 to be flight certified in its new category.

(Facing page) One of Bob Bradford's fine Otter renditions, done in the 1950s while he worked in DHC's art department. (DHC)

Years later, when Bill Burlison was asked to summarize the project, he admitted that it was a large program for such a small number of aircraft with the US manufacturer so close to the border. "It was a good project," he added, "for the Canadian aircraft manufacturers and a good deal for de Havilland. We worked well with Grumman and were exposed to a company with a higher technology. We learned more about big jigs and production methods during this period than ever before. We were able to upgrade things on the Beaver and Otter lines a dozen different ways because of our association with Grumman."

Another Success Story

Throughout 1953 and 1954, 50 Otters were delivered to a variety of customers, both civil and military. Max Ward set something of a precedent by bringing a bushplane the size of the Otter to Yellowknife. His opposition were equipped with prewar types of varying shapes and sizes and were quick to pass judgement on the expensive new Otter. They were outspoken that it would never pay its way, but Ward had other ideas and

Two RCMP officers accept the log books for their first Otter from Buck Buchanan while Geoff Priestley looks on. (DHC9269)

with the Otter line and de Havilland Canada. It was not long until Widerøe's neighbours, the Royal Norwegian Air Force, were also buying Otters for exacting search and rescue duties out of Bodø.

Other customers in 1954 included Imperial Oil, the RCMP and Laurentian Air Services. By the time 1955 rolled around the RCAF had 34 Otters on their inventory.

Otter vs Helicopter

By any standard, the Otter had made a commendable start but the big Beaver customer, the US Army, had not shown more than average interest. Russ Bannock kept the subject alive on his frequent visits to Washington, where he checked in regularly with the director of Army aviation. The Army liked the Otter but recollections of the controversy surrounding the Beaver order were still fresh in everyone's mind. Any purchase would involve a competition and there were no competitions coming up for medium-sized aircraft in the fixed wing category. As the two men talked it occurred to the director that there was to be an exercise "Skydrop II" between two types

An RCAF Otter of 115ATU on UN duty in the Middle East makes a low pass over a Mediterranean beach. (DND PL107581)

of helicopter in late summer of 1954. "Perhaps," he said, "if de Havilland would make an Otter available for Operation Skydrop II, it could be slipped into the contest and provide an interesting comparison from everyone's point of view."

Needless to say an Otter was made available with a demonstraton team composed of Bannock as director of military sales, pilot Doug Givens and maintenance engineer Bob Irving. It was a gruelling month's work, taking part in every conceivable form of military support aviation. The Otter proved immediately that it could operate in confined spaces hitherto restricted to helicopters. As the weeks went by, observers could see that the Otter was carrying bigger loads from nearly all the same areas and doing it with relative ease. The helicopters were plagued with mechanical delays but the Otter went through the entire month with nothing more than daily maintenance.

The Army's aviation group was bubbling with enthusiasm at the Otter's performance under such unusual competitive circumstances but they were not the only ones watching. By coincidence the Army Corps of Engineers were also in search of a special aircraft for a project of their own. They were confronted with an extensive mapping assignment north of the

Brooks Range in Alaska and it became obvious from the display that the Otter had put an end to their search. The two Army interests combined to spark a quick purchase of six Otters in a case of history repeating itself.

These were to be off-the-shelf civil machines for a series of evaluations, particularly in the Alaska survey. The first was turned over to the US Army in a brief ceremony on January 25, 1955, followed quickly by the other five.

The US Navy did not wait long to put in their order, for they too had been impressed by the battle with the helicopters at Fort Bragg. They needed the Otter for the Antarctic, where the US was taking part in a multinational exploration program. The US flag was being carried by the Navy, which started with four Otters and increased the number to 11 as the program grew. By the time the first Antarctic Otters were delivered in early 1956, they had thoroughly proven themselves on both sides of the Arctic Circle.

Wardair now had three machines in Yellowknife and Canadian Pacific Airlines were operating three in remote areas in northern B.C. Charter companies and private corporations used Otters extensively throughout the Northwest Territories in the search for

natural resources, while countless others wearing RCAF colours spent most of the year on skis. Elsewhere on the Arctic Circle the Norwegians were building up a reputation of their own with the Otters of Widerøe's in regular scheduled service and the RNoAF in patrol and rescue work.

The First Strike

It was not until 1941, with the Anson program under way, that talk of a shop union became an issue. The first inroads were made when the employees were handed union leaflets at the corner of Sheppard and Dufferin as they left for home in the evening. There was still much of the family spirit throughout the plant and it was unanimously decided that an employee relations committee be formed under Edgar Featherstonhaugh that would meet regularly on shop problems. It functioned successfully for some time but changed during the Mosquito days to an employee-run UAW-CIO local.

As the staff grew again following the war, the same union continued to represent the workers, and by all accounts the relationship went very well into the fifties. But pressures built by 1955 to the stage where negotiations between the company and the union became difficult. The meetings that year stalled on one major issue: the union insisted on seeing the company books. Phil Garratt was remaining clear of all involvement, but his long years of struggle to provide employment left him a little biased on the management side of the argument. Finally negotiations reached the point where George Bird, head of the UAW in the US, came up for a major meeting with local union officials and company representatives. Garratt had stayed out of all talks up to then but agreed to attend one meeting. The preliminaries were dispensed with by about mid-morning and all made their way to the table as befitted a meeting of such importance. The proceedings were opened by Bird with a formality that indicated years of practice.

At the first indication of a discussion, Phil Garratt was up on his feet. "Just a minute," he said, "before we waste a lot of time, let's get a couple of things straight. We know nothing about strikes, you do. We don't want a strike, you do. We don't know how a strike will hurt us, so that is up to you. If the question to be decided

here is whether you can see the company's books, the answer is NO! I don't know what you are going to do, but I think I'll go have a drink." And he walked out.

Needless to say everyone was dumfounded; glances went from one to another. Doug Hunter became red in the face; silence was complete for the better part of a minute. The meeting continued and a strike decision was called. It was the end of June and the first strike in the company history. When told of the decision, Garratt's comment was, "They'll be back by September—it gets pretty cold then." It was Armistice Day, November 11, before the strikers returned—a day that Garratt felt was significant—and it was getting cold.

It turned out to be an awkward strike because it was the first for both parties. The union tried to keep everyone from entering the plant but an arrangement was later made to allow entrance to supervisory personnel. In order to avoid trouble, the engineering department moved quickly to an office in the Eglinton-Bathurst area. For many years de Havilland had retained legal title to the dormant Central Aircraft Limited which had been used during the war as part of the Mosquito program. The engineering staff simply reported for work each day at the new address as members of Central Aircraft. The strike left a lot of non-union people immobile but a bad forest fire season in northern Ontario made work for the pilot staff. Those who could be spared were asked to assist the Ontario Department of Lands and Forests in aerial firefighting. Dave Fairbanks recorded 73 hours of such work, flying a Beaver and Norseman in what he later described as some of the toughest flying in his career.

The Trans Antarctic Otter

The de Havilland Otter arrived on the aviation scene while there was still a lot of old-fashioned glamour connected with flying, particularly in the field of exploration. The histories of exploration aircraft make interesting reading and none more typical than the story of serial number 126.

In July of 1956 an RAF crew arrived in Downsview to pick up this special orange-coloured Otter and ferry it to England. The aircraft had been purchased by the British Commonwealth Trans Antarctic Expedition as part of

the upcoming International Geophysical year. Forty nations were to combine their efforts during 1957-8 for a scientific exploration of the south polar continent.

The expedition was the brainchild of Sir Vivian Fuchs, who dreamed up the idea in 1954 while waiting out a blizzard in Graham Land, Antarctica. Its purpose was to mount a combined Commonwealth effort to complete the first surface crossing of the Antarctic continent from Shackleton Base on the Weddell Sea to McMurdo Sound on the Ross Sea. It was to be supported by Great Britain, New Zealand, Australia and South Africa and financed by a mixture of government and private donations. The New Zealand portion would be headed by the famous conqueror of Mount Everest, Sir Edmund Hillary, using a Royal New Zealand Air Force DH Beaver.

The RAF agreed to supply a crew of four plus two supporting Auster single-engined planes and miscellaneous radio equipment. The Otter was to be the only one operated by the RAF and they used it for the next two years with outstanding success. It was fitted at Downsview with a 177-gallon internal tank, giving it twice the normal flight endurance, and prepared for the Atlantic flight. S/L John Lewis was commander with F/L Gordon Heaslip, Flt. Sgt. P. Weston and Sgt. E. Williams. Navigator S/L Robert Seymour was along to work out the details of their Atlantic crossing.

Their route from Downsview was Goose Bay, Labrador; BW-1 of Narssarssuaq, Greenland; Keflavik, Iceland; Prestwick, Scotland; ending up at de Havilland headquarters, Hatfield. Here the Otter was completely winterized to expedition specifications with a heavy-duty battery, a radio altimeter, a SARAH (Search And Rescue Aircraft Homing) beacon and receiver, a radio compass and a Bendix Polar Path Gyro. Otter 126 now took on the identification XL 710, was crated and was put aboard the ship *Magga Dan*, which set sail from London on November 15, 1956.

By now 40 nations were preparing for the International Geophysical Year which was to start July 1, 1957, and end in December 1958. The exercise was to provide a harsh proving ground for some 22 other Beavers and Otters. The US Navy was handling much of the United States' commitment and had been taking part in Operation

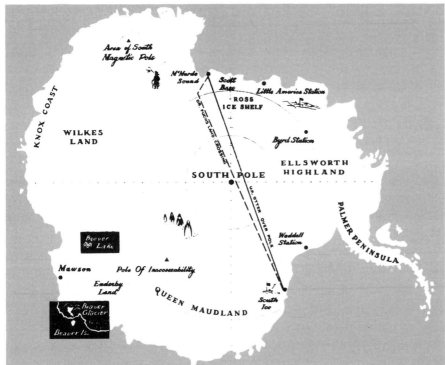

The British Commonwealth Trans Antarctic Expedition Otter seen in Antarctica alongside a Beaver. XL710 eventually worked its way back to Canada in 1963 as CF-PNV. (via DHC)

The map shows air operations involving Otter XL710.

(Bottom left) One of the Australian Antarctic Beavers is poled to shore during this quaint barge operation. (via DHC)

A New Zealand Beaver carries a sled under wing during Antarctic operations. (via DHC)

Deep Freeze since February 1, 1955, making preparations. They started with four Otters and added nine the following year. Australia, New Zealand, Chile and Japan all had Beavers and, by early January 1957, the British Commonwealth Otter arrived at Shackleton Base on the Weddell Sea with Sir Vivian Fuchs and his party. The same RAF crew under S/L John Lewis continued with the aircraft, this time without the services of navigator Seymour. On the other side of the continent Sir Edmund Hillary was setting up his headquarters at Scott Base on McMurdo Sound.

The plan for the expedition was to establish a sub-base between Weddell and the South Pole and move from there to the actual polar crossing. Sir Edmund, in the meantime, would have arranged the necessary depots from the Pole to Scott Base and would assist during the balance of the mission. Otter XL 710 surveyed the preliminary route during 19 flights, each averaging 6½ hours. It set up a depot 300 miles closer to the Pole, later called South Ice Base, and stocked it ready for the next summer's drive.

During the Antarctic winter of 1957 the Otter was stored and covered in a pit, but with the approach of summer in September it was made ready for the support of Fuchs' land mission. When the party moved out, Shackleton Base was closed down and operations centred for the next few weeks on South Ice Base. Once again when the land party left for their push to the South Pole, S/L Lewis and his crew supported them until it was time to join Sir Edmund Hillary on the other side of the continent. This flight required a little waiting for weather, but they got away on January 6, 1958. Their effort was historic as it was the first attempt at a non-stop crossing of Antarctica in a single-engined aircraft.

They passed over the overland party after 2 hours in the air and reached the South Pole station 2 hours and 40 minutes later. Exactly 11 hours and 1 minute after takeoff, XL 710 touched down at Scott Base, a flight of 1430 statute miles. The Otter continued to work with the New Zealand Beaver throughout the rest of the party's overland mission until the expedition was triumphantly welcomed at Scott Base headquarters.

The end of the expedition did not complete the history of Otter 126; it

simply changed allegiance, joined the US Navy and took on the number 147574. In its original orange colour '574 served from July 1958 to April 1960, flying 148 hours for VX-6 Squadron in the Antarctic. Once again a change of nationality occurred, when New Zealand needed an aircraft to replace one of its Beavers. A USAF C-124 Globemaster flew the Otter to Wellington for a complete overhaul by the staff at de Havilland Aircraft Company of New Zealand.

When 126 emerged from the shops, the airframe only had 408 hours. It flew in RNZAF colours for the first time in November 1961, all ready to return to Antarctic duty, but before the new identification, NZ 6081, could be installed, politics and a change of policy by the New Zealand Department of Defence brought another stage in its career. The closing of their Antarctic flight detachment rendered the Otter surplus and it was put up for sale by tender under New Zealand registration CK-CFH.

Georgian Bay Airways of Parry Sound, Ontario, tendered a bid, bought it sight unseen and had it shipped to Montreal. The registration changed to CF-PNV on March 12, 1964, in time to do a summer's work along the Hudson and James Bay coasts, working out of Moosonee. Most of its life in Ontario was spent on amphibious floats or wheel-skis, fulfilling a number of contracts from the resort areas of Muskoka to Frobisher Bay in the Arctic.

In December 1969 'PNV moved west to La Ronge, Saskatchewan, where it ranged far and wide for the next six years. It was while with La Ronge Aviation Services that it suffered its only major damage. On May 14, 1976, while taking off from the strip at Lynn Lake, it stalled after takeoff due to improper loading and fell back onto the runway. There were only minor injuries to the nine people on board but the aircraft was withdrawn from service and its registration cancelled.

Old 126 had now served 20 years and looked as if it was destined for retirement as a crippled derelict in the back of a hangar. A new career loomed when title of the aircraft was transferred to Cox Air Resources Limited of Edmonton. At latest report it is being restored as the second Cox Turbo Otter and, if this comes to pass, it will be interesting to watch the

next stage of this aircraft's colourful history.

Team Work
Those who knew Phil Garratt well always marvelled at his tact and diplomacy when dealing with the people in the plant, particularly when there was something difficult or out of the ordinary to be done. He would usually prefix his request with "When you have time . . ." or "Wouldn't it be nice . . ." but when the "chips were down" and the company's reputation was at stake, a sort of mutual understanding took over. One old-timer in the shop summed it up in a few words: "We got to know Phil Garratt because he would come down on the floor and talk to us." The Plexiglas car top for the royal tour in 1951 was a case in point, but there were others.

One such occasion was the visit of the DH Comet 3 to Downsview in 1955. The pressurization problems of the earlier Comet 1s had been rectified after an exhaustive program and the parent de Havilland was sending their new model on a flight around the world to re-establish the airliner's prestige. The Canadian portion of the trip was to involve Vancouver, Toronto and Montreal before the final dash home to England. The flight in Comet G-ANLO had gone amazingly well with John Cunningham, de Havilland's chief test pilot, in charge and Peter Bugge as second pilot. R.W. Chandler was radio navigator. A number of the world's top airline captains rode on various legs of the flight, along with DH sales personnel and seven aviation specialists in everything from aerodynamics to engines.

The landing at Downsview December 18 was in the nature of a courtesy stop, giving recognition to the Canadian branch of the family. A good crowd was on hand to meet the sleek jet as it arrived from Vancouver and the crew, who only two days before had been basking in the sunshine of Hawaii, were treated to a cold Ontario Sunday. Full opportunity was given the Toronto and Montreal airline executives to inspect the new Comet during the next two days before its flight to London on the 22nd. Shortly after takeoff from Dorval that night, the Comet 3 experienced its only mechanical problem of the tour. The jet pipe of number 3 engine became detached and the subsequent blast blew the large engine cowling doors

open. After dumping fuel Cunningham landed the Comet back at Montreal. Here the decision was made to remove the damaged doors and make a three-engine ferry to Downsview for repairs.

"Looking back to that December," recalled John Cunningham after his retirement in 1980, "I well remember the remarkable effort made by the Downsview staff, over Christmas, in repairing the damage done to our Comet. The weather was bad on the 23rd but I eventually arrived on three engines at Malton Airport because Downsview was below operational limits. I was driven to the de Havilland plant and met by Phil Garratt and Russ Bannock, shortly after dark. Phil was pouring me a welcoming drink but, before I was able to accept, I looked out of the window and realized that the visibility had improved somewhat and I could see lights on the other side of Downsview. We checked with the Met. office at Malton who said there would be a temporary lifting of the cloud and an improvement in visibility. We dashed back to Malton, got 'NLO fired up on three engines and took off. I remember flying down the expressway at about 300 feet until we came to the shopping centre, made a sharp left turn and saw the lights of Downsview. And so it was that our Comet arrived back at

The world-girdling Comet 3 arrives at Downsview for a brief stopover in December 1955. It was back later for repairs and stayed over Christmas. (DHC2380)

Captain John Cunningham waves a farewell thank you to de Havilland employees as he prepares to leave for Montreal and the final leg of his world flight. (DHC2381)

Downsview on the night of the 23rd, ready for repairs. I was finally able to accept Phil Garratt's offer of a drink.

"By a lot of hard work over Christmas, the DH Canada team cleaned up the engine bay, bolted the jet pipe back to the engine, repaired and refitted the engine bay doors so that on the 27th we left for Dorval. We took off on the night of the 27th and, after a 6 hour, 20 minute flight, arrived at London Airport. We flew to Hatfield later that morning and gave a press demonstration flight there the next day—a fine tribute to the splendid work put in by the DH Canada team. I have many happy memories of my visits to Downsview since 1946, but Christmas 1955, when Peter Bugge and I enjoyed the day with Phil and Jessie Garratt and family, will always remain in my memory."

Bill Bozanin was on the repair crew that Christmas and remembers it as a hectic but exhilarating experience. "We had a team organized as soon as we heard of the problem and went to work the moment the Comet was pushed into the hangar. From six to eight of us worked around the clock with about 12 hours non-stop and little time off to sleep. Bill Stewardson kept us supplied with coffee and snacks, but I recall we were all able to make it home for our Christmas dinner. There was a lot of damage to the rear of the nacelle but we got it all cleaned up on the 26th and then they were off for Montreal."

As a pleasant postscript to the whole affair, the world flight won John Cunningham the US Harmon International Trophy for 1955.

137

Tragedy and Hard Work

With the unfortunate strike behind them in 1956, everyone settled down for a busy productive year. The first Grumman Tracker was close to its test flight and the Beaver and Otter lines were moving favourably again; military deliveries were getting back into full swing. During mid-February this new surge of optimism was shattered by the crash of a US Army Otter and the loss of four lives—all within sight of Downsview.

It was the first fatal accident since the war at the DH Canada field involving an aircraft manufactured at the plant. When the control tower phoned in the first stunning news that an Otter had broken up in the air, a sombre group gathered in the general manager's office. It was Tuesday, February 14, and three of the dead were US Army pilots from Fort Riley, Kansas, who had arrived only the day before to start flight training. Bill Ferderber was the DH Canada pilot killed and the aircraft they were flying was number 92 with US Army markings 53252.

Ferderber had been given the training assignment and spent the morning with Major A.G. Aticisson and Captains J.P. Dowling and C.E. Durand, preparing them for their familiarization flight. They had been in the air for about an hour in the Downsview area at approximately 3000 feet when security guards saw a wing separate from the Otter and the remains spin down into a field. The fact that it came apart in the air was extremely serious, in view of the fine record and the 75,000 hours of flying time Otters had accumulated in service.

Forty members of the company engineering staff were soon joined by experts from the RCAF, DOT, National Research Council, USAF, US Army and US National Advisory Committee for Aeronautics. Fred Jones of the Royal Aircraft Establishment, Farnborough, England, was also there to help put everything in sequence, go over every square inch of wreckage and determine what failed first.

Some idea of the task they faced can be determined by the records of the photographic department alone. During the investigation some 2200 photographs were produced, 2100 feet of film and 5000 feet of oscillogram recording film. Photos were made of all the structural static tests and over 1500 feet of film were taken in the air to record flight manoeuvres during the aerodynamic trials. Even the services of aviation artist Bob Bradford were brought in to piece together, in graphic form, the logical sequence of events and present a step-by-step interpretation of the aircraft's fatal plunge.

The suspected cause was an inadvertent release of flaps, and a series of tests was conducted by pilots George Neal and Bob Fowler in a specially reinforced Otter in an attempt to duplicate the situation. Neal and Fowler, securely strapped into their specially instrumented Otter, arranged bunts on signal, which George could manage with relative ease. After a series of these he reasoned that, although recovery was within the capability of the pilot anticipating the manoeuvre, the abnormality of the original case, coupled with the surprise element, would render recovery out of the question. A contributing factor at the time of the accident would undoubtedly be the forward centre of gravity condition due to the fact that it was a training flight. It is not difficult to picture three keen students, one in the copilot's seat and two by the cockpit door, looking over his shoulder.

The investigation was going on almost around the clock when a second Otter accident was reported. This time the location was Goose Bay in Labrador but the circumstances were all too similar, a training flight, a sudden bunt and a breakup of the structure. Fred Buller and Dick Hiscocks went to the accident scene, armed with the investigation data up to that point, and gathered more convincing evidence.

With everyone giving the investigation the highest priority, the pattern of events slowly emerged. The primary cause was metal contamination holding a valve in the wing flap jack open. When the pilot selected the flaps up, there was no restriction in the hydraulic circuit and the flaps retracted immediately. With the extreme downwash suddenly removed from the tail, the nose pitched down with disastrous results. Combined with the element of surprise and the forward centre of gravity, this caused overstressing and an immediate breakup of the wing structure. In the Toronto accident, it was calculated that the wing passed under the fuselage and made sufficient contact with the fin area to completely remove the tail section.

After the long months of investigation, the details of the accident finally settled into place. The design group set to work to eliminate any such occurrence in the future. An interlocking mechanism coupled an elevator tab to the flaps, automatically compensating any abrupt changes of trim without pilot input. The same device was used later in the Twin Otter.

The Move to Missiles

Shortly after the Tracker program was announced, a new division at Downsview led de Havilland Canada into the sophisticated field of missiles. It all started because of the close ties with de Havilland Propellers Limited, who were leaders in British missile technology. The new Guided Missile Division at DH Canada was able to provide the Canadian government with technical units drawing on British missile experience and technical know-how. The classified nature of the work led, naturally, to little publicity and not much was known, even in Downsview, of what went on behind the doors marked "Secret." The new division played a major part in the Grumman Tracker program with the installation of the intricate avionic equipment.

The sphere of this new operation included control engineering, electro-mechanics, optics and infrared studies, as applied to guidance, auxiliary power, fusing, missile ancillaries and

Bob Bradford's view from space showing Canada's Alouette satellite with its STEM antennas, both of which were major de Havilland Canada projects. (DHC)

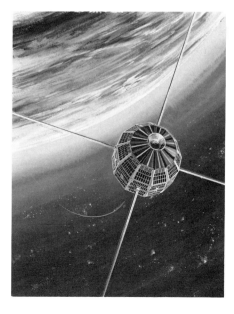

fire control. The new division took part in the Velvet Glove and Sparrow II missile programs. They also took part in US Navy missile developments, always classified "highly secret." Two specialist areas for the Canadians were missile auxiliary power units and infrared calculations. Specialty work was started on new type inverters and alternators. It was the only integrated infrared research and application capability in Canada. The department worked in conjunction with British de Havilland Propellers on the Firestreak air-to-air missile, used on the Sea Vixen.

In 1960 the name was changed to Special Products Division, embracing all the former activities and expanded to include the operations of the former Engine and Propeller Division carried on at the north plant.

The STEM
Throughout the late 50s, de Havilland was getting a reputation in the art of forming sophisticated metals into difficult shapes. Bob Prout was always taking on these new challenges but a call he received at a quarter to five one evening from Dr. Phil Lapp of the Special Products Division had him stumped—temporarily. When Prout checked with Dr. Lapp next morning, Lapp explained that de Havilland had acquired the rights to produce an idea that had been patented by George Klein of the National Research Council. He wanted a long metal strip that would coil in and out like a carpenter's rule and form a rigid pole. "Once I knew what he wanted," recalls Bob, "I figured we could do it and headed back to the shop. It took quite a while but finally we made it work and it became STEM (Storable Tubular Extendible Member)."

The success of STEM was immediate. The de Havilland self-erecting antennas went on to become an important element in every subsequent US/Canada space satellite program. In its final form, STEM consisted of a stowage drum, an unfurling element, a drive pinion and a guide roller. It was designed for either motorized extension and retraction or self extension in which the tightly wound metal tape used its inherent energy to propel itself and form a 360° tube as it extended. The STEM devices also served as land antennas, vehicular masts or even hand-held exploration communicators. They varied from 15 inches to 850 feet.

A companion project added to the Division's prestige when they built the hull for Canada's first satellite, Alouette I, also equipped with STEM antennas. A 75-foot STEM unit was produced for the Canadian Javelin rocket tests.

To ensure a Canadian "presence" during the installation of the Boeing Bomarc missiles in Canada a consortium company called DCF Systems Limited was formed. De Havilland's Special Products Division was the lead member with CAE (Montreal) and Ferranti Packard (Toronto) as the other participating companies; their initials formed the name for the new company.

The 30 to 40 Canadians from the consortium assisted Boeing in installing the Bomarcs in their shelters at North Bay, Ontario, and La Macaza, Quebec, in 1961 and 1962. The bases were turned over to the Royal Canadian Air Force upon their completion.

In 1962 the facilities of the Special Products Division were expanded by the acquisition of Canadian Applied Research, a company that had been formed in 1947 as part of the Avro-Malton complex. The combined organization, under the new name SPAR (Special Products and Applied Research) was headed by vice president Doug Annan. They took over 260,000 square feet of space in their new head-

Otter 3682 runs up while sitting atop its test stand at Downsview. This experiment enabled a study of STOL characteristics while the Otter remained on "terra firma." (DHC7472)

quarters at Malton and employed up to 600 people.

In a few years Larry D. Clarke had moved up from contract administrator to manager of SPAR Division. By then the division had built up considerable assets and equipment but throughout the troubled years of the Douglas contract (dealt with later) had always operated in the background. Clarke came up with an offer to purchase the division for $1,350,000, which was approved by Hawker Siddeley. From 1969 onward SPAR became a separate entity with Larry Clarke as its head. A number of de Havilland specialists accompanied him and together they moved to the forefront of the space industry. In a tough survival environment SPAR has continued to mix sound business with scientific ability. Their latest accomplishment is the world-recognized CANADARM, used successfully on the space shuttle.

Slower STOL
The DHC-3 Otter was well received in the industry from the day of its very first flight. Experienced operators, like Max Ward and Viggo Widerøe, sized it up immediately as the best aircraft yet developed for their needs. The US Army watched it compete with the helicopter and, along with the Navy, bought it in quantity. While the Otter's reputation grew, others were watching its progress on the scientific side—those who wished to probe more deeply into the new technology of STOL. The National Research Council and the Defence Research

major change at this time was the installation of a General Electric J85-GE-7 turbo jet in the rear of the fuselage with the jet efflux directed out each side through fully modulated diverters. An extra lever in the cockpit enabled the pilot to direct the jet thrust either forward or back. This configuration examined in-flight reverse effects in combination with slipstream deflection. Test pilot Bob Fowler did the flying during 1961 and 1962 and the results were very encouraging. A minimum speed as low as 48 mph was obtained.

About 200 hours of test flying had been completed when Pratt & Whitney announced their new PT6 turbine. Fowler's involvement in the test flying

Looking like a huge bat, STOL research Otter 3682 flies along the taxi way behind DHC's flight test hangar. (DHC11217)

Otter 3682 after conversion to twin PT6 engines, J-85 turbo jet, and unique undercarriage. (DHC19156)

Board in Ottawa had always worked closely with de Havilland on the aerodynamic aspects of short takeoff and landing. With the advent of the Otter they sought to explore the subject further, realizing that slow flight stability and control was one of the truly new developments in the design of aircraft since the end of World War 2.

Discussions on the subject between the Canadian Defence Research Board and DHC as early as 1956 resulted in a joint research program. It revolved around the existing Otter technology and went deeper into the areas of slow flight and steep approach. A report at the time spelled out their reasoning: "The purpose of the DRB/DHC program is to assess the aerodynamic performance, stability and control problems of STOL aircraft with the object of finding new refinements in the art." RCAF Otter 3682 was extensively modified for a program that was to have three stages. The beam-type landing gear, looking like small floats, was capable of absorbing steeper descent touch-down speeds. The tail section was placed high out of the propeller slipstream and involved butterfly-type elevators. In the initial stages, measurements were made of the aerodynamic characteristics of the Otter in its standard configuration. Next, a series of novel aerodynamic features was planned to study slip-

stream deflection and boundary layer control.

In the slow-flight experiments a large bat-wing flap was installed, then the whole aircraft was mounted on a stand and towed behind a truck at 35 mph to study the flight characteristics close to the ground. These experiments determined the type of gear and the size of the larger tail section still to be designed. When the aircraft was ready for flight trials, George Neal conducted a series of short flights close to the ground then, later, at altitude, gathering data. This series terminated in 1960.

The second stage used modified Otter wing flaps and had the undercarriage strengthened to twice the standard energy absorption. The

of the new engine began and it opened new avenues of thought at de Havilland. The engines were not available commercially but two test models were rented and installed in the experimental machine, allowing the existing data to be enlarged with the additional slipstream of two propellers, while still maintaining the J-85 engine. The program terminated in 1963, about the time talks started on the design of a twin-engined Otter. The twin-engine configuration was the most noticeable feature to emerge from the experi-

(Facing page) A forest fire rages as an Otter of the Ontario Department of Lands and Forests is readied for a fire fighting mission. CF-ODL has served with the Ontario government since May 1953, frequently in the role of water bomber. (DHC7770)

140

Beavers are crated for shipment around the world, including one for Pakistan. (DHC)

mental program, even though it was only a minor part. The greatest advantage was the data and experience gained during 300 hours of flying in the slow flight regime and its relation to the landing manoeuvre. Bob Fowler's contributions were in the interpretation of human reactions to steep descent and the coordination needed for landings in this configuration.

An improved version of the Caribou was planned at one stage, built around two J-85 jet engines with adjustable nozzles in the rear of the fuselage, as in the special Otter. It would have been an interesting version of an already impressive shortfield performer but the engineering manpower was diverted to the T-64 turbine engine experiment. Altogether the experimental Otter added considerably to the company's depth of STOL technology that will continue to be reflected in the product line.

The Export Business
As assemblers of British-made products from 1928 until the war in 1939, DHC's sales objectives lay naturally within Canadian borders. Even postwar sales were planned around the Canadian market until circumstances forced a broader look at the situation. The first indication that the rest of the world was interested came with the sale of 15 Fox Moths in 1947-1948 to

India, Southern Rhodesia and New Zealand. When the Chipmunk went into production 90 of the first production batch went for export, and the design was even exported to the UK so it could be built there for the "soft currency" countries.

A large department became necessary to pack and crate Beavers for overseas shipment around the world. The first 100 Beavers went mainly to the hungry Canadian market from 1948 to 1951, with only 18 to the United States and abroad. Of the second 100 delivered, 65 were exports. The same general pattern developed with the Otter, where exports jumped from 34 in the first 100 to 88 in the second. Beaver and Otter sales continued strongly into the 1950s and it was obvious that DH Canada was firmly in the export business.

Two new offices sprang up because of the US military commitment to the L-20 Beavers. Wing Commander Derry Wray managed the increasing business at Ottawa, while Col. Joe E. McDonald acted as US liaison in Washington. When Derry Wray died in 1951 Garratt approached Donald L. "Buck" Buchanan, who was secretary-manager of the Royal Canadian Flying Clubs Association, and invited him to become the Ottawa representative. Buchanan obtained his early education in Guelph and was in editing and publishing before the outbreak of war. He joined the RCAF in 1940, serving as a flight instructor first at Mount Hope, then at Oshawa,

Dunnville and Trenton, until 1943. A posting overseas to 419 Squadron put him into Lancaster heavy bombers and later he moved to 420 Squadron on Halifaxes in July 1944. He became a squadron leader, served as flight commander of "420" and won a DFC before his discharge from the service in July 1945. He took up publishing briefly again in Canada but returned to aviation in 1946 to manage the RCFCA.

Buchanan's chores with DHC in Ottawa were many and varied: from DOT liaison and chasing contracts through the government maze to entertaining guests and monitoring US military payments through the Canadian Commercial Corporation. The main sales responsibilities rested back at headquarters with Russ Bannock as director of military sales and Punch Dickins as director of civil sales. A.F. "Sandy" MacDonald acted as sales manager but most of the orders from outside the country came through the agents around the world shared with the parent company.

In April 1955 Sandy MacDonald took over the post of public relations and Buck Buchanan moved to Downsview from his job in Ottawa to become sales manager. This was the unprecedented growth period with over 800 Beavers and 75 Otters in operation around the world. When a major sale to Malaysia began to drag, Buchanan asked for the services of G.V. "Geoff" Priestley, who up to that point had been doing contract

Throughout the 1950s and 1960s Beavers and Otters found their way to dozens of countries. Seen here are some of these exports: Beaver 500 was VP-FAE, one of six of these for the Falkland Islands Government Air Service; P-03 of the Argentine Air Force; ZK-BFN (formerly CF-HGW) dropping fencing supplies in New Zealand; AP-AKQ sold to Pakistan in February 1958; and Otter number 168 seen at Cebu in the Philippines in April 1957. (DHC, Andras Keleman, via DHC, Peter Keating, David Luchabough)

Lots of work. This scene at de Havilland in 1954 shows plenty of activity. Beavers, Otters and Chipmunks are being finished. Down the line an RCAF North Star and Vampire are being overhauled. (DHC)

administration at a desk outside Punch Dickins' office.

The volume of paper work, which grew as the shipments of aircraft increased, and the wide geographical coverage held a message for Buchanan that he could not ignore. "The Canadian and US orders were easily managed from Toronto," said Buchanan, "but when the amount of paperwork on some of the foreign sales began to equal the weight of the airplane, we had to get a little more efficiency into our dealings with new customers. Under the arrangements existing at the time, the solicitation of new business in the foreign field was handled by DH area representatives, whose services and costs were shared with the parent company. The same applied to agents who held exclusive sales rights in their respective countries.

"The DH area representatives were experienced, able and energetic, but they had interests other than DH Canada to serve. We also enjoyed close ties with our agents but they, too, had other principals to serve. We were relatively 'new boys' in the game and often wondered if we were getting the dedication to the DH Canada

cause that we wanted. The development of international business clearly indicated that we get out and 'beat the bushes' on our own with representation directly from the Downsview headquarters.

"In 1960 a Beaver order for the Ghana Air Force was a typical case and proved to be a turning point in our sales approach. It started shortly after the world tour with an early morning telephone call I received from an old fishing friend, Air Commodore Fred Carpenter of the RCAF. Fred was at the United Nations in New York on business and indicated that there was the possibility of a sale to Ghana. I rushed to New York and that afternoon I was introduced to the general commanding the armed forces of Ghana. He was visiting his country's mission at the U.N. and before the day ended, I had negotiated the sale of 14 Beaver aircraft. The general and his staff were in the process of establishing the Ghana Air Force and discussions indicated the likelihood of requirements in the near future for Otter, Caribou and Chipmunk aircraft as the new service progressed.

"When the contract documents were ready I sent Geoff Priestley to Accra for the signing. He was fully briefed on the situation and, in addition to the signing, visited the Ghana Air Force main base at Takoradi. We

became involved with the development of their air force, which netted us two million in Otter sales and a Caribou order of five and three quarter million dollars. The Ghanaians also bought Chipmunks from England to become the first organization, civil or military, to operate all our Canadian types."

After the considerable sales effort to Ghana, Buchanan received approval to broaden his international coverage and enlarge his sales staff; Geoff Priestley took charge of Africa and the Middle East, while Tony Verrico moved from the test flight department to begin a search for customers in the Far East. John F.B. Shaw joined the company after a career on helicopters with the British military. Buck selected him for the South America territory, which involved learning to speak Spanish. Shaw tackled the assignment in two stages. First he took a university language course in Toronto; then he lived for 12 weeks in the homes of the agents in Caracas and Bogotá where only Spanish was spoken. He combined his new-found knowledge with his flying background and was soon selling DHC products to 14 countries in South America.

The North American market remained strong but was becoming a special field. Buchanan brought George Hurren from the Ottawa office where

he had been managing the company affairs since 1955. Like Buchanan he had built up considerable wartime experience and associated himself with the Royal Canadian Flying Club movement. He held the position of manager when he was asked to take over the Ottawa office of DH Canada, filling the shoes Buchanan had vacated in the capital city. Hurren's sales responsibilities at Downsview began with Canada and slowly enlarged to encompass the whole of North America and the Caribbean.

The marketing team that began in the early 1960s remained relatively intact for the next 20 years. The salesmen soon became as well known in their territories as they were back at Downsview: Tony Verrico and Peter Adams in the Far East, Geoff Priestley

DHC tech rep Ben Cox receives a plaque for his service in Alaska from Col. Wayne Dowling, US Army. Cox became the first manager of de Havilland Aircraft Inc., Chicago, DHC's US subsidiary. (DHC)

Russ Bannock

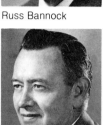
George Hurren

Geoff Priestley

Tony Verrico

John Shaw

Buck Buchanan

Soon after its formation in 1959 the Ghana Air Force ordered Chipmunks, Beavers, Otters and Caribous. The Chipmunks were British-built, but the total of 34 DHC aircraft represented a major success for the sales department. This fine view shows Beaver, Otter and Caribou in formation. All three types have since been replaced in GAF service. (DHC)

in Africa, and John Shaw in South America. George Hurren looked after Canada and the USA, and all reported through Buchanan to the vice president sales, Russ Bannock. The group built up a formidable record of both domestic and export sales, with exports growing from 40 per cent in 1960 to 85 per cent ten years later. In the period after 1970 when Buchanan became vice president of sales the yearly sales averaged $60-80 million with a peak in 1976 of $130 million.

Military STOL

If ever the Canadian de Havilland company wants to look back for the period it came of age, the answer is somewhere in the Caribou program. In the wake of earlier successes, the decision to move into the big league with a large twin-engine design was accepted without a qualm by everyone concerned. Certainly the drama began with a formidable cast of players, but much was to be learned before the box office tallied the receipts or the final curtain fell. No project came closer to bankrupting the company, yet the Caribou is credited with setting de Havilland Canada on the trail to its present world status in the industry.

Planning for the fourth DHC design did not come about easily, nor did it happen overnight. With the Otter safely launched, the engineers began thinking of a twin-engined machine that would continue the workhorse heritage and incorporate their growing lead in short-takeoff technology. Aircraft size did not bother the designers but the choice of power plant did. As far back as 1954 a study was conducted involving an airplane of 13,000 pounds gross weight with two P&W R-1340 engines. It showed very little gain over the single-engine Otter and was scrapped while still on paper.

A second study set the gross weight of 22,000 pounds with two 1200 hp engines and full transport carrier certification. This study was discontinued at an early stage as commercially unattractive but the search went on for a proper engine/airframe combination. Five power plants were eventually considered and even a four-engine configuration was visualized at one time. If the engine was a dilemma, so also was the choice of customer. The average Canadian bush operator would never be able to afford such a large aircraft and the big-money customer at Downsview was now the US Army. The Grumman Tracker program was going well by this time and a feeling of optimism prevailed at all levels of the organization.

While deliberations for a new design continued, Russ Bannock made regular trips to Washington as befitted his title, director of military sales. He was pleased to hear the glowing reports of the Beavers and Otters in Army service and he often detected the words,

"This is what we want next." The ultimate in the Army's eyes, according to these discussions, was a three-ton tactical transport with rear loading which fortunately was in line with DH Canada thinking. With this rather limited input, the design team settled on two P&W R-2000-7M2 engines of 1450 hp each which would give a maximum weight limit of 28,500 pounds. Turbine engines were ruled out at this stage but an adjustable rear loading ramp with inward folding doors was considered a must.

A quick general specification was drawn up in early 1957, complete with drawings, and duly presented to the right people on Bannock's next visit to the Pentagon. First impressions

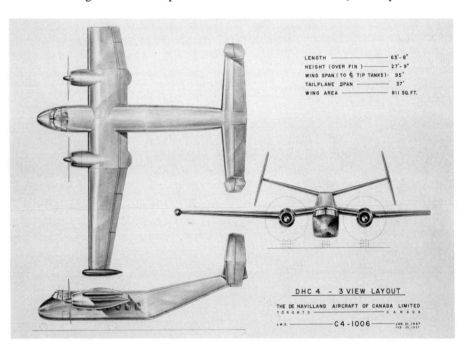

The early layout drawing of the Caribou showing the twin tail arrangement that figured in this design. (DHC678)

brought undeniable signs of interest along with an informal suggestion that Russ "stick around" for a few days. His vigilance paid off three days later when he was invited to meet with the Director of Army Aviation and the Secretary of the Army. Things moved quickly at this meeting for Russ was confronted almost immediately with the question "How much for five and when could we get them?" This time it was Bannock's turn to say "stick around" as he headed for a telephone booth in the

corridor and placed a call to Doug Hunter in Downsview. The full weight of the urgency was impressed on the director of engineering along with the suggestion that the price be set at half a million each, with delivery in 24 months. Some serious discussions took place in Garratt's office during the next hour and Hunter returned the call to Washington with, "Phil says it's OK." Within three months a Pentagon order arrived for the first five Caribous.

Design in a Hurry

Wind tunnel models were used to establish airfoil properties of the Caribou and, because of the suddenly crowded timetable, a unique method of testing was developed. The model was mounted on the front of a truck with all its connected gadgetry and driven up and down the runway. The method worked so well that soon a similar system was flown on the back of an Otter, giving a quick source of aerodynamic data. Two types of tail configuration were considered: a twin fin with an upswept stabilizer and a more conventional single vertical tail. The latter was eventually chosen along with a retracting undercarriage. Large double-slotted flaps covered the whole span, with the outboards serving as ailerons, similar to the Otter. A good deal of attention was given to cargo loading and cabin size. The original

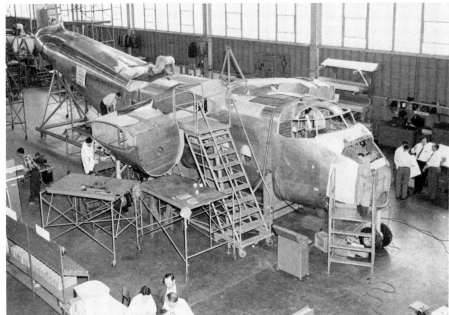

layout drawings were dated January 21, 1957, and, in an all-out effort involving nearly everyone in the plant, the prototype was readied for flight towards the end of July 1958. On July 30 at 2:30 p.m. the test crew of George Neal, Dave Fairbanks and H. Brinkman took Caribou number 1 on a two-hour first flight.

A wave of exhilaration swept through the organization at this milestone. No one could begrudge them their feeling of pride on September 17 when the press were invited to witness the Caribou in action. Even the British Comet was over to round out the display and add to the excitement. The Chipmunk, Beaver and Otter performed in turn with special emphasis on short landings and slow flight manoeuvrability. Rain showers forced the guests inside the hangars during the main event but the Caribou performed anyway to rave reviews in the papers next day.

A small run of 20 machines was begun, including the five evaluation air-

craft for the US Army, which now called the aircraft the YAC-1. There were still cries of concern from the US aircraft industry and considerable opposition to the Army buying another Canadian-made aircraft, even though there were no competitors in the category. When the first of the five Army machines arrived at test flight, it joined in the certification flying which had now reached the stage where the Canadian Department of Transport chief evaluation pilot was taking part in the flying.

Trouble

The target for licencing the Caribou was the US civil certification rule governing twin-engined transports, then called CAR 4b. It was the world-accepted standard and was approved by Canada's DOT, who began working regularly with de Havilland on the step-by-step certification procedure. Chief pilot George Neal and his test crew were busy, for this was the first time DHC had taken on such a formidable set of regulations. Even the DOT were breaking new ground in the certification of an original design in the 24,000-pound gross weight, twin-engine class.

The tests progressed satisfactorily throughout the rest of 1959, even though the equipment and techniques to do the job were not as sophisticated as in later years. The flutter tests, in which the aircraft is flown to its maximum designed dive limit, were completed to '4b standards and the program moved to stalls. Neal found the "power off" stalls borderline but controllable with aileron. They were written up as such in the general reports. The "power on" stall was limited by rudder control but considered within the bounds of certification at the time. A year-end meeting was held to summarize the certification progress and Neal prepared a list of 24 items needed before finalization, including a stick-shaker stall warning.

It was during the early testing that a decision was made to add 42 inches to the cabin length, forward of the wing, in order to obtain the proper centre of gravity range. The added section was introduced in serial number 3, which joined the test program as CF-LKI-X (and with the US Army number of 57-3079). The certification program was

Bob Bradford rendition of the Caribou in its natural element.

nearing the end and Neal was working with DOT test pilot Walter Gadzos in clearing up the outstanding items. One of these was a repeat of the dive to 280 mph to test for flutter due to the lengthened fuselage and the fact that additions had been made to the tail-plane trimming.

Tuesday, February 24, started out like any other for Neal and Gadzos, who were pleased with the progress they were making. The dive presented no anxiety in view of the fact that

Neal had already completed the same manoeuvre with the prototype. At 10,000 feet in their dive (at 265 mph) a high frequency buzzing developed in the elevator control which Neal diagnosed as spring tab flutter. This excited the elevator, and even though the speed was immediately reduced, the excessive vibration continued.

At 180 mph an audible structural failure occurred on the port elevator and a resulting change in the control column oscillations. Slowing the aircraft and even shutting off the engines made no difference to the fluttering elevator and the decision was made to

148

abandon the aircraft. By this time they had lost considerable altitude. Gadzos had a little trouble with the escape hatch in the cockpit floor. When it did open he went through with the push and hung upside down momentarily by his legs.

George Neal prepared to follow through the open hole but paused for one more check, shut off all switches and fuel, tucked his pencils and clipboard under the co-pilot cushion and jumped at 3000 feet. As the silk snapped open and eternal quiet prevailed, he watched 'LKI continue on its final path with a flapping noise like a broken window blind.

Both pilots landed safely, although Gadzos injured his legs in the hasty bail-out. George made his way to the nearest farm where he nonchalantly telephoned the news to Dick Batch of Engineering, giving a capsule report of the events and an approximate lo-

cation of the wreckage. A combined Ontario Provincial Police/DHC search operation soon located the crumpled Caribou in a field south of Udora, near Uxbridge, in time to stop early arrivals from walking off with souvenir sections of aircraft. Thanks to George Neal's presence of mind in shutting things down there was no fire even though the wreckage reeked of gasoline fumes. It was all duly recorded in the newspapers of the 25th.

Now the reporters who had been so kind on press day, had something a little more lively to work on. They cited the 4000 jobs involved at Downsview and called Washington to see if the crash would cancel the Caribou order. "Losing an aircraft is nothing to get panicky about," was the reply. "We've lost a lot in the early stages." One press call to general manager Garratt asking if the company would still continue to make the Caribou brought a quick reply: "Why not?"

The collected evidence under knowledgeable eyes soon began to tell the story. The details fell into place after the surrounding area had been searched completely and all parts returned to Downsview. On March 29 the port elevator horn and horn shield were

found north of Musselman's Lake, 13 miles from the crash site. Another valuable find during May, in the same general area, produced the spring tab strut from the port elevator and the tab balance weight. Added to the pilot's report, it was all the evidence the engineers needed to determine the cause and correct the fault.

It was a typical case of aerodynamic sleuthing and, like most accidents, this one began for the simplest reasons. Evidently the longer control cable required by the lengthened fuselage reduced the dampening of the spring tab in the elevator circuit, allowing both to flutter at a much lower speed than those in aircraft number 1. It was enough to start the buzzing George Neal felt and the high-speed control oscillations at 265 mph. The mass balances and strut found near Musselman's Lake indicated that they were torn off early in the sequence, aggravating the flutter and leading to a failure of the tube that linked left and right elevators. From then on the left side was free to flutter like a "window blind" even though George had some control with the starboard elevator. The extreme pull forces required to raise the nose of the aircraft at the height of the activity also uncovered a control column fault. The control wheel pulled out of the column, forcing Neal to switch to the co-pilot wheel. He found the aileron controls jammed at this stage and the decision was made to abandon the aircraft.

The incident proved a costly portion of the company's learning curve on

The Honourable George R. Pearkes, Minister of Defence (left), Phil Garratt and Air Marshal H.L. Campbell officiated at the Caribou presentation ceremonies on press day. (DHC8862)

The second test Caribou demonstrates its abilities to a military group at Camp Borden, Ontario. (DHC9112)

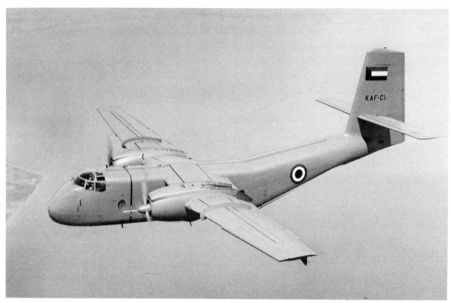

Caribou development. The top photo shows the number 1 prototype with the short nose and clean leading edge of the wing. The second photo shows a Kuwait Caribou with the extended nose section and modified wing with stall bars, wing fences and drooped leading edge. (DHC8635 via Jan Stroomenbergh, DHC16189)

When Canada's General Guy Simmonds, Chief of Staff, learned of the US Army interest in the Caribou (designed specifically for army support on a large scale) he ordered studies within his own command and pledged $2.5 million to de Havilland in support funding. The RCAF soon learned of the Army's sudden interest in operating large aircraft and promptly put a stop to the scheme. Fortunately for de Havilland and the program generally, the financing went through just the same. The money was well spent, for during the Belgian Congo relief mission the RCAF came through with a quick order for four aircraft, designated the CC-108-1A. This stop-gap assistance helped somewhat but no new orders came from the US even though US Army enthusiasm was as strong as ever.

An Exercise in Banking
In a few short weeks the burden shifted to the shoulders of the director of finance, whose introduction to the Caribou problem had been rather unusual. Frank Stanley was returning to Toronto along Highway 401 after a few days away from the city. He had heard of the Caribou crash but did not know many details. Somewhere west of Oshawa he found himself driving behind a truck carrying unmistakable portions of DH Caribou. He could hardly contain his curiosity until he reached his home telephone, little knowing he would soon become an active participant in the Caribou drama. The DH Canada financial position became so tight that the Royal Bank of Canada, with whom they had dealt for years, said, "No more money!" Frank Stanley, the man between the company and the banks, became very busy.

The banking industry has lived for years with the term "risk capital" and here was a situation to test any bank. The de Havilland search for new support went as far as the great Barclays group in England, where one of the directors was none other than Lord Portal, Viscount Hungerford, ex-Chief of Air Staff, RAF. Lord Portal had visited Downsview on March 17, 1954,

large aircraft but the problems were quickly diagnosed and, just as quickly, put right. A larger washer corrected the control column problem and a series of stiffening modifications precluded any further flutter. Flight testing continued on the next aircraft from the production line and Clay Staples of the FAA and an assistant were up for a ride in the aircraft. The time was nearing when US approval would be sought. Staples' preliminary introduction was favourable but he did not agree with the criteria that had been written up for the stalls.

He insisted that they be completed using the FAA procedures in the approaches to stalls and the actual stalling of the aircraft itself. The Caribou would not meet these requirements and a new program in that particular area had to be carried out. With still only five aircraft on the order books,

a new program on top of the already heavy expenditure presented a major crisis. Test pilot Bob Fowler and project engineer Bob McIntyre took over a new and intensive flight program, while George Neal was given a much needed holiday to recuperate from his harrowing experience over Uxbridge.

By mid-summer of 1959 the US approval for stalls had been received but the job had not been easy. Ted Johnson teamed with Fowler in flying over 1000 stalls in every conceivable configuration. Bob McIntyre carried on the diplomatic role with weekly trips to Washington, reporting regularly to the FAA on the growing file of test data. The Caribou that emerged from it all was certainly the most stall-tested aircraft in the FAA 4b category. It now had wing fences, stall bars, a drooped leading edge and two stick-shaker stall warning devices.

where he had been flown in the Otter and thoroughly briefed on company activities. The decision was placed with this ex-airman, whose judgements in the banking world were reputed to be on a par with his wartime decisions in the High Command. He ruled favourably in de Havilland's case, which, according to hard-pressed Frank Stanley, "saved the day." It was a major corporate move and changed de Havilland's banking pattern from that day onward. The same group of banks, Barclay's-Canadian Imperial Bank of Commerce, has continued to look after the company's extensive banking commitments under the capable direction of Frank Udell, who was with Portal on that 1954 visit to Downsview.

Royal Assignment 1959

Eight years after the incident of the plastic car top for Princess Elizabeth

in some of the travel arrangements?" The timing was awkward, in the aftermath of the Caribou crash, but the reply went back that DHC would be pleased to take part.

Test pilot Bob Fowler was chosen for the job and went through briefings with the RAF Royal Flight on matters of protocol. It was discreetly pointed out that Prince Philip, who was an experienced pilot on the Heron, would probably wish to fly the airplane but that in no case should he be allowed to do so when the Queen was on board. Fowler got a call to the Caribou test program at the last moment and the assignment fell to Dave Fairbanks. He was joined by F/L Heath of the RCAF as co-pilot and, with DHC service representative Terry Rawlins, took the Heron to Whitehorse, Yukon, to be ready for a flight on July 19, 1959.

The period was only months before the birth of Prince Andrew and, as

ing of the 31st they flew the Queen and the Duke of Edinburgh to New Glasgow and, later in the day, to Sydney, N.S. This time Prince Philip joined the Queen and her lady-in-waiting in the cabin, along with Lt. Com. McPherson of the Royal Navy and Terry Rawlins.

"It was a trip to remember," said Rawlins many years later. "Everything went smoothly including hoisting the little flag over the cockpit as we taxied in. My own introduction to the Duke didn't go so well for I wasn't with him on the Whitehorse flight and he didn't know who I was. After I had attended to my duties at Charlottetown and climbed on board, Prince Philip looked down the long cabin and said, 'Who the hell is he?' Fortunately the equerry explained that I was the engineer and I was allowed to stay." At the end of the day's flying the crew said good-bye to the royal

A very important visit from the heads of Barclays Bank, March 17, 1954. Left to right: F. Udell, manager of Barclays in Canada; Russ Bannock, DHC; H.A. Stevenson, president, Barclays Canada; Lord Portal of Hungerford, Barclays England; Phil Garratt and George Mickleborough, DHC. (DHC)

and Prince Philip, DH Canada got another request involving the royal couple, this time, Her Majesty the Queen and the Duke of Edinburgh. Another tour of Canada was in the offing and the organizers turned to de Havilland for the use of the demonstrator D.H.114 Heron, CF-IJR.

Most of the flying for the tour was to be done with Air Canada but some airports were too small for their Viscount airliner. The four-engined Herons formed a major part of the British Royal Flight and the call came through from Ottawa, "Would it be possible for DH Canada to take part

the Queen was feeling indisposed that morning, it was decided that Prince Philip would proceed alone on the day's itinerary. From then on there was no doubt who would fly the plane and the question never came up. His Royal Highness simply took his place in the left-hand seat and began starting the engines. Fairbanks went along in the right seat for what turned out to be a very relaxed ride, completely devoid of any protocol. Prince Philip proved to be a good pilot even though his radio transmissions favoured naval language rather than the terminology of the airways. They flew first to Dawson, then Mayo, before returning that evening to Whitehorse.

The assignment was not over for, after a return to Downsview, Fairbanks, Rawlins and F/L Heath positioned themselves in Charlottetown on July 29 for the second stage. On the morn-

The DH Heron demonstrator used by Queen Elizabeth and the Duke of Edinburgh in 1959. (DHC11795)

couple and made their way back to Downsview for a late night landing.

Another Demonstration

Dave Fairbanks was a native of Ithaca, New York, and the son of a Cornell University professor. During the early war years he had skipped school to hitchhike with a couple of friends to the Canadian border. They intended to enlist in the Royal Canadian Air Force but were turned back at Buffalo with only pennies in their pockets. Fairbanks' second attempt to become a pilot was a little more formal. This time he had his widowed mother's approval and in February 1941 he enlisted in the RCAF at Hamilton, Ontario.

1 Rearward retracting, steerable nosewheel
2 Nose gear torque arms
3 Nose gear drag strut
4 Nose gear forward door
5 Taxi light
6 Ram air intake - flight compartment ventilation
7 Ram air intake - combustion, flight compartment
8 Flight compartment heater fuel control unit
9 Flight compartment heater - 50,000 B.T.U. capacity
10 Fire extinguisher - flight compartment heater
11 Flight compartment heat/ventilation ducting
12 Electrical equipment bay
13 Nose hatch
14 Windshield wiper motor
15 Windshield wipers
16 Pilot's/copilot's instrument panel
17 Pilot's rudder pedals
18 Rudder control quadrant
19 Pilot's control column
20 Copilot's control column
21 Pilot's seat
22 Copilot's seat
23 Nosewheel steering handwheel
24 Elevator forward control quadrant
25 Elevator trim tab handwheel
26 Elevator control cables and pulleys
27 Flight control cables and pulleys
28 Radio center console
29 Pitot head for pilot's instruments, left side and for copilot's instruments - right side
30 Static vents
31 Access panel to flight compartment underfloor area
32 Air charging panel - wheel brakes
33 Flight compartment floor hatch
34 24 VDC, 36 ampere-hour, lead-acid battery. Optional 24 VDC, 34 ampere-hour Nicad battery available
35 Main inverter
36 Standby inverter
37 Gyro compass unit
38 Hydraulic system reservoir - system is fed by two engine-driven hydraulic pumps at a pressure of 3000 p.s.i.
39 Equipment rack/escape ladder
40 Flight observer's seat - in stowed position
41 Avionics racks, right hand
42 Overhead console
43 Emergency escape hatch
44 Circuit breaker panels
45 Electrical junction box, No. 10
46 Electrical junction box, No. 2
47 Electrical junction box, No. 1
48 Electronic timer - wing and tail deicing
49 Electronic timer - propeller deicing pump
50 Lightning arrester - HF antenna
51 HF antenna - No. 1
52 HF antenna - No. 2
53 Toilet compartment - customer option
54 Toilet compartment door
55 Toilet
56 Washbowl
57 Cabin heater installation, 200,000 BTU capacity - optional
58 Cabin heat ducting
59 Cabin hot air louvers
60 Troop seats - 32 side-facing
61 Tie-down rings
62 Jettisonable emergency hatch
63 Front spar frame - wing/fuselage attachment
64 Rear spar frame - wing/fuselage attachment

65 Engine/nacelle fire extinguishers
66 Fire extinguisher discharge lines to engines - two shot system
67 Aileron control quadrant and gust lock lever
68 Wing fore flap - root
69 Wing fore flap - inboard
70 Wing fore flap - mid
71 Wing fore flap - outboard
72 Wing trailing flap - root
73 Wing trailing flap - inboard
74 Wing flap bellcrank - root
75 Wing flap bellcranks interconnecting push-pull rods
76 Wing flap bellcrank - mid
77 Wing flap bellcrank - outboard
78 Wing flap actuator and bellcrank
79 Horizontal stabilizer screwjack - varies horizontal stabilizer incidence with flap position
80 Wing fore flap push-pull rods
81 Wing fore flap hinge arms
82 Aileron - mid
83 Aileron - outboard
84 Aileron geared tab
85 Aileron/rudder interconnect tab - right wing only
86 Aileron trim tab - right wing only
87 Aileron trim tab actuator and position indicator
88 Aileron geared tab actuating beam

89 Outboard aileron control linkage
90 Mid aileron control linkage
91 Aileron bellcrank - mid
92 Aileron push-pull rods - mid
93 Aileron bellcrank - outboard
94 Aileron push-pull rods - outboard
95 Wing fuel tank ribs
96 Wing position lights
97 Gyro compass flux valve
98 Wing hinged leading edge
99 Wing leading edge deicing boots
100 Wing deicing distributor valves - outboard
101 Wing deicing suction and pressure lines
102 Wing deicing distributor valves - inboard
103 Propeller deicing tank installation - one each wing
104 Propeller deicing pump and electrically - operated motor
105 Landing lights - one each wing
106 Wing fences - to improve lateral characteristics in stalls
107 Forward retracting main landing gear

108 Main landing gear door
109 Main landing gear drag strut
110 Main landing gear shock strut
111 Outer wing joint fitting
112 Engine nacelle hinged cowlings - upper, both sides
113 Engine nacelle hinged cowlings - lower, both sides
114 Hamilton Standard 43D50-651, fully-feathering, reversible pitch propeller
115 Propeller dome
116 Propeller controller
117 Pratt and Whtiney R-2000-7M2, 14-cylinder radial, air-cooled engine with single-stage, single-speed supercharger
118 Engine air exhaust pipes
119 Engine auxiliary firewall
120 Engine mounting frame
121 Engine support members

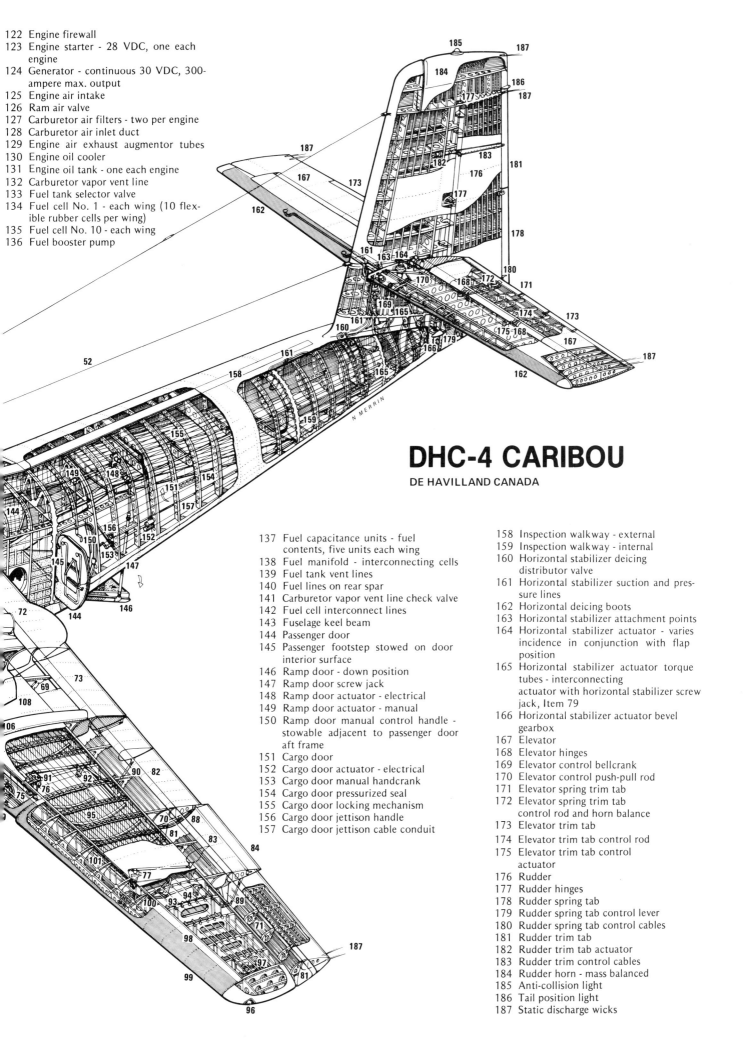

122 Engine firewall
123 Engine starter - 28 VDC, one each engine
124 Generator - continuous 30 VDC, 300-ampere max. output
125 Engine air intake
126 Ram air valve
127 Carburetor air filters - two per engine
128 Carburetor air inlet duct
129 Engine air exhaust augmentor tubes
130 Engine oil cooler
131 Engine oil tank - one each engine
132 Carburetor vapor vent line
133 Fuel tank selector valve
134 Fuel cell No. 1 - each wing (10 flexible rubber cells per wing)
135 Fuel cell No. 10 - each wing
136 Fuel booster pump

DHC-4 CARIBOU
DE HAVILLAND CANADA

137 Fuel capacitance units - fuel contents, five units each wing
138 Fuel manifold - interconnecting cells
139 Fuel tank vent lines
140 Fuel lines on rear spar
141 Carburetor vapor vent line check valve
142 Fuel cell interconnect lines
143 Fuselage keel beam
144 Passenger door
145 Passenger footstep stowed on door interior surface
146 Ramp door - down position
147 Ramp door screw jack
148 Ramp door actuator - electrical
149 Ramp door actuator - manual
150 Ramp door manual control handle - stowable adjacent to passenger door aft frame
151 Cargo door
152 Cargo door actuator - electrical
153 Cargo door manual handcrank
154 Cargo door pressurized seal
155 Cargo door locking mechanism
156 Cargo door jettison handle
157 Cargo door jettison cable conduit

158 Inspection walkway - external
159 Inspection walkway - internal
160 Horizontal stabilizer deicing distributor valve
161 Horizontal stabilizer suction and pressure lines
162 Horizontal deicing boots
163 Horizontal stabilizer attachment points
164 Horizontal stabilizer actuator - varies incidence in conjunction with flap position
165 Horizontal stabilizer actuator torque tubes - interconnecting actuator with horizontal stabilizer screw jack, Item 79
166 Horizontal stabilizer actuator bevel gearbox
167 Elevator
168 Elevator hinges
169 Elevator control bellcrank
170 Elevator control push-pull rod
171 Elevator spring trim tab
172 Elevator spring trim tab control rod and horn balance
173 Elevator trim tab
174 Elevator trim tab control rod
175 Elevator trim tab control actuator
176 Rudder
177 Rudder hinges
178 Rudder spring tab
179 Rudder spring tab control lever
180 Rudder spring tab control cables
181 Rudder trim tab
182 Rudder trim tab actuator
183 Rudder trim control cables
184 Rudder horn - mass balanced
185 Anti-collision light
186 Tail position light
187 Static discharge wicks

He soon became a skilled pilot with 826 hours of instructing to his credit but his dream was the action of an overseas posting. It came at last in 1943, when he joined a Canadian Spitfire squadron in England. He soon began downing enemy aircraft, moved to a Tempest squadron and added locomotives, road transport, ships and buzz-bombs to his growing score. He was shot down while accounting for his 15th victory and spent two months in a German prisoner-of-war camp. He was repatriated as a squadron leader with a DSO and two bars after the war and joined de Havilland in 1955.

Though the Caribou stall problems had been solved by mid-summer of 1959 the promised orders from the US did not come. Undelivered aircraft on the line provoked another crisis, which forced a showdown in the manner of the Beaver and Otter sales. The need for a competition was still being stressed by the opposition at the Pentagon but, because the Caribou had been designed specifically for the Army, there was no competing type. Finally, in obvious desperation, Secretary of Defence Charles Wilson said, "Bring the plane down and demonstrate it."

If ever a trade became a polished art at de Havilland, it was the demonstration of their STOL airplanes. The pilots in test flight used to call them "dog and pony shows" and every opportunity was taken to do demonstration circuits for visiting guests on a short grass strip close to the hangars. The same kind of show could easily be moved to Washington. By now Dave Fairbanks was manager of flight operations and he planned the demo with a flair that was to become his trademark in the years ahead. Permission was obtained from the FAA authorities to use a parade square in Washington with a level grass section of 900 feet. Fairbanks arrived in a Caribou in front of the military observers, took out 32 equipped troops, circled and landed; he loaded once again with cargo and vehicles and went through the same routine. The next day the procedure was demonstrated in every detail for General Howes, Secretary of Defence Wilson and a number of congressmen. The convincing display put an abrupt end to the discussions; the Army could now buy the airplane they so badly wanted and began ordering them in

An early morning departure for the crew of the world tour Caribou. Left to right: Dave Fairbanks, captain; Mick Saunders, first officer; Dave Kendrick, engineer; H. Brinkman, who joined the tour through Germany only; and Norm Paterson, engineer. (DHC)

batches of 50. The US Army Certificate and designation KAC-1 coincided with the official delivery of the first three machines in September of 1959, which would lead to a total of 165 before the program ended.

The Caribou World Tour

During the dark days following the Caribou crash and the subsequent drain on company finances, many serious discussions took place about sales strategy. Seven months of flying the airplane had given everyone complete confidence that the Caribou was everything the engineers had predicted. The big unknown was the number the US Army might order. In any event, world sales would certainly be needed to make the project viable, and it was time for the sales department to take centre stage.

The spotlight fell on Russ Bannock, then director of military sales, and Buck Buchanan, who managed all sales on the international side. Both were well steeped in the sales expertise of the de Havilland empire and well qualified for the task. They had the established worldwide agency organization of the parent company backing their effort, along with considerable experience in the export of Beavers and Otters. These earlier aircraft had all been delivered by ship but now the company had a product that could fly oceans and navigate the world airways. Like any new concept, STOL had to be seen to be believed; the Caribou must be ably demonstrated on a worldwide basis if it was to be sold. Bannock and Buchanan came to this decision early in their discussions and soon had

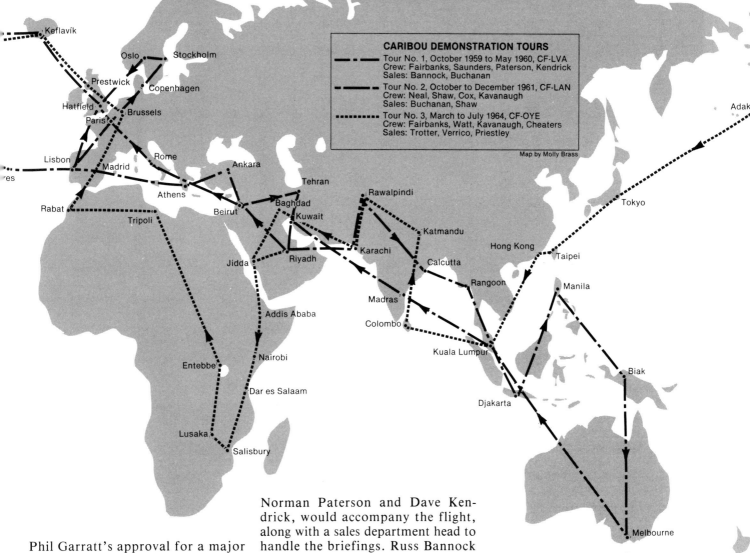

Map by Molly Brass

CARIBOU DEMONSTRATION TOURS
- — ··· — Tour No. 1, October 1959 to May 1960, CF-LVA
  Crew: Fairbanks, Saunders, Paterson, Kendrick
  Sales: Bannock, Buchanan
- — — — Tour No. 2, October to December 1961, CF-LAN
  Crew: Neal, Shaw, Cox, Kavanaugh
  Sales: Buchanan, Shaw
- ······ Tour No. 3, March to July 1964, CF-OYE
  Crew: Fairbanks, Watt, Kavanaugh, Cheaters
  Sales: Trotter, Verrico, Priestley

Phil Garratt's approval for a major demonstration tour.

Planning for the tour was developed from Downsview by correspondence, using the services of the de Havilland area representatives, along with the agents concerned. Whenever available, the assistance of Canadian government representatives, ambassadors, commercial counsellors and trade commissioners was requested. Operations planning was carried out by flight operation manager Dave Fairbanks and his staff, who arranged special navigational charts, clearances, manifest forms, crew visas, right down to the careful selection of a spares package to be carried on board. It was to be the longest tour the company had ever attempted and would cover 30 different countries in the course of the next four months. It was timed to coincide with the first Caribou deliveries to the US Army.

Dave Fairbanks was to captain the aircraft, along with a seasoned ex-RCAF pilot, A.W. "Mick" Saunders, as his first officer. Two of the company's top maintenance engineers,

Norman Paterson and Dave Kendrick, would accompany the flight, along with a sales department head to handle the briefings. Russ Bannock was to manage the first phase through part of Europe and Buck Buchanan was to take command of the tour starting with Lisbon. Their mount for this ambitious program was the ninth Caribou from the production line, CF-LVA, with only 15 hours of test and demonstration flying. The tour got off on October 22, 1959, to a rather poor start with the weather, and then on arrival in the Azores it required a complete engine change, with a new "power egg" flown in from Canada. They got away to Lisbon on November 2 and arrived in England on the 4th. It is significant that their British stop was Hatfield, where demonstrations were arranged in Germany, the Netherlands, Belgium and France, mostly to the US Army units stationed there.

The log book entries began to match any flying carpet story. Throughout Portugal, Algeria, Libya, Greece, Turkey, Lebanon, Iran, Kuwait, Bahrain, Qatar and Oman they went, seeking out difficult landing strips to astound everyone with the Caribou's

versatility. They preferred fields designed for Beavers and Otters, for usually nothing bigger had ever used them. Any DC-3 strip they called a "piece of cake;" they sought instead high mountain clearings with difficult approaches. Each country provided a new challenge, in its flying facilities or its geography: to Pakistan, India, Kashmir, Burma they went . . . to Thailand, Malaysia, Singapore and North Borneo. Their regular reports to Downsview made interesting reading and provided a special article for the parent company's *Gazette*.

Dave Fairbanks described the trip as "right out of an adventure book," with paradrops, food drops, loading and unloading vehicles, transporting awkward cargo and just plain passenger flights. Their life took on all the aspects of a travelling caravan—arrive, unload equipment, meet the officials and arrange the details of a demonstration. The next morning, up at dawn to fly all manner of cargo to the smallest airstrips their hosts could find. They would climb with heavy loads on one engine while observers sucked oxygen from primitive bottles and noted performance figures for their own enlightenment. When the show was all over, they would pack up everything again and move to the next stop on the tour.

Sarawak in North Borneo, the Philippines, Dutch New Guinea, Australian New Guinea, Australia, Timor, Bali and South Borneo and back to Madras, India . . . they had now been away four months and were performing near miracles, still on schedule, no delays and no sickness—until March 2. On that day Fairbanks visited the local hospital for what he thought were stomach cramps and ended up with an emergency appendix operation. A quick conference was called and an immediate decision made: "Press on with the tour." Buck Buchanan took on a dual role. He had maintained his pilot's proficiency since his Lancaster days of World War 2 and by now had plenty of experience with the Caribou. Mick Saunders took over as captain and Buchanan moved into the right seat—it was "business as usual." From Madras they travelled to Bombay and Karachi, followed by demonstrations in Kuwait and the deserts of Saudi Arabia. Then it was Syria, Lebanon, Greece and Italy.

Dave Fairbanks joined them again March 14 in Rome and they went on through Paris to England. This completed their scheduled tour but they made another swing through Germany, Switzerland, Denmark, Finland, Norway and Iceland before finishing up with a flight back to Downsview via Frobisher Bay. All told, they had been away 221 days, travelled 50,000 miles in 40 countries, and visited 154 airports. In 479 demonstraton flights they had completed 664 landings, carried 6683 passengers, and feathered one propeller 500 times.

The crew received an enthusiastic welcome home, for things had taken a decided upswing in the Caribou saga. The first quantity order of 50 US Army machines had been received and word had just arrived that a set of turbine engines was to be installed in a Caribou. It is significant that three of the major purchasers of the Caribou, India, Australia and Malaysia, were visited on that first demonstration tour. It had been a very convincing

display and one that prompted a similar world flight four years later.

The Resolution Island Airlift
Much of the DH Canada story has taken place far from the airport boundary of Downsview. The whole world has been the testing ground and the very nature of the product provides many a tale of adventure in faraway places. Most of the time it was the customer who built the reputation that surrounded the de Havilland airplanes—the bush pilots in the Arctic and military crews on their support missions. De Havilland pilots often joined in the action, particularly on the demonstration and proving flights. A typical operation originating out of Downsview and involving DHC people was the Resolution Airlift of 1961.

Resolution Island lies off the southern tip of Baffin Island at the junction of Hudson and Davis Straits. It was one of the Distant Early Warning sites where the Federal Electric Corporation was responsible to the USA on matters of supply. It had a gravel landing strip of 1300 feet, long enough for an Otter, but Nordair, the commercial operator on the contract, were suddenly faced with a 25,000-pound airlift of bulky equipment from the main base at Frobisher Bay. It was a difficult job calling for STOL and Nordair contacted de Havilland engineering about the use of a Caribou.

Up to this time only six Caribous had been delivered to the US Army and four to the RCAF; none had been used commercially. All had departed for sunny climes with only hot weather

CF-LAN, on contract to Nordair, offloads freight during the Resolution Island airlift. (DHC)

to worry about. When the demonstrator aircraft, CF-LAN, was leased to Nordair for the Resolution flight, it was to be the first such operation in the sub-zero Arctic. Bob Fowler was to captain the flight with Bill Weitsel of Nordair as first officer. The rest of the de Havilland crew was Norm Paterson, Bob McKenna and Len Trotter. Photographer Reg Corlett was along to record the event on film.

The flight arrived at Frobisher on January 29, 1961, and reconnoitred their assignment. Frobisher was a DOT field with navigational aids, a 9000-foot runway, and a heated hangar, if needed. Their other destination, even in the most flattering terms, could only be described as a windswept, snow-covered, ice-locked outpost, with the airstrip located on the perilous hump of a high, narrow promontory. One end of the runway pointed to a sloping valley, while the other presented an 800-foot drop to the sea. For half the length, the airstrip was only 100 feet wide, walled by rock, well above the Caribou's wing tips. One windsock on a cabin gave the wind direction—it usually blew straight across the runway at an average 25 to 35 knots. Whiteouts of blowing snow were prevalent and the mixture of warm and cold ocean currents often blanketed the strip with fog. Maximum VFR conditions each day in January ranged from 7:30 a.m. to 3:30 p.m.

It took 15 days to complete the mission with six round trips averaging 2 hours 30 minutes each flying time. It took 40 minutes to load at Frobisher, but only 12 minutes to unload at the strip through the large rear door. All unloading was conducted on the runway with the engines idling. At the

156

Close-up study of one of the US Army's pre-production Caribous. (DHC)

RCAF Caribou 5323 runs up on the ramp at RCAF Station Trenton, June 1, 1963. It was taken on strength in November 1960 and ten years later sold to Tanzania. During a border skirmish with Uganda it reportedly was lost when it crashed into a hilltop while transporting ammunition. (Nick MacDonald-Wolochatiuk)

Resolution strip the average temperature was -24°F and at one time it went as low as -37°F (with no calculation for chill factor). The runway was of compacted snow and the turning space varied from precarious to non-existent. The Caribou was not equipped with reversing propellers at that time.

Despite the handicap of strong crosswinds and turbulent air, at no time did the Caribou use more than 700 feet of the available runway. The operation was indeed a test of men and equipment and a lot of data was acquired on the limits of the oil dilution system and how the equipment reacted to the cold-soaked Arctic environment.

A Caribou Tale

As the US Army received more and more of their multi-purpose aircraft from de Havilland, so their interest grew in the professional aspects of Short Take Off and Landing. They were pioneering military STOL and took great pride in their short landing techniques. When the first Caribou with reversing propellers was tested by the US Army in July 1960, the pilots sought every opportunity to put this new facility to the test. Representatives from DH Canada and the Army were conducting hot-weather evaluation at Yuma, Arizona, and the service crews often took off on their own for a little practice.

It was during one of these practice sessions that the rescue service got a

US Army Caribous on location in Viet Nam where up to 40 DH Canada technical representatives and service personnel served during the conflict. In the above photo a Sikorsky Skycrane airlifts a damaged Caribou in the combat zone. (DHC)

call from a farmer in the area that an aircraft had crashed in the desert and disappeared in a cloud of dust. The helicopter rescue squad was alerted and began a search with fears that it might be the Caribou. It was a great relief to all when the Caribou came in to land in the midst of all the confusion. The helicopter proceeded to the so-called crash site and found only Caribou tire tracks in the sand. The cloud of dust that so alarmed the farmer had been thrown up by the mighty wash from the reversing props as they braked the aircraft.

STOL in Combat

While Korea brought the Beaver into combat, it was Viet Nam that tested the Otter's ability under fire. The first eight US Army U-1A Otters were assigned in 1963 to a small American combat contingent known as Farm Gate. Over 100 Otters eventually served in Viet Nam in a number of roles, including electronic eavesdropping. Throughout the war some 25 Otters were lost in action and related accidents. Twenty others were transferred to Cambodia under US foreign aid.

As United States military involvement in southeast Asia began to grow in the early 1960s, the Caribou was soon given its baptism of fire in Viet Nam. The first US Army C-7 Caribous

arrived there in the spring of 1962 and in less than four years six squadrons were in use with the 834th Air Division. These were transferred to the 483rd Tactical Airlift Wing in January 1967, based at Cam Ranh Bay. For the duration of the war the Caribous were to provide valuable airlift capability throughout South Viet Nam in many combat operations, including the notorious siege of Khe Sanh.

During the Viet Nam war twenty C-7 Caribous of the US Army/USAF were destroyed in combat or in operational mishaps. By war's end numerous Caribous had been captured intact by the North Vietnamese, as three of

the six American Caribou squadrons had been handed over to the South Vietnamese Air Force.

The Caribou has continued to serve with distinction in the USAF and in recent years has equipped several reserve squadrons as well as special units such as the Army's Golden Knights parachute team. The last USAF Caribou are presently serving with the 357th TAS at Maxwell AFB in Alabama. These aircraft will be retired in October 1983 and replaced by C-130s.

RCAF Caribou Operations

Caribous have also given exceptional service to the Canadian military, par-

US Army parachutists take to the silk from a Caribou's convenient rear exit. (DHC)

Thirty parachutists pour from a La Sarre Caribou at the third annual "Boogie d'Alma" sport parachuting meet at Alma, Quebec, September 1982. (André Gaudet)

Early Caribou cockpit arrangement. (DHC)

ticularly on United Nations duties. They were a vital aspect of UN air support in the Middle East. They backed up UN observation teams into the late sixties, running schedules to El Arish, Gaza, Beirut, Jerusalem, Cairo and Cyprus. RCAF Caribous also supported UN missions in Yemen and West Pakistan. On these duties life was far from routine for these were operational zones and real hotspots. On May 18, 1967, Caribou 5321 was intercepted by a fighter aircraft while flying from Raffa to Gaza and was in danger of being shot down.

Captain Bob Simpson dived for the deck and evaded the fighter, which had already fired warning shots. On another occasion an RCAF Caribou was destroyed on the ground during action between India and Pakistan.

One of the major RCAF/CAF Caribou operations took place in Peru after the disastrous earthquake there in June 1970. When word of the trouble filtered to the outside world on June 7, Transport Command immediately dispatched number 5327 from Trenton to Lima. It was the first international relief aircraft to arrive and began

hauling medical supplies from Lima to a crude strip bulldozed out of an orchard at the 8700-foot level near the devastated town of Anta. Soon five CAF Caribous, with 70 personnel, were on the scene, each aircraft flying two return trips daily to the interior and taking in supplies, then flying out the victims. In the first six days, 806 sick or injured victims were flown out in 41 missions and 90 tons of supplies were moved. The CAF relief operation under Lt. Col. W.I. Butchart continued its work in Peru until June 26. It had functioned almost perfectly but for one minor landing incident. The efforts of 424 Squadron at Trenton were roundly praised by world relief organizations and a number of Peruvian and Canadian decorations were conferred upon many of the 424 participants in the relief operation. Ironically, when the Caribous returned to Trenton in late June, they were greeted by their first CAF Buffalo replacement, which had arrived June 23.

Persistent Caribous

In 1970 the Canadian Armed Forces Caribous were sold to Tanzania where they served for many years. Some of these Caribous, and others originally sold overseas, have been gradually working their way back to Canada and the United States. In recent years several have been operating in the Canadian Arctic. Canadian bush operators have been finding out that the STOL qualities built into the Caribou

(Top photo) RCAF Otter 3745 flies alongside Caribou 5321 on Middle East duty with the United Nations in the mid-sixties. DHC aircraft have served the UN on many of its operations since the Korean War. (via DHC)

Offloading a diesel engine from a Kelowna Flightcraft Caribou at the Cadillac Mine in the Yukon. (R. "Goby" Gobalian)

(Facing page) Caribou 57-3082 in its Arctic colour scheme. This aircraft was also used to evaluate a ski undercarriage. (DHC)

Flightcraft's Caribous have been indispensible in supplying the isolated Cadillac Mine. Its rugged airstrip, located in a narrow winding valley, challenges the imagination of any pilot trying to get in. (R. "Goby" Gobalian)

for the military, their rugged gear and loading capability, are just right for northern freighting. Jean-Marie Arseneault, who has 5500 hours flying time on them for La Sarre/Propair in northwestern Quebec, describes a typical operation: "The Caribou is ideal for outsize cargo. On one job we took a helicopter from Val d'Or in

Installation of GE T64 turbines in the Caribou confirmed the efficiency of the engine and led to the DHC-5 Buffalo. (DHC)

Quebec to Rae Point in the Arctic islands, a 2500-mile flight. The chopper was at work 26 hours after we left Val d'Or and the customer probably had the most economic air transport deal he could have found anywhere."

Bob Ambrose of Kelowna Flight Services also operates Caribous in out-of-the-way parts of Canada. His first aircraft, C-GVYZ, has been in use since March 1980 and is a former Kuwait Air Force Caribou. Much of its work has been into the Cadillac Mine, 210 miles north of Fort Nelson in the Yukon. Jean-Marie Arseneault and Bob Ambrose concur on the Caribou. Not only is it a good all-round transport, but it will likely be around

a long time yet—so long as R-2000 piston engines are available. Failing that, some enterprising fellow is bound to install a pair of simple, light-weight turbines on the Caribou and launch it on another career.

Army Aviation Develops

A study of US military history during the 1950s shows one of the major changes to be the rise of Army support aviation. This began with the arrival of the Beaver, for up to then the air arm had been restricted to small reconnaissance aircraft. Despite opposition by US industry, the Army had won the right through full-fledged competitions to purchase all three of the de Havilland STOL types. The continual opposition they experienced only strengthened their resolve, for they were using the aircraft effectively —in some cases spectacularly—and were proving their point. The Army developed a close bond with de Havilland, who were, in fact, designing specifically for the Army in a way no US manufacturer had ever done.

Unfortunately the growth of Army aviation antagonized the US Air Force. During years of working with de Havilland, the Army had developed its own brand of aviation, was becoming extremely good at it and was buying bigger and bigger aircraft. A confrontation was brewing because the Air Force felt its specialty was being infringed. The Army felt confident that it had the situation well in hand. Back at Downsview, de Havilland remained friendly with both sides and stayed out of the inter-service politics.

This was the situation in February 1961 when the announcement of a combined development program moved DH Canada into the turbine age and gave a new lease on life to the Caribou. Since 1957 General Electric had been developing a high technology engine under a contract with the US Navy Bureau of Weapons. The turbo-prop/turboshaft engine was to be called the T64 and had been designed for low fuel consumption, high reliability and ease of maintenance. It had a two-stage high-efficiency generator turbine and delivered 2344 shp plus 565 pounds thrust.

The General Electric Company were looking for a fixed-wing evaluation aircraft and had their eye on the DHC Caribou; it was not long before a single-source contract was drawn up with de Havilland as a joint effort between the US and Canadian governments. News of the joint conversion program was welcomed by DHC engineers, who were in a slack period and down to a staff of 250. They had been considering turbine power for the Caribou themselves and here was an opportunity to put their ideas to work under the watchful eye of their best customer, the US military.

Participants in the program would be the US Navy, under whose auspices the T64 was developed, General Electric's small aircraft engine department at Lynn, Massachusetts, and DH Canada, responsible for designing and carrying out the conversion and conducting the test flying. The RCAF would supply Caribou serial number 1 as the test-bed airframe. It was to be the company's first experience with turbine power and the T64-GE4 fitted their requirements.

Considerable modification work was needed to convert RCAF Caribou 5303 but it emerged with its new turbine look by September 1961 ready for testing. Chief engineering test pilot Bob Fowler took it into the air on September 22 and continued with 220 hours of very interesting flying. With the added thrust from the more powerful engines great care had to be taken: it was possible to exceed the designed speed limitations for the aircraft with only one engine operating and to attain the design dive speed with both engines while still in level flight. It took only three minutes to climb to 15,000 feet. Needless to say all parties were pleased with the results and, after the evaluation contract, Caribou 5303 was reconverted to its original configuration.

The Buffalo
The T64 might have been a US Navy development engine but the Army were closely monitoring its test in the Caribou. They had ambitions to operate an advanced version of the aircraft capable of carrying vehicles and they now had a turboprop engine with the right performance. In keeping with US Army policy of constant improvement, they presented their requirements in the form of a design competition.

They specified a STOL transport capable of carrying the tactical loads of the Boeing Vertol and Chinook helicopters. It should be capable of transporting a Pershing missile, a 105mm howitzer and a 3/4 ton truck. The

The prototype Caribou with its new T64 turbine engines enjoyed exceptional climb performance. (DHC13917 via R.J. Fox)

aircraft must have turbine engines, rear loading and a payload of five tons. De Havilland put all their accumulated data into a proposal called the Caribou II and entered it in the competition during May of 1962. The other finalists of the 25 competing companies were Fairchild, Grumman and North American Rockwell. The

Engineering and production heads at the rollout of the first DHC-5 Buffalo. Left to right: W.T. Heaslip, N.E. Rowe, R.D. Hiscocks, W.C. Burlison, F.H. Buller, W. Bozanin and T.G. Higgins. (DHC17362)

evaluation took the better part of a year but ended with a contract for de Havilland in March 1963 to supply four prototype machines. This made the fourth competition in as many airplanes that DH Canada had won for the supply of the US Army. The new airplane was to be developed for $22.5 million on a one-third share basis among the Canadian government, the US Army and de Havilland.

The US Army was pleased with the arrangement but the US Air Force grew more and more restless. Design work went ahead with great speed at DHC for the project, now called the Buffalo, was a natural extension of the company's STOL line. It was

(Facing page, top) One of the original pre-production Buffalos overflies Niagara Falls. When the US Army lost its authority to operate large fixed-wing aircraft no production order was received from Washington. (DHC)

(Facing, below) A Canadian Armed Forces Buffalo on duty at Ismailia, Egypt, April 20, 1978. DHC aircraft have often been used to support UN operations in rugged or isolated regions. (Larry Milberry)

(Top) A 413 Squadron search and rescue Buffalo at CFB Summerside. (Larry MacDougal)

(Below) An exceptional view of a Buffalo delivered in 1982 to Egypt. (DHC)

assigned the US designation CV-7A and took only one year to bring to the testing stage. It flew successfully on April 9, 1964, with Bob Fowler, Mick Saunders and Bob Dingle as crew. Testing with the cooperation of the US Army and Canadian government authorities was toward an FAA CAR 4b certification. The program went well and by the time the approval was obtained in April 1965, four prototypes were flying. It was during this period that the Canadian government authorized an initial order of 15 Buffalo aircraft for the RCAF, thus enabling the company to begin a production line.

Four evaluation models were delivered to the United States for comprehensive service tests totalling 500 hours of flying. The military proving cycle was so trouble-free that a 90-day trial period was ordered for two aircraft in an actual combat environment. The first Buffalo departed Fort Rucker, Alabama, on November 12, 1965, and arrived in Nha Trang, South Viet Nam, on the 17th. It was demonstrated to senior military personnel on the 18th and went to work the next day carrying 17,400 pounds of cargo and 112 passengers in five hours of flying. The second Buffalo arrived on the 22nd and went into service two days later.

Both aircraft teamed perfectly with the Caribous of the 92nd Aviation Company detailed for support work into the Viet Nam interior. The jungle airstrips varied from 1000 to 3000 feet and the support action involved cargo, troops, supply drops and LOLEX (Low Level

The fourth preproduction Buffalo during field trials with the US Army. (DHC17822)

The RCAF takes over the first production run of CC-115 Buffalo aircraft in 1967. (DHC28856)

Extraction, in which the cargo is pulled from the rear loading doors by a parachute) deliveries, often on short notice. The test aircraft were an inspiration to all, for they carried greater loads and did everything with a little more flair than the hard-working Caribou. On the low-level missions, under enemy attack, the Buffalo's steep descent and pull-up kept it out of the range of enemy fire.

Detailed reports of the period make fascinating reading, for the aircraft were deliberately put into front-line action. Loads of 10,000 pounds were routine. Air drops included 3/4-ton army trucks and on one single paradrop mission the Buffalo dropped 64 Vietnamese paratroops. When a special fueling operation was called for, 45-gallon drums were hauled into a strip at 25 drums per aircraft. A good day's work, according to one crew, was 60,000 pounds of cargo and 170 passengers in 4:50 hours flying time. Even the maintenance turned out to be quite reasonable for a new aircraft type so far from home with only 10-15 per cent of the available spares used. Needless to say, the operational commanders were pleased with the results.

When the aircraft returned to Fort

Rucker in mid-February, they had flown 605 hours with 416 sorties, carried 1045 tons of supplies and 2831 passengers. Both arrived back on US soil in serviceable condition with only minor battle damage recorded. The commander of the 5th Special Forces Group is understood to have requested the Buffalo on a regular basis to support his units. The request was never put into action for it came at a difficult time in the history of the US military and the Buffalo story in particular.

The Air Force had not been idle throughout this period, for their stepped-up studies showed that they could meet their logistical requirements with the Lockheed C-130 Hercules. This decision coincided with the arrival in Washington of a new Secretary of Defence, Robert McNamara. His background had been with the Ford empire and with RAM Consultants, who had done recent work for the Air Force. While de Havilland looked worriedly across the border at this new turn of events, a compromise was reached between the two services. The Army would acquire all helicopters for their tactical support and the Air Force would take over all fixed-wing operations, including the Caribous that were still in the

system (to be called the C-7A). The Buffalo literally got lost in the shuffle from then on; all liaison work on the aircraft ceased.

It was a major setback for de Havilland to lose such a valued customer on such a large project with politics as the only reason. The shock severely retarded further engineering development on the Buffalo but production was under way and a search began for other customers. The deliveries to the Royal Canadian Air Force of its CC-115 Buffalos began in 1967 and were of the 5-A model, incorporating improvements from the brief Viet Nam testing. By 1968 other sales had materialized in Brazil, with two orders of 12 each, and Peru, which bought 16. Buffalo production was temporarily terminated in August 1972 with the delivery of aircraft number 59 and remained that way until the introduction of the 5-D model.

As the sale of Buffalos tapered off through 1972, more and more thought was given to the obvious improvements that could be incorporated. If the plans of the US Army had been allowed to run full course, constant improvement would have been a matter of routine. It was also obvious that the original specifications, written around a STOL tactical requirement for rough terrain, were penalizing the aircraft particularly in the normal transport category. The design criteria allowed for much greater payloads from normal paved runways, resulting in two sets of performance figures. One would be an Assault STOL version at 41,000 pounds gross weight for unprepared fields and the other at 49,200 pounds for paved runways.

Once the decision was made, more than 60 improvements were incorpor-

ated into the Buffalo, including anti-skid brakes, Beta control propellers and a new auxiliary power unit. The major change was the upgraded General Electric engine, the CT64-820-4, increased from 2970 shp at sea level and 86°F to 3133 shp. The new Buffalo would be called the "D" model and a new production batch was ordered to incorporate all the planned improvements. Production of the Buffalo began again in 1976.

The amazing Buffalo, with its history of technical progress and political setbacks, continues in production. Like the Caribou of former years it toured widely and it has recorded sales to 17 countries outside North America. The year 1982 ended with the sale of ten Buffalos to Egypt and brought the cumulative total over 18 years to 121.

A World Record

Buffalo serial number 60 was used for the prototype testing of the new model and showed improved performance in all areas of flight. Pilot Tom Appleton was doing high-altitude handling tests at 30,000 feet and noted that his time in climbing to the test area had been exceedingly short. Reflecting on the higher flat rating of the new engine and the D model's higher power-to-weight ratio, he realized the climb must have been close to a world record. A search of the figures revealed that the Group 2 climb record for turboprops in the unlimited weight class was held by the Lockheed P-3C Orion at 10 minutes, 26 seconds to 9000 meters (29,500 feet). He felt the new Buffalo could beat it easily.

Appleton requested permission to apply for a record attempt in conjunction with other high-altitude test work to be done on the aircraft and applied to the Fédération Aeronautique Internationale, the official world body on such trials, through the Canadian representative, the Royal Canadian Flying Clubs Association. By early February the necessary recording and calibration equipment was in place and on February 16, 1976, W.P. "Bill" Paris of the RCFCA was in attendance at de Havilland to act as official FAI steward.

The crew of the record breaking Buffalo 5D after completing the climb to height record February 16, 1976. Left to right: Barry Hubbard, Tom Appleton and Bill Pullen. (DHC43343)

1 Weather radar
2 Glideslope antenna
3 Ram air intake - to refrigeration unit
4 Ram air intake - to flight compartment and cabin
5 Refrigeration unit
6 Water separator
7 Silencer
8 Air duct to cabin
9 Air ducts to flight compartment
10 Windshield wiper motor
11 Nose hatch
12 Electrical equipment bay
13 Nose gear forward door
14 Taxi light
15 Rearward retracting, steerable nosewheel
16 Nose gear torque arms
17 Nose gear drag strut
18 Access panel to flight compartment underfloor area
19 Air charging panel - wheel brakes
20 Flight compartment floor hatch
21 VOR antenna
22 Pilot's rudder pedals
23 Rudder control quadrant
24 Rudder control cables and pulleys
25 Nosewheel steering control
26 Pilot's/Copilot's instrument panel
27 Radio console
28 Pilot's control column
29 Copilot's control column
30 Pilot's seat
31 Copilot's seat
32 Standby compass
33 Pitot heads for pilot's instruments, left side and copilot's instruments, right side
34 Elevator forward control quadrant
35 Elevator control cables and pulleys
36 Flight control cables and pulleys
37 Elevator trim tab handwheel
38 Overhead console
39 Avionics racks, right hand
40 Emergency escape hatch
41 Equipment rack/escape stair
42 Circuit breaker panels
43 Flight technician's seat - stowed

55 Main distribution box
56 DC power distribution box
57 AC variable frequency distribution box
58 Propeller control panel
59 AC distribution box - 400 Hz
60 Transformer/rectifier units
61 Fire extinguisher bottles
62 Troop seats - 34 side facing, plus provisions for fitting 7 forward facing seats down center

74 First aid kit
75 Oxygen outlets in cabin wall
76 Passenger door
77 Passenger door jettison handle
78 Passenger footstep stowed on door interior surface
79 Parachute jump signal lights
80 Control panel - cabin lighting and doors
81 Rear distribution box
82 Tie-down stowage
83 Portable fire extinguisher
84 Passenger oxygen bottles
85 Pendulum release unit
86 Parachute anchor lines - both sides
87 Ramp door - down position
88 Ramp door screw jack
89 Transverse drive shaft-ramp door
90 Electrical actuator - ramp door
91 Manual actuator - ramp door
92 Cargo door - up position
93 Rear emergency hatch - in cargo door
94 Electrical actuator - cargo door
95 Handcrank - cargo door

44 Crew oxygen bottles
45 Avionics racks, left hand
46 Charging panel - crew oxygen
47 Static vents
48 VHF antenna
49 Toilet compartment - customer option
50 Toilet compartment door
51 Washbowl
52 Toilet
53 Engine bleed air duct in cabin
54 Main pressure regulator - engine bleed air

63 Tie-down rings
64 Cabin air louvers
65 Jettisonable emergency doors
66 Front spar frame - wing/fuselage attachment
67 Rear spar frame - wing/fuselage attachment
68 Wing flap actuator and torque tubes
69 Aileron control quadrant
70 Gust lock lever
71 Wing flap sensor
72 Refuel/defuel line from fueling adapter
73 Master fueling valve

96 Pulleys and transverse cables - cargo door
97 Elevator servo actuator - autopilot
98 Rudder servo actuator - autopilot
99 Elevator trim actuator - autopilot
100 Vertical gyro units - autopilot
101 Aileron servo actuator - autopilot
102 HF coupler and receiver/transmitte
103 HF antenna - No. 1
104 HF antenna - No. 2
105 Lightning arrester
106 Hydraulic lines to rudder actuator

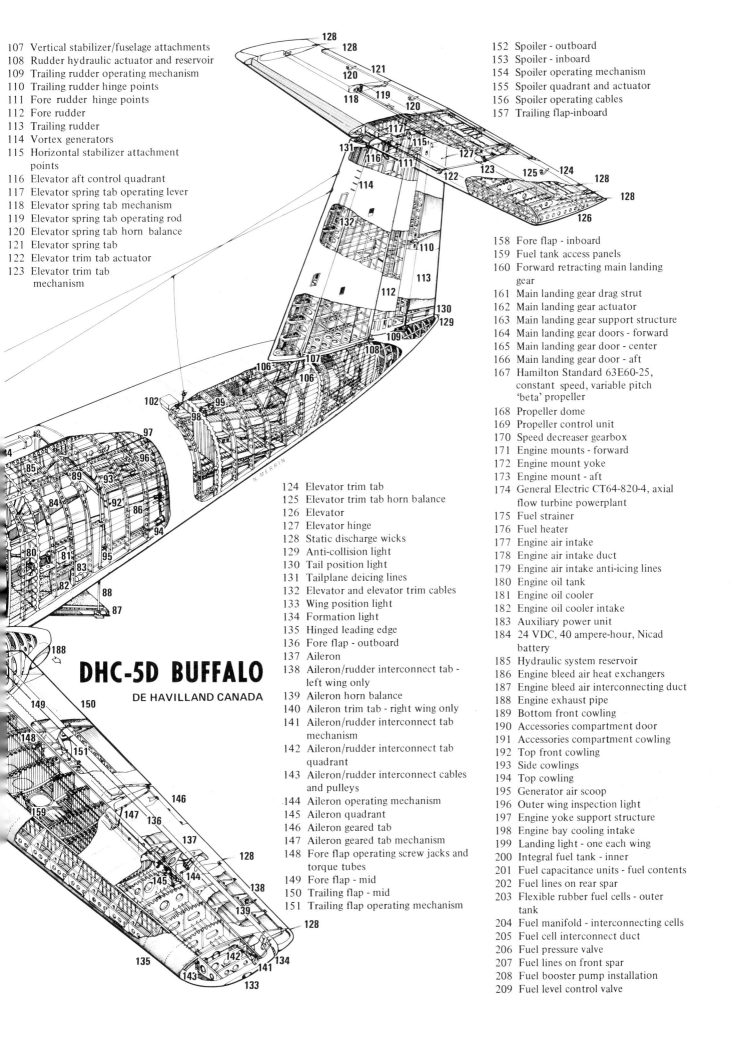

107 Vertical stabilizer/fuselage attachments
108 Rudder hydraulic actuator and reservoir
109 Trailing rudder operating mechanism
110 Trailing rudder hinge points
111 Fore rudder hinge points
112 Fore rudder
113 Trailing rudder
114 Vortex generators
115 Horizontal stabilizer attachment points
116 Elevator aft control quadrant
117 Elevator spring tab operating lever
118 Elevator spring tab mechanism
119 Elevator spring tab operating rod
120 Elevator spring tab horn balance
121 Elevator spring tab
122 Elevator trim tab actuator
123 Elevator trim tab mechanism

152 Spoiler - outboard
153 Spoiler - inboard
154 Spoiler operating mechanism
155 Spoiler quadrant and actuator
156 Spoiler operating cables
157 Trailing flap-inboard

158 Fore flap - inboard
159 Fuel tank access panels
160 Forward retracting main landing gear
161 Main landing gear drag strut
162 Main landing gear actuator
163 Main landing gear support structure
164 Main landing gear doors - forward
165 Main landing gear door - center
166 Main landing gear door - aft
167 Hamilton Standard 63E60-25, constant speed, variable pitch 'beta' propeller
168 Propeller dome
169 Propeller control unit
170 Speed decreaser gearbox
171 Engine mounts - forward
172 Engine mount yoke
173 Engine mount - aft
174 General Electric CT64-820-4, axial flow turbine powerplant
175 Fuel strainer
176 Fuel heater
177 Engine air intake
178 Engine air intake duct
179 Engine air intake anti-icing lines
180 Engine oil tank
181 Engine oil cooler
182 Engine oil cooler intake
183 Auxiliary power unit
184 24 VDC, 40 ampere-hour, Nicad battery
185 Hydraulic system reservoir
186 Engine bleed air heat exchangers
187 Engine bleed air interconnecting duct
188 Engine exhaust pipe
189 Bottom front cowling
190 Accessories compartment door
191 Accessories compartment cowling
192 Top front cowling
193 Side cowlings
194 Top cowling
195 Generator air scoop
196 Outer wing inspection light
197 Engine yoke support structure
198 Engine bay cooling intake
199 Landing light - one each wing
200 Integral fuel tank - inner
201 Fuel capacitance units - fuel contents
202 Fuel lines on rear spar
203 Flexible rubber fuel cells - outer tank
204 Fuel manifold - interconnecting cells
205 Fuel cell interconnect duct
206 Fuel pressure valve
207 Fuel lines on front spar
208 Fuel booster pump installation
209 Fuel level control valve

DHC-5D BUFFALO

DE HAVILLAND CANADA

124 Elevator trim tab
125 Elevator trim tab horn balance
126 Elevator
127 Elevator hinge
128 Static discharge wicks
129 Anti-collision light
130 Tail position light
131 Tailplane deicing lines
132 Elevator and elevator trim cables
133 Wing position light
134 Formation light
135 Hinged leading edge
136 Fore flap - outboard
137 Aileron
138 Aileron/rudder interconnect tab - left wing only
139 Aileron horn balance
140 Aileron trim tab - right wing only
141 Aileron/rudder interconnect tab mechanism
142 Aileron/rudder interconnect tab quadrant
143 Aileron/rudder interconnect cables and pulleys
144 Aileron operating mechanism
145 Aileron quadrant
146 Aileron geared tab
147 Aileron geared tab mechanism
148 Fore flap operating screw jacks and torque tubes
149 Fore flap - mid
150 Trailing flap - mid
151 Trailing flap operating mechanism

The crew for the attempt in Buffalo C-GBUF-X was Captain Tom. E. Appleton, co-pilot W.E. "Bill" Pullen and engineer Barry Hubbard. Appleton lifted off the runway at Downsview for a direct climb to 30,000 feet. The tapes started to record from brake release and printed the times through every altitude on the climb. The entire flight took only 17 minutes from take-off to touchdown and covered just 13 miles. Even without the instrumentation and tapes they knew they had bettered the Orion's time. It turned out to be a margin of 2 minutes and 22.5 seconds.

The time to 3000 meters (9,800 feet) had been 2 minutes, 12.75 seconds; to 6000 meters (19,700 feet), 4 minutes, 27.5 seconds; and to 9000 meters (29,500 feet), 8 minutes, 3.5 seconds. These constituted three records in each of the two categories. One for the turboprop "unlimited" class and one for the new class (no previous record) for turboprops in the 12,000-16,000 kilogram class. During those 17 minutes of flying, Appleton and his crew had broken six "time to height" records and established the Buffalo as a top world performer.

The Bell-Bottom Buffalo

An interesting design project involving the Buffalo brought DH Canada into close contact with Bell Aerospace Company of Buffalo, New York. Bell had been experimenting for years with an air cushion landing system (ACLS) on smaller aircraft to the point where the system was now ready for test on a large scale. A Canadian Forces CC-115 Buffalo was chosen as the vehicle and a combined US/Canada research and development program was organized. Bell Aerospace built the air cushion trunk, while Pratt & Whitney Canada supplied the two ASP-10 air supply systems using ST6 gas turbine engines driving axial fans. De Havilland contracted to do installation work and the test flying for system function and aerodynamic stability. The proving flights were conducted in 1975 by the USAF 4950th Test Wing at Wright Patterson Air Force Base. The overall cost was shared by the United States Air Force and Canada's Department of Industry, Trade and Commerce.

It was a challenging exercise for de Havilland's experimental test department under technical project manager C.J. "Chris" Austin. First, the two

slim turbine engines were installed on the fuselage under the big Buffalo wings and ductwork was attached to a 32 by 14-foot inflatable "doughnut" on the underside of the aircraft. In normal flight the two-way-stretch rubber/nylon composite skirt clung closely to the bottom of the fuselage like a well-fitting girdle. For landing the air cushion was inflated to about 160 pounds per square foot, and escaping air from over 700 small holes around the ground contact area provided a supporting "lubricant." Bob Fowler did the aerodynamic testing on the regular gear and proved the aircraft's flight stability with the trunk in both positions before turning it over to the USAF.

Unfortunately most of the de Havilland personnel who had watched the test vehicle take shape were unable to witness the field trials in 1975, in which

The Bell ACLS (Air Cushion Landing System) on a modified Buffalo, with the inflatable trunk extended. The port compressor turbine under the wing can be clearly seen, as well as the added floats and skids. (DHC39423)

it was tested on all manner of rough terrain by the USAF. The big Buffalo, looking more like an ungainly hippo, proved it could traverse pavement, grass, mud and snow—even six-foot-diameter craters. It tracked sideways in a crosswind and achieved its braking through inflatable skids in the trunk. Wingtip floats and skids kept the wings level on ground or water.

The tests fulfilled all expectations for performance and controllability within the limits of the program and showed that the ACLS concept was compatible with the STOL high-wing turboprop. For military purposes the bell-bottom Buffalo proved it could handle emergency rescue roles in a variety of terrains although considerable trunk material development would be required to achieve adequate life. After CF 115451 was restored to Canadian Forces configuration in the Downsview shops, it was no longer the showpiece it had once been, but it was still pointed out to visitors as the ACLS Buffalo with the comment, "It used to take off and land on a cushion of air."

Enter the Commuters

The Turbo Beaver

One of the bright spots in Canadian aeronautical design and development during the 1960s was the introduction of the Pratt & Whitney PT6 turbine engine. In those days the engine company was called United Aircraft of Canada Limited and was part of United Technologies Incorporated; the design of the PT6 engine was a Canadian contribution to the proud line of Pratt & Whitney engines. Its creators contemplated a worldwide market but perhaps the greatest interest came from Canada itself.

Turbine technology was developing rapidly and there was no doubt that turbine engines, with their greater efficiency, were taking over from piston engines. The group at Longueuil had done their market studies well and the bush flying trade in Canada was ready for the change. No one knew this better than de Havilland Canada, who were working closely with United, but there were others who were keenly interested in the higher power/weight ratio offered by the PT6 engine.

De Havilland Canada became involved early in the life of Pratt & Whitney's small turbine. DHC received the contract to convert a standard RCAF Beechcraft 18 into a PT6 test vehicle. Bill Billings was in charge of the engineering and, while plans were under way to prepare a special nose mounting, Bob Fowler acquainted himself with a standard Beechcraft so

that he could pass on the eventual flying qualities of the conversion. All the preliminary testing, including a light-up of the test engine, was completed at Downsview and the aircraft was turned over to John McNeil, the P&W test pilot who did the engine calibration flying.

This early introduction to the light turbine era started many a huddle among the engineers at de Havilland Canada, particularly those associated with the experimental STOL Otter, who wanted to round out their test program with a pair of these engines, knowing that the benefits would be impressive. The company's involvement with the PT6 gave it an inside track to the new engine data. The engine seemed tailor-made for the DHC designs and it was not surprising that the company began getting customer enquiries. Pacific Western Airlines, for example, not only suggested that their piston Beavers be converted to turboprop, but sought permission and help to do the work themselves.

The first meeting on the subject occurred in December 1962 and correspondence continued between PWA and DHC through March of 1963. It soon became evident that it was not simply a case of installing a new engine mount and cowling. A DHC conversion kit was considered so that operators could modify their own aircraft, but by March 14, when a complete proposal for a turbine-powered Beaver was issued, the project had become much more complex.

The changes, besides the new engine and nacelle, would include a new fin

and rudder together with a 28-inch fuselage extension forward of the wing. The enlarged cabin space allowed two more passenger seats and under-floor storage for an extra 29 imperial gallons of fuel. The payload would be 157 pounds better than the standard Beaver at all ranges up to 500 miles and the economical cruise speed would be increased, but the gross weight would have to be held at the same 5100 pounds. The PT6-6 turbine engine at 550 shp (with growth potential), against the R-985 piston engine at 450 hp, guaranteed an excellent takeoff performance which was particularly attractive to the Ontario Department of Lands and Forests. They would be able to add dozens of smaller lakes to their northern duties and ordered a study on converting their existing Beaver fleet.

About this stage, Pacific Western Airlines bowed out of the proceedings and an April meeting of the de Havilland management committee approved three months' design work to bring about the necessary Beaver modifications. The final decision to proceed was made with an internal factory instruction for a 16-plane production program. Work proceeded quickly. The Turbo Beaver, CF-PSM-X (to record the initials of Peter S. Martin, the project engineer), was test flown on the last day of 1963.

The major operator of the Turbo Beaver was the Ontario Ministry of Natural Resources, which took delivery of its first of 17 on June 4, 1965.

The first Pratt & Whitney PT6 turbine in the nose of a Beech 18 and the test crew: J.A. MacNeil and R. Fowler. (DHC13672)

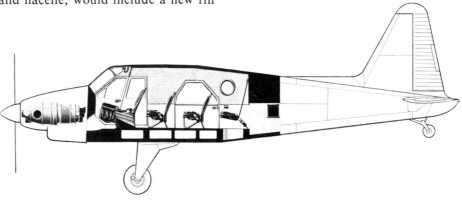

An early cutaway drawing of the Turbo Beaver showing the extended fuselage, the PT6 installation and the tail section of the Leonides Beaver II. (DHC)

In the final analysis, the extensive improvements involved in the conversion along with the costly turbine engine made it an expensive airplane even though it was an exceptional performer. It still had to compete with its piston cousins in the call-and-haul trade and these were now becoming available in quantity from surplus US Army stocks. The sale of Turbo Beavers slowed enough in 1967 that Hawker Siddeley decided to close down the production line.

The Birth of the Twin Otter

"There is a time in the affairs of men," said Shakespeare, "which taken at the tide leads to fortune." In similar vein he went on, "We must take the current when it serves or lose our ventures." No words could more aptly describe the logic behind de Havilland's Twin Otter.

The Twin Otter emerged in what many considered too much haste, but the time was right and taken on the "tide" of market demand. The DHC-6 was the most significant happening in a decade at Downsview and the project that was to see de Havilland through a long, difficult period. It came at the height of the Caribou sales, when DHC was riding the crest of US Army enthusiasm for STOL aviation. It bridged two distinct marketing periods: the US military business and the emerging commuter airline business.

The de Havilland engineers had always visualized an Otter with two engines and the Caribou was the direct result of one such study. It was realized quite early in the Otter program that it was a large airplane for one engine and that its payload on floats was limited. Max Ward and other operators in the north wanted multi-engine safety. They were pleased with the cabin volume of the Otter but needed a heavier payload capability to remain competitive. The lack of an engine with a suitable power-to-weight ratio had always been the obstacle to designing a twin-engined aircraft in that weight category, but the news of Pratt & Whitney's PT6 turbine design started everyone thinking along new lines.

"The break came in Viet Nam," recalls Russ Bannock, "where we had a lot of Otters and Caribous. De Havilland had a very efficient group of technical representatives and field

The final configuration of the Turbo Beaver tail can be seen in this view of demonstrator CF-ROM and prototype CF-PSM-X. Sixty Turbo Beavers were completed, mostly for customers in the Canadian north. (DHC)

maintenance personnel there in 1963 and I was over on one of my regular trips. I flew from base to base in US Army Otters, for it was the only way we could get around easily. The officers with whom I flew were all high in their praise of the airplane but were unanimous on two points. They talked constantly of two engines in the Otter for greater safety and would have preferred a tricycle undercarriage to combat the ever-present crosswinds.

"On the long flight home in a dreary military transport, I couldn't get one Army general's proposals out of my mind. I drew up numerous plans and sketches based on my talks, to present to the engineers when I got back to Downsview. Dick Hiscocks, 'Nero' Rowe and Fred Buller were all in agreement; in fact Peter Martin began, immed-

iately, preparing a set of preliminary designs. I felt sure that I could sell something like this in quantity to the US Army and it was a natural for commercial bush operations. We were working very closely at the time with Pratt & Whitney on their PT6, for it offered 50 per cent more power for 35 per cent less installed weight. Bob Fowler had a lot of experience with two of them in the STOL research Otter. The results were just what we were looking for.

"It was an extremely busy period for us at de Havilland. We had moved into a new type of management under Hawker Siddeley and announced a program to build DC-9 wings at Malton. We had contracted to build four Buffalos, a hydrofoil for the Canadian Navy and we were also into guided missiles. We had just completed installing a turbine engine in the Beaver and here we were planning a new airplane. The interest in a two-engined Otter was completely genuine; we had to get going at that time or we would

Twin Otter number 9, CF-UXE, is seen in TAA markings. It was displayed as such at Farnborough but was delivered instead to Air Caledonia in January 1968 as F-OCFJ. Most recently, it has served in the French Polynesian islands with Air Tahiti. (DHC)

"Whiskey Whiskey Papa," the Arctic's most famous Twin Otter. Bought by Weldy Phipps' Atlas Aviation in 1973, it was the first Twin Otter to enter commercial service in Canada. (DHC)

lose the market."

An important meeting on the subject of a twin-engined Otter was convened on July 22, 1963, attended by C.H. Dickins, R. Bannock, W.T. Heaslip, F.H. Buller, D.L. Buchanan, L. Trotter, R.D. Hiscocks, P. Martin and N.E. Rowe. All aspects were discussed including the possibility of starting a brand-new design. This was ruled out because time was short. A retracting gear was discussed but the speed loss for short-haul STOL operations was not worth the redesign involved. Because more cabin and baggage space was desired, it was decided to extend the Otter fuselage and the size increase meant increasing the wingspan. Good STOL performance was deemed essential and it was decided to plan around a possible sale of 300 aircraft.

The decisions were acted upon promptly by the design office, which nonetheless maintained the basic bushplane simplicity. A rugged fixed gear with compression blocks in the mains and a steerable nose-wheel provided a starting point. Guidelines were quickly drawn up in which the Otter wingspan was increased by seven feet and the overall length by five feet. The fuel capacity was increased, all doors were enlarged and a new tail section was designed. US Army interest was maintained during this time through regular progress reports. As far as they were concerned they wanted it right away.

This urgency brought about a novel proposal that they begin immediately building five test aircraft. The object was to fly the first aircraft as soon as possible and have the static testing of structural components completed as the work progressed. Phil Garratt thought it was a good idea but came

Early artist's concept of the Twin Otter by Bob Bradford. The positioning of the lift struts and engines was later changed. Registration letters used were for the chief engineer at the time, N.E. Rowe. (DHC)

The prototype Twin Otter on its first flight. This aircraft is now in the National Aviation Museum, Ottawa. (DHC Z1040)

The engineering team responsible for the Twin Otter design. Left to right: R.E. Klein, J.B. Houston, W.T. Heaslip, N.E. Rowe, F.H. Buller, P.E. Martin, A.L. Watson, R.D. Hiscocks. (DHC)

manager, and in 1957 to Hawker Siddeley, Montreal, where he rose from plant manager to vice president.

The plant experienced a 5-week strike, which ended in September, a month before the Douglas Aircraft Company took over the DC-9 wing program at Malton (see chapter, "The Changing Times"). It had been a traumatic year, almost overshadowing the test and certification work on the Twin Otter, but there was more to come. In late November George Luesby made another entry in his diary of the engineering department: "On November 22, 1965, P.C. Garratt posted a brief

up with the inevitable questions: "What is it going to cost?" and "Can you find out by next Friday?" It was one more challenge to the seasoned group at Downsview, who had faced this sort of thing before; the old fire was ignited once again! The heads of departments, Bill Houston on pricing, Fred Buller on engineering and Bill Burlison on production, got their people working and came up with a figure of six and a half million in time for the next board meeting.

The board of directors studied the committee's proposal, which was based primarily on the US Army interest. The subject was thoroughly discussed while Phil Garratt sat back listening. He pushed his chair up to the table, looked around the room and raised the deciding question, "Any objections?" The silence in the room dictated the answer, the minutes were recorded, the Twin Otter was on its way.

The one prototype and four pre-production aircraft were to be called the Series I, with a PT6-20 engine and a limiting takeoff weight of 11,000 pounds. By February 1965 final assembly of the prototype was started, and there was enough optimism that a production go-ahead was issued for ten additional machines. On April 29, 1965, a small roll-out ceremony took place, with Sir Roy Dobson, chairman of the worldwide Hawker Siddeley organization, of which de Havilland

was by now a part, joining with the DH directors for an official photograph. Bob Fowler and Mick Saunders tested the aircraft for the first time a month later on May 20, the start of an intensive certification program.

On Friday, May 21, one day after the first flight of the Twin Otter, word came from England that Sir Geoffrey de Havilland had died at the age of 82. In July George Mickleborough resigned and on the 29th of that month a major management change took place. William Benton Boggs, formerly vice president of transportation equipment, Hawker Siddeley, Montreal, was appointed the new de Havilland president and chief executive officer.

"Bill" Boggs was a graduate of McGill University, B.Eng. (Mech.), who served during World War 2 as a squadron leader in the aeronautical engineering branch of the RCAF. He was awarded the OBE in 1944 and went on to be assistant superintendent, maintenance, Trans Canada Air Lines. Successive moves took him to Canadair, where he became production

notice that he was retiring at the end of the year. This represents the end of the 'father' image in the company and is deeply regretted by everyone. He was the stabilizing anchor for the whole organization." Garratt's official retirement was to take place at the end of the year and he would continue as a director with an office in the Hawker Siddeley building in the city.

The Department of Transport certification for the Twin Otter came through on April 7, 1966, and four days later Dave Fairbanks demonstrated the aircraft to a growing airline in the mid-western USA—Air Wisconsin. In September he swung through Boston, New York and the far west, demonstrating the Twin Otter all the way to California. The following month he did a four-day sweep to seven US military bases. Once again the friendly element in the Pentagon showed their continued interest by asking for a quotation on 100 Twin Otters.

The request was hardly in the mail before talk of another competition complicated the issue. Intense lobbying took place in Washington to have the Army rule out the STOL requirement. Suddenly, the takeoff limitations were extended to 2200 feet at 50 feet screen height. These new guidelines allowed a Beech entry and the finalists in the competition were the Beech King Air and the Twin Otter.

The contest narrowed to a battle of prices and, although Bannock pressed for a strongly competitive price, he was no longer in control of the project. With the retirement of Phil Garratt, Bannock did not have the backing he once enjoyed. A new price study turned out to be considerably higher than the King Air. Needless to say, the matter was closed without the usual fly-off.

As with the Buffalo of the same period, the expected orders did not come, even though countless military demonstrations south of the border proved the Twin Otter's performance to Army and Air Force satisfaction. It did not take a clairvoyant to read the message: the days of the large military orders had come to an end.

The game was not lost just because the US military orders died on the vine. The Twin Otter—which some publications referred to as the ugly duckling—was performing beyond all expectations and the price was right for the times. Once again it was up to the sales department to come through. While Dave Fairbanks was demonstrating in North America and Grant

The prototype Twin Otter undergoing float tests on Toronto Harbour. (DHC25004)

Davidson south of the equator, Buck Buchanan made sure that the Twin Otter got to the Hanover Air Show of 1966, with Mick Saunders and Bob Irving as the demo team. Through the efforts of David Price and Laurie Jones of Hawker de Havilland Australia, Trans Australia Airlines placed an order for four which got world sales off to a good start. The good news was followed by the announcement that the Chilean Air Force had ordered five. Sultan Ghazi of Afghanistan was at Hanover and wanted the Twin Otter for his country's landlocked, mountainous terrain. General Air of Germany also prepared to place an order.

Back home the Ontario Department of Lands and Forests backed their early interest by taking delivery of the first Series I machine as soon as it was certified for floats—renewing a historic involvement with DHC that went back to the Moth. Trans Australia Airlines took delivery of serial number 6, now called the Series 100, with a gross takeoff weight increased to 11,579 pounds. In Canada the market began as expected—in the north. "Weldy" Phipps, who was making a name for himself flying small aircraft on oversize tires in the Arctic, placed an order for number 12. Max Ward had been a major customer for the single-engine Otter and constantly needled de Havilland to install two engines. He encouraged the development of the Twin Otter on floats and took delivery of serial number 35 in April 1967. This proved only a starter and, as was the case with the Otter, he

pioneered its use on floats and skis in the high Arctic and was soon back for more.

The bulging order book for the new airplane kept the plant busy, but the change of attitude in the Pentagon was of great concern. Russ Bannock, as director of sales, had been counting heavily on military business for the Twin Otter and he would have to find new customers in the civil field. It was not planned that way, but a new kind of customer developed almost simultaneously for the Twin Otter—the United States "commuter" services.

A New Market

Civilian sales had always been a substantial part of DH Canada business, but from now on they would have to be increased if anything like the existing production volume was to be maintained. The two de Havilland people most involved with the civilian side were Buck Buchanan and George Hurren. Buck held the reins on world marketing while George was in charge of sales throughout Canada, the USA and the Caribbean. When asked one day how de Havilland got into the airline commuter business, Buck's quick reply was, "If you were going to be perfectly honest, you would have to call it luck." To this George added, "Luck and Joe Fugere!"

The story goes back to 1965-66 when the Twin Otter was first exposed to world markets on the air show circuit. The Reading Air Show of 1966 was typical, as United States operators peered bug-eyed through the Twin Otter door and remarked on such a

Joe Fugere (right) and his first Twin Otter with Phil Halsey, manager, customer support. (DHC39860)

large cabin for a 12,500-pound-class airplane. Air taxi services had sprung up all over the US, particularly on the lower California coast and in the busy eastern corridor from New York to Boston. One of the most typical in the New York area was Pilgrim Airlines, headed by Joe Fugere. Fugere was one of the first to size up the potential of the Twin Otter as a commuter aircraft and he became one of its most enthusiastic supporters. This ex-Navy aviator, who had bought out New London Flying Service in 1962, defied the cynics of the day by calling his expanded air taxi service "Pilgrim Airlines" and selling flights from New London to New York/Idlewild. It was a struggle at first but by 1965 his rapidly growing airline needed increased seat capacity. He wanted to buy Twin Otter number 6 but had to settle for a later place on the line. He began his inaug-

C-FAUS, Twin Otter number 34, seen in flight near Toronto. It had recently been refurbished after a career in the US as a commuter. It joined Lambair in 1971 and spent many years operating in northern Manitoba and the Northwest Territories. In this view it's equipped with an oversized nosewheel for Arctic operations. (DHC)

Veteran Series 200 aircraft HH-AIY awaits passengers at a remote airstrip near Jeremy in Haiti in May 1981. This aircraft went into service in the US in 1968, serving in the southern states and in Alaska. It returned to Canada for several years more hard work, then was sold to Haiti Air Inter. (Peter Crampton)

Twin Otter number 586 in the colours of the Fuerza Aerea de Chile approaches to land at Downsview on a predelivery flight, 1978. The Twin Otter has won global acceptance among the military as a utility transport. (F.T. Guthrie and Associates)

ural run with serial number 14, from Groton/New London to New York's JFK International, and was the first to operate the Twin Otter in scheduled service.

Air Wisconsin, which had taken delivery of number 13, also began their scheduled flights on the same day and at the same hour, but the difference in time zones would tend to shade the statistics in favour of Pilgrim. Within six months, these two airlines had taken delivery of their second Twin Otters, which set a convincing precedent in the new short-haul services. Both Preston Wilbourne of Air Wisconsin and Joe Fugere of Pilgrim became respected spokesmen on commuter airline affairs. Fugere was nominated first chairman of the Commuter Airline Association and served three years as a member of the Urban Transportation Advisory Council.

With its 15-20 seats, at a price of just under $300,000, the Series 100 Twin Otter provided an attractive money-maker for the aspiring US commuter lines. Orders from fledgling airline groups began flowing into the de Havilland sales department, where juggling priorities on the order book became the outstanding problem of the day. Competing airlines grew up in the Boston and Los Angeles areas, all using Twin Otters, and a surprising number of orders was coming from small airlines in other countries.

These squat-looking turbines with their distinctive fixed gear were soon being seen in the islands of the Caribbean, in Mexico, Italy and Hawaii. Indonesia started an airline in the jungle with its Twin Otters, as did Afghanistan in their isolated back country. A small French airline, Air Alpes, devised an alpine landing strip on the side of a mountain, bringing customers within minutes from its cities to some of the best skiing hills in the world. The exciting touchdown on the edge of a cliff with an uphill

Search and Rescue threesome. These Canadian Forces Series 300 aircraft formed up for the camera just before their delivery in May 1971. Since then, the Twin otter has served the Canadian Forces as a tough and reliable workhorse at home and abroad with the UN. (DHC)

Air Alpes uses Twin Otters to take skiers to remote locations in the French Alps. Here a Twin Otter is shown on the sloping Alpine runway, and F-BOOH, a Series 100 aircraft, is seen at the chalet. (DHC33494 via Air Alpes, DHC)

run to the ramp soon became routine, as did the departure of the Twin Otters down the slope and off into space, like a mammoth ski jump.

During the years that de Havilland had spent demonstrating their particular brand of STOL, the major effort had been directed to their military customers, particularly the US Army. There were no special rules governing civil STOL when the Twin Otter began carrying passengers and it was regarded simply as a normal category "CAR 3" airplane. No credit was given for the fact that its ground rolls were significantly shorter than other CAR 3 types or that its approach angle had a built-in steeper gradient. The Twin Otter brochures carried two sets of field performance figures, one headed STOL and the other CAR 3, or US Civil Air Regulations criteria for general purpose aircraft. It was sometimes difficult to explain that the airplane de Havilland had designed for a STOL landing distance of 1050 feet (over a 50-foot obstacle to a stop on the ground) was certified in CAR 3 at 1940 feet. Later, under US Special Federal Air Regulations No. 23, the landing distance became 1500 feet. If the airplane could talk, one could imagine it saying to the pilot, "What rules are we working under today, Boss? I can give you three choices." Most operators carrying commercial passengers were dealing with runways of 3000-4000 feet, well above any short-field limitations, so there was little pressure for STOL.

One small airline came into being in the United States because it was able to use the short-field capacity of the Twin Otter. Houston, Texas, had just opened its new International Airport and a group under Jay Seaborn sought to connect the busy Clear Lake/NASA space centre with the new terminal complex and with the old Hobby Airport closer to downtown. They built their own 2500-foot flight strip opposite the manned spacecraft centre, calling it the Clear Lake Metroport, and put four Twin Otters to work on a typical shuttle service. They flew the 32 miles from Clear Lake in 11 minutes and flights between the two air-

ports in 9 minutes. Their aircraft were in the air from 6:00 a.m. until midnight making 75 flights daily and became a familiar sight around Houston International. The short runway concept proved itself from the beginning in their case, and later, as Metro Airlines, their Twin Otters pioneered the new procedure of using special short strips in a quiet corner of the airport away from the big airliner traffic. Metro thus established the first total STOL operation in the United States.

A STOL Showcase

DH Canada is still proud of the Norwegian operation that took the DH STOL concept and built an airline around it. Norway's mountainous shoreline had been a transportation problem for centuries, and although seaplanes had played an important role in recent years, they had their limitations. Widerøe's Flyveselskap A/S had pioneered a successful float service up and down the rocky coast

and helped break the isolation of the scattered coastal communities. The seaplanes showed the Norwegian government the advantages of air transportation, at a time when they were concerned with improving services to remote areas.

The Norwegians were involved in a study of the subject when Mick Saunders and Bob Irving arrived to demonstrate the Twin Otter. They saw the aircraft immediately as the answer to their problem. If the communities would build small landing strips, a specialized air service could be set up which would cut long sea voyages to a matter of minutes. Health services, particularly in emergencies, could be improved and the inhabitants would lose that feeling of isolation from the commercial centres. After they studied the four Norwegian Air Force Twin Otters that arrived in Bodø during 1967, their minds were made up.

While one group began searching for landing sites, the Ministry of

178

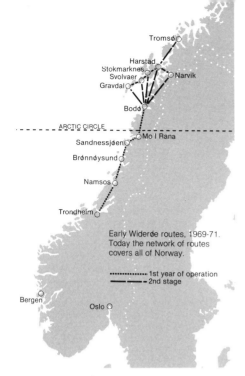

Early Widerøe routes, 1969-71. Today the network of routes covers all of Norway.
.... 1st year of operation
—— 2nd stage

Widerøe's senior pilots take delivery of their first Twin Otter in June 1968. Left to right: Eric Langset, K.F. Baastad and Odd Schyberg. (DHC29372)

The vivid design of the first Twin Otter for Norontair. (DHC36331)

Transport and the Directorate of Civil Aviation prepared an operating structure. They studied the Twin Otter runway lengths and came up with a practical length of 800 meters (2600 feet) which they set as a standard. They even coined their own terminology, calling the system their "short field services." Widerøe's, as Norway's oldest independent operator, was asked to handle the new operation in all areas relating to staff and services. The company was reconstructed with a wider range of shareholding which included local interests and the other airlines in the country—SAS, Braathens SAFE, and Fred Olsen. A practical plan with national unity as the common goal was evolved for the provision of a government subsidy.

On June 1, 1968, a group from Widerøe's and the Directorate of Civil Aviation arrived at Downsview to do some training and take delivery of their first Series 200 Twin Otter. By now the airport plan was completed south of Bodø. The first service was begun linking five communities south to Trondheim. Each field had a paved landing strip, a control tower and a terminal building; each had VASI approach aids, a DME and a localizer. Citizens groups, unlike their counterparts in North America, encouraged the building of airstrips and the provision of fire fighting services. The DCA was represented at each field and the whole well-organized system was tied into the national airlines for everything from weather information to seat reservations.

The Norwegians' thoroughness paid off during the inaugural year 1969 when the lone aircraft, LN-LMN, carried 25,000 passengers and some 300,000 pounds of freight. Their Twin Otter was in the air 12 hours a day, 6 days a week. During this high utilization, which involved 120 landings a week, Widerøe's experienced only a single one-hour delay for technical reasons. Flight cancellations for weather occurred only three days during the first year. The inhabitants along the route were delighted with the service and the farsighted Norwegian government continued planning to project the service north of the Arctic Circle.

Four Series 300 Twin Otters were ordered in 1971 for a new service north of Bodø, linking the isolated Lofoten Islands and the communities along the northernmost tip of Finnmark. The main operations base at Bodø was enlarged, with a sub-base and hangar at Hammerfest, Europe's northernmost city. The maintenance was of the highest order, the pilot training and operating techniques on a par with the major airlines. Step by step the Norwegian showpiece of short field services grew to a total of 35 airports (20 north of the Arctic Circle), using as many as 12 Twin Otters. The aircraft proved equal to the task and laid the groundwork for the larger Dash 7 to follow some years later.

It was not the passenger-carrying aspect alone that provoked the sudden interest in de Havilland's up-graded Otter, for by the end of 1968 seven air forces throughout the world had purchased 25 of them. Also by the end of 1968 seven oil companies had purchased them and many others were leased in the search for petroleum on

four continents. Mining companies eyed the easy transportation the Twin Otter provided in their search for minerals. The International Nickel Company had C-FINB equipped with intricate magnetometer equipment, with so much external rigging that it was soon dubbed the "flying clothesline."

A determined effort by the government of Ontario in 1971, ably assisted by two Twin Otters, started a successful commuter service in that province. It was aptly named Norontair under the Ontario Northland Transportation Commission branch with the goal of linking widespread northern communities. The first two Otters in their garish orange colour with large mauve and white loons painted on the side were operated under a lease arrangement by White River Air Services of Sault Ste. Marie.

The service started by linking Sudbury, Earlton, Timmins and Sault Ste. Marie and soon gained respect for on-time, efficient service. In due course the line expanded to cover the whole of northern Ontario with a new eye-catching paint scheme and more Twin Otters.

As orders tripled and then quadrupled, unprecedented pressure was put on the production department, whose planning had not counted on such an upswing in sales. Additional space was leased back in the old north plant, which began to take on the activity of the Mosquito days. The early figures of Twin Otter production grew from three a month to a peak of ten. The best year by far was 1968 when 102 sales were recorded. Everything about the Twin Otter was working in its favour and encouraging new customers. Its size and self-sufficiency made it useful for photography and fire bombing from the air, for ice patrols and remote supply. Many thought that a nosewheel ski on an aircraft the size of a Twin Otter would be a problem, but soon they were using skis in the Arctic and Antarctic in some of the toughest conditions the world could offer.

With the strike and plant shutdown in 1972, Twin Otter sales dropped to 12 for the year and in the 1975 strike to 34. In 1976 deliveries were up again to 41, including the first two to the US armed services. It was almost a case of history repeating itself when a request for search and rescue aircraft came from Alaska. Back in 1949 it had been Beavers for the US Air Force; this time it was for de Havilland's old customer, the US Army. Two specially fitted Twin Otters (designated UV-18A) went to the Alaska Army National Guard for logistical

flights to remote villages throughout northern Alaska. They had oversize tires for rough terrain and were capable of switching to skis or floats as the occasion required. In presenting the log books to Lt. Col. E.J. Dolan Jr. of the National Guard Bureau, vice-president Doug Annan took the opportunity to recount the long association between the US Army and de Havilland. It was a fitting postscript, one year later, that the US Air Force took delivery of two Twin Otters (designated the UV-18B) for paradrop training at the US Air Force Academy, Colorado Springs. The Twin Otter, which had come into being because of

US military interest, was once again wearing the colours of the US Army and Air Force.

Float Flight to the Amazon
Delivery of three Twin Otters to Peru was one of the most interesting of the many such flights carried out by de Havilland Canada pilots. Departing from Toronto's Island Airport on Lake Ontario the three float-equipped Twin Otters were ferried over a route of more than 3500 miles to Iquitos, on the Amazon River, in Peru. They had been ordered by the Peruvian Air Force—the fourth operator to fly the float version of the PT6-turbine-

Survair's "flying clothes line" Twin Otter on Toronto Harbour. Loaded with advanced electronics, it was used in the airborne search for minerals. (DHC)

A Royal Nepal Airlines Series 300 aircraft waits on a Himalayan STOL strip. The company's fleet is a lifeline for remote villages in one of the world's most inaccessible lands. The Twin Otter shown entered service in May 1971. (DHC)

A Peruvian Twin Otter 200 of Group Aereo 42 on the Rio Marona near Iquitos where it was supporting oil pipeline construction in 1976. (R.J. Fox)

powered STOL airplane, and the fourth military operator.

It was the longest delivery flight ever made by float-equipped aircraft from de Havilland's Toronto plant, although the Peruvian Air Force was an old customer of the company, having operated Beavers in the Amazon River basin for many years. The delivery assignment meant a great deal of advance planning and it soon became obvious that long-range floatplane flights are a rarity these days.

Pilot George Northrop and engineer Harold Williams were assigned to deliver the first aircraft and to remain in the town of Iquitos for a period of training and flight evaluation. Flight operations manager Dave Fairbanks and engineer Ben Cox delivered the remaining aircraft at intervals.

The first Twin Otter got away on Monday, November 13, 1967, and flight-planned for the first logical stopover point, Charleston, S.C. which showed a seaplane base ten miles southwest of the city. The first leg, incidentally, was the longest of the trip—better than 800 statute miles.

On arrival in Charleston it soon became obvious that although the necessary facilities for customs and fuelling existed, they were not geared in any way as a seaplane base. The US Coast Guard came to the rescue by coordinating all the necessary arrangements and countering the many telephone calls that "a plane had crashed into the bay."

Unforeseen delays in obtaining highway approval for airport refuelling trucks and finding a decent road close to the water's edge were only part of the headache. Even the Department of Agriculture got into the act when oranges and other edibles were found aboard the aircraft. And there was a loud moan from all concerned when they learned that two more of the large floatplanes were to follow, requiring similar assistance. But by the time the second aircraft arrived, a kindly barge operator offered his services and greatly eased the confusion.

Next stop was the popular holiday resort of Nassau which has a "seaplane base" in the busy harbour off Bay Street. But many years have passed since the area was used for flying boats and the pilots again found difficulty in refuelling from a tank truck on the shore.

Out of Nassau, the journey was lengthened by the need to fly around Cuba, but a Jamaican Defence Force pilot, George Brown (who had recently taken delivery of his own Twin Otter), organized a suitable strip of beach on the edge of the Palisadoes Airport which could be reached by the regular fuel tender. The procedure worked so well that by the time the second aircraft arrived, Fairbanks was able to receive not only airport control instructions but docking directions from a walkie-talkie on the shore.

A choice of two routes lay ahead after Kingston, one down the Pacific coast through Turbo and Buenaventura and the other following the Magdalena River to Palanquero. The inland route had been recommended,

since turbine fuel was available at the Colombian military base 64 miles from Bogotá. The base was known to have a large river and a ramp that had once been used for floatplanes.

Out of Jamaica, neither the weather reports nor the radio facilities proved reliable. An occasional glimpse of the winding river through the clouds proved the best navigational aid and on the arrival of each aircraft, Palanquero was wide open to receive the Canadian visitors.

If the flight through the Colombian Mountains required a degree of alertness, it was mild compared with the welcome at Palanquero. The town and military base were as expected, but the river at this time of the year was in a state of flood. The rainy season had been reckoned with, but not the debris seen floating down the river.

Northrop and Fairbanks found moderately clear spots to set down, but had to manoeuvre carefully to avoid fully grown palm trees floating in the water, complete with coconuts. The river flow was at least 20 knots and required considerable power from the PT-6 turbines to keep the aircraft stationary against the flood.

When it was learned that the river height would fluctuate during the night, guards were posted to keep the floats secure. The precaution proved timely, for the water had risen five feet by departure time. Fuelling went well the next day, and after another battle with the floating debris, they took off on the final hop to Iquitos.

The mountains surrounding the Colombian capital of Bogotá called for an early climb to 10,000 feet and all three flights were conducted between cloud laters at this altitude until the jungles of the Amazon began to show. Mile after mile of trees and winding rivers pointed to the value of seaplanes in country where the only other travel is by way of slow river boat.

The Peruvian Air Force base at Iquitos provided a welcome sight for the weary Twin Otter crews as they circled the town for a landing. Here the river is wide and inviting and proper facilities exist for the care and servicing of floatplanes.

In the Amazon Delta of South America, the Twin Otters and their crews provide a vital transportation link between the widely scattered communities.

A spectacular photo by Ron Nunney showing one of the early Series 200 Twin Otters for Peruvian service on the Amazon River. (DHC28013)

Twin Otter Variations

It has been stated that the Twin Otter was designed in a hurry to catch the market and take advantage of Pratt & Whitney's new light turbine engine. The aircraft was introduced during a period of rapid change in light transport aircraft in every aspect from navigation avionics to brakes. The Twin Otter kept pace with its competition in the fast-moving commuter trade and improved models followed in quick succession. Each new model was given an identifying number but the changes came so thick and fast that the Product Support Department issued a bulletin on their respective differences.

The prototype and four preproduction aircraft were called the DHC-6 Series 1, had PT6-A-20 engines and a gross weight limitation of 11,000 pounds. The first production series was called the DHC-6 Series 100, approved July 29, 1966,

with the PT6-A-20 and a gross weight limit of 11,579 pounds. These aircraft had very few changes from the Series 1; all had the short stubby nose and they ran from serial number 6 to 115 inclusive. In the Series 200, which started with number 116, a longer nose was the pronounced change, which, together with added space in the rear compartment, doubled the baggage capacity to 126 cubic feet. The PT6-A-20, with its "toothpick" Hartzell propellers and 550 shaft horsepower, was still the powerplant of the 200 series (to number 230) but Pratt & Whitney were working on a version of increased horsepower.

The new P&W PT6-A-27 (25 per cent more horsepower at 5 per cent increase in weight) was the next major change in the Twin Otter line, boosting the speed to 150 knots and allowing a gross weight at takeoff of 12,500 pounds. These aircraft, from number 231 onwards, are known as the Series 300. Aircraft 130 and 210 were also converted to these specifications during the certification program. The most prominent exterior changes were the "paddle blade" pro-

pellers and larger exhaust stacks, and the addition of wing fences and vortex generators on the tail surfaces. There were new seating arrangements and cabin refinements inside while the pilots had improved instrumentation, including automatic feathering switches.

New requirements for emergency exits were introduced in the US for commercial or CAR 3 airplanes, and although the Twin Otter already had five such openings (including the crew doors), DH built two more under the wings and closed off the one in the roof. The new regulation called Special Federal Air Regulation No. 23, governing general aircraft in commercial flying, came in about the same time as the Series 300, which met all the requirements to carry passengers for hire in an approved service. All previous series could be retrofitted with kits supplied by de Havilland. To the casual observer Series 110, 210 and 310 further complicated the numbering — these were Twin Otters that complied with British airworthiness requirements, produced initially for customers in

Australia. French Twin Otters also had special certification which, combined with existing approvals, allowed worldwide coverage outside the Communist countries. One last variant was developed for the Airtransit experimental STOL exercise — these aircraft were called the Series 300S. The S stood for STOL and the aircraft had all the requirements necessary to meet the FAR 25 requirement.

HMCS *Bras d'Or*

Since the invention of the marine screw propeller, engineers have striven to increase the speed of ships in rough seas. In only 60 years, flying has progressed from the Wright Brothers beyond the Concorde to the moon, but ships with displacement hulls have always been limited to a maximum speed by the physics of water. In Cape Breton, N.S., the versatile Alexander Graham Bell was one of the first to reduce hull resistance by lifting it out of the water on "hydrofoils." Indeed in 1919 his *Hydrodome 4* reached a record speed of 61.5 knots on the calm waters of Lake Bras d'Or.

In the 1950s the Canadian Defence Research Board developed hydrofoil craft to explore their behaviour in rough water. Nine years later DRB

scientists concluded that a 60-knot, open ocean, hydrofoil ship was feasible for anti-submarine warfare. The concept was based upon surface piercing foils for simplicity and to provide acceptable ship motions in both the foil-borne attack mode and the long-range hull-borne search mode. The proposal, based upon aircraft technology, was blessed by the British and US navies, which gave moral and technical support to the project.

De Havilland Canada then entered the field with a three-year feasibility and design study, sponsored by the Department of Supply and Services, working closely with DRB researchers and the Canadian Navy. Their concept was based upon a canard arrangement of surface piercing foils to provide stability in all conditions. There were commercial hydrofoils in service at the time but they were limited to sheltered waters. Surface effect ships, such as hovercraft, were being proved in moderate seas but open-ocean use dictated enormous craft of great complexity to cope with steep waves.

At the time the hydrofoil study was awarded to de Havilland the Engineering Department was occupied with the DHC-5 Buffalo. Fortunately some talented engineers were available from

the cancelled Avro Arrow program and a 12-man group was formed under Dick Becker, who had just completed the development work on the CS2F Tracker program. This group, backed by the company's technical resources, set out to assess and develop the novel requirement.

During these studies, craft motions in a random seaway were simulated in Toronto on what was probably the world's largest computer at that time. The simulated motions were checked on the largest of many models, a quarter-scale craft, in the approaches to Halifax Harbour. Other model trials were conducted in Ottawa, Stockholm, New York and London in some of the world's best hydrodynamic facilities. Key features of the design included a steerable superventilating bow foil weighing 7 tons, hydrofoil sections capable of operating at 60 knots and supercavitating propellers capable of absorbing 15,000 horsepower at 1800 rpm.

In 1963 the Defence Department accepted the findings of the study and awarded a design and construction contract to de Havilland for the Fast Hydrofoil Escort (FHE 400), a 200-ton Antisubmarine Warfare (ASW) hydrofoil ship. The study group of

HMCS Bras d'Or

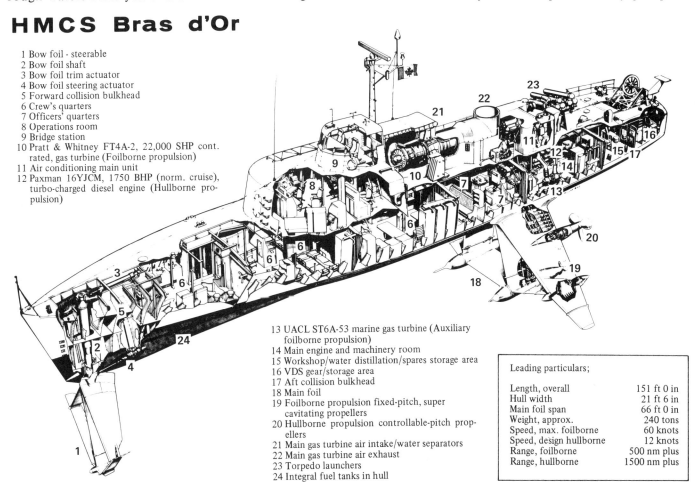

1 Bow foil - steerable
2 Bow foil shaft
3 Bow foil trim actuator
4 Bow foil steering actuator
5 Forward collision bulkhead
6 Crew's quarters
7 Officers' quarters
8 Operations room
9 Bridge station
10 Pratt & Whitney FT4A-2, 22,000 SHP cont. rated, gas turbine (Foilborne propulsion)
11 Air conditioning main unit
12 Paxman 16YJCM, 1750 BHP (norm. cruise), turbo-charged diesel engine (Hullborne propulsion)

13 UACL ST6A-53 marine gas turbine (Auxiliary foilborne propulsion)
14 Main engine and machinery room
15 Workshop/water distillation/spares storage area
16 VDS gear/storage area
17 Aft collision bulkhead
18 Main foil
19 Foilborne propulsion fixed-pitch, super cavitating propellers
20 Hullborne propulsion controllable-pitch propellers
21 Main gas turbine air intake/water separators
22 Main gas turbine air exhaust
23 Torpedo launchers
24 Integral fuel tanks in hull

Leading particulars;	
Length, overall	151 ft 0 in
Hull width	21 ft 6 in
Main foil span	66 ft 0 in
Weight, approx.	240 tons
Speed, max. foilborne	60 knots
Speed, design hullborne	12 knots
Range, foilborne	500 nm plus
Range, hullborne	1500 nm plus

12 expanded in time to 150 engineers and technicians during the detail design stage. Phil Halsey was the first program manager during the early phases of construction of the prototype. Dick Becker became assistant chief designer. Transmission design and construction were awarded to General Electric in Lynn, Massachusetts, as they were the acknowledged experts in hydrofoil transmissions. A 2000-bhp engine turned two quiet controllable-pitch propellers for the hull-borne mode. A 22,000-shp P&W gas turbine drove twin supercavitating propellers at 1800 rpm in the foil-borne mode.

De Havilland designed the ship and built most of the foils and the complex systems, except for the propellers and the hydraulic and electrical components, which were subcontracted. The largest item was the welded aluminum hull, built by Marine Industries, Sorel, Quebec. Special automatic welding machines were built at Sorel to fabricate the huge skin panels from extrusion and plate. Aircraft type subassembly jigs were used for welded frame assemblies. Shipyard skills in handling large components were invaluable in mating the hull to the foils. De Havilland tradesmen and engineers moved to Sorel at this stage for the fitting out and activating of the systems.

A serious fire gutted the engine room in 1966, delaying the roll-out and launch to mid-1968. The cost of repairs used up funds allocated to installation of the fighting equipment (developed by Canadian Westinghouse as prime contractor). A decision was made to defer installation of the integrated navigation and torpedo fire control equipment and the towed sonar until the FHE 400 had shown its paces in the open ocean. A special floating slave dock was built for the hydrofoil. After weighing, aircraft style, at 273,345 pounds, the ship was placed on the dock, launched from the marine railway at Sorel and towed down the St. Lawrence River to the Halifax Naval Dockyard, to the toasts, in English and French, of the Marine Industries and de Havilland teams.

After the party Harry Beffort, who had succeeded Phil Halsey as program manager, returned to other duties at Downsview. Dick Becker became program manager for the sea trials phase and drove the 800 miles to Halifax with the senior engineering staff and tradesmen to set up shop in the Halifax Naval Dockyard. Here the ship was commissioned HMCS *Bras d'Or*, in recognition of Alexander Graham Bell's pioneering efforts. The Navy crew, under their CO, Cdr. Tino Cotaras, had been appointed during the fitting-out phase in Sorel. De Havilland retained responsibility for testing and maintenance during contractors' trials in calm water. Shakedown trials of the systems and late delivery of the foil-borne transmission delayed the start of high-speed trials until April 1969, with Cdr. Gordie Edwards as the captain. On July 9, 1969, he

"flew" *Bras d'Or* at a record speed of 63 knots, exceeding her design speed.

More important were the subsequent rough water trials in typical North Atlantic winter weather—wind, sleet and 15-foot waves. The commander of a nearby destroyer signalled that the 200-ton *Bras d'Or* looked more comfortable at 40 knots than his 3000-ton ship at 18 knots, taking "green ones" over the bow. After a succession of short cruises, Cdr. Edwards arranged to cut the "Halifax umbilical cord" and took the ship on a triangular course to Bermuda and Norfolk, Virginia, returning to Halifax 14 days later. Several thousand people visited the ship in Bermuda. The Norfolk visitors were senior NATO officers and attachés from a dozen countries.

Apart from stress corrosion cracking in the main foil, none of the teething problems were related to the advanced features of this state-of-the-art design. The ship performed as predicted by de Havilland, and the joint Navy, DRB and de Havilland trials team worked well together and had a lot of fun. Regrettably defence priorities changed in the 1970s. The project was literally shelved and the *Bras d'Or* set on its slave dock on the Dartmouth side of Halifax Harbour, where, at the time of writing, it remains.

The FHE 400 hydrofoil *Bras d'Or* as it appeared in the foil-borne mode at 40 to 50 knots. (DHC32572)

Otter 3679 in search and rescue colours typical of the RCAF around 1960. This Otter was later sold to India.

A DHC-4 Caribou in standard US Army paint scheme circa 1960.

Illustrations by D.P. Bromley

A DHC-2 Beaver of the British Army in camouflage paint.

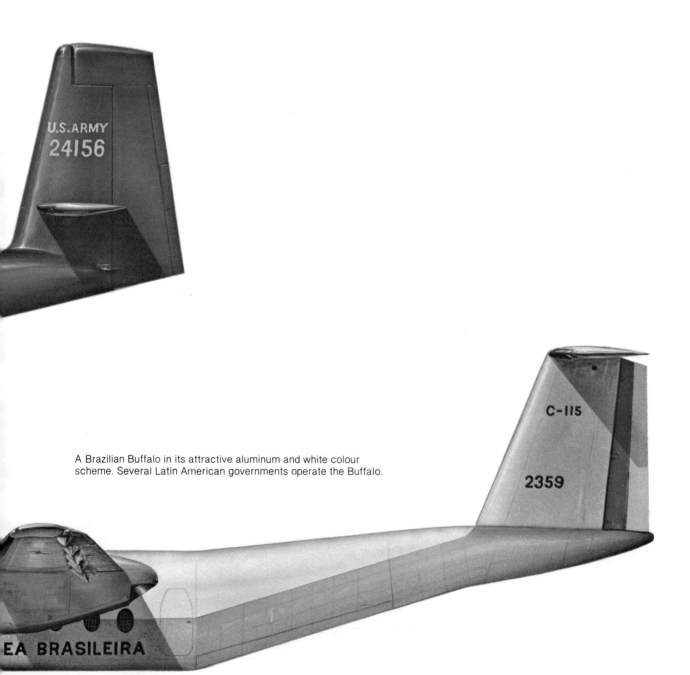

A Brazilian Buffalo in its attractive aluminum and white colour
scheme. Several Latin American governments operate the Buffalo.

In Airline Markings

DHC-6 Twin Otter 300S of Airtransit.

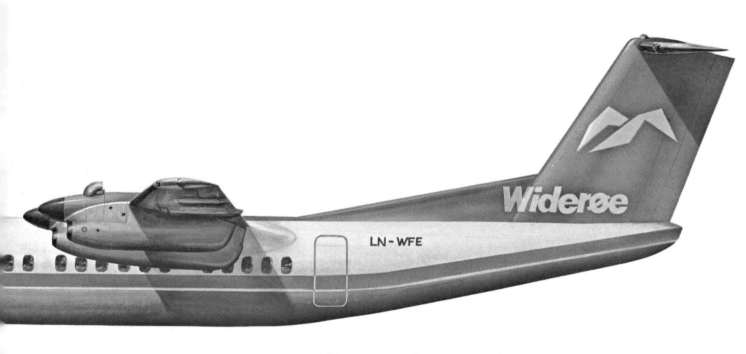

Widerøe of Norway has operated the Otter, Twin Otter and, shown here, the Dash 7.

Norontair is the first Dash 8 customer. It operates a far-flung network across northern Ontario.

Illustrations by D.P. Bromley

Airline STOL

Rio Airways of Texas progressed from Twin Otter to Dash 7 in 1982. (DHC)

In the early days of commercial aviation, when flying was still very much "by the seat of the pants," there were often arguments over which was the best Canadian bushplane. Some aircraft had more horsepower while others had larger wings; all seemed to lift off sooner or later if given a long enough run. Design concepts of the day remained very much the same as the engineers compromised between speed and payload, but World War 2 was to change all that. Aircraft technology advanced in a hurry to the benefit of the entire industry. The airlines profited immensely after the war from the advances in design, and the benefits of this new technology spilled over into general aviation.

The Canadian bush operators who opened the north immediately after the war had to do so with whatever prewar equipment they could acquire. The Beaver brought a welcomed change but some of the old attitudes still lingered: pilots were pleased with the way de Havilland's new bushplane got out of a small lake, but most gave credit to the powerful Wasp Junior in the nose rather than to its aerodynamic innovations. Many oldtimers still felt that the secret of a steep takeoff was to gain lots of speed while still on the runway and that it was compromising safety to operate this new aircraft at low speeds.

The fact that these special low-speed qualities in the Beaver were a design feature was realized early by the US military, particularly the Army. Their experience soon convinced them that the positive low-speed control they were experiencing was not due to

power alone. It became clear that the wing/flap combination and airfoil had much to do with the equation. The Otter, when it arrived, only helped to prove the point, for it had even more aerodynamic advancements.

Other companies were also designing aircraft that would take off and land in short distances and were doing it in a number of ways; and all these aircraft became lumped together in a new category—STOL, for Short Take Off and Landing. The term was not completely descriptive but it did help to differentiate from the VTOL or Vertical Take Off and Landing helicopter. (The word "vertical" is clearly defined as straight up and down, but in the case of STOL the question has often been asked, "How short is short?") The advanced flap design of the de Havilland system had been refined and improved through each successive model until it became a distinctive company trademark. The moving of control surfaces through large angles provided a high level of control with no unorthodox handling characteristics. No new operating techniques are forced on a transitioning pilot with de Havilland STOL and the nosedown attitude with the use of flap even improves his view of the runway.

Metro 66

Demonstrations to the US forces had won orders for the Beaver, Otter and Caribou, after competitive demonstrations. It had taken these small "spectaculars" to sell to the military and it was beginning to look as though a similar show would be needed to convince the world of civil aviation. Up to this point, US military pilots were almost alone in pioneering the art of STOL.

A few of the forward thinkers and airway planners in the USA were also studying short field techniques and could see a practical application to one of their major concerns—congested air traffic at major airports. The leader in this minor crusade was Oscar Bakke, Eastern Regional Director of the Federal Aviation Agency. He held the view that air traffic generated by the commuter airlines, intercity short-haul operations and air taxi flights would soon have to be separated from trunk-line operations. He saw STOL as a possible answer but his promotions and traffic seminars were only receiving lukewarm attention. He realized that STOL was not clearly understood and that a full-scale demonstration was needed to sell the concept. He picked New York City as the site for his showpiece, in what was to be known as Metro 66.

Metro 66 was staged ostensibly to demonstrate aerial support in a disaster-relief situation but, at the same time, to show the feasibility of full-scale passenger operations by air. Bakke's object was to prove that, with all regular forms of transportation disrupted, STOL and VTOL aircraft could give air access to the city centre of New York and so provide logistic support in a major emergency.

Two hundred representatives of the US Federal Government, the New York State Government, and the City of New York gathered in downtown Manhattan on September 5 and 6, 1966, to review one of the most momentous exercises to date in the deployment of STOL utility aircraft. All manufacturers of STOL and VTOL equipment were invited to participate, but de Havilland aircraft provided the largest contingent. George Neal flew

189

the STOLs to use the pier. It delivered 70 passengers in five missions. Governors Island, a mile off the southern tip of Manhattan Island, provided the biggest landing area for STOL aircraft —four baseball diamonds in a row on the East River with a 1900-foot grass area. This was the site of the most spectacular demonstration and the most substantial cargo operation of the exercise. Dave Fairbanks and Norm Paterson landed a 6000-pound, 80-piece field hospital unit in the Buffalo. The unit was subsequently transferred to a Sikorsky S-64 Skycrane, which delivered it in an underslung cradle to the Belleview Hospital in Manhattan.

Consternation was caused by the Buffalo landing in the East River Park. Some residents, seeing such a large aircraft disappearing in a cloud of

The largest of the STOL aircraft in Metro 66 was the Buffalo shown here landing and taking off at East River Park in New York. (DHC25663, 25498)

the Turbo Beaver, Mick Saunders the Twin Otter and Dave Fairbanks the Buffalo. Joe Fugere from nearby New London joined the exercise with his new Twin Otter in Pilgrim Airways colours.

The landing sites included three areas accessible to VTOL aircraft only and four accessible to STOL and VTOL aircraft. Of the STOL strips, Pier No. 26, alongside the Hudson River, was the shortest with 900 feet of runway available. It was also the site on which most attention was centred as it was the type of STOLport Bakke visualized for commercial use. Most of the passenger movements were seen at this location.

Sixty-four missions were successfully flown into Pier 26, during which 300 passengers were brought in from six staging areas, Teterboro Airport, Linden Airport, Flushing Airport, Kennedy International Airport and two military airfields in the New York area. This impressive performance was concentrated into a 3½-hour period on the first day.

The cast of this show comprised Helio Stallions and Couriers, Fairchild-Hiller Turbo Porters, a DH Canada Turbo Beaver and the star performer, the DHC Twin Otter, the largest of

The Twin Otter lands on South Street opposite Roosevelt Drive. (DHC25508)

dust on the baseball diamond, called radio stations to report a crash. But the Buffalo came to a full stop somewhere around second base of the third diamond and took off again, using only half the space available. The only dangerous aspect of this operation was several near-collisions among rubber-necking motorists on the adjoining East River Drive. Just to prove that the landing was quite routine, Dave Fairbanks took the Buffalo in a second time, which movie cameras recorded for posterity.

The next day saw most of the STOL activity concentrated on a 1200-foot strip on South Street, opposite Roosevelt Drive, where turbulence caused by the tall buildings demanded considerable pilot skill. There were 17 scheduled landings and takeoffs from South Street, and again the Twin Otter was the largest aircraft to use the strip, delivering two loads of 14 passengers each.

During the two-day exercise, more than 40 aircraft, including six STOL types and six VTOLs, performed a total of 440 takeoffs and landings at eight different downtown Manhattan sites. In 220 missions, 765 passengers were moved and many tons of cargo delivered. When the results were examined, it was apparent that Metro 66 Airlift had achieved its objective. All operations had been conducted without incident to aircraft, property or operating personnel. It was also noted that the passengers and cargo carried were only a fraction of what could be transported in a real emergency. The exercise opened the eyes of a lot of people to the potential of STOL airports and this was exactly what Oscar Bakke had set out to do in the first place.

The exercise did not provide the immediate results he sought, and the surge of community opposition eventually ended his pioneering. It was only many years later that the use of separated approach patterns and stub runways was realized—in basically the same area where his vision had sown the seed.

It did not take long for New York streets and parks to get back to normal after Metro 66 but the memory of the successful STOL demonstration made a distinct impression on the minds of transportation planners. As air traffic congestion grew in the areas of Washington and New York, so the thinking turned to special airway routings and STOL airstrips. In October

1967 the US Civil Aeronautics Board summoned 16 airlines, nine cities and two departments of the federal government to an investigation of air traffic in the entire eastern corridor from Washington to Boston. The purpose was to explore the use of STOL and VTOL outside the main city terminals using new routes and landing strips. A companion study was begun in Canada by the Department of Transport to link Ottawa, Montreal and Toronto.

Back at Downsview it was "business as usual" with the emphasis in 1967 shifting from engineering to sales. The usual liaison with the US military was maintained but it had become obvious that new customers would have to be found for the Buffalo and the Twin Otter. These export sales started with the order for 12 Buffalos for Brazil, which was soon increased to 24. Production of Beavers and Otters ended in 1967 with deliveries of 19 and 3 respectively for the year. Nine Caribous were exported in 1967 while Turbo Beaver deliveries increased to 13.

Other items of special interest that summer were the July 21 "roll-out" ceremony of the hydrofoil *Bras d'Or* at the dockyards in Sorel, Quebec, and the sale on October 10 of the Special Products Division, as SPAR, to

a group of employees under Larry Clarke. It was during 1967 that Bill Burlison had to retire for health reasons, ending a long and productive career with DHC. On December 5 of that year another major change in top management occurred when Russ Bannock resigned to start a private sales and consulting business in Toronto.

A Downtown Airliner
By 1968 the hearings on the Northeast Corridor study by the US Civil Aeronautics Board were in full swing. They were looking into the feasibility of downtown air service between the major cities from Boston to Washington. De Havilland Canada participated actively in the investigations and two airlines began serious studies. Eastern Airlines' approach was a series of shuttle runs without passengers between Washington and New York using the French 52-passenger Breguet 941. This aircraft had made a favourable impression at the previous Paris Air Show and McDonnell-Douglas were even interested in building it in the USA as the M-D 188E. Eastern demonstrated the Breguet to government officials in Washington at the end of August and carried out six weeks of trial runs, using a newly-built 1095-foot STOL strip at La Guardia Airport as their home base.

American Airlines showed their interest with a slightly different approach. They based their concept on the New York Metro 66 exercise and, mindful of the Buffalo demonstration into the East River park, looked at the de Havilland plans for a civil version of the Buffalo. The exercise on

A model of the DHP 35 proposal that led to the Dash 7. It was to carry 38 passengers and had a fixed undercarriage. The dimensions approximated the present Dash 8. (DHC30683)

the New York pier had convinced them to study the floating STOLport idea and they chose a site in the Chelsea section of the Hudson River. Artists' concept drawings for the project were hardly dry when the citizens group for the "preservation of Chelsea" went into action. They caused such a political clamour that the airline soon lost interest.

The studies at de Havilland for the conversion of the military Buffalo soon shifted to an entirely new STOL passenger aircraft twice the size of the Twin Otter and more in keeping with

the "Corridor" concept. The project received enthusiastic backing from president Boggs and by 1967 had moved out of the preliminary stage to a full-scale product allocation. The project that was eventually to become the DHC-7 emerged in January 1968 as DH project 35. The proposed aircraft had an interesting configuration, which was to change many times.

In its proposal stage, the aircraft started as a T-tailed transport of 26,500 pounds gross weight that would carry 39 passengers over a 200-mile range. Photos of the original model show a novel fixed "grasshopper" undercarriage, and a high wing was to house four PT6A-30 engines of 780 hp each. Planning moved into the product development stage with the financial aid of the Department of Industry, Trade and Commerce and preliminary specifications were reviewed in the light of the latest CAB rulings in the US. Extensive worldwide market studies were begun in late 1968, based on the concept of providing improved interurban and regional air transportation. These studies led to revisions in the specifications of the planned airplane, with an increase to 48 passengers and a gross weight of 38,000 pounds. Throughout the program the performance target was built around 2000-foot runway limitations and an extremely low noise level.

The project moved forward during 1969 with wind tunnel testing at the National Aeronautical Establishment and completion of a full-scale engineering mock-up. Design Engineering finalized the basic lines, the wing structure and the intricate flap geometry. Thousands of drawings emanated from the enlarged drafting department and the undercarriage design reverted to a conventional wide-track, retractable format. An engineering go-ahead was given early in the year and a search made for a manufacturing partner. Early discussions took place with the SAAB organization in Sweden, who were contemplating a similar project. They decided not to proceed and negotiations were conducted with Messer-

schmitt Bolkow-Blohm of Germany on a joint venture basis. No agreement was concluded.

Other troubles were in the offing, for even though the planning went forward with enthusiasm, all was not well in the boardroom at Downsview. Although an extensive sales tour had been launched in September 1969, word came from Hawker Siddeley England in December to shelve the project. Though de Havilland Canada had been a self-sufficient producer of aircraft for so many years, it was still British owned. The de Havilland organization had long since been swallowed up by the giant Hawker Siddeley organization run by astute businessmen whose first responsibility was to their shareholders. Hawker Siddeley had the competing HS-748 and a new short-haul project, the HS-146, that was jet powered and bigger. Continued successes through the years at Downsview had put a distinctive stamp on DH Canada, but they were now muddying the waters of the parent pool. The Hawker Siddeley logo at Downsview had become the symbol of an absentee landlord. Constant directives came from England that they were not interested in a short-haul transport but neither the president nor the Canadian government seemed to pay any attention. As interest in an all-Canadian STOL transport and national STOL policy grew at Downsview, so the British interest waned. Hawker Siddeley had moved the Canadian company out of the small aircraft market by shutting down Turbo Beaver production and were not ready to invest in a STOL airliner. For the first time in 42 years a major difference of opinion had arisen between the parent company and its Canadian branch, and the situation was also beginning to strain the good relationship that had always existed between DH Canada and the government in Ottawa.

All this made life difficult for president Boggs, who was trying to build up the company's capability and was receiving every encouragement from

the Canadian government to launch a new product. The British directors were unable to sway the government but took action by asking president Boggs to leave. They sought a new man to manage the only portion of their empire still bearing the single name de Havilland on its masthead. The official date of Bill Boggs' resignation was May 1, 1970, and Bernard B. Bundesman, who managed sales of the Hawker Siddeley D.H.125 business jet at La Guardia Airport in New York, took over as president.

Bundesman began his aviation career with Douglas Aircraft Company in 1934 and was associated with the Bell Aircraft Corporation in Marietta, Georgia, during World War 2. In early 1951 he joined the Lockheed Company in Georgia and worked his way up to chief salesman on the Jetstar program, which was Lockheed's early entry into the business jet market. "Bundy" was well liked in corporate aviation circles, and when the Hawker Siddeley Group began marketing their D.H.125 in the USA, he was appointed president of Hawker Siddeley International Limited. Of entirely US background, Bundesman moved as a stranger in troubled times to the Canadian branch of a British organization to carry out their directions, which in the final analysis could only be described as "winding down" the company.

The Canadian government stepped in on July 23, 1970, with the announcement that funding would continue on the DHC-7 project until September 30, 1971. The move saved jobs and kept the thousands of engineering man-hours intact. Other changes in this period brought D.N. "Doug" Kendall to the board of directors along with Bill Heaslip, vice president engineering, and Buck Buchanan, vice president sales.

It was during 1970, according to Fred Buller, chief designer, that the STOL concept made its greatest historical step forward. Close liaison with the American Federal Aviation Administration brought the right meeting of minds to produce a clear definition of STOL. De Havilland acted as a catalyst at these meetings to bring on decisions on runway size, approach angle, height over the threshold and a mound of other details hammered out in friendly consultation. By September 1971 the FAA had finalized its decision into Part 298 of the regulations.

An Airtransit Twin Otter over Canada's Parliament Buildings, a few miles from the Rockcliffe terminal airport. (DHC38295)

Other projects at Downsview were keeping everyone busy but there was a feeling of uncertainty at the middle levels of management. The new 300 Series Twin Otter, with improved performance and gross weight, was selling well and even Caribou sales, with the US orders filled, were 295 and climbing. By the end of 1970 the 24 Brazilian Buffalos had been delivered and a new order of 16 obtained from Peru. This was a commendable performance on the part of production and sales, but everyone knew that their future hung on the decisions being made in the engineering department. All their eggs were in one basket with the DHC-7 and the political climate was unsure. The company's stature and its past record were carrying government support for the time being, but how long would it last?

There were very few DHC-7 mile-stones in 1971. Government help was renewed as a Flight Development Project, while full-scale market studies were enlarged. A similar FDP go-ahead for the development of the PT6A-50 engine was given to Pratt & Whitney in 1972, lending support to an all-Canadian engine/airframe combination. Another positive step, announced March 30, was a joint marketing agreement between de Havilland and the Boeing Company of Seattle, Washington. The move came at a crucial point in de Havilland history, for it marked the company's full-scale entrance into the airline market. DH in no way competed with Boeing and there was much to be gained from the expertise of this prestigious manufacturer of big jets.

By coincidence the announcement came as another Boeing/de Havilland project, the augmentor wing, reached an important stage. On May 1 a modified Buffalo with Rolls-Royce Spey engines and a special "blown" wing took to the air for the first time from a 2000-foot strip of Seattle runway. Most of 1972 was complicated by the longest strike in de Havilland's history, lasting eight months. Major sales opportunities were lost but promised deliveries were completed by supervisory personnel. On the brighter side, the year ended with an announcement on October 16 by the Minister of Industry, Trade and Commerce that two pre-production DHC-7 aircraft would be built for test and type certification purposes. No production decision was taken at that time.

Airtransit

Nineteen seventy-three was another year of ups and downs, with the bad news first. Early in April, the US Civil Aeronautics Board was forced to terminate its plans for a Northeast Corridor STOL project, due mainly to strong community opposition to air operations outside the major airports. Locations outside major airports were one of the CAB's main objectives in eliminating traffic congestion. It was a major blow. Planning for a Canadian STOL demonstration linking Montreal and Ottawa was well on by this time and it began to look as though Canada must back her years of STOL experience with her own demonstration of inter-urban transportation. Six special Twin Otters for the Ottawa-Montreal project were delivered by mid-year and work began on two STOLports, one in the old Montreal Expo parking lot and the other on the main runway of the historic Rockcliffe airport.

The STOL service called Airtransit demonstrated a total system concept involving the latest in navigation aids, special traffic control, STOLport management, government regulations and, above all, an aircraft capable of landing within a 2000 foot runway limitation. The six Twin Otters were modified to provide the most complete STOL package possible at the time and were called the Series 300S model. In broad terms they included technical refinements to improve short takeoff and landing capability and additional safety features associated with transport category airplanes (under Part 25 of the FAA regulations).

These were the most sophisticated Twin Otters ever to leave the production line at Downsview. After all, this was a scientific evaluation that would pave the way for the DHC-7; every item had to duplicate the '7 as closely as possible in being "state of the art." Pilots of standard Twin Otters eyed with envy the features in the 300S that could make their work easier: high capacity brakes, an anti-skid braking system, wing spoilers, propeller de-icing, electrical and hydraulic system improvements, emergency brakes, propeller auto-feather time delay and improved power-plant fire protection.

The key to precise navigation and to schedule reliability was the use of sophisticated avionics. The units chosen for the Airtransit demonstration were current off-the-shelf items from leading manufacturers. The detailed selection of navigation aids, including the ground approach method, was the result of a lengthy evaluation by the Department of Transport. The Twin Otter 300S was equipped with the usual avionics for air transport category IFR operation plus dual Collins 109 flight directors. Each aircraft had the latest area navigation system made by Litton Industries, providing pre-planned, card operated automation. Perhaps the most sophisticated feature of all was the microwave landing system, quite new in Canada, called CO-SCAN, designed and built by Cutler Hammer's AIL Division. With this type of guidance the aircraft can select the most appropriate path to the runway and avoid locations on the ground that present obstructions or are highly sensitive to noise.

By combining area navigation with microwave instrument landing systems, and by using a new low-level air routing, the Twin Otters could fly from the runway at Montreal on a pre-determined routing to the runway in Ottawa and remain completely clear of the standard air traffic patterns.

There were numerous delays in starting Ottawa's STOL experiment, caused by everything from strikes to shortages of steel. History even repeated itself: just as the Ontario Department of Lands and Forests had once built hangar doors too small for their Beavers in 1948, so Airtransit duplicated the feat in 1973 for their Twin Otters. This time the doors did not have sufficient clearance for the high Otter tail. Needless to say, the slip-up was soon corrected, and by mid-summer the service was ready to begin.

The two-year, $25.5 million project was handled as a subsidiary of Air Canada, with Gary G. Vogan as president. Walk-in terminals were built at either end of the system. The newly hired pilots were given special training and practiced back and forth between Ottawa and Montreal for weeks before taking on fare-paying passengers.

The interiors of the six Twin Otter 300Ss were furnished in comfortable style with only 11 seats instead of the usual 19. It was realized that these numbers would not be economic but, in the case of seating, the object was to duplicate as closely as possible the coming DHC-7. When the passenger service finally began on July 24, 1974, it was an immediate hit with the brief-case trade in both cities. The flight time was 46 minutes, which, with the minibus time at both ends, brought the downtown-to-downtown time to 1 hour 25 minutes. This compared favourably with the regular airline time of 2 hours and the automobile at 2 hours 30 minutes. An innovation was a one-way fare of $20 including ground transportation.

At first 16 Twin Otter flights were scheduled per day but the response to the service was so encouraging that they were soon boosted to 30. There were the inevitable rush hours and slow weekends, but the load factor, overall, for the first year was 58.2 per cent. The experiment was providing a wealth of data for what was becoming a new Canadian concept of transportation. All eyes were on the project—probably the least concerned was the regular passenger who was getting the kind of service he wanted and let it go at that. The critics looked mostly at the cost figures and scoffed at the limited number of passenger seats. The planners held to their vision of a complete STOL package and did their advanced thinking in terms of a 48-passenger DHC-7. The newspapers had a heyday reporting both sides. When the project ended on April 30, 1976, it had completed all of its objectives and had proven that STOL could operate in the same sky as the major carriers in a complex area like Montreal and do it on a round-the-clock basis. For the forward thinkers the demonstration was an ideal showcase for Canadian technology—a concept pioneered in Canada with Canadian-manufactured aircraft and engines, ready for export.

The Dash 7

In May of 1973 the first engine run of the PT6A-50 was successfully completed by Canadian Pratt & Whitney in Montreal and preparations were

Canada's western operator Time Air uses Twin Otters and Dash 7s throughout Alberta. Their contact with de Havilland goes back to the days when George G. Ross used a Puss Moth in his ranching business. (DHC)

(Below) The Wardair Dash 7 airlifts supplies for a group of scientists a few miles from the North Pole. Photographer George Hunter raised a special flag for the occasion. (George Hunter via DHC)

The Vickers Viscount fitted as a flying test bed for the PT6-50 turbine engine. (Pratt and Whitney Canada)

made to install it on the nose of a Vickers Viscount for air testing. Since its introduction into service in 1964 Pratt & Whitney's PT6 engine had become the world's most popular and thoroughly tested aircraft power plant. As propulsion requirements changed so the models grew in size, even though the basic concept remained the same. The PT6A-50 was planned around the DHC-7 and was a natural evolution of the '40 series. The state of the art in engine manufacture had reached the point where the airframe designer could make some specifications of his own: the '50 engine was an example, for it had a special reduction gearbox to accommodate very low-speed, low-noise propellers. Because of the increased gearbox diameter and large propeller manoeuvre loads, a twin exhaust port was also incorporated. These exhausts were directed upward over the wing to discharge noise and emission away from the aircraft. A host of other improvements included simplified power management and propeller control systems.

In the light of history 1973 was a year of distinct progress. From the early stages of development the new design had been known by the product number DHC-7. On October 1, 1973, it was given the name Dash 7 and from then on all references to the aircraft in promotional material used this designation. The marketing program had been accelerated from the beginning of 1973 and a worldwide sales program began on May 22, 1974. The sales effort for the new plane during this stage was consolidated under one department with Joe

Andrews in charge. Regional teams were formed and the whole effort was coordinated with the Boeing world sales organization. Since the arrangement was made with Boeing in 1972, there had been much exchange of expertise in sales engineering and marketing. The task of promoting a new type of aircraft into a sceptical market was a challenge for both companies and de Havilland profited immensely from the arrangement, which continued into 1981.

As de Havilland moved into the 1970s, all major head office directives still came from England, usually during the visits of Sir Arnold Hall and Stuart Kennedy. Toward 1973 talk of selling the company grew to the point where a price was negotiated with the Canadian government and a deadline set of June 28, 1974, as part of continued Dash 7 funding.

To the surprise of a few, and possibly even Hawker Siddeley itself, the Canadian government exercised its option on May 27, 1974, to purchase de Havilland Canada outright and began similar negotiations for the purchase of Canadair Limited.

With de Havilland Canada now wholly Canadian-owned and a major government investment involved, there was less doubt about the future of the Dash 7. Work proceeded at full speed and the program began to acquire considerable momentum by the end of 1974. Pratt & Whitney delivered the first PT6A-50 engine in September, followed by the DHC directors' approval on November 26 of a production launch involving 25 aircraft. By this time the first pre-production aircraft was on its feet and ready to move. By Christmas of 1974 it went into the paint shop for a colour scheme similar to the Airtransit Twin Otters. The orange-red Dash 7 made its public debut February 5, 1975, when the Honourable Alastair Gillespie, Minister of Industry, Trade and Commerce, unveiled the "Quiet STOL Airliner" to 600 guests. It was a colourful affair with a certain amount of drama as a curtain was drawn and floodlights revealed the glistening aircraft. One of those attending the unveiling ceremonies, who had more than the average interest, was flight operations manager Dave Fairbanks. In his war days and his commercial flying career, Fairbanks had won a reputation as a skilled flyer and brilliant demonstration pilot. He had been scheduled to go to

Ethiopia that week to promote an Otter sale but had bowed out because of a medical appointment in Toronto. He had been working closely with the Dash 7 design team and taking part in the cockpit layout discussions. He was looking forward to this new aircraft after his years of demonstrating the previous types. His Caribou world flights, his Farnborough demos and the Buffalo landings in the New York park were just a few of his accomplishments with DHC.

He stood at the door as the crowd gathered for the Dash 7 ceremony, greeting friends and acting the part of company host. He circulated during the display of the aircraft and joined the crowd for the cocktail party that followed. Another of his specialties was playing the piano, although he never performed professionally, and he was prevailed upon this evening to sit down and go through his lively routines, completely by ear. To those who knew him, his showmanship at the keyboard matched his flair in the cockpit.

When he reached home that night there was a message from his doctor, who had been trying all evening to contact him. The message read, "Report immediately to the hospital." His tests indicated that he had suffered a recent heart attack. Fifteen days later David C. Fairbanks, war ace and world flyer, was dead at the age of 52.

The Dash 7 Flies
Other dates will be added to the chronology of the Dash 7 but none more important than the first flight on a cold, bright afternoon, March 27, 1975. DH Canada test pilots Bob Fowler and Mick Saunders were on board with flight engineers Jock Aitken and Bob Dingle. The onlookers that day were almost all employees who were used to STOL and expected a short takeoff: what they had come to witness was the extremely quiet noise level. As C-GNBX-X climbed high for its 2 hour 20 minute test flight, the only noise came from the Twin Otter flying photographic chase with flight operations manager George Neal and chief photographer Ron Nunney aboard. Extensive test flying began immediately and the second prototype joined the program on June 26.

By the fall of 1976 the aircraft had accumulated 1000 test hours and the Ranger reconnaissance version was announced at the Farnborough Air

Show. Another big day was May 2, 1977, when the Department of Transport Chief of Airworthiness, Ken Owen, presented the type approval certificate to de Havilland's Dash 7 project engineer, G. Ron Jackson, in a ceremony at Downsview. One month later the first production aircraft was rolled out at a family day gathering of employees.

In June of that year the number 1 demonstration Dash 7, C-GNBX, made its international debut at the 32nd Paris Airshow. It performed from June 1 to 12 in the flying display and introduced hundreds of people to quiet STOL. It left immediately after the show for a tour of the European air transport industry. To France, Turkey, Greece, Yugoslavia, Norway, Sweden, Denmark and England it travelled, giving show flights and demonstration rides to a cross section of the industry. In England it concentrated on the small feeder-line runs and headed for an important demonstration trip to Scotland's North Sea oil installations. Twin Otters were already operating in the area and Loganair's chief pilot, Ken Foster, accompanied Tom Appleton on a four-airport tour of the area. Bad weather complicated the day's flying with fog, rain and hail. It put both the crew and aircraft to the test and served to show off the '7 to even greater advantage than was intended. Two important demonstrations were completed in Iceland and Greenland on the return to Downsview, where they arrived on July 25. During the 55 days away, the airplane flew over 160 hours, completed 200 flights in 11 countries and carried nearly 4000 passengers. A look at the press reports when the flight was finished revealed that the Dash 7 was, as hoped, being regarded not merely as "another turboprop replacement" but with its quiet operation and short runway performance, as a new concept in short-haul transportation. By the end of 1977 Rocky Mountain Airways' first Dash 7 was in Denver, Colorado, preparing to begin commercial service and three more deliveries were in the preparation stages.

The Proving Ground
For every new type of aircraft there is still much selling to be done, even though the company product record has been good. De Havilland had proven the short landing and takeoff

concept with the Beaver and Otter lines and had shown that the technique could be applied equally well with big aircraft such as the Caribou and Buffalo. For the most part their experience lay in military STOL, but now their latest product was in the most sophisticated form of all, a 50-passenger pressurized aircraft designed specifically for short-haul airlines and conforming to the most stringent civil regulations. The first sales drive had revealed a wait-and-see attitude among the carriers. The argument often heard was "Who needs the extra cost of STOL —We always have lots of runway."

The de Havilland/Boeing sales effort from the beginning was twofold. It had to promote the idea of STOL itself, along with the hardware capable of small field operations and the use of secondary runways. The aircraft had to meet all the tough airline standards of round-the-clock operations, including dispatch reliability (the percentage of scheduled flights completed without a mechanical delay exceeding five minutes). The order book was slow in filling as the Dash 7 approached certification; a convincing display would be needed from those early airplanes. Gone were the experimental exercises of Metro 66 and Airtransit, the meetings on regulation and instrumentation. The airline world would be watching the first customers.

It was not by luck alone that the first four operators of the Dash 7 were ideally suited to demonstrate the aircraft. It was a natural phenomenon of free enterprise. All had used the Twin Otter before and simply expanded their operations because a new, bigger and better product existed. Rocky Mountain Airways had pioneered the use of the microwave landing system and short runways in the mountain resorts around Denver with six Twin Otters. They projected the '7 into identical route structures, descent patterns and short runways with a minimum of effort. Spantax Airlines of Spain was the second operator with a distinctive short-haul operation that it had pioneered with one Twin Otter. Wardair, which had set a new standard of northern transportation in Canada with their Twin Otter fleet, took on an even broader range of activity with their first cargo/passenger Dash 7. The fourth '7 went to the oil fields of the Middle East with Emirates Air Service, a specialist service requiring

short hauls and coping with a wide variety of runway conditions. The question of how such a big aircraft could pay its way in each environment was uppermost in everybody's mind but improved overall economics emerged in all cases.

Rocky Mountain Airways' president, Gordon Autry, had watched the aircraft's certification process during 1975-76 with interest; all the advance figures told him it was ideal for his competitive Denver-Aspen resort run. He placed an order for the first delivery position and, as soon as it could be arranged, the demonstration aircraft went to Denver to verify his calculations. Autry took delivery of serial number 4 in a special ceremony on January 18, 1978, and began the first Dash 7 revenue service on February 3.

To this established carrier with extremely short runs and a tight time schedule, dispatch reliability was a major challenge. The route, the Talar microwave landing system and the steep approaches to the short runways had all been proven. Now it was time to establish what the first aircraft from the production line might manage in the way of reliability. President Autry made the point in his first report to de Havilland that, although he had to introduce the Dash 7 into service during the busiest month of the year, he was able to start with a dispatch reliability of 98.5 per cent —including all the variables of the learning curve. By October that same year Rocky Mountain reached 100 per cent dispatch reliability while operating 9.9 hours a day, 7 days a week, with very short stage lengths. It was exhilarating news for the DHC engineers who had been plugging tirelessly with that goal in mind, but they were quick to credit the outstanding work of the Rocky Mountain staff under Autry and his director of maintenance, Dennis Wells.

During the first year of operation, the aircraft made a total of 4250 flights with an average flight time of 40 minutes. After the first seven weeks, Rocky Mountain ordered their second Dash 7 and took an option on a third. After exactly one year of operations, in December 1979, they took delivery of their second machine and were the first airline to have two Dash 7s in revenue service. Their successful pioneering in the short-haul transport field won them the Air Transport World

Wardair Canada took delivery of the first Dash 7 to be operated in Canada at a ceremony on May 23, 1978, with a replica of the first Ward Fox Moth close by. (DHC46461)

Award as "Commuter Airline of the Year."

The Dash 7's third customer, Wardair Canada, was another experienced operator of Twin Otters which had updated the old term "bush flying" and proven that it could be done on a large scale through modernization and organization. Serial number 7 was the first Dash 7 to go into service in Canada and the circumstances could not have been more appropriate. The operator was one of the company's best customers and the aircraft was to be named after one of Wardair's pioneer pilots, Don Braun, who had done much to establish the Otter and Twin Otter in the north. Max Ward accepted the aircraft in a ceremony at Downsview on May 23, 1978, with Mrs. Braun performing the christening. It went north to work out of Yellowknife and, after the training and certification flights, flew its first revenue mission June 20. The company's target for a profitable northern operation was 200 hours per month, so the two crews under chief pilot Dave Watson had a formidable challenge.

The first revenue flight, to a number of Alberta airfields, carried an advance party of officials planning the royal visit by Queen Elizabeth in July. The next, on the 23rd, was a charter taking foreign diplomats on tour through the high Arctic. On July 31 the royal tour began with Queen Elizabeth, the Duke of Edinburgh and Prince Andrew. Dave Watson, Wardair's northern

operations manager, was captain on the flight, which involved ceremonial stopovers at Peace River, St. Paul, Lloydminster, Vegreville and Namao in Alberta.

With the glamour events over it was time to begin cargo operations and start the Dash 7 living up to the Twin Otter reputation. The inaugural exercise was ideal for such a test as it involved an all-freight contract from Yellowknife to the Echo Lake copper and zinc mine on the shores of Great Bear Lake. The contract involved flying general freight in and returning with containers of mineral concentrate. The unpaved airstrip was 3000 feet long, or DC-3 length. The Dash 7 was soon going in and out with maximum payloads of 12,000 pounds (double the DC-3 payload) and making ten round trips a day. The operation into Echo Lake went off without a hitch.

Another unique proving exercise came in the summer of 1979 with a contract to fly to the North Pole for the Department of Energy, Mines and Resources. There was a time when such an exercise would have warranted headlines but in 1979, for Wardair Canada and the Dash 7, it was routine. The Earth Sciences Division of DEM&R were placing 50 Canadian scientists and others from the USA and Norway as close to the Pole as possible. They were to spend two months working on a series of projects named Lorex 79 and were to be serviced by Canadian Forces Hercules doing LAPES (Low Altitude Parachute Extraction System, formerly called LOLEX) supply drops. Dr. Hans Weber was in charge and

went north in March with one of Bradley Air Service's Twin Otters to prepare a site. They found a patch of level ice about 800 yards long and 60 yards wide, just right for the Dash 7, and prepared to set up camp. It was Wardair's job to bring in the original base camp.

The Dash 7, with two crews under Dave Watson, arrived at the Canadian Forces base at Alert, N.W.T., and began operations during the period of 24 hours of daylight. They remained 11 days and flew 19 round trips of 2½ hours each from Alert to the polar ice strip, with routine 25-minute stopovers on the ice runway. On the final trip the crew positioned themselves directly over the Pole and, just for the record, did the first round-the-world Dash 7 flight before returning home to Yellowknife. Once again the '7 with *Don Braun* on the nose came through with a "no snag" report, ready to take on its next northern conquest.

In four different parts of the world and in a wide variety of uses the '7 established itself in a matter of months. The air transportation community had indeed been watching; the flow of orders began. Rocky Mountain's convincing display and deregulation of the industry in the USA brought back an earlier de Havilland customer, Air Wisconsin, and a few new names. The Canadian Forces took two for use in Europe and the order book soon took on the international scope associated with the Twin Otter. The airplane that had weathered so many political storms shrugged off early media criticism and simply went out and proved itself in its own element—the skies and short runways of the world.

The Changing Times

The British de Havilland board of directors after the retirement of A.S. Butler. Left to right, rear: F.E.N. St. Barbe, W.E. Nixon. Front: C.C. Walker, Sir Geoffrey de Havilland and F.T. Hearle. (via British Aerospace)

For over 30 years DH Canada lived under the proud banner of the British company, steeped in the prestige of Sir Geoffrey de Havilland (knighted in 1944) and his associates. The family image that Phil Garratt encouraged at Downsview was simply a reflection of longstanding company philosophy that went back to the days of the Moth. The pattern of DH management throughout the world was as remarkable as the organization itself,

One of the first postwar overhaul projects was a Catalina for the Royal Netherlands Navy for use in the Dutch East Indies. (via L.B. Best)

for it grew from a set of old-fashioned values. It was not the later style of space-age aviation but it was ideally suited to the period. These happy circumstances could not last forever, but while they remained few appreciated the uncluttered nature of the system at Downsview.

Martin Sharp, in his book *"DH, An Outline of de Havilland History"*, summed up the parent company's relations with its offshoots in one sentence: "The central policy for each of the overseas companies had always been to serve aviation in the land of its adoption." The same view continued through the war years. Frank Stanley, DHC's man of finance in the 1950s, described this parent/branch relationship after the war: "The parent company never expected any returns

from us," he said, "and resisted the efforts of British banks to acquire Canadian profits. DH England made loans to us from time to time and were repaid, but held the policy of ploughing profits (whenever there were any) back into the next design project. Their aim was self sufficiency, not a source of head office revenue."

"The annual meetings with England were simplicity itself," recalls Russ Bannock, "and more like an annual family reunion. Whoever was over from the Canadian board would report on the year's work. Sir Geoffrey and his directors would ask questions, offer advice and that would be it. We would touch base with their sales group and ask a few questions of our own. It was always a very productive session."

While attention in Canada was focused in the postwar period on the manufacture of large passenger aircraft and jet fighters—particularly Avro's delta-wing Arrow—Phil Garratt was moving de Havilland Canada along an unspectacular path almost of his own choosing. He used to enjoy a walk through his plant and complained once that the place was getting too big; he did not know everyone any more. On one such trip he recognized one of the sweepers and asked about the man's health. "My health's fine, Mr. Garratt," he said, "but they tell me I must retire next month due to my age. Is there anything that can be done, sir?" Garratt dropped in to see Frank Stanley on his way back to the office and argued the sweeper's case. His reasoning was simply that the

By the late 1940s a wide variety of overhaul work filled the hangars at Downsview. (DHC257)

man would be able to sweep the stairs just as well next year as this and it did seem a little unfair when the man wanted to keep on working. Stanley sympathized but suggested that the only option would be to make the sweeper assistant to the general manager.

The Overhaul Business

As manufacturing built up in the mid-1950s, the volume of overhaul work fell. The Tracker project and the expanded effort on the Caribou placed

heavy demands on the staff and facilities. The company had weathered its first strike and work was proceeding at an unprecedented rate in comfortable new quarters.

Routine and uninspiring as overhaul work may have been, the revenue from these contracts was responsible for DH Canada's healthy recovery after the war. Fairchild, by comparison, attempted to bolster its return to civil aviation with pre-fabricated housing and went out of business in 1948.

The overhaul of Catalinas at Toronto Island in 1946 led to a steady flow of similar Canso work, which was the backbone of the overhaul program for the next ten years. The Canso line started with six conversions for the Danish Air Force. Canadian Pacific Airlines needed four for northern Quebec and war hero Johnnie Fauquier needed two for mining exploration. Rexco had one outfitted for South America and another was fitted out in a de luxe configuration for Richmond Exploration. Eleven were converted for the RCAF, and so it went until 74 of the big Consolidated boats had been refurbished.

Twenty-six North American Harvards went through the shops in 1948-49, along with two rare birds, a Fair-

child 71C bushplane and a Vickers Valetta. From 1951 to 1954, 50 Avro Lancasters were overhauled while 16 others were modified. The Grumman G21A Goose was much in demand for executive conversion and four were completed. Eight Douglas DC-3s received complete overhaul as did 10 of the Canadair CL-2 North Stars. A North American B-25 Mitchell went through the shops along with a total of 13 Noorduyn Norseman Mk.IVs.

The move by the RCAF in 1948 to obtain 86 of the D.H.100 Vampires put the company into jet maintenance. The whine of jet engines was new to Toronto but, with all the assembly and overhaul taking place at Downsview, jet flying in the area became routine. Russ Bannock flew the first Vampire to arrive in Canada for the RCAF in February 1948 and the DHC test pilots became one of the first civil groups in Canada to enjoy the prestige of pure jet propulsion. From 1949 to 1956, 71 Vampires went through their overhaul cycles at Downsview and 60 received 400-hour

A detailed look at the Beaver's wheel/ski arrangement. (DHC)

A Bradley Air Services Beaver with its over-sized tires for Arctic use. This tire was developed by Weldy Phipps in the late 1950s. (K.M. Molson)

Agricultural chemical spray tank installation for Beaver use. (DHC)

Beaver conversion done in Australia in 1968 by Aerial Agriculture. A Garrett TPE 331-61 was fitted, along with a new tail. After tests, the Beaver was reconverted to standard configuration. (Peter Ricketts via Peter Keating)

Polish PZL-3S engine Beaver conversion done by Airtech Canada of Peterborough. First flown by Paul Hartman in September 1982, the -3S Beaver offers operators attractive possibilities. (K.M. Molson)

One of Airtech's 600 hp PZL-3S Otters in flight. Airtech has a 1000 hp Otter conversion in the planning stage. (via Airtech Canada)

inspections. By the time overhaul work dried up in 1956, a total of 340 aircraft of 15 types had been processed.

Beaver 1000

On November 10, 1956, the entire company joined in a happy ceremony to present Beaver number 1000 to "the Boss" in recognition of his years of leadership. The registration carried his initials, CF-PCG. During the preliminaries leading up to this gala occasion, Phil Garratt was asked what colour he wanted on his personal aircraft. The reply was a typical Garratt quote: "You can paint it any colour you like as long as it is yellow!" One year later the parent de Havilland company paid him a similar honour with a full directorship in the British company.

Garratt was typical of the old school that managed with a "father" image, a firm hand and an adroit smile. Responsibility charts were not for him, and when asked for his methods, he said simply, "I run the company and my managers can come and see me at any time." Bill Burlison was a typical manager of the period who was in charge of all production. "There was no one between Mr. Garratt and myself," recalled Bill, "and he made it clear I could go to him any time I liked. This was quite true, but you can be sure I checked everything out at my own level before I would dare call on him for a decision. Only Phil Garratt could make such a system work!"

It was not a period of marathon meetings. Most of the important decisions were made over the big round table in the directors' dining room. Often when an awkward situation arose, Garratt would invite the participants to dinner at the Granite Club and by morning the problem would usually be settled. He tried to keep everything simple and was a great believer in the personal approach. He discouraged any memo of more than a page, and when someone once offered to lend him a book, his quick reply was, "But I have a book."

In May 1957 an interesting experiment was conducted at Downsview for the US Army under a contract to test a "spy plane" Otter. The object was to obtain complete silence and involved a large, five-bladed, fixed-pitch propeller. It didn't have the performance of the standard propeller (in

Beaver and Comet 1 on the ramp together at Tokyo in 1951. Bruce Best arranged for this photo session, flying over from Korea to meet the Comet. (US Army)

Beaver No. 1000 shown over downtown Toronto in 1956, was registered CF-PCG and presented to P.C. Garratt for his personal use. (DHC4636)

During the first stages of the quiet Otter experiments an outside exhaust system was used. Later a silencer inside the cabin was combined with the five-bladed propeller in this US Navy research program. (DHC5207)

An early radar experiment for the US Army had pods on each wing of an Otter for 360-degree surveillance. (DHC6292)

fact it was very restricted) but with the exhaust muted in a series of noise dampeners the aircraft was exceedingly quiet.

George Neal and Bob Fowler flew the test series and described the uncanny silence both inside and out. There was no sound but the internal clatter of the engine, a sound that is usually well hidden in the regular configuration. The propeller, though interesting, never went past the experimental phase. In a companion exercise about the same time, a special 360-degree radar installation was tested in a US Army Otter involving two radomes, one on each wing.

Life in the engineering department during the 1950s was also uncluttered, as is shown in veteran George Luesby's notes of the period. Luesby headed the drafting department from the war days and kept an interesting diary of engineering highlights. "The design team had become quite cohesive," he wrote in a summary of the times, "and all had a complete understanding of each other's capabilities which contributed to a productive output. The computer had not yet been introduced; the manufacturing and skilled trades had the flexibility to permit rapid changes with a minimum of paper work. Moreover, the management heads were 'gentlemen of the old school' in every respect. That applied to the parent company and here in Canada, where exercise of the humanities was combined with their foresight and good judgment. It permeated down through the whole organization and the success of the products was a reflection of the people involved."

This was the family atmosphere that prevailed at Downsview up to 1958, with the entire aviation industry in Canada on a decidedly upward swing. The advent of the Caribou was almost overshadowed by the high-profile Avro Arrow a few miles away at Malton, but de Havilland felt comfortable in its STOL niche. It felt confident in the move to larger aircraft for it was basking in the success of its previous types. The Chipmunk trainer was now with seven air forces and numerous civil schools. The Beaver was making a name for itself in the Antarctic, where three newly discovered features — a glacier, a lake and an island — had all been named after it. The world press was telling of the Otter that flew non-stop across Antarctica, over the South Pole. Grumman Trackers were being delivered regularly to the Royal Canadian Navy. All these successes seemed to reach a crescendo on the day the Caribou was demonstrated to the press — things had never gone so well. These were heady days in the Toronto area for all who laboured in the manufacture of aircraft. The end was to come abruptly on February 20, 1959 — Avro Canada's Black Friday.

Black Friday
The gloom and doom that followed the cancellation of the Avro Arrow program has been told and retold with varying degrees of emotion. The traumatic effect on the industry as a whole was to continue well past the first stage of shock; few escaped some part of the Arrow backlash. To the remaining Avro officials and skeleton staff at Malton, the job of putting the corpse to rest was depressing in the extreme. Here was a large plant with the potential for high technology, coupled with a production reputation that went back to the days of World

Sir Roy Dobson, the dominant man at A.V. Roe of Manchester, England, became the head of the Hawker Siddeley world empire. (Hawker Siddeley Canada Ltd. 38129)

War 2. How could it be brought back to life?

The sonic boom of the Diefenbaker edict halting the Arrow was felt on both sides of the Atlantic and particularly in the boardrooms of the Avro empire in England. They had enough problems at home to deal with and simply told Malton to find something to do — anything. It was not the most inspiring assignment in industrial Toronto, moving into the competitive trades of pots, pans and home hardware. Boat construction was started with little enthusiasm and less success. The once-proud Avro had been dealt a mortal blow. The whole industry mourned.

Dramatic events in the aviation industry seldom go singly, as was soon to be seen at de Havilland Canada. The shock of the 14,000 layoffs at Malton was still a topic of conversation when the first US Army Caribou ploughed pilotless into the woods near Uxbridge. The backing of the de Havilland empire was needed in the months that followed to fend off financial disaster and put that project back on track. During the next two years, while both Toronto companies were adjusting, the Avro and de Havilland parents back in Britain were facing another kind of problem.

The British Labour government chose this critical time to overhaul their country's aviation industry with a program of amalgamation. The long-standing names of Avro and de Havilland would soon disappear from the scene and be swallowed up by 1966 in one giant company under a new banner — Hawker Siddeley Aviation. Both remained for some time as the Avro Whitworth Division and the de Havilland Division but the rationalization project soon combined them under one management following the recommendations of the British Defence White Paper. Sir Roy Dobson, the former Avro head, was ultimately in charge of the whole organization.

Although Canadians had no part in the rearrangement of British aircraft manufacturing, the repercussions were felt in the Toronto area for years to come. Hawker Siddeley soon became a diversified group in Canada of which aviation was only a part. De Havilland Canada was allowed to keep its name as a member of the group but was now only one spoke in a much bigger wheel. Avroites in their haughty moments had often called de Havilland Canada the "box factory" in reference to postwar Fox Moth production. Since the days of the wooden Fox, however, Downsview had forged a new identity for itself with its successful bushplanes. After the cancellation of the Arrow many Avro specialists made their way to de Havilland, where they were welcomed into the expanding work force. The Grumman Tracker contract was a financial success and Caribou sales were now in high gear; the situation at the bank, under the watchful eyes of George Mickleborough and Frank Stanley, was the best it had been in years.

Engineers to Britain
During 1959 contracts for US military Beavers and Otters had come to an end and Caribou costs grew to the point where cutbacks were made in the engineering department: the staff fell from a high of 400 in mid-1958 to a low of 225 in December 1959. In England the D.H.121 Trident was in the early design stages and the parent company requested engineering help from Downsview. The group from DHC, under M.C.W. "Mike" Davy, left Canada in November and included K.J. Bullock, G.B. Jackson, G.A. Hilliam, Tony Liddell, A.J.W. Melson, Bill Snyder and Allan Skeggs. They took on an assortment of tasks but most worked on the empennage area of the Trident. They remained a year in England and returned in time to take part in the installation of the T64 turbine engine in the DHC-4 Caribou.

Another request from England about the same time involved tool processing and coordination for the manufacture of the D.H.125 business jet. DH Canada's manufacturing engineering section sent Bill Simpson, Gordon Hogan, Derek Thoms, Roy Hickman and Tom Salsbury on loan to assist in the project.

A Caribou demonstration tour was launched during October to December 1961 into every country in South America but Bolivia and Paraguay. George Neal was captain of this trip with John Shaw as first officer. Ben Cox and Bill Kavanaugh were the engineers and Buck Buchanan was in charge on the sales side. Though the tour went well no Caribou sales resulted because everyone was awaiting the emerging turbines, but it paved the way for later products. With turbine Twin Otters, 100 sales resulted in a 12-year period. Three were presidential aircraft, and Peru had the largest Twin Otter floatplane fleet in the world with a total of 17. Argentina, alone, took about 20 Twin Otters.

The Thin Edge of the Wedge
If ever there was an opening line, "There I was minding my own business," it applied to the next round of events to confront Garratt and company at Downsview. It was mid-1962 and Sir Roy Dobson was in Canada for a critical board meeting. Things had been going poorly at Malton and the problem of what to do with the Avro plant was high on the agenda. Sir Roy's style was not the easy-going manner of Sir Geoffrey, nor did Hawker Siddeley follow the pattern of DH England which left the Canadians very much on their own. A tough new policy had come to Downsview and a wily, freewheeling leader was now in command. The subject of the Malton plant was not mentioned at the morning meeting — it was in the dining room later that things began to happen.

After the pre-lunch refreshments had been measured out, Sir Roy, gazing across the 96 acres of de Havilland property, opened the inevitable conversation.

"Garratt," he said abruptly, "I want you to buy Avro."

Garratt looked at the ice in his drink as he thought for a moment and replied, with his usual grin, "How much?"

All ears perked at the sight of a couple of masters at work and Dobson replied with two words in his broad Yorkshire accent, "Book value!"

There was silence for a few moments and, as if on cue, Frank Stanley said in a meek voice, "And what is 'book value,' sir?"

Once again, after a slight pause, Sir Roy launched a leading question: "How much do you have in the bank?"

This proved a critical point in the conversation because the director of finance had to admit to a healthy balance of $12.5 million.

"That's 'book value'!" said Dobson and the deal was closed.

Once the sale was consummated and Dobson back in England, management had to decide what to do with their new investment. The boat building enterprise at Avro was not going well and by now sparrows were the only things with wings in the empty bays at Malton. De Havilland, the once humble "box factory," suddenly found itself in the driver's seat with more power than it had ever expected or wanted.

A July 1962 editorial in the respected *Aircraft* magazine put the change of owners at Malton in perspective:

"FULL CIRCLE: The news early this month that the de Havilland Aircraft of Canada Ltd. was taking over the Malton facilities of Avro Aircraft brought to an end — just 16 years and 7 months after it started — the meteoric career of the Malton-based company.

"The principle reason for Avro Aircraft's untimely demise was, of course, the cancellation three years ago of the Avro Arrow. This traumatic experience was one from which the company never recovered in even a small way. Undeniably the problems faced by the management were staggering, but even making allowance for this, the company's performance in the last three years has been disappointing. Post-mortem reveals that the feeling is very widespread that the Avro name is still anathema in Ottawa, and to a very large extent this was behind Avro Aircraft's failure to re-establish itself in the smallest way. The change of name of the parent company from A.V. Roe Canada Ltd., to Hawker Siddeley Canada Ltd. tends to suggest that not only the outsiders felt this was the case.

"NOTHING BUT GOOD: The takeover of the Avro facilities bodes nothing but good for the giant Malton complex, which has about half as much plant space again as de Havilland Canada operates at Downsview. This means that de Havilland Canada will now have expanded plant space in the order of 2.5 million square feet, about 30 percent less than Canadair, but nevertheless still impressive by any standards. More important, perhaps, than the Avro plant itself, is the variety of very modern manufacturing and production tooling which it contains. Giant stamping presses, skin mills, etc., many bought especially to handle the advanced fabricating techniques required for the Arrow, are now at de Havilland Canada's disposal.

"The future never looked brighter for de Havilland Canada. With its greatly expanded facilities, an important development contract from the US Army for the turboprop Caribou II (won, incidentally, against the competition of 24 American companies), and the first civil sale of the piston-powered Caribou I sewn up, the company can take quiet pride in its progress. Few aircraft companies are built on a bed-rock foundation, but de Havilland Canada is one of those that is."

The Bobcat
One of the first steps for de Havilland was to take stock of their new acquisition — its equipment, manufacturing potential and contracts. There were still CF-100s in the plant at Malton for servicing and the installation of ECM (Electronic Counter Measures) equipment. Alex Watson

was appointed project manager and, with Ron Gibson as project engineer, worked with Air Materiel Command in Ottawa to complete the contract. There were tip-tanks for the CF-104 and a small contract with Republic Aircraft in the USA.

Another project was far removed from aviation and eventually required the maximum in de Havilland ingenuity in the form of the machine shop expertise of Bob Prout.

Prout was a veteran of the war years, going back to the Ansons and Tiger Moths. He had worked closely with Reg Robinson in setting up the machine shop for Mosquitos and had become a specialist in metal fabrication. He was asked to go to Malton to review a Hawker Siddeley project that had been in progress for ten years, first at Canadian Car in Montreal and now at Avro. It was called the Bobcat.

After all this time the Bobcat had become a controversial project. It was an all-purpose half-ton military carrier for personnel, supplies and armament. It was an amphibious tracked vehicle, light enough for transport by air yet strong enough to withstand the rigours of combat.

When Prout sized up the project he could see it was a long way from completion. The special armour plate from England had not arrived, contracts in the USA were still unfulfilled and the gearboxes were still untried.

The controversial Canadian Bobcat during its unsuccessful field trials. (via R. Prout)

His report sparked a re-evaluation of the work and, as so often happens in such cases, he was "borrowed" from Downsview to take charge of the project.

The Bobcat became a major challenge for the next year with its all-welded construction, its amphibious skirts and complicated gearing. Finally the 20 vehicles were completed and delivered to the prime contractor, Hawker Siddeley. From there they were turned over to the military for a period of harsh operational testing. The Bobcat ended up as one of those great ideas that never made it to the production line. By this time the DC-9 wing contract had arrived at Malton and Prout was busy himself with a new challenge.

People who knew Phil Garratt's method of operation and his dominant presence at Downsview could see a new problem growing in the complexity of Hawker Siddeley ownership. The past successes from Chipmunk to Caribou had been accomplished with DH Canada almost supreme unto itself. It would be difficult to find any subsidiary company that enjoyed such complete command of its destiny with the head man so completely "the Boss." But new names were entering the Canadian scene and new management structures would soon put an end to the simplicity of the past.

When efforts to refloat Avro Canada had proved unsatisfactory in 1961, Sir Roy Dobson had managed to lure Theodore Jonathan Emmert

The de Havilland Aircraft of Canada Limited board of directors, July 1963. Left to right: N.E. Rowe, vice president, Engineering; R. Bannock, vice president, Military Sales; C.H. Dickins, vice president, Sales; G.J. Mickleborough, vice president, secretary treasurer; P.C. Garratt, chairman and managing director; T.J. Emmert, chairman, Hawker Siddeley Canada Ltd.; W.W. Parry, vice president, legal counsel; O.M. Solandt, vice president Research and Development; F.A. Stanley, vice president, Finance. (DHC)

from the vice presidency of Massey-Ferguson to become president and chief executive officer of A.V. Roe Canada. The move had put Emmert and Garratt on an equal footing, both reporting to Dobson in England, but the next year, when Emmert became president and chief executive of Hawker Siddeley Canada, it was a different matter. The two men, whose paths had hitherto never crossed, were now thrust together at the highest level. Observers knew them as two different personalities from two different backgrounds and speculated over how they would get along. Garratt was invited to the Hawker Siddeley Canada board and Emmert joined the board of DH Canada on August 16, 1962.

"Ted" Emmert was born in Illinois in 1915 and gained his education at South Dakota and Washington Universities. He joined Boeing in 1935 as a production worker and in eight years became assistant to the executive vice president. In 1947 he joined Canadair as director of organization,

which took him to the office of vice president and director within a year. The year 1950 found him, while still an American citizen, with Ford of Canada as their executive vice president. This position lasted for nine years until he was named vice president of Massey Ferguson — and thence to A.V. Roe Canada. The responsibilities in his latest assignment involved more than aviation, for his portfolio covered such diversified companies as Avro Aircraft, Orenda Engines, Canadian Applied Research, Canadian Car Co., Orenda Industrial, Canadian Steel Improvements, Canadian Steel Foundries, Canadian Thermo Control Co., Dominion Steel and Coal Corp., Canadian General Transit Co. and Canadian Steel Wheel.

The Douglas Wing Contract
De Havilland Canada and Phil Garratt had the obvious ability to manage Hawker Siddeley's airframe commitments in Canada, while Orenda handled things on the engine side. Together they had the unenviable responsibility of restoring a state of normality to the Toronto aviation scene. Larry Clarke was given the assignment to search out a company interested in the Malton plant. By coincidence it happened that Douglas Aircraft of California were seeking a subcontractor for their new DC-9 with a suitable plant and a willingness to share the financial load.

The Avro/de Havilland facilities at

Malton seemed tailor-made for Douglas under the circumstances. Partial manufacture at Malton would provide an excellent bargaining point in selling the airplane to Trans Canada Air Lines, who were calling for a major Canadian content in any fleet replacement. The opposition, General Dynamics, with their Canadair plant at Montreal, were certainly not in the running, so the DHC/Malton arrangement looked ideal. Douglas soon invited the entire DHC management team to Los Angeles to discuss such an arrangement.

It was the first meeting between Donald Douglas Sr. and Phil Garratt, who reportedly got along well. A development-sharing contract was drawn up between Douglas and de Havilland Canada for construction of wings and rear fuselage components in Malton. It was one of seven such subcontracts entered into for the building of the DC-9. Each participant was to use its own capital to fund the engineering, tooling and qualification testing of its own components. Douglas would purchase the completed portions under a fixed-price contract covering a specific number of units. Payment would be completed on delivery of the aircraft to the airline. On top of this, each subcontractor was to share in the cost of the aircraft certification testing, proportionate to its own participation, this cost to be returned later as part of deferred payments. It all

The round-the-world Caribou 'OYE after returning to Canada. (Larry Milberry)

sounded straightforward and little was said at the time of the fact that Douglas (and therefore DHC) was competing for much the same market as the de Havilland Trident being produced by the British de Havilland division of Hawker Siddeley.

It was in March 1963 that the cost-sharing arrangement between Douglas and de Havilland Canada was announced with all the fanfare and enthusiasm that a post-Arrow industry could muster. A wave of enthusiasm swept through Toronto at the thought of reactivating the troubled Malton plant, particularly with a partner of such international prestige as Douglas. Phil Garratt himself was less enthusiastic, for he never did like building parts for other people's airplanes. He admitted that his prejudice was of a personal nature; he also realized that pressure was mounting south of the border against further military purchases outside the USA and, in the words of one director, "that Beaver, Otter and Caribou sales would not last forever." He made his one and only trip to Malton, reasoned that there was more than enough to keep him busy at Downsview, and handed the management of the contract over to Punch Dickins. Punch looked on the assignment with some misgivings but was given a free hand and the pick of company personnel. Don Long would be project engineer while Bill Houston would look after planning and methods. Bill Burlison and Alex Downey departed the Caribou line at Downsview to manage production and inspection respectively. Bob Prout was already over at Malton finishing up the Bobcats and began checking out the machine shop potential.

George Robinson was to act as Hawker Siddeley's financial watchdog while Larry Clarke, Doug Annan, Bill Jackson, Harry Beffort and Duke Riggs were to take on responsible positions in the newly formed Malton Division. A recruiting campaign was begun for engineering and production personnel, particularly within the ranks of DH Canada itself.

Promotions were the order of the day at Downsview as longtime specialists left for new duties at Malton. Plant enthusiasm was at an all-time high for new challenges were appearing simultaneously on four fronts. As well as the Douglas cost-sharing arrangement there was the contract to build four pre-production Buffalos for the US Army. The following month work started on the Turbo Beaver while preliminary designs began for the upgrading of the Otter with two of the new lightweight P&W turbines. The big push was the DHC-5 Buffalo, for there was every

The de Havilland sign on the familiar Avro hangars. The first set of Douglas DC-9 wings is prepared for shipment by rail from the Malton facilities to California. (DHC20079)

indication that it would go on to even greater success than the Caribou.

By March 28, 1964, it was time for another world demonstration of the Caribou. This time the aircraft was CF-OYE and the crew for the tour consisted of Dave Fairbanks, captain; Jack Watt, first officer; Bill Kavanaugh and Ron Cheaters, flight engineers. The sales team was Len Trotter, technical sales manager; Tony Verrico, regional sales manager Far East; Geoff Priestley, regional sales manager Africa. This time they went round the world, starting their demonstrations at Tokyo and ending up in Brussels. They visited 28 countries and flew 38,000 statute miles with 200 demonstrations for a total of 320 flying hours.

The successful first flight of the Buffalo in April 1964 started a new wave of enthusiasm at Downsview, but dark clouds were forming over the Malton operations that foretold a stormy period for DH Canada. The contract with Douglas had started well, with good relations established and plenty of know-how available. It soon became obvious, however, that the contract had been prepared in too much haste. There were many hard-to-live-with clauses in view of the unknowns in the project, which cost millions before they were resolved. Both Douglas and de Havilland were 15 per cent short on their man-hour figures and the tooling estimate of $9 million was used up the first year. The prime contractor, Douglas, did not have an easy time, for the deep stall problem with T-tail jets was complicating their own program and causing delays. Production began to settle down at three wing-sets per month when suddenly the demand went up to five, then nine.

These roller coaster activities were putting a strain on management, even though life at Downsview was going surprisingly well. Hawker Siddeley Canada exercised its authority with two major moves to overcome the Malton problem. As previously mentioned, it brought in William B. Boggs, formerly vice president of transportation equipment, Hawker Siddeley Montreal, on July 29, 1965, to become president of DH Canada. (Phil Garratt remained as a member of the board). Their second move was to engage US production expert Hugh Whittier to take charge of Douglas wing production. President Boggs rearranged his management team in an effort to boost production at Malton, allocating new responsibilities and sending over additional people from Downsview. Douglas was happy with the workmanship on the wings — in fact compliments were received from resident airline representatives — but deliveries fell behind. Comparisons were always being made between American and Canadian methods of manufacture and it was generally conceded that US companies got more per man-hour from the worker than did their Canadian counterparts. Whittier took the US approach and went through the plant drastically rearranging the manpower. These moves did not sit well with the union and more problems arose.

By September of 1965 the situation at Malton had deteriorated to the point where even the once-happy relationships among the top personnel were suffering. On the financial side the problem fell under that part of the contract termed the "risk factor" and no money was yet received from Douglas. When $50 million were needed at the bank even to carry on, the situation became critical. Phil Garratt admitted that "we are in the wrong swimming pool," and his comment was as brief and to-the-point as most of his statements. "We have got to get out." A proposition was made that Douglas buy out the operation or increase the agreed price. They chose the former but DHC retained title to the property.

The whole sad story was told in the announcement that followed in the press: "De Havilland Aircraft of Canada has relinquished its partnership with Douglas Aircraft Co. in the production of the Douglas DC-9 jetliner. DHC has been engaged in production of the wings, rear fuselages and empennages of the DC-9 at its Malton plant since July last year and has delivered a number of sets. But recent doubling of the aircraft's production schedule, plus increasing complexity resulting from the demand of various models in the series, have combined to require an investment twice that originally projected for the DHC portion of the program.

"Accordingly, the two companies have agreed that Douglas should take over full responsibility for expanding DC-9 production, and the portion of the Malton plant devoted to the program will be leased and operated by Douglas Aircraft Co. of Canada Ltd. Initially the lease will be for five years, with option to renew for three terms of five years each. Douglas will reimburse de Havilland for its investment in the program; under the original arrangement, DHC would not have been paid for the components until the sale of completed aircraft to the airlines. DHC will be able to return to the concentration of its full resources on its expanding STOL utility transports and other projects."

Some de Havilland Canada work was continued at the Malton facility for some time after Douglas took over, for there was still lots of vacant space. A large section of the office was maintained for engineering of new projects, including the hydrofoil and augmentor wing. The huge spares inventory, from Chipmunk to Buffalo, which had only recently been established under one roof in Malton, stayed there for a number of years. The large hangars backing onto Derry Road were handy for storing Caribous and Twin Otters but required a time-consuming shuttle service back and forth between the two airports, particularly with the growing traffic at Toronto International Airport.

During the months that followed the collapse of the Douglas contract, people continued to ask, "What happened?" Many close to the scene still maintain that DHC could have solved the production difficulties and maintained control of both the property and the wing contract. Douglas was not anxious to locate in Canada but had no alternative at the time. When they got into difficulty themselves some years later and were forced to join with the McDonnell company, the Canadian operation was one of the points that did not sit well with the famous "Mr. Mac" of St. Louis.

Powered-lift Research

A long-term V/STOL research program known as the "augmentor wing" began at Avro Canada in 1960 with theoretical studies into ducted jet flaps and powered lift. Thrust deflection or thrust vectoring, as it is called, was an essential element of the new concept.

With the shut-down of Avro, the project leader Don C. Whittley moved to de Havilland to continue the work and become program manager, advanced research and technology. In 1965 a combined program was started, bringing together the US National Aeronautics and Space Administration (NASA) and the Canadian Department of National Defence. A large scale model with a wing span of 42 feet was built by de Havilland for test in a 40 by 80-foot wind tunnel at NASA's Ames Research Center in California. The success of these tests warranted a "proof of concept" aircraft to examine the principle in actual flight.

The US and Canadian governments entered into an agreement whereby NASA and the Canadian Department of Industry, Trade and Commerce would modify a C-8A Buffalo for flight research. DITC contracted with de Havilland and Rolls-Royce of Canada to provide the propulsion system and new engine nacelles. NASA contracted with the Boeing Company of Seattle to modify the aircraft, install the wing duct system and

Crown Prince Birendra of Nepal, who became King in 1972, is welcomed during a 1968 visit to Downsview by president William B. Boggs. (DHC29829)

209

perform initial flight tests. Two Rolls-Royce Spey turbofan engines were modified at the Rolls plant in Montreal to supply an air distribution system that would vector cold by-pass thrust through the augmentor flap and direct hot propulsive thrust (about 60 per cent of the total) to rotating nozzles (similar to those on the Harrier V/STOL fighter). The concept became known as the augmentor wing because the combination of a blown wing and vectored thrust serves to "augment" both wing lift and wing thrust at the same time.

The wing changes involved reducing the span by 17 feet and replacing all of the original wing structure aft of the rear spar. Here the air distribution ducting was installed along with augmentor flaps, ailerons and spoilers. Fixed full-span leading edge slats were installed. Very little of the new wing looked the same. When the special engine nacelles, complete with their modified Speys, were shipped from de Havilland, the final assembly took place at Boeing Field and the aircraft was rolled out of the factory doors in Seattle to be prepared for flight.

A wave of enthusiasm went from desk to desk at de Havilland Canada, May 1, 1972, with the word that the Augmentor Wing Buffalo had flown in Seattle. Boeing's pilot, Thomas E. Edmonds, tested the aircraft for basic airworthiness and flight characteristics before delivery to the Ames Research Center, Moffett Field, California. An interesting eight months of flying followed with a number of US and Canadian test pilots, including de Havilland's Bob Fowler, participating in the evaluations.

Cost restraints had dictated a rather austere test vehicle in which to test Whittley's design concepts. The landing gear did not retract and most of the systems were modified from the original Buffalo. The engines, which had been chosen for their ease of modification, were noisy and subject to high fuel consumption. The cost-cutting features did not detract in any way from the low-speed performance and handling qualities; in fact in all vital parameters the aircraft either met or bettered expectations. The rotating thrust nozzles allowed a steep descent at high power settings. Cross ducting in the wings combined the cold flow with the hot thrust of the engines to compensate for roll and yaw asymmetrics.

The photo above and the diagram illustrate the augmentor wing principle. Air is blown through the ducted augmentor flap while most of the thrust is obtained from the rotating nozzles. (DHC)

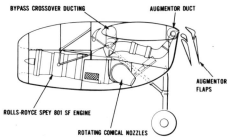

The Spey-powered Buffalo regularly performed STOL-type approach and landing manoeuvres on a 7½-degree glide slope at speeds ranging from 55 to 65 knots. Takeoff ground rolls averaged 600 feet and 900 feet to a screen height of 35 feet. (With the use of higher flap settings, these values were later reduced to 300 and 450 feet respectively.) When all these factors were established, the program moved to aerial navigation and automatic terminal guidance during 1975. By 1976 a total of 250 flying hours had been accumulated and all areas of certification were examined.

The joint government contracts ended in 1980, bringing the first stage of the program to a successful conclusion. With over 900 hours of flying, the test vehicle was flown back to Canada in 1981 by Canadian Forces test pilot Major Larry Dufrimont, first to Downsview and then to the Canadian Forces base at Mountainview, Ontario. Here it began a 30-month project-definition exercise sponsored by the Canadian government to assess the commercial aspects of a new generation aircraft in either a military or civil configuration. Don Whittley and his team visualize an advanced STOL

The augmentor wing Buffalo in a dramatic takeoff photo. (DHC)

The Shah of Iran during his visit to Downsview in conversation with Phil Garratt and the Hon. Paul Hellyer, Minister of National Defence. Frank Stanley in the rear chats with an RCMP officer. (DHC21119)

transport in the Boeing 737 class with modern high bypass engines giving fuel economy and a noise level approaching that of the Dash 7. Whittley also points out that other applications are possible including a Lockheed C-130 Hercules replacement or a smaller naval support aircraft.

Project manager Don Whittley has received wide recognition for his work in augmentor technology. In 1973 he was presented with the Canadian Aeronautics and Space Institute McCurdy Award for his contribution to Canadian aviation. In 1975 he was invited to present the 32nd British Commonwealth Lecture at the Royal Aeronautical Society meeting in London.

Another Royal Visitor
With a reputation for slow-flying airplanes that could take off and land in extremely short distances, it was common to welcome interested visitors from foreign countries, particularly dignitaries who were themselves pilots. Prince Bernhard of the Netherlands had been in to fly the Otter with minimum publicity, but when the colourful Mohammed Reza Pahlavi, Shah of Iran, arrived on May 26, 1965, it was a different matter.

The Shah and his entourage were in Toronto on a number of missions including a trip to Downsview for a flight in a company aircraft. In view of the large retinue and the style of the East, the telephone calls in advance of the visit were frequent and detailed. All efforts were made to provide a welcome befitting a world figure and no one was closer to the barrage of phone calls than Garratt's secretary, Enid Koyl. The luncheon would be easy to arrange, for such functions were routine, but one last-minute request posed a new problem.

It was mentioned that the Shah's practice was to take a short nap after lunch and it would be appreciated if the appropriate facilities were provided. There was no "snooze room" at Downsview and there wasn't much time. Mrs. Koyl made a quick trip to a furniture store, bought a couch of the right size and had it delivered to the general manager's office. The couch drew a raised eyebrow and "What's all this?" from Phil Garratt, who agreed that their honoured guest should be invited to take a rest in the office if he so desired.

Mrs. Koyl prepared to do her part and kept an eye on the dining room for her cue. To her dismay the party headed straight for the line of aircraft, where a crowd gathered and photo bulbs flashed. Bob Fowler showed the Shah the Otter and Russ Bannock took him through the Caribou. Dave Fairbanks took the royal visitor (and his bodyguard) for a flight in the Turbo Beaver and, combining salesmanship and diplomacy, Punch Dickins joined the bodyguard in the back.

Apparently the Shah had shrugged off the invitation for a nap as the temptation of adding another aircraft to his list of conquests was too great. This left the enterprising secretary with another problem: an unused couch that wasn't appropriate in the head office, didn't match anything and nobody wanted it. It took considerable sales expertise to dispose of the "surplus material," which ended up in Doug Annan's recreation room.

T.J. Emmert, chairman of Hawker Siddeley Canada, presents P.C. Garratt with a model of his Beaver at his retirement party March 16, 1966. DHC president W.B. Boggs sits at right. (DHC)

A touch of nostalgia as Max Ward sits in a replica of his first Fox Moth and Phil Garratt joins him for a photograph at the christening of a Wardair 747 in Garratt's name. (Wardair)

Phil Garratt Retires

Phil Garratt's last full year at Downsview was a mixture of pride and frustration. He saw the Twin Otter, which he had launched, start on its successful road to world sales. He heard the success stories of the Buffalo in Viet Nam and saw the last of 1350 aircraft delivered to the US Forces. He weathered the storm of being moved into the role of an advising director and saw his longtime friend and associate, George Mickleborough, retire the day the change took place. The DC-9 wing program had been a burden he neither wanted nor enjoyed, for it only complicated his tenuous position with the new masters in England. He still kept an active presence at Downsview and flew his Beaver regularly. Whenever he was out of town it was his practice to phone his secretary at the Hawker Siddeley head office and have her read any special mail. On one such call in mid-November 1965 a letter from Hawker Siddeley in England looked important so he asked that it be read to him. It was from Sir Arnold Hall, asking him to submit his resignation from management. There was a pause at Garratt's end of the line and the simple question, "Is that all?" And so it was that the man who always said that he would retire at 90 prepared a short notice for everyone in the plant, November 22, 1965, announcing his retirement at the age of 71. In recognition of his long years in command, he was allowed a place of honour on the company's board of directors, but his days of "biting the bullet" were over.

Additional recognition came to P.C. Garratt as he entered retirement. He had received the Trans Canada (McKee) Trophy in 1951 and the McCurdy Medal in 1960. In 1966 he was the first winner of the newly established C.D. Howe Award to recognize leadership in the manufacturing field. That same year he was named the winner of the McKee Trophy, making him the second dual winner of the trophy. (T.M. "Pat" Reid, 1942-43, was the other.)

The Bombings

North Toronto was wrapped in fog on the morning of September 24, 1968, as Frank Stanley prepared to leave for work. The vice president of finance had enjoyed a good night's sleep and his mind was occupied with plans for the coming day. As he looked out of the window to check the fog, he remembered he was to take his wife's car to work that morning and it had been parked in the driveway overnight. He had trouble starting the engine but gave it little thought until it began hesitating at the first stop sign. The car's behaviour diverted his mind from the day's problems to the thought that there must be water in the gas. The Corvair continued to run, but when he parked along the east wall of head office, he thought, "I'll have to get that car down to the garage tonight."

When Stanley reached the second floor he was accosted with the question, "How about you? Were you bombed last night?" According to a police officer, a number of small bombs had exploded on the lawns of Hawker Siddeley executives and Larry Clarke's car had run out of gas two blocks from his home. "Not me," said Frank, but suddenly he remembered his halting trip along Wilson Avenue. A quick return to his parked car confirmed the worst: when he finally managed to spring open the engine compartment a mess of broken wires and twisted metal confronted him—it was a wonder the poor car ran at all.

Stanley returned to his office with the news, "Yes, you can count me in," and joined the police investigation. He returned home with one of the officers and there, on the side of the driveway, was a piece of two-inch cast iron pipe seven inches long and capped at each end, the remnants of an amateurish schoolboy bomb. When the story hit the *Toronto Star* afternoon edition, it revealed that ten senior officers of the Hawker Siddeley organization had been subjected to similar bombings at 4 a.m. that morning, but nobody was injured. Some bombs had damaged lawns and shrubs, some broke basement windows, and others had been planted in cars. The Hawker Siddeley list involved the homes of A.A. Bailie, J.H. Ready, Evan Bull, W.D. Walker, D.G. Kettering and W.W. Muir. The de Havilland homes included president W.B. Boggs, who had lawn damage, Larry Clarke (his car), Paul Davoud (two basement windows) and Russ Bannock, who had resigned the year before to start his own company (shrub damage and a broken window). It was only through further investigating that another three de Havilland names were added to the list—Phil Garratt, who had retired in 1965, Alex McIntosh and, of course, Frank Stanley. Those officers who lived in apartments, including Ted Emmert, Hawker Siddeley president and chief executive officer, were not bombed.

Metro Detective Kenneth Craven described the bits of pipe as protest bombs intended to frighten. They were composed mainly of ammonia salts and acid, separated by a thin piece of metal. The pipe bombs were cradled in stands made of coat hangers so the acid would eat through the thin metal and unite with the ammonia. The 14 bombs had gone off in a period of four hours throughout a wide area of Etobicoke, North York and Toronto. One policeman and a reporter were starting to examine an unexploded bomb when second thoughts caused them to take cover. It exploded harmlessly only moments later but left a hole in the ground.

It was the period of the early draft dodgers from the USA and, according to police evaluation, the bombings were a demonstration against the sale of Caribous for use in the Viet Nam war. Police Chief Mackey felt it was the work of students, but obviously under the direction of a well trained subversive. Police kept the executives' homes under surveillance for another week but, although a reward of $10,000 was offered, no culprits were ever apprehended. Frank Stanley and Alex McIntosh had to have extensive work done on their cars but the broken glass and lawn damage was a less costly item. The closest the police came to solving the issue was to find where the pipe was purchased—in the University of Toronto area.

Waterfront Activity

Time was when the motorist driving along Toronto's waterfront would see numerous floatplanes bobbing at their buoys, presenting an ever-changing colour spectacle. In the thirties it was the air harbour at the foot of Yonge Street and in later years, the Island Airport ramp. There was always action around the floatplane dock: boats back and forth, planes under tow, the going and coming of aircraft. Times have changed and very seldom does the motorist view much floatplane action in Toronto Harbour. One reason is the fact that there was sometimes too much action: the kind that gives insurance underwriters sleepless nights.

Every year, with regularity, one or more aircraft would sink during the autumn windstorms. Often they were

de Havilland types and sometimes they were owned by the company. The Moths with their lower wings were extremely vulnerable for they would literally fly at their buoys during a storm and once they dipped a wing in the water would soon turn turtle and slowly sink. Hornet Moth CF-BFK was a case in point in 1937, but there were others.

The Beavers and Otters, with their metal construction, were a little less costly to salvage under such circumstances but sinkings occurred even into Twin Otter days. On one of these occasions, operations manager Dave Fairbanks got a frantic call from the Island that a Twin Otter was sinking and they were having trouble getting it to the ramp. By the time Dave got there the tail and one wing were submerged but clear of the buoy. He was taken out and climbed into the tilting cockpit for a try at starting the still-dry engine. Although the battery was under water, he got the engine started and pointed the aircraft at the ramp. With full power and very little control, he managed to get enough of the high float on the ramp to prevent the aircraft from sinking and saved a costly salvage operation.

The next time there was no warning. A Twin Otter, destined for Peru, sank during the night. It had been fully loaded, ready for an early morning takeoff, but at first light only a wing tip and part of an engine remained above the surface. It took a lot of drying out and many man-hours of work before it was serviceable again. Times have indeed changed at the Toronto Island Airport, where the talk today is more of short-haul air services. Water operations are minimal. Floatplanes are not stored at the buoy any more (they are hauled up the ramp) and the insurance people rest more easily.

Showmanship

Life in Flight Operations at Downsview was never dull nor was the pilot's job description confined to testing airplanes. The flying assignments were many and varied. Pilots were a vital part of the sales team and assignments took them to the far corners of the world. The man who allotted the tasks during the surge of Twin Otter demonstration tours was operations manager Dave Fairbanks, who fitted himself into the assignments regularly to keep up his proficiency. He had taken

A Twin Otter destined for Peru is winched slowly from the waters of Toronto Harbour after sinking overnight. (DHC39290)

The Twin Otter demonstrator bows to the crowd after completing its demonstration routine. (DHC39547)

part in all the major demonstrations since the days of the Otter and was internationally recognized as one of the best in the business.

It was late 1973 and a crew change was needed in Peter Adams' Far East sales area. George Northrop had been demonstrating the Twin Otter for a month and was called back for another assignment. There was still another swing to be done through the Middle East following the Japanese aerospace show the second week in October. Fairbanks arrived in Tokyo on the 7th ready for whatever was needed at the Truma Air Force base, an hour's drive from Tokyo.

The three competing aircraft—Short Skyvan, Britten Norman Islander and Twin Otter—were to perform on the 10th. Asked what sequence he would prefer, Fairbanks said, "Last." The Skyvan went first, and when the pilot of the BN Islander did his routine, it consisted of circles and dives on the Twin Otter waiting in the ready area with engines running. If this display was intended to rattle the Twin Otter crew, the BN pilot had underrated Fairbanks.

Dave had his own series of manoeuvres and usually chose last spot on the program so he could improvise as the occasion demanded. The royal

box with the dignitaries, including the Crown Prince, was positioned for the best possible view. Fairbanks now knew what he had to do. His short takeoff was followed by a series of dumbbell turns including a fast and slow flypast. On the last climb he feathered both engines and continued in the turns as before. At the correct moment his crewman Bruce Jack returned the propellers to normal and CF-DHA settled in to the shortest of landings at the far end of the runway. Fairbanks then did three more takeoffs and landings on the same runway, ending up in front of the crowd. A slight turn faced the Twin Otter to the box and, with precise manipulating of reverse thrust and brakes, Fairbanks bowed the Twin Otter to the crowd. He had used the manoeuvre before but in Japan it was an instant hit. The crowd applauded and all began bowing in return. Six Twin Otters finally went to Japan.

Realignment

The most traumatic period in the history of DH Canada was the transition from a thriving private enterprise organization through the amalgamation process to a government-owned establishment. In the final analysis the Hawker Siddeley years combined with the changing times to upset the orderly development of the previous 30 years. It became well known during the early planning of the Dash 7 that the

Hawker Siddeley Group was willing (if not anxious) to sell de Havilland Canada. A joint offer by Air Canada and Canadian International Comstock Company was made through Ottawa and another feeler was extended by Douglas Aircraft, but the only actual commitment resulted when Ottawa underwrote the first two Dash 7s for $75 million: under this agreement the Canadian government held an option to buy de Havilland which was valid until June 28, 1974.

As that day drew close, Clive Baxter in his Ottawa column in the *Financial Post* speculated that the government would pick up the option and mentioned a study on Canada's aircraft manufacturing future being conducted by the Department of Industry, Trade and Commerce. The full story came out in the *Globe & Mail*, Toronto, on May 28, 1974, when aviation reporter Ken Romain outlined the government's move to make aircraft manufacturing in Canada purely Canadian:

"The federal Government has taken its first steps toward reshaping the Canadian aviation industry and bringing part of it under Canadian control.

"The Government announced it will exercise its option to purchase de Havilland Aircraft of Canada Ltd., Toronto, at an estimated cost of $38 million, and will seek an option to purchase Canadair Ltd. of Cartierville, near Montreal, at a cost of $32 million.

"Ottawa [plans to offer] them for sale as a package to Canadian interests, stating it only plans to operate them on an interim basis.

"The announcement of the Government's intentions was made by Industry, Trade and Commerce Minister Alastair Gillespie. The option to purchase de Havilland was negotiated two years ago and was to expire on June 28.

"Mr. Gillespie said control of de Havilland will be transferred to the Government within 30 days of the effective date of the notice.

"A new board of directors consisting of Canadian businessmen and senior company officials will be appointed to assume control on an interim and trusteeship basis."

After all the rumours and speculation, the actual transition of ownership on May 27, 1974, went extremely well. On the date of the actual transfer three new directors—Dr. J. Herbert Smith, R.M. Barford and J.G. Grandy —were appointed to the board, but the operating management remained the same. President Bernard Bundesman was asked to continue on an interim basis and it became Dr. Smith's responsibility as chairman to guide the company into a new era. Current programs at Downsview continued as before while Ottawa began negotiations with Canadair. The government had negotiated an October 15 deadline with General Dynamic Corporation of St. Louis, owner of the Montreal company, for a maximum price of $38.15 million.

When that sale was accomplished, inquiries were invited for an all-Canadian buyer and even a joint ownership. Seven proposals were made by various Canadian companies as a "package deal" but very few details emerged. The aviation press was critical of any suggestion that the companies be merged. Nothing ever came of the proposals that ended up on Industries Minister Alastair Gillespie's desk and he calmed the waters with the statement that the government would continue an "interim operation" until a suitable purchaser could be found in each case.

These proceedings were in the negotiation stages when word came that Phil Garratt had died in Toronto. He had been off the board since April 6, 1971, and had received further honours in his final years. He received the prestigious Canada Medal in 1971 and was inducted into Canada's Aviation Hall of Fame in 1973. The memorial service, held five days later, was described by his friend, columnist Bruce West, in the *Globe & Mail*, November 21, 1974.

"Last Thursday I went up to Christ Church, Deer Park, to attend a memorial service for Phil Garratt, who died a week ago at the age of 80. The big church was packed to the doors, with a crowd containing an impressive cross-section of the whole Canadian aviation industry, pilots, air engineers, company executives. They came to honour the memory of this big, friendly man because he, perhaps more than any other individual in this country, had personified the hopes, the struggles and the amazing successes of the aviation industry in Canada for more than half a century."

An era had certainly ended with the death of Garratt but a new one was beginning under government ownership. The Dash 7 flew for the first time on March 24, 1975, but the fact that there were no solid orders was drawing unfavourable comment in the press. Nothing came of the private offers to purchase either de Havilland or Canadair and it became apparent that both would have to be operated as crown corporations for some time to come. The economic climate was poor with only 2600 employees at DH Canada and 2700 at Canadair.

As far as de Havilland was concerned Twin Otter sales were steady, the Buffalo was being upgraded and two Dash 7s were well into their certification program. Russ Bannock rejoined the company as director of sales on July 11 in time to witness the regular strike, which lasted for four months (half the length of the previous one in 1972). "Bundy" Bundesman retired as president on January 6, 1976, and was replaced by Russ Bannock. Dr. J. Herbert Smith remained as chairman of the board. John A. Timmins joined as director of sales, and the early Dash 7 sales team was absorbed into the overall marketing group. Joe Andrews and most of the former team left the company but Mike Kilburn, one of the originals from DH sales in England, remained in Downsview. It was time for the company to settle down and adjust to all the changes.

Ontario Transport Minister James Snow accepts another Twin Otter for Norontair and receives the log books from president Russ Bannock. (DHC45114)

President B.B. Bundesman (left) with test pilots Bob Fowler and Mick Saunders. (DHC42155)

215

Today and Tomorrow

A Tyrolean Airways Dash 7 climbs away in this Ron Nunney action photo. (DHC)

Fifty Years in Canada

De Havilland Canada began its second half century on a wave of acclaim for the Dash 7. The Canadian press, which had leaned heavily in past years on the lack of pre-production orders, were now calling the growing sales a "turnaround." Everything was reported under headlines about "taxpayers' dollars" when the company became fully owned by the Canadian government, but now the emphasis was on how much employment the airplane would generate and the value of export sales to the country's economy.

By now the '7 had been certified, demonstrated at the 1977 Paris Air Show and shown to a sizable portion of the aviation world. The first delivery to Rocky Mountain Airways was history and sufficient orders were on hand to guarantee a busy 1978. Newspaper reporters began to emphasize the fact that 55 man-years were needed to build just one '7 and that five of the first half dozen ordered were bringing in export dollars. Even the controversy over

whether Toronto Island Airport should be used for intercity STOL service took on a new light when Bob Fowler demonstrated the '7 there in 1977. The plane's arrival was marked with a turn-off at the first intersection and Fowler continued during passenger flights to use less than half of the available 4000-foot runway. Even more convincing to first-time observers was the low noise level, less than the snarling single-engined floatplanes so common in the area. It had become obvious that de Havilland no longer had a "paper airplane" but a well designed product for a special market. Howard Tinney, who led the Boeing group during the years of '7 cooperation, in referring to world markets called it "the only game in town."

The fact that Twin Otter sales were closing on 600 during January 1978 and Buffalo sales were steady improved de Havilland's standing in the popularity polls; the anniversary year was beginning to look promising. Early in the year the plant at Downsview took on a gala appearance with flags and gold "50 year" stickers everywhere. Bob McIntyre and his anniversary committee had been meeting for months; their program emphasized an impressive first half

century. A family day was planned and a booklet on the company history was produced. The actual date that DHC began the second half century went unnoticed during the blustery months of February and March.

In February 1928 British de Havilland Moths had been shipped across the Atlantic for use in Canada. In February 1978 the process was reversed when a DHC Twin Otter was delivered for use in Britain. Chipmunks and Beavers had been used in the mother country and now Twin Otters were seeing commercial use there. Brymon Airways of Plymouth took delivery of their second Twin Otter for use on the cross-Channel routes. The historic delivery took place 50 years to the month after Bob Loader's arrival in Canada with his crate of two Cirrus Moths.

April provided another landmark when the first of four Twin Otters went to the People's Republic of China, fulfilling five years of sales effort. China's search for geophysical aircraft began in 1973 with a delegation of ten specialists and interpreters who visited Downsview for a series of demonstrations and presentations. They were headed by the China Geophysical Survey Company on behalf of that country's Bureau of

Geology and sponsored by the Canadian Department of Industry, Trade and Commerce.

The complexity of their requirements in the geophysical line involved close liaison with Scintrex Limited of Concord, Ontario, and other suppliers of scientific equipment. Len Trotter, assistant vice-president, marketing and sales, coordinated the negotiations through 1974-76, which involved numerous meetings with government and industry officials in Canada and China. After one of the most complex sales efforts in the life of the Twin Otter, the sale of three aircraft was announced at the Paris Air Show in 1977. The first two aircraft, which were equipped for photographic survey, were rolled out on February 8, 1978, and delivered to China by DHC crews via Europe and the Middle East two months later. The third was the most complete geophysical Twin Otter ever to leave Downsview. A fourth machine followed.

On April 1 Herbert Smith retired as chairman of the board and was replaced by Douglas Kendall, who had been a director since September 1970. Max Ward dropped by during May to accept his first '7 and one month later, June 24, the official 50 year ceremony took place. The gates were opened that afternoon to an estimated 10,000 people as the employees took their families on a tour of the factory, viewed special displays

The geophysical Twin Otter which went to the Peoples' Republic of China is shown on a test flight over Downsview. (DHC)

and watched an air show. Lucky draws were held for Twin Otter rides while thousands of hot dogs and gallons of soft drinks were consumed. A highlight of the afternoon was the handover ceremony of Twin Otter 600 to Aero Mech of Clarksburg, West Virginia, part of the Allegheny Commuter network. Two of the original DHC employees, Frank Warren and George Mickleborough, were introduced to the audience by president Russell Bannock.

A New President

It was a good party by any standard but a complicated six months lay ahead. The presidency changed hands when Russ Bannock returned to his aircraft sales and consulting service on July 14 and a new chief executive officer moved in. The company magazine, *High Lift,* introduced John W. Sandford to the DHC family and their customers:

"John W. Sandford was appointed president of the de Havilland Aircraft of Canada Limited in July. The appointment was something of a 'homecoming' for Mr. Sandford who began his career in North America when he emigrated from England to join Avro Canada in 1957 — just two years before the cancellation of the Arrow fighter program in 1959. In John's own words, 'When Avro offered me $5000 a year, I couldn't believe such a vast sum of money.'

"Like some of his contemporaries here at Downsview, John Sandford made his first acquaintance with aviation at the age of 14 in Britain, as an apprentice with Westland Aircraft. From here he went on to take a masters degree in aeronautical en-

gineering at the Cranfield Institute of Technology (then the College of Aeronautics).

"His early career in Canada disrupted by cancellation of the Arrow program, John joined North American in the United States (subsequently North American Rockwell) and went on to establish an outstanding reputation in the US aerospace industry.

"As director of engineering for advanced launch systems John was responsible for the development of improved boosters for the Saturn rocket that took men to the moon, research on nuclear-powered rockets and the study of spacecraft for interplanetary flight.

"From here (now with the Space Division of Rockwell International Corporation) he went on to concentrate his efforts on the Space Shuttle program. As the company's proposal manager, he was responsible for the winning proposal to NASA for the design, development and production of the shuttle vehicle system. This, John admits, was the highlight of his career in the US. 'After all, how many times do you get the opportunity to bid on a $10 billion program — and win?' He hastened to point out that he received no commission on this sale!

"But it was time for a change and at his own request John transferred to Rockwell's General Aviation Division — 'because I wanted to try something different.'

"Then, in 1975, John Sandford was appointed president of Canadian Admiral Corporation where, we understand, he was involved with the manufacture of something called a

'refrigerator' and — even worse — a 'dishwasher'!

"On the question of his decision to join de Havilland, John had this to say . . . 'When the opportunity to join de Havilland as president and chief executive officer came along, after I'd been with Rockwell for nearly 17 years, I researched the matter pretty thoroughly. What I saw was a company that has been successful in the aircraft business for 50 years — and that's quite a record. A company with two well established airplanes and a new one all competing for world markets. I was convinced that the company and its products had a bright future and was prepared to couple my own future with it.'"

It was a busy month for John Sandford, settling into his new job. The Spantax Dash 7 had been delivered and Emirates Air Service were getting ready to put theirs into operation. In the US President Jimmy Carter had just signed a controversial bill deregulating the country's airlines. A backlog of Twin Otter orders was developing and the Buffalo line was moving well, but this was the year for union negotiations. Once again, as had happened in 1975 and 1972, negotiations broke down and picket lines formed. It was not the best of welcomes for the new president but he took the situation in his stride and began an intense communications program to let everyone know what was going on. DH Canada kept up its reputation at the year's Farnborough Air Show while the "monthly" staff at home pitched in to cope with existing aircraft deliveries and spare parts orders.

A trend in the airline industry at the time of deregulation proved advantageous to de Havilland: the trunk airlines began associating themselves more closely with the commuter lines as they dropped their less productive runs. Cooperation with the major lines was eagerly sought by the small airlines, who gained the use of computer booking services and terminal facilities in exchange for the transfer of passengers: the true definition of a feeder-line. The introduction of the Dash 7 with its quiet, short-field capability provided a new dimension to the feeder-line concept and growing sales indicated its acceptance by the major regional carriers.

Like the Twin Otter before it, the Dash 7 proved just right for an unexpected swing in market conditions.

John W. Sandford, who assumed the presidency of de Havilland Canada on July 14, 1978. (DHC46710)

A contributing factor was a change in US regulations that permitted commuter airlines to use 56-seat aircraft; previously they had been restricted to aircraft with no more than 30 seats. The fact that the '7 could be operated into any Twin Otter runway gave it a distinct advantage over the competition. Everyone agreed it was the quietest airliner in the business and talk began, once again, on the use of reliever runways at large airports. Not only did US orders come in, but the long worldwide sales promotion began to pay off with orders from Norway, Austria and England. By the time the differences with the union were settled in November and everyone was back at work, president Sandford had an announcement of such importance that a fullfledged press conference was called.

Expansion Again

Coinciding with this conference, a report was issued to the employees which contained possibly the best news they had received in a decade. It announced new orders and options for Dash 7s which would require a $6.5 million plant expansion. The production rate of the '7 was to go from one to two a month and Twin Otters from four to five. The Sandford announcement served to vindicate the once criticized '7; orders now stood at 32 and 13 of these were from com-

muter airlines in the United States.

The plant expansion announced at the press conference by senior vice president Doug Annan involved an assembly area, a small-parts manufacturing area and an additional 65,000 square feet of storage. New subcontract work was announced along with the prospect of 300-400 new jobs at Downsview. The good news was reported by an eager press along with an item of historical significance. When John Sandford announced that sales for the fiscal year ending May 30 totalled $125 million, with a profit of $2 million, and that more than 85 per cent of production was exported, he indicated clearly that de Havilland Canada had turned the first half century on a sound footing. Industry Minister Jack Horner injected his contribution to the occasion with the statement that the federal government had no plans to return the plant to the private sector.

The buoyant feeling at Downsview that came with $100 million in new aircraft sales continued throughout 1979. It was all very similar to 1929, when a large backlog of orders fuelled enthusiasm for expansion. Fifty years later it was a backlog of Twin Otter and Dash 7 orders that provided welcomed employment but put a strain on existing facilities. Like 1929 it was a year of decision: management was faced with extending the life of existing products while solving the ever-present problem of space and equipment. The engineers were asked to explore the growth potential of the product line and Maurice Crawford took over details of the expansion. The main decision for management was a little more difficult — a new aircraft design that would see the company through the next decade.

The Dash 8

A good deal of attention had always been given to future projects at DH Canada under a group of advance design engineers. Two of their proposals (called DHPs) had been executive aircraft models during the Bundesman years. Two were turbine engine conversions for the Caribou and Otter. A 50-passenger turbofan had been considered in 1970 as well as a single-engine Otter replacement model, the DHP 56 with a turbine engine and a long, square fuselage. DHP 35 had developed into the Dash

Investigating new projects is a continuing process, and only a certain number find their way into production. Here are four that did not. (Clockwise, from top left) An experimental model investigating ducted fan engines on a Dash 7; DHP-48, a twin-turboprop executive aircraft from the early 1970s; a jet trainer, successor to the Chipmunk, 1954; and DHP-52, a twin-turboprop amphibian for the corporate and commuter market, 1973 (DHC and R.J. Fox)

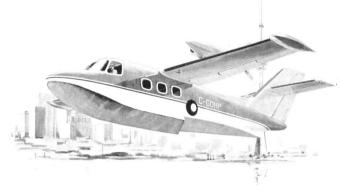

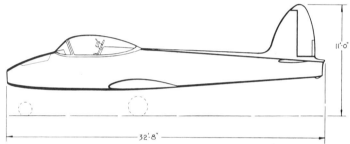

7, while DHP 58 in 1978 was a twin-turboprop, 30-passenger commuter. The company's pre-eminence in the regional airline field had been established with the Twin Otter and Dash 7; it seemed logical to continue in that area by exploring DHP 58 further. Studies showed a distinct gap between the $2 million and $5 million commuter airliner, somewhere between the Twin Otter and the Dash 7.

While Brian Eggleston and his advanced design group were putting together a technical outline called Dash X, a team of experts, including Bob McIntyre, Ron Jackson, John Shaw and John Glaser, headed across North America gathering airline reactions. Their reports were favourable; the timing for such a product was considered sound. The new short-haul airliner would be in the 20-40 passenger bracket and retain a degree of commonality with the Dash 7. In this way the engineering talent of the past years would be preserved and the hard-won short-haul technology expanded. It was realized that competition would be strong in this market where other nations were already at work.

John Sandford summed up the situation in a paper, "The Changes Ahead," for the annual meeting of the Canadian Aeronautics and Space Institute, May 3, 1979. He reviewed the plans for existing products, including a civil version of the Buffalo called the Transporter. He described a family of aircraft options at de Havilland in the regional transport field similar to the well-known Boeing line of big jets. He pointed to the growth potential of the Dash 7, which could be expanded to the 70-passenger class and provide a choice of four aircraft in the commuter airline range. He called it a "step up or sell up" approach and the key would be the 35 passenger Dash X, soon to appear as the 36 passenger Dash 8.

The May announcement was followed by another presentation at Paris in June where the three existing DHC types, sporting matching paint schemes, put on an imposing display. Back at Downsview the ramps and taxiways were a mass of colour with aircraft for every corner of the world in the testing, training or delivery phase. Signs of new construction were everywhere; the parking lots were

crowded to the point where new ones were planned and staggered working hours were implemented.

For the rest of the year there was steady progress, but the new Conservative government under Joe Clark was in power in Ottawa, with all the uncertainties of changing cabinet ministers and policy reversals. The Progressive Conservatives' Sinclair Stevens had long been a critic of everything that took place at Downsview and it was only reasonable to expect the worst. The newspapers reported talk of "privatizing" all government-owned aircraft manufacturing. When asked for his views on such a sale, John Sandford took the view that any new owner should be a "buyer of quality." "There are many people who can buy us," he said, "but very few people who can afford us. We have to order the material for the Dash 7 two years before we sell it. It takes a great deal of front-end investment before the plane goes out the door."

The go-ahead for a full-scale Dash 8 development program came in September 1980. Market forecasts showing that over 70 per cent of

1 Weather radar
2 Glideslope antenna
3 VOR antennas
4 Weather radar receiver/transmitter
5 Transformer/rectifier unit
6 Electrical contactor box - DC
7 28 VDC, 40 amp/hr Nicad battery
8 28 VDC, 13 amp/hr Nicad auxiliary battery
9 Ground crew interphone
10 External DC power receptacle
11 Forward retracting, steerable nosewheel
12 Access panel to rudder pedals and control cables
13 Access panel to aileron quadrant and flight control cables, pulleys and rods
14 Electrically-operated windshield wipers
15 Static ports, one each side
16 Pitot head for Captain's instruments, left side and First Officer's instruments, right side
17 Rudder pedals
18 Captain's control column
19 First Officer's control column
20 Flight controls in underfloor area
21 Center console - engine & propeller levers, flap lever, gust lock lever and elevator trim handwheels, etc.
22 Captain's and First Officer's instrument and glareshield panels.
23 Overhead console - DC system and control, ice protection, windshield heat, fuel control, battery, exterior and panel lighting, AC system and control, air conditioning, etc.
24 Captain's seat
25 First Officer's seat
26 Nosewheel steering control
27 Captain's chart case stowage
28 Circuit breaker panels - both sides
29 Emergency hydraulic handpump handle
30 Emergency nose landing gear release and handpump system
31 Flight compartment crew escape hatch - inward opening, removable
32 Control pulleys and cables - flaps, ailerons, engine controls
33 Control pulleys and cables - gust lock, engine controls, brakes
34 Flight compartment/cabin door - with integral forward observer's seat
35 Toilet - externally serviced
36 Toilet compartment folding door
37 Main electrical distribution panels - accessible through toilet compartment wall
38 Buffet unit - hot beverage containers, soft drinks and liquor stowage, etc.
39 Aisle service trolley - optional
40 Wardrobe compartment with cabin attendant's switch panel above.
41 Avionics compartment
42 Cabin attendant's folding seat with interphone
43 VHF No. 1 antenna, VHF No. 2 antenna on fuselage underside
44 Passenger emergency exit - Type II, floor level
45 Eighteen pairs of forward facing passenger seats - 36 seat configuration
46 Airstair door - manually operated, counter balanced
47 Airstair door external release handle
48 Airstair door internal release handle
49 Seat rails
50 Air conditioning air outlets

51 Emergency exits - Type III
52 Emergency exit internal release handle
53 Emergency exit external release handle
54 Front spar frame - wing/fuselage attachment
55 Wing/fuselage attachment points - front spar
56 Rear spar frame - wing/fuselage attachment
57 Wing/fuselage attachment points - rear spar
58 Engine control pulleys and cables
59 Wing front spar
60 Wing rear spar
61 Aileron splitter quadrant and gust lock
62 Aileron/spoiler and disconnect clutch
63 Flight spoiler control cables
64 Power control unit - flap drive

65 Flap line primary drive shaft, driven from power control unit, - a secondary flexible drive provides power to the flap screwjacks should the primary drive shaft fail

66 Flap screwjack - non-reversible, two per each inboard flap section
67 Flap screwjack - non-reversible, two per each outboard flap section
68 Flap drive transfer gearbox - transfers power to flexible drive should the primary drive shaft fail, - includes flap position sensor
69 Inboard flap section - constant chord, supported by cantilever rollers located in tracks mounted on the fuselage side and inboard side of nacelle
70 Outboard flap section - tapered, supported by rollers in tracks mounted on the outboard side of the nacelle and at wing stations YW261.0 and YW369.0
71 Flap track No. 4 roller carriage mounting at YW261.0
72 Flap track No. 5 roller carriage mounting at YW369.0
73 Left aileron
74 Right aileron
75 Aileron hinges
76 Aileron spring tab - left aileron
77 Aileron spring/trim tab - right aileron
78 Aileron output quadrant and control rod
79 Aileron spring tab operating lever

80 Roll spoilers - outboard, operate in conjunction with ailerons at air speeds below 200 knots. At speeds in excess of 200 knots, ailerons operate alone
81 Outboard spoiler actuator - hydraulic, No. 2 system

82 Roll spoilers - inboard, operate in conjunction with ailerons and outboard roll spoilers at air speeds below 130 knots
83 Inboard spoiler actuator - hydraulic, No. 1 system
84 Ground spoilers - outboard
85 Outboard ground spoiler actuator - hydraulic, No. 2 system
86 Ground spoilers - inboard, operate with outboard ground spoilers to provide wing lift dumping on landing. Operation is automatic through sequenced switches on the engine power levers and main landing gears
87 Inboard ground spoiler actuator - hydraulic, No. 2 system
88 Left and right elevators
89 Elevator horn mass balance
90 Elevator trim tabs
91 Elevator trim tab mechanism
92 Elevator spring tabs
93 Elevator spring tab mechanism
94 Elevator trim tab actuator - non-reversible
95 Elevator control input mechanism
96 Elevator control push rod
97 Elevator control quadrant
98 Fore rudder
99 Trailing rudder

DASH 8
DE HAVILLAND CANADA

N. MERRIN

100 Trailing rudder gearing push rod - upper
101 Trailing rudder gearing push rod - lower
102 Rudder actuator - hydraulic, No. 1 and No. 2 systems
103 Rudder control quadrant
104 Fore rudder hinges - four places
105 Trailing rudder hinges - three places
106 Horizontal stabilizer deicing boots - pneumatic

107 Deicing lines - horizontal stabilizer
108 Deicing lines
109 Deicing distributor valves and water separator
110 Pressure regulators - rudder hydraulics
111 Emergency location transmitter antenna
112 Emergency location transmitter
113 Flight data recorder
114 Cockpit voice recorder
115 Primary/secondary heat exchanger - air conditioning
116 Air cycle machine - supplies cooling air to air conditioning system
117 Air circulating/mixing unit
118 Rear pressure bulkhead
119 Baggage compartment rear bulkhead
120 Baggage restraint nets and posts - optional
121 Baggage restraints - cargo door
122 Baggage compartment door - inward opening, rolls upward on tracks to clear baggage door opening
123 Baggage compartment door tracks and rollers
124 Access panel to rear baggage compartment

125 Pipe lines in dorsal fin - one bleed air to air conditioning system, two deicing to horizontal stabilizer deicing and four hydraulic to rudder hydraulic actuators, etc.

126 Engine/nacelle fire extinguishers
127 Deicing lines - pneumatic
128 Wing leading edge deicing boots - pneumatic
129 Deicing isolate valve
130 Deicing distribution valves
131 Deicing water separator
132 No. 2 hydraulic power system ground service panel on nacelle right wall. No. 1 hydraulic power system ground service panel is installed in left engine nacelle.
    Hydraulic power is provided by two engine-driven hydraulic pumps, delivered to the systems at 3000 psi.

133 No. 2 hydraulic system reservoir
134 Hydraulic ground pressure connector
135 Pressure refuel/defuel fuel filler
136 Fuel master shut-off valve
137 Refuel/defuel lines
138 Fuel tanks, integral - one each wing. Total usable fuel, 5790 lb. (850 U.S. gallons). Optional 8200 lb. long range capacity available.
139 Fuel surge bay
140 Fuel collector bay - containing fuel high pressure ejector pump and electrical auxiliary pump
141 Magnastick fuel quantity backup indicating system - operable from ground
142 Capacitance probe - fuel contents, 6 per tank
143 Fuel vent and fuel pressure relief valves and fuel low pressure ejector pump
144 Fuel vent lines
145 Access panels to fuel tank
146 Access panel to fuel tank end rib
147 Overwing fuel filler - each wing
148 Landing lights - two each wing
149 Wing stall bar
150 Lift transducer - left wing only
151 Wing position lights
152 Tail position light - lower
153 Tail position light - upper
154 Anti-collision light - upper
155 Static discharge wicks
156 H.F. antenna
157 Rearward retracting main landing gear
158 Main landing gear drag strut
159 Main landing gear support structure
160 Main landing gear doors
161 Engine firewall
162 Engine nacelle lower cowling - hinged
163 Engine air intake - deiced
164 Engine nacelle top front cowling
165 Engine yoke support structure
166 Engine mount yoke
167 Engine access panels
168 Engine nacelle side cowlings - hinged
169 Engine nacelle rear side panels - hinged
170 Engine mounting support structure - aft
171 Pratt & Whitney PW120, 2000 SHP, free-turbine powerplant
172 Propeller reduction gearbox
173 Hamilton Standard 14SF, fully-feathering, constant speed, propeller - electrically deiced
174 Propeller pitch control mechanism
175 28 VDC starter/generator - one each engine
176 115/200 VAC generator - one each engine
177 Engine air exhaust ducting
178 Speed decreaser gearbox cooling air intake
179 Wing inspection light - each nacelle
180 Access panel to tail cone
181 Space provision for optional APU
182 Taxi light

production would be delivered to scheduled airlines had much to do with the airplane's final configuration. The Dash 8 design specification included certification under FAR 25 requirements for operation from a 3000-foot runway at sea level and ISA +15°C conditions. The capability would allow the new airplane to operate economically at crowded hub airports on short, independent stub runways using the procedures developed by US operators of the Dash 7.

The new concept could best be described as a multi-purpose regional transport airplane, optimized for regional airline operation yet adaptable to anything from unpaved runways to business flying and the military. Low-speed controllability in the approach mode would continue to be a distinct de Havilland feature while the minimum-drag airframe would provide a quick climb to altitude and higher cruise speeds. The design required an engine with maximum fuel efficiency and it was decided the Dash 8 would have two of the Pratt & Whitney PW 120 engines, each delivering 2000 shp to 82°F. By the end of 1980 the construction of a wooden mockup was well under way in the experimental bay of the test flight hangar.

Airworthiness — An Explanation
Through all the years that de Havilland Canada sold products from

the parent company the original airworthiness certification was completed in England. It was recognized by Canadian authorities and DHC's responsibility was to maintain the airworthiness specifications laid down. Even when DHC produced the D.H.83C Fox Moth after the war it was simply an extension of the original British airworthiness certification.

It was not until the Chipmunk, Beaver and Otter days that the company became involved with original certification procedures, but these were relatively simple compared with later years. The Chipmunk and Beaver were certified to conform with British Civil Air Regulations (BCAR) and the Otter with the International Civil Aviation Organization (ICAO) requirement. The United States Federal Aviation Authority rules were also accepted as standard in Canada and were spelled out in what was then called the FAA Civil Air Regulations (CAR for short). The de Havilland types fell in the category of "normal utility and acrobatic category airplanes" and thus complied with Section 3 of the regulations or CAR 3.

When the Caribou was designed it was a different matter. Although it was primarily a military design, it would need airworthiness standards to comply with "transport category airplanes," which came under regulations Section 4b or CAR 4b. When the Buffalo came along the target was also for full transport category certification and it went to the 4b standard in Subsection SR 422, the turbine category covering the differences in

airplane performance. Some time after the Twin Otter was certified the US federal regulations were completely overhauled and called FARs (Federal Air Regulations) from then on. The old CAR 3 became FAR Part 23 and CAR 4b became FAR Part 25.

A new requirement was introduced in 1969 for light twin CAR 3/FAR 23 types capable of carrying more than 10 occupants. It was a mandatory upgrading of CAR 3 and involved additional safety features such as autofeathering propellers, improved electrical circuitry, additional emergency exits, etc. Thus the Twin Otter, with its original CAR 3, now conforms to Special FAR Part 23, British ARB and French DGAC airworthiness approval.

The Dash 7 received full airline certification under FAR Part 25, but as there was no category for STOL, a special condition was applied to allow for the steeper approach and shorter landing. In the case of the Dash 8 this special condition does not apply and the initial certification will be as a standard FAR 25 airplane, together with FAR 36 governing noise standards, and SFAR 27 covering such things as fuel venting and exhaust emissions.

Passages
The 50-year celebration that marked the company's growth brought with it one of life's mathematical factors called retirement. Long-service

The Pratt & Whitney PW120 advanced technology engine and Hamilton Standard 14SF propeller in the testing rig before installation in the Dash 8. (DHC51886)

The Twin Otter fitted with a chin radar and internal fuel tanks takes on ice patrol duties off the Greenland coast. (DHC45996)

employees had always enjoyed recognition with a yearly retirement party. Now, many of the people who had played a major role in the formative years were passing the responsibility to younger hands.

Even before the 50-year mark the names of George Mickleborough, Frank and Ab Warren, George Blanchard and John Slaughter were on the retirement list. Buck Buchanan, George Hurren and Len Trotter took reluctant leave of the sales organization they worked so hard to build and Harry Beffort retired from his years of union negotiations. In October 1979 Dick Hiscocks retired and the office of vice-president engineering was taken by M.C.W. "Mike" Davy. In December Fred Buller retired as chief designer and was replaced by John Thompson. Buller and Hiscocks had worked together in design engineering since the Chipmunk/Beaver days. Alex Watson, engineering manager, prepared for his retirement in January 1980, which would be followed in February with a retirement party for veteran test and demonstration pilot Don Rogers. Another veteran from DH England, Phil Halsey, whose experience went back to the Mosquito and later the Comet, attended these affairs and prepared for his own retirement in June 1982.

Communications

Good employee communications was one of Geoffrey de Havilland's policies that went back to his first company. It started with the *Airco Rag* during the years with the Aircraft Manufacturing Company in World War 1 and, later, the de Havilland *Enterprise*. The in-house *Enterprise* became so sought after by the aviation trade that the de Havilland *Gazette* emerged as a sales promotion medium. It became a high quality publication with glossy paper, good photographs and accurate technical articles. It had a steady run of cartoons by noted aviation cartoonists and a nice blend of English humour on the back pages.

The magazine had to be suspended during the slump in the thirties but Martin Sharp took over as editor in 1937 and brought it back to life until another curtailment during World War 2. Sharp revived it again during the era of the DH Comet and Canadian bushplanes, when it reached its highest level. It was taken over by

Hawker Siddeley in 1960 and ended one year later.

The Canadian scene was covered in the early issues of the *Gazette* with photos and news stories as far back as 1928. The policy of an in-house communication was responsible for the *De Havilland Mosquito* in Canada during the war years at Downsview and surviving copies are now collectors' items. Various news sheets followed during the fifties and sixties with Fred de Jersey and Ernest Ball publishing such items as the *Progress Report* and *High Lift* in more recent times. Economic conditions have once again curtailed the larger communications but the internal *Downsviews* still carries plant news to the employees.

Boom Times

On December 13, 1979, the Conservatives were toppled in Ottawa and talk of selling the company faded into the turmoil of parliamentary business. The year had produced 16 Dash 7 sales and seen the delivery of 52 Twin Otters and 8 Buffalos. Other statistics as the Christmas holidays approached placed sales at $247 million and staff at 4600.

For three years in a row the trend at DH Canada had been positive and rewarding. The Dash 7 was selling well and performing according to early predictions; the Twin Otter and Buffalo were moving steadily. All these things provided stability and accounted for early confidence in the new Dash 8. No one could blame the board of directors and the management committee for feeling optimistic.

When the Aviation and Space Writers Association visited the de Havilland plant on May 30, 1980, there was another important announcement about the Dash 8: formal commitments had been received from purchasers for 55 of the aircraft, representing a sales value of $400 million. It was a heady period, for never before in de Havilland Canada's history had so many advance orders been received for an airplane that was still only in the early stages; the Dash 8 was off to a decidedly better start than the '7. Coupled with this announcement was word that a second site was planned to look after the necessary expansion. John Sandford explained that 12 locations were under consideration and that a decision would come in July. This started a

Nine 45-gallon drums inside a Twin Otter, all connected to the main tanks, provide fuel capacity for long delivery flights. (DHC23662)

scurrying by numerous Ontario municipalities and howls from Mayor Mel Lastman of North York (which includes Downsview) at the thought of losing any de Havilland jobs.

The controversy was resolved early in 1981 with the decision to build at Downsview. Sixty-five Canadian municipalities had applied, particularly Peterborough and Windsor which had put on strong presentations. The problem from the beginning had hinged on the need for 100 acres of land on the Downsview site owned by the Department of Defence. When this land was made available, the most prudent line of action was to remain at Downsview.

It did not take long to plan the office and hangar space. The new complex contained an additional warehouse, a low bay and high bay hangar, along with the much needed office space. It was to total 669,000 square feet and cost $75 million. An encouraging announcement in December 1980 had recorded four Dash 7 sales and options to Atlantic Southeast Airlines of Atlanta, Georgia. Also at that time Air Wisconsin ordered a tenth Dash 7, making it the largest regional operator in the USA using the '7.

The optimism of the new year was reflected in an article by Ron Lowman in the *Toronto Star* in January 1981 based on an interview with Dawson Ransome, head of Ransome Airlines. Ransome operated 15 aircraft under the Allegheny banner in the competitive Philadelphia-Washington-New York circuit. Three of his aircraft were Dash 7s and he was in Toronto

The Dash 8 prototype in its preliminary colour scheme.

ordering three more. The article was headed "US BOSS LOVES OUR DASH 7S" and went on to explain that Ransome's enthusiasm for the '7 was such that he would have loved to take on something as interesting as the proposed Toronto-Ottawa-Montreal STOL service. He talked about the aircraft's tight turn capability, which was impressing US controllers and made for less complicated arrivals and departures. "The short-haul business is booming," said Ransome, who explained that he was trying to replace his French Nord 262s with Dash 7s.

Antarctic Action

Service crews from DH Canada have often been called upon to perform outstanding maintenance feats far from home, particularly during the Viet Nam War and the days of the Caribou. It happened again in the summer of 1980 but this time the locale was 1500 miles from the South Pole.

It all started with a minor mishap to the touring Transporter, which was on O'Higgins Island in the Chilean section of the Antarctic. The main port landing gear had broken through the ice crust during taxiing, which resulted in propeller and engine damage. Replacing a propeller was routine but getting 7 1/2 tons of supplies and equipment to retrieve the airplane proved to be a minor expedition. Crawford Byers was despatched to Alaska to acquire a set of Caribou skis while Doug Fleming prepared a new propeller and Norm Bailey organized all the gear and equipment that would be needed for

Members of the Transporter recovery team on O'Higgins Island survey the wrecked tent after the storm, before resuming work. (DHC49354)

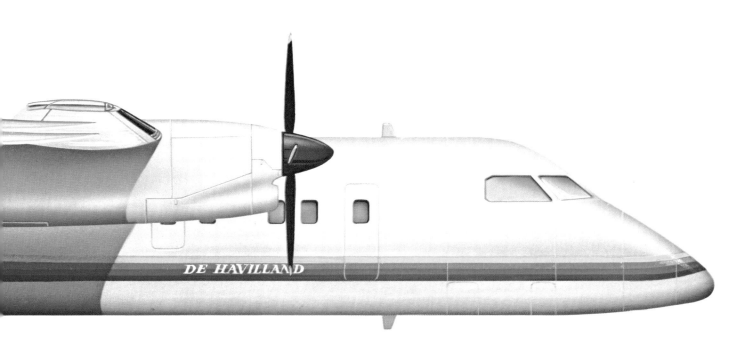

Illustration by Peter Mossman

the changeover. Everything was shipped to Chile where it was forwarded, first by Chilean Lockheed C-130 Hercules from Punta Arenas to Base Frei, then by Twin Otters of the Chilean Armed Forces.

The de Havilland crew built a tent around the engine, but on August 12 winds of 100 mph wrecked the tent and prevented work for three days. When the wind relented there was a massive snow removal job to be done before the new propeller and the skis could be fitted. It was the first time a set of skis had been used on a DHC-5 but they allowed pilot Bill Pullen to ease the aircraft out of the snowdrift and head north to a warmer climate. Fleming and Bailey described it as "just another job" when they got back to Downsview but confessed to an aversion to shovelling snow.

Another unusual exploit involving a DHC aircraft was the Transglobe Expedition of 1979-82, described by its patron, Prince Charles, as "a suitably mad and splendidly British idea." Headed by Sir Ranulph Twisleton-Sykeham-Fiennes, the adventurers set out to circle the globe via both poles,

Transglobe Twin Otter which supplied Sir Ranulph Fiennes' trek across the Antarctic. (DHC50077)

225

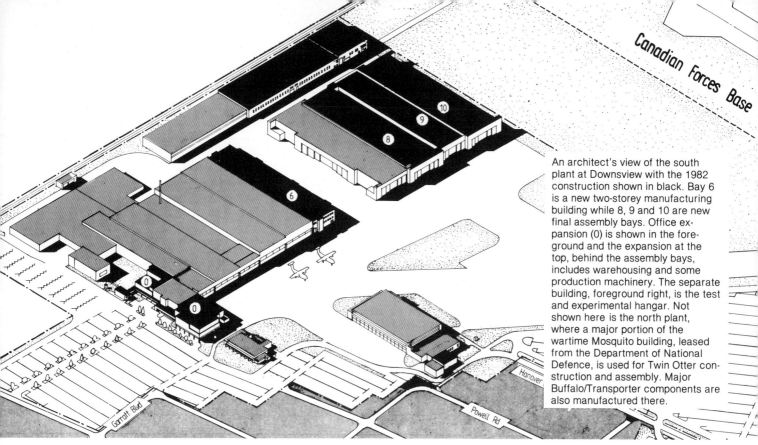

An architect's view of the south plant at Downsview with the 1982 construction shown in black. Bay 6 is a new two-storey manufacturing building while 8, 9 and 10 are new final assembly bays. Office expansion (0) is shown in the foreground and the expansion at the top, behind the assembly bays, includes warehousing and some production machinery. The separate building, foreground right, is the test and experimental hangar. Not shown here is the north plant, where a major portion of the wartime Mosquito building, leased from the Department of National Defence, is used for Twin Otter construction and assembly. Major Buffalo/Transporter components are also manufactured there.

A close-up of the wheel/ski combination fitted to the first British Antarctic Survey Twin Otter in 1968. (DHC30590)

The Transporter, the civil version of the Buffalo, is seen in this shot by Terry Shwetz making a LAPES cargo delivery. (DHC52213)

by foot, ship, Land Rover, snow-mobile and sledge. In the Antarctic they duplicated Sir Vivian Fuchs' crossing, supported this time by a Twin Otter. The aircraft, in brilliant red, white and blue, was sponsored by the Chubb Group of Companies and had seen service in the North Sea oil business with Loganair. It was fitted for Arctic work in Canada and was operated on the expedition by pilot Giles Kershaw and flight engineer Gerry Nicholson, who were regular visitors to Downsview as crew of the British Antarctic Survey.

A Change in the Weather

The company's annual report in May 1981 showed sales for 1980 at a record high of $347 million and provided continued optimism through the summer of 1981. Everyone in the industry thought the once-dreaded fuel crisis was under control, even if prices remained high. The United States had welcomed back the Iran hostages and the newly elected Reagan administration was forcing interest rates upwards when the August air traffic controllers' strike dealt the teetering airline industry a severe blow. Perhaps the parties involved misread the times, for the strike started a dramatic tumbling of the

cards that reached right back to the production line at Downsview.

Commuter airlines, with their quick, frequent services, were the first to be hurt in the strike, and an up-and-coming Dash 7 operator, Golden Gate Airlines, was the first airline casualty. Golden Gate served Los Angeles and 18 other western cities with Dash 7s. By the fourth week of the strike their losses had reached $40,000 a day and they were forced to suspend all services indefinitely. The trunk airlines were also suffering and United Airlines laid off 2100 personnel within days. Soon 14,000 airline layoffs were announced.

A very cold wind blew into Downsview the day Golden Gate folded for they operated nine '7s and had ordered five more. Their closing made things very difficult for de Havilland by thrusting these aircraft on a softening market and causing a reshuffling of the delivery list. Another blow was a rapid decline in Twin Otter sales. So many orders were cancelled in one short period that production was chopped from six to three per month and 214 workers were laid off from the line. The news got worse when President Reagan fired the striking controllers and even more confusion hit the US airline industry. The business that Dawson Ransome said was booming in January was now under severe economic strain. Cutbacks continued throughout the industry and 450 more layoffs were announced at de Havilland during October.

The first Dash 8 is rolled out during the gala ceremony at Downsview on April 19, 1983. (DHC52454-21, Tony Honeywood)

The entire aviation industry was badly hit by the economic recession of 1982 and since manufacturing was such a big employer, much was written in the press about the problems. In a *Financial Post* interview John Sandford apportioned blame for the situation on a percentage basis. Twenty percent he blamed on the controllers' strike, 40 per cent on predatory financing (governments competing by supporting their countries' products with unrealistically favourable financing), 20 per cent on high interest rates and 20 per cent on the general decline in the economy.

Long before the onslaught of these economic storm signals, the wooden mock-up of the Dash 8 had been built in the de Havilland experimental hangar. This led to a metal mock-up in 1982 while the jigs and fixtures were being prepared and the subcontractors organized. On December 1, at the Airline Association convention in San Francisco, John Sandford announced the roll-out date of April 19, 1983. It was also announced that the first Dash 8 was to be delivered to the Ontario government's regional airline, Norontair, following type certification. The action moved to Hangar 8 where the eighth such drama

in the company's history began to unfold—preparing a new aircraft design for its first flight.

Despite the depressing drop in Dash 7 and Twin Otter sales, interest in the Dash 8 remained high with an unprecedented list of firm orders and options. Excitement built at Downsview as the test aircraft came together over the winter of '83 until it was time for its trip to the paint shop. Here, along with its attractive paint scheme, it received one more sample of a company tradition. The last three letters in the registration C-GDNK were in honour of the retiring Chairman of the Board, Douglas N. Kendall, who had served since 1970.

When the time came to unveil the Dash 8 for public viewing the event developed into a twofold presentation. A private in-house ceremony for the employees and their families was held Saturday, April 16, with the Honourable Pierre Elliott Trudeau officiating. The visit by Canada's Prime Minister demonstrated his interest in the industry and served to recognize the people who had worked so hard to make the event possible. It also acted as a full dress rehearsal for industry guests the following Tuesday.

The roll-out ceremonies on April 19

Two fine views of the Dash 8 during early test flying. Above it is posed off Lake Ontario's scenic Scarborough Bluffs, while the second view shows it in landing configuration. (DHC52763-1 and 52744, Charles Bryant and Ron Nunney)

were vividly described by *The Canadian Aircraft Operator.* "It was pure theatre," said Canada's general aviation newspaper. "Looking on were 1,600 guests representing customers, suppliers and good friends of de Havilland Canada from all over the world.

"The big production bay was blacked out. The curtain withdrew dramatically to reveal 411 Reserve Squadron band marching out playing a jaunty rendition of 'Those Magnificent Men in Their Flying Machines,' while behind the band a tug-towed Dash 8 emerged from the shadows in a silhouette created by brilliant backlighting. As it came to a full stop before the applauding audience, the house lights were brought up to reveal the aircraft in all its gleaming splendour, its pristine white finish offset only by a tapered nose-to-tail yellow / orange / red / burgundy colour speed band."

The Dash 8 Flies

On June 20, 1983, the Dash 8 made its first flight—still ten days ahead of a schedule set three and a half years before. Veteran test pilots Bob Fowler and Mick Saunders were at the controls with Don Band and Ches Pyne at the engineer stations. Two chase aircraft followed the new airliner, a Buffalo for photography and a Dash 7 with President Sandford and Douglas Kendall on board. "Delta November Kilo" flew a triangular course over Peterborough and Lake Scugog, completing a series of prescribed manoeuvres en route. It also performed several optional tests and landed after 90 minutes with Fowler's comments, "A lovely test, the best we have ever done."

The Test Program

When asked how the first flight compared with that of the Dash 7, Fowler was quick to point out the difference in the design specifications of the two airplanes. "We were able to predict much more in advance with this aircraft." he said. "The engine controls were calibrated ahead of time in the test rig and worked perfectly. The flight controls felt so good after our skips that we knew we were in for a good ride."

The euphoria of that excellent flight was not allowed to linger. Testing began immediately. It was to be a long program, with 1670 hours of flying over the next 14 months involving five aircraft. State-of-the-art improvements were introduced, to add efficiency and speed the FAR, Part 25 certification.

Engineering Test Flight under manager W.M. "Wally" Gibson had developed into a very efficient unit with a blend of experienced leaders and new test specialists. The design engineers were also a seasoned group under program manager G.R. "Ron" Jackson. The program began with J.P. "Jack" Uffen as director of Development Engineering, who made major contributions to the Dash 8 on the management side. When he retired in 1984, R.G. "Dick" Batch took over the responsibility and D.R. "Roy" Madill moved to manager of Technical Design. Senior aerodynamicist T.R. "Tom" Nettleton played a central role in the design of both the Dash 7 and Dash 8. In the test department itself the two seasoned members, M.P. Rosemeyer and Jock Aitken, led a highly qualified team.

The second pre-production Dash 8 began flying on October 26, the third in late November. The fourth was scheduled for the end of the year. By November 15 the first two machines had a total of 120 hours of flying and the program was in full swing.

Deliveries Begin

By the time the first Dash 8 flew, there were 53 confirmed sales and 60 options. In other times that would have been an excellent start for any program but the enthusiasm was dampened by the announcement of a $265.2 million loss for the company during the seven-month period ending December 31, 1982. One week earlier a similar loss at Canadair, for 1982, was reported at $1.4 billion. These announcements cast a dark cloud over the Canadian aerospace industry—the thunder and lightning were to follow in due course.

The airline upheaval in the United States put so many Twin Otters and Dash

To speed the pre-test period, a heavily instrumented engine test rig was built for the new technology P&W 120 engine. By the time the aircraft flew, most of the operating parameters for the electronic engine and propeller controls were in place, requiring only in-flight data. (Charles Bryant–DHC)

President John Sandford beams with pride as he welcomes the test crew back from the first flight of the Dash 8. Left to right: Mick Saunders, Bob Fowler, Sandford, Don Brand, Ches Pyne and Ron Jackson. (Tony Honeywood–DHC)

7s on the used market that new sales in that segment almost dried up. All production lines at Downsview were cut back drastically and the Dash 7 stopped completely. The assembly bays and service ramps grew quiet even though the test hangars remained busy. Empty desks reflected a dwindling office staff and spaces began to show in the once-full parking lots.

The press went into high gear the moment cost overruns at these two government-owned companies began to show. The national challenge to Canadian technology was lost in the shuffle and everything, once again, was reported in tax dollars. Even before the rollout, John Sandford had written a letter to the Toronto Star countering an unfavourable article that called de Havilland a "money losing company."

"I can only say the company has made a profit in each year since 1974 when it was acquired by the crown. Since acquisition, total profit is approximately $16 million.

"At this point, like so many aerospace companies throughout the world, we are suffering the effects of a world economy in recession. In spite of that, as recently as May of this year, we announced record sales. Since the crown acquired de Havilland eight years ago the company has

recorded about $1.6 billion in sales of aircraft and services—$1.4 billion of this has been in the highly competitive export market. In this same period we generated 32,000 person-years of work for de Havilland employees, and almost 20,000 person-years of work have been generated within out suppliers' factories across the country. About 900 Canadian suppliers participate with de Havilland in building some of the best aircraft that fly around the world today."

The letter received no headlines and it wasn't the last time the term "money losing company" would be used.

One bright spot was the delivery of the first Dash 8 to Norontair, October 23, 1984. Ontario Premier William Davis joined the official ceremony and watched John Sandford hand over the log books to Northern Affairs Minister Leo Bernier. The first airline flight of a Dash 8 occurred on December 19, when the aircraft completed its scheduled run from Sault Ste Marie to Kapuskasing. On the same day, another handover ceremony saw the first Dash 8 delivered to a United States operator when Eastern Metro Express took possession of their first in an order of eight.

Management CDIC Style

From the day the operation of de Havil-

The handover ceremony of the first Dash 8 to Norontair, October 23, 1984, was attended by hundreds of guests, suppliers, customers and employees. Ontario's retiring Premier, William Davis, joined the ceremony to watch John Sandford hand over the log books to Ontario's Northern Affairs Minister, Leo Bernier. Left to right:Wilf Spooner, chariman of ONTC, Leo Bernier, William Davis with John Sandford following the ceremony. (Tony Honeywood–DHC)

land Canada and Canadair entered the public domain it fell under the control of the Canadian Development Investment Corporation (CDIC), responsible to the Minister of Industrial Expansion. The preservation of a Canadian aerospace industry was a genuine reason for the purchase of these companies in the first place and the intention was to move both into the private sector when the time was right. De Havilland continued in a favourable financial position in spite of the fact that the Dash 7 was a slow starter. The buoyant commuter airline industry of 1979–80 encouraged equity inputs as in any other corporation. Canadair was well into its Challenger program on the same basis but was running an even greater deficit due to performance shortfalls in the test program.

The downturn in the North American economy wasn't making life easy for Joel Bell, the CDIC boss in Ottawa, who was caught with two very expensive product development programs carrying a high Canadian profile. The media were in full cry at the amount of government assistance and instant experts emerged of every political hue.

Back in the short-lived Tory regime of 1981, when talks of "privatization" were raised, John Sandford had made the remark "Many can buy us but few can afford us," and explained one of the basic rules of modern aircraft manufacture. "It takes a great deal of front-end investment before

the plane goes out the door." The statement applied even more now that a market recession had entered the equation. The break-even point on sales of the new Dash 8 was set around 300 machines, so the front-end investment was bound to be high.

With all the howls from the media, Bell made a move that was never completely understood by the aviation fraternity. In the latter part of September the press was informed that John Sandford would become vice-chairman to see the Dash 8 program into airline service and concentrate on marketing. An interim president would be announced later. Sandford was an ideal choice to market the Dash 8 now that it was flying. After all, it was his pet project from its very first year. Bell's master plan also involved Sandford heading a program to bring the two government companies closer together.

The timing was critical for any such plan, as an election was coming and the Liberals were down in the public opinion polls. There were worried looks in both Downsview and Ottawa. The position of president remained open until August when it was announced that D. Bryan Long, a senior advisor at CDIC, would fill the role on an interim basis. About the same time it was announced that the Dash 8 had cracked the military market with an order of six aircraft from the Department of National Defence, four as transports and two as trainers. An additional two would go to the Department of Transport for airway calibration. It would be a nice order to talk about at the coming Farnborough Air Show.

Farnborough 1984
If ever there was a watershed of the 1980s for de Havilland Canada, it was the British Farnborough show of 1984. Every second year, when the producers of aviation hardware meet in England, it is the custom of the participants to announce their latest sales conquests. De Havilland had more than the DND sale to talk about. One was a confirmed Dash 8 sale to an old customer, Tyrolean Airways of Innsbruck, one to North Africa and two to a Far-East operator. Twin Otter sales had revived with orders from China and Ethiopian Airlines.

By all previous standards this was a good sales announcement, but a pall hung over the Canadian chalet on the top of Farnborough's famous hill. It was election week in Canada and a clear trend for change was indicated. The mood of the Canadian contingent was not improved when the attending Buffalo crashed doing

a STOL demonstration landing. If nothing else it demonstrated the structural integrity of the aircraft, for the three occupants crawled out unhurt.

News came during the flurry of this unfortunate incident that the Conservatives had won an overwhelming victory back in Canada. From that moment on, a new era was under way in Canadian aerospace and a new pattern began to unfold at de Havilland.

The Rocky Road to Change
While campaigning for election, Michael Wilson, the eventual finance minister, promoted a plan to merge de Havilland and Canadair as a first step toward privatization. This idea received wide editorial support and, by coincidence, was similar to the plan Joel Bell had in mind.

It didn't take long for the Progressive Conservatives to settle into their new role on Parliament Hill and allot the portfolios. Gone were the grand plans of a consolidated aerospace effort; the Minister of Regional Industrial Expansion, Sinclair Stephens, quickly returned to a pledge he had made during his lean years in opposition. He put de Havilland up for sale along with some 54 other crown corporations.

The Liberal incumbents of CDIC, and those associated with de Havilland, soon left the scene. Joel Bell left in October and Paul Macklin Marshall (president and CEO of Westmin Resources) was appointed in his place. By January the position of DHC president was resolved with W.B. "Bill" Boggs coming out of retirement to take the role he vacated in 1970. It was a supreme challenge for the veteran Boggs, who had headed Canada Systems Group during the intervening years.

During the next two years de Havilland was to suffer comments like "money losing," "debt ridden" and the old favourite, "awash in red ink." Even Peter Newman in his colourful prose called de Havilland Canada, "Ottawa's perpetual problem child." The magazine Canadian Aviation, editorialized that governments traditionally get behind their aerospace industries in difficult times and that, in spite of the heavy expenditures, de Havilland was "on the brink of a profitable future." Even the harshest critics praised the excellence of the new Dash 8. Few reported the track record of self sufficiency the company had achieved over 50 years and that the "problem child" held its own long after Ottawa rescued the company from Hawker Siddeley in 1974.

The costs of bringing the Dash 8 to life outweighed the sales income in the

	Sales (millions)	Profit
1975–76	$90	$465.000
1976–77	$121	$2.7 million
1977–78	$125	$2.2 million
1978–79	$172	$3.8 million
1979–80	$248	$1.7 million
1980–81	$358	$6.4 million
1981–82	$450	$2 million

latter half of 1982 and 1983. A good sales year of $204 million in 1984 eased the loss to $40 million but the decline continued into 1985.

During March, a short 15-day strike took place with negotiations hinging on job security if the company should change hands. Some interesting Twin Otter and Buffalo sales were recorded, and the next month John Sandford announced he was leaving for a position as vice-president of Fairchild Industries Inc. Prior to his departure the plans for a stretched version of the Dash 8, the 300 series, were well under way and announced to the press during May.

The Bidding and Choosing
The "for sale" sign at de Havilland did not bring an immediate response for there were no quick returns in the offing. A lot

of specialized items had to be considered that only experts in the field fully understood. It was going to be a slow process. There were a number of interesting "nibbles" according to Paul Marshall but that was all he would divulge. By the spring of 1985 he was able to announce seven companies in the running. At one time it looked like British Aerospace might be interested in buying back the company but that did not last long. In June the Boeing Commercial Airplane Company of Seattle indicated its interest, and by August Marshall had narrowed the list to four or five serious proposals.

By November 1985 the bidding for the two aircraft companies on the CDIC sales list began to heat up. President Paul Marshall announced that Boeing was interested only in de Havilland and a consortium headed by West German entrepreneur Justus Dornier proposed buying both de Havilland and Canadair. Boeing was a long-time friend of de Havilland and already established in Canada. The Dornier group's proposal was one that had been broached many times but never taken seriously, to operate the two concerns in their respective locations under the umbrella of a single holding company.

While Boeing remained a leading contender, the Amsterdam-based Fokker BV

joined Versatile Corporation of Vancouver and unidentified backers in filing an application under the name of Rimgate Holdings Ltd. Boeing soon became the front runner for, as Marshall put it, their offer was "superior."

A New Owner
At 3:30 p.m., Monday, December 2, 1985, the Hon. Robert de Cotret, president of the Treasury Board of Canada, announced at a news conference in Ottawa that the federal government had reached an agreement for the purchase of de Havilland Canada by the Boeing Company. At exactly the same moment, de Havilland Canada's president Bill Boggs was informing more than 4000 employees at a special meeting called in Bay 7. The simultaneous announcements ended weeks of speculation and rumours about the future of the company.

On the morning of the joint announcements, Boggs joined Richard Albrecht, chairman of Boeing of Canada, and Paul

A 1986 view of the plant that employs over 4800 and has close to 1100 suppliers and subcontractors from coast to coast in Canada. In person-years of work, the Twin Otter represents 32:9, the Dash 7, 165:6 and the Dash 8, 112:7. For every 100 jobs in Downsview, 70 others are created elsewhere in Canada. (Charles Bryant–DHC)

The special ice reconnaissance patrol Dash 7R delivered to Environment Canada. The high "crow's nest" observation deck and the side-looking radar are the outward points of recognition. Inside, the cabin is full of electronic patrol equipment for ice detection and plotting in Canada's coastal waters. (Charles Bryant–DHC)

The Boeing of Canada board meeting of January 1987 appointed Ron B. Woodard as president of the de Havilland Aircraft Company of Canada. Woodard had spent 20 years in the aerospace industry, gaining executive experience in program management and international sales, and came to de Havilland from Boeing's Materiel Division. Boeing chairman Richard Albrecht announced that William Boggs would remain a member of the board and become vice-chairman of Boeing Canada. (DHC)

Marshall of CDIC in a meeting with supervisory staff and later a gathering of newsmen in the sales mockup area. Public reaction to the news was swift and varied. Opposition parties in the House of Commons called the sale a "give-away" yet financial analysts called it a "good deal" for all concerned.

Negotiations continued for the rest of the month amid speculation that it might be possible to cancel the deal. Sinclair Stephens was in hospital at the time and pressed for a December 31 closing date. The opposition in Parliament was so great that a delay in signing was granted to allow for a committee of investigation.

Everyone pressed for details of the purchase arrangement and the following list was issued to the employees by Boggs, Albrecht and Marshall:

PRICE: The total purchase price is $155 million, consisting of a $90 million down payment and promissory notes totalling $65 million over 15 years. The notes carry no interest but will be adjusted to reflect inflation. This $65 million will be forgiven if Boeing invests $325 million for Canadian goods and services unrelated to the current operations of de Havilland or Boeing in Canada.

Projects such as the just-launched Dash 8 series, for example, or modifications and improvements to the line, will not be eligible for this debt relief.

ROYALTY PAYMENTS: Boeing is to pay a royalty of $275,000 for every Dash 7 sold beyond number 122 (108 sold to date). A royalty of $225,000 will be paid on any Dash 8 or derivative beyond aircraft number 400. All on-going

development costs are to be paid by Boeing.

ADDITIONAL INVESTMENTS: Boeing has announced plans to invest $115 million in product development and upgrading facilities at Downsview. They have just announced the launch of the Dash 8 series 300 and will also be picking up all future losses of the company.

SALES FINANCING: De Havilland will continue to be eligible for EDP and EDC support, as in the past. In addition, Boeing has given up substantial tax benefits except to use those tax benefits to support sales financing for Canadian purchasers of de Havilland products.

DIPP GRANTS: Certain product development costs may be shared by Ottawa on a project-by-project basis, providing that eligibility requirements are met under the Defence Industries Productivity Program. These grants can cover up to 50 percent of the development costs but are expected to be repaid from products sold. DIPP grants are now available to all other companies manufacturing in Canada, and will be reinstated for de Havilland under the new ownership.

LAND VALUE: Land speculation has been eliminated as an issue in this agreement. Under the terms of the letter of intent, if any of the lands acquired by Boeing become surplus to future requirements, the government may repurchase those lands at a price stipulated in the agreement.

Finally, on January 31, the formal signing took place and Boeing became owner of the de Havilland Aircraft of Canada Limited in its 58th year. The two

proud names in aviation history would now be working as one but each would retain its product identity and family heritage. The Downsview complex would now be known as THE DE HAVILLAND AIRCRAFT COMPANY OF CANADA, A DIVISION OF BOEING OF CANADA.

The Boeing Company

When the Boeing Commercial Airplane Company of Seattle, Washington, purchased de Havilland, it was no stranger to Canada. William Edward Boeing had flown into Vancouver in 1919 with the first international mail flight and ten years later returned to establish Boeing Aircraft of Canada Ltd. Throughout the 1930s the company built a number of U.S.-designed aircraft, the C-204 flying boat and the 40H-4 mailplane. They developed a Canadian-designed flying boat, the Totem, which made quite a hit at the time but did not go into production. The depression reduced the company to repair and overhaul status but by 1937 a new plant was established at Sea Island Airport to build the British Blackburn Shark.

The company reached its peak during World War 2, using the original building and expanding to a number of small plants at Victoria, Chilliwack and Nelson. The total manufacturing space during the war was 878,479 square feet and employment reached 10,315. Boeing of Canada made numerous parts for the Avro Anson, tailplanes for the D.H. 98 Mosquito and wing spars for the Noorduyn Norseman. Their facilities included a major overhaul shop and, along with the 17 Blackburn Sharks, they built 307 Consolidated Catalina flying boats and amphibians. All operations ceased after the war and the Sea Island factory was sold to Canadian Pacific Airlines.

The company returned in 1960 as Boeing of Canada Ltd., with a helicopter overhaul facility at Arnprior, Ontario. In 1971, the Winnipeg Division was formed to make high strength-to-weight fibre-composite plastic components, many of which are used in the Dash 7 and Dash 8. A smaller company, Boeing Computer Services, Canada Ltd., has offices in Vancouver, Calgary and Toronto.

In recent years, Boeing established a close association with de Havilland on the augmentor STOL program and built the intricate blown wing. The Seattle sales organization also joined DHC in extensive world-wide marketing assistance for the Dash 7. When the two companies merged in 1986, Boeing had 1000 employees in Canada which, with the Downsview staff, brought the total to 5500.

A reasonable calm prevailed after the signing of the agreement, for increased aircraft deliveries and new sales were beginning to tell the story. The Financial Post said, "The decision of the federal government to sell de Havilland Aircraft was a sound one. The sale to the Boeing Company could be a good deal for de Havilland and the country. Instead of hand wringing a little clapping would be in order." These sentiments were echoed by John Sandford, now president of Fairchild Republic Co., who said, "Boeing is the best thing that could have happened to de Havilland."

The rush of orders through the last six months of 1985 brought steady deliveries into the next year. By May, three Canadian carriers had ordered a total of 46 Dash

The de Havilland employees shared a portion of company history October 3, 1985, when Dash 8 serial number 50 became part of the fleet of Horizon Air, the Seattle-based regional airline. It was the 7000th aircraft manufactured at the Canadian Downsview plant and was part of an original order of ten (with an additional ten options). (Tony Honeywood–DHC)

8s to a tune of $410 million, bringing the sales and options to 144. By June the Downsview payroll had grown to 4800 and the parking lots were full again. By the end of the year export deliveries had broadened to New Zealand and Papua New Guinea. In two years the Dash 8 had 30 per cent of the market share in its class. An interest in the 300 series was beginning to show, with 23 firm orders and 15 options.

Other Sales
The Dash 7 market revived in 1985 with sales to New Guinea, China, Cairo and a very special ice reconnaissance model, the 7-R, to the Canadian Ministry of the Environment. As 1987 began, 107 Dash 7s had been delivered to 22 countries. The largest operator is Pan Am Express (formerly Ransome Airlines) with 10 Dash 7s in its fleet.

A boost for the 20-year-old Twin Otter came with the 1985 edition of Esso Air World's annual survey of the "Turbine-Engined Fleets of the World Airlines." The numbers from Aviation Data Service of Wichita, Kansas, reported 488 Twin Otters in airline service, well ahead of the Fokker/Fairchild F-27. In spite of the downturn in the economy, 30 Twin Otters left the Downsview lines between January 1983 to October 21986. During the same period, eight Buffalos and 17 Dash 7s went to world markets.

October 1986 was a benchmark for the entire de Havilland team as it recorded the delivery of the 7000th aircraft manufactured at Downsview. The customer was Horizon Air and the aircraft was the fifth Dash 8 in their order of 10. The occasion also served as an official opening of Bay 9, which had remained unused since 1982 with a dirt floor. Horizon's president, Mike Kuolt, accepted delivery of the airplane and gave a spirited motivational message to the 4000 company employees gathered for the occasion.

The Montreal-based Innotech Aviation Ltd. conducted considerable market and technical research for the corporate Dash 8 and became the exclusive distributor. Four custom-fitted models went through their shops in 1986, for Mobil Oil, the government of Alberta and LTV Aerospace.

During the controversy of the de Havilland sale, one commentator made the remark that Boeing was buying an opportunity to spend money. It did not take long for that sequence to begin. A news report noted that the new owner was spending $20 million at Downsview on numerical control equipment, automatic riveting, increased capacity for compos-

ites and more computerized manufacture. A new optimism prevailed in the offices and on the shop floor that echoed into the marketplace.

The City Express Story
In the years before the Dash 7, much de Havilland talk hinged on the word STOL and the Short Take Off and Landing airplanes the company built. The STOL technique had been used successfully by the U.S. military but still remained outside the public transportation realm. An entire department at DHC was dedicated to planning commercial STOL and Bob McIntyre spearheaded a series of promotions, complete with practical demonstrations.

The Airtransit experiment with Twin Otters (page 195) proved the STOL intercity concept but had limited impact without a 50 passenger aircraft available. Endless negotiations and studies were carried out on the possibility of a Toronto-Ottawa-Montreal system using the Toronto Island Airport but the opposition

A team of City Express commuters over the Toronto waterfront. The first two Dash 8s joined the fleet simultaneously and went on a ten-flights-a-day service between Toronto Island and Montreal. Their two Dash 7s fly eight Toronto-Ottawa flights a day. (Tony Honeywood–DHC)

was tough. While approvals inched closer to reality, a small Peterborough airline, Air Atonabee Ltd., using 19-passenger Saunders ST-27s (turbine converted D.H. Herons), obtained permission to fly into the Island Airport on a regular basis. Soon it had added Ottawa and Montreal to its schedules, using "Airtransit" style buses at each end of the run.

Air Atonabee was successful but limited until an experienced airline man, Victor Pappalardo, saw the potential and bought the airline, changing its name to City Express. Soon Pappalardo had a couple of Dash 7s on the run and the de Havilland concept of a STOL service began to take shape. The world's quietest airliner came and went unobtrusively, the

fares were kept low and a series of innovations brought prompt passenger response. The timing coincided with transport deregulation steps in Canada and City Express became a showcase of private enterprise in the short-haul field.

City Express demonstrated the concept McIntyre was trying to promote in the 1970s and in no small way influenced development of a similar service being planned in London, England. Unfortunately Bob McIntyre did not live to see the complete fulfillment of his Toronto or London dream; he died on September 23, 1985.

The London Docks STOLport

While de Havilland was promoting city-centre STOLports during the 1970s the deserted Royal Docks of London were always considered an ideal site. The Thames Upper Docks lie within six miles of Trafalgar Square and had become the focal point of a giant revitalization program. By 1980, the British government created the London Docklands Development Corporation (LDDC) to breath new life into the entire Thames estuary. An airport was discussed on the basis of the de Havilland STOL concept but it wasn't until the introduction of the Dash 7 into British airline service in 1982 that the plan was taken seriously. Trial landings conducted on a disused wharf by Brymon Airways convinced the construction firm of John Mowlem and Co. to plan a full STOL-port service for the LDDC.

There was the usual hue and cry from

the environmentalists, followed by a public enquiry and an inspector's report. Even then there were delays through 1984/85 as the Greater London Council fought the project in the high court. General permission was given in May 1985 and by March 1986 detailed planning permission was secured. One month later John Mowlem and Co. had the empty warehouses removed and by the end of 1986 the runway concrete was completed on the wharf between King George V and Royal Albert Docks.

The delays enabled the British Environment Ministry to establish the noise and runway restrictions while the CAA

The first Dash 8 for the Canadian Forces was delivered in April 1987 for service with 412 (Det.) at CFB Lahr, West Germany, where it took over duties form a Dash 7. (Tony Honeywood–DHC)

The Dash 8 Series 300 prototype was built by inserting two plugs into the fuselage of the Dash 8 prototype. The plugs add about 11.5 feet to the length of the aircraft and allow 50 seats. (DHC)

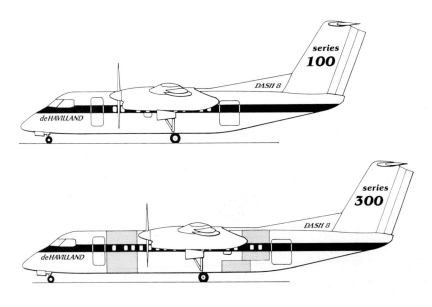

235

evaluated the technical aspects of glide slope and traffic congestion. By the time the service opens in the fall of 1987, a new life will dawn for the Royal Docks and a new travel pattern will come to the great city of London.

Competition is keen among the airlines wishing to operate the new service, but for the foreseeable future the only large passenger aircraft to fully meet the stringent requirements is the de Havilland Dash 7.

Ground School
Throughout the days of the Otters and Caribou, de Havilland operated its own ground school and organized conversion training for pilots. The advent of the Dash 7, and particularly the Dash 8, brought a new sophistication that called for specialized training services. In the fall of 1985 de Havilland signed a contract with Flight Safety International for comprehensive pilot and maintenance training on Twin Otter, Dash 7 and Dash 8 aircraft. The contract called for the construction of a 25,000 square foot state-of-the-

The Dash 8 Series 300 makes an impressive entry before an audience of employees, suppliers and customers at the rollout ceremony, March 22, 1987. (Ron Nunney–DHC)

art training centre next to the cafeteria building at Downsview. Full classroom and simulator facilities on all types will be available to corporate, military and commuter customers to speed their aircraft into service.

This side view shows off the sleek lines of the Series 300. (Larry Boccioletti–DHC)

Three-views of DHC Aircraft

Drawings by N. Merrin

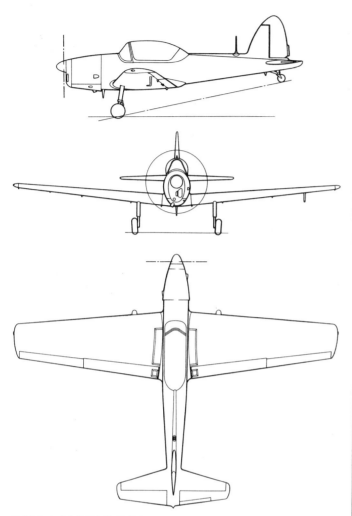

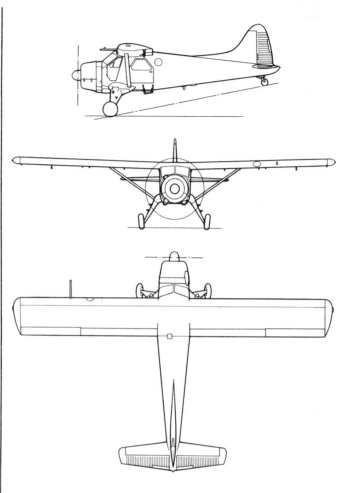

DHC-1 CHIPMUNK

Engine   Gipsy Major 1C
  (reciprocating)
Brake horsepower   140
Propeller   Fixed pitch wood or
  metal

External Dimensions

Wing span	34 ft 4 in
Length overall	25 ft 5 in
Height overall	7 ft 0 in
Tailplane span	11 ft 11 in
Wheel track	8 ft 11 in
Wheel base	17 ft 20 in
Wing area (total)	172.5 sq ft
Aileron area (total)	13.9 sq ft
Flap area	22.0 sq ft
Fin area	5.9 sq ft
Rudder area (inc. tab)	6.8 sq ft
Tailplane area	17.0 sq ft
Elevator area (inc. tab)	15.2 sq ft

Weight

Empty weight	1184 lb
fuel	180 lb
oil	23 lb
crew	380 lb
misc.	163 lb
Maximum takeoff weight	1930 lb
Maximum wing loading	11.2 lb/sq ft

Maximum power loading	13.8 lb/bhp

Performance

Maximum speed S/L	140 mph
Maximum permissible dive	200 mph
Normal cruise (at 5000 ft)	122 mph
Climb speed	80 mph
Glide speed	70 mph
Rate of climb S/L	900 ft/min
Service ceiling	17200 ft
Takeoff distance to 50 ft	870 ft
Landing run	930 ft
Maximum range	485 miles

Recommended Aerobatic Speeds

130 mph for a slow roll
140 mph for a loop
150 mph for a roll off the top of a loop

Fuselage Dimensions

Maximum width	2 ft 6 in
Maximum depth	4 ft 7 in
Maximum section	9 sq ft

DHC-2 BEAVER (Landplane)

Engine   P&W R985 Wasp Junior
  SB-3 (reciprocating.)
Brake horsepower   450
Propeller   Hamilton Standard,
  constant speed, counter
  weight, 2-bladed.

External Dimensions

Wing span	48 ft 0 in
Length overall	30 ft 4 in
Height over tail	9 ft 0 in
Tailplane span	15 ft 10 in
Wheel track	10 ft 2 in
Wheelbase	22 ft 9 in
Wing area (total)	250 sq ft
Aileron area (total)	24.6 sq ft
Flap area	20 sq ft
Fin area	16 sq ft
Rudder area (inc. tab)	9.4 sq ft
Tailplane area	25.4 sq ft
Elevator area (inc. tab)	23.0 sq ft

Weight

Basic operational	3000 lb
Maximum takeoff	5100 lb
Maximum landing	5100 lb
Maximum wing loading	20.4 lb/sq ft
Maximum power loading	11.3 lb/bhp

Performance (Max. takeoff weight)

Maximum speed S/L	140 mph
Maximum permissible dive	180 mph
Maximum cruise S/L	135 mph
Economical cruise (5000 ft)	130 mph
Stalling speed	60 mph
Rate of climb S/L	1020 ft/min
Service ceiling	18000 ft
Takeoff run	560 ft
Takeoff to 50 ft	1015 ft
Landing run	500 ft
Landing from 50 ft	1000 ft

Payload/range, normal tanks, 45
  min reserve

100 miles — 1675 lb
300 miles — 1500 lb
470 miles — 1350 lb

Internal Dimensions

Cabin length	9 ft 0 in
Maximum width	4 ft 0 in
Maximum height	4 ft 3 in
Floor area	31.5 sq ft
Volume	134 cu ft
Cabin doors (L)	40 in x 39 in
(R)	40 in x 39 in

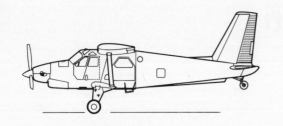

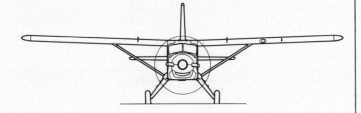

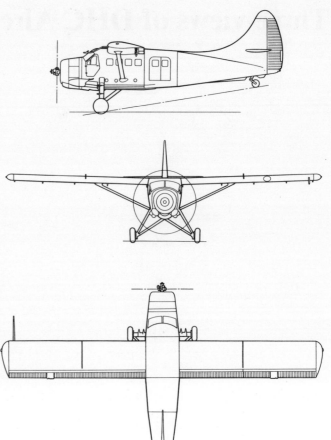

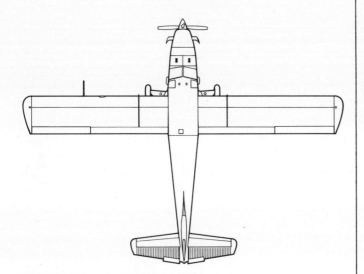

DHC-2 Mk III TURBO BEAVER (Landplane)

Engine   P&W PT6A-20 (turboprop)
Shaft horsepower   550
Propeller   Hartzell, 3-bladed, full
feathering and reverse

External Dimensions

Wing span	48 ft 0 in
Length overall	35 ft 3 in
Height over tail	11 ft 0 in
Tailplane span	15 ft 10 in
Wheel track	10 ft 2 in
Wheelbase	22 ft 9 in
Wing area (total)	250 sq ft
Aileron area (total)	24.6 sq ft
Flap area	20.0 sq ft
Fin area	21.5 sq ft
Rudder area (inc. tab.)	11.0 sq ft
Tailplane area	25.4 sq ft
Elevator area (inc. tab.)	23.0 sq ft

Weight

Basic operational	2760 lb
Maximum takeoff	5370 lb
Maximum landing	5100 lb
Maximum wing loading	21.5 lb/sq ft
Maximum power loading	8.3 lb/hp

Performance

Maximum speed	170 mph
Maximum permissible dive	180 mph
Maximum cruise	157 mph
Economical cruise (5000 ft)	151 mph
Stalling speed	60 mph
Rate of climb S/L	1220 ft/min
Service ceiling	23,900 ft
Takeoff run	500 ft
Takeoff to 50 ft	1030 ft
Landing run	360 ft
Landing from 50 ft	870 ft

Payload/range, normal tanks, 45 min reserve

200 miles —	1850 lb
400 miles —	1545 lb
600 miles —	1210 lb

Internal Dimensions

Cabin length	11 ft 6 in
Maximum width	4 ft 0 in
Maximum height	4 ft 3 in
Floor area	40.5 sq ft
Volume	174 cu ft
Cabin doors (L&R)	46 in x 40 in

DHC-3 OTTER (Landplane)

Engine   P&W R1430 Wasp S1H1
(reciprocating)
Brake horsepower   600
Propeller   Hamilton Standard,
hydromatic, 3-bladed

External Dimensions

Wing span	58 ft 0 in
Length overall	41 ft 10 in
Height over tail	12 ft 7 in
Tailplane span	21 ft 2 in
Wheel track	11 ft 2 in
Wheel base	27 ft 10 in
Wing area (total)	375 sq ft
Aileron area (total)	26.3 sq ft
Flap area	98 sq ft
Fin area	33.2 sq ft
Rudder area (inc. tab)	27.0 sq ft
Tailplane area	39.0 sq ft
Elevator area (inc. tab)	46.0 sq ft

Weight

Basic operational	4431 lb
Maximum takeoff	8000 lb
Maximum landing	8000 lb
Maximum wing loading	21.3 lb/sq ft
Maximum power loading	13.3 lb/bhp

Performance

Maximum speed S/L	153 mph
Maximum permissible dive	192 mph
Maximum cruise S/L	132 mph
Economical cruise (5000 ft)	138 mph
Stalling speed	58 mph
Rate of climb S/L	735 ft/min
Service ceiling	17,400 ft
Takeoff run	630 ft
Takeoff to 50 ft	1155 ft
Landing run	880 ft
Landing from 50 ft	440 ft

Payload/range, normal tanks, 45 min reserve

200 miles —	2920 lb
500 miles —	2580 lb
875 miles —	2100 lb

Internal Dimensions

Cabin length	16 ft 5 in
Maximum width	5 ft 2 in
Maximum height	4 ft 11 in
Floor area	79 sq ft
Volume	345 cu ft
Cabin doors (L)	46.5 x 45 in
(R)	30 x 45 in

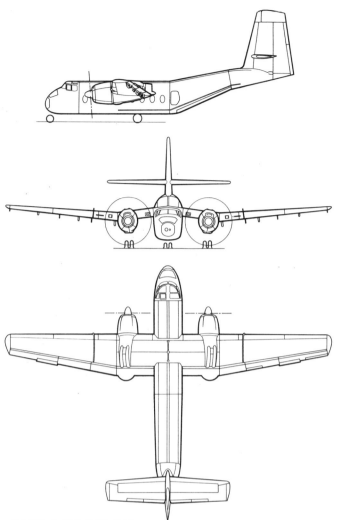

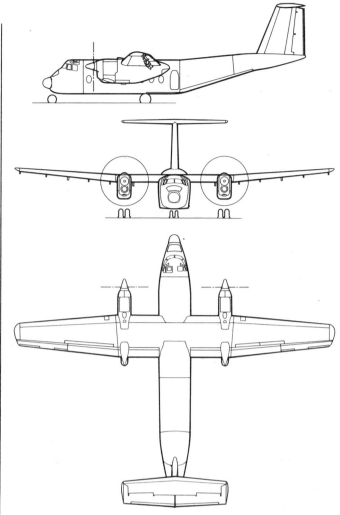

DHC-4 CARIBOU

Engine 2 x P&W R-2000 7M2
(reciprocating)
Brake horsepower 1450
Propellers Hamilton Standard,
3-bladed, full feathering and
reverse

External Dimensions

Wing span	95 ft 7½ in
Length overall	72 ft 7 in
Height over tail	31 ft 9 in
Tailplane span	36 ft 0 in
Wheel track	23 ft 1½ in
Wheel base	25 ft 8 in
Wing area (total)	912 sq ft
Aileron area (total)	91 sq ft
Flap area (total)	285 sq ft
Fin area	127 sq ft
Rudder area (inc. tab.)	84 sq ft
Tailplane area	144 sq ft
Elevator area (inc. tab.)	86 sq ft

Weight

Basic	17,630 lb
Maximum takeoff	28,500 lb
Maximum landing	28,500 lb
Zero fuel weight	27,000 lb
Maximum wing loading	31.2 lb/sq ft
Maximum power loading	9.83 lb/bhp

Performance (Maximum Weight)

Maximum speed	216 mph
Maximum permissible dive	240 mph
Economical cruise speed (10,000 ft)	182 mph
Stalling speed	68 mph
Rate of climb S/L (2 engines)	1355 ft/min
Rate of climb S/L (1 engine)	235 ft/min
Service ceiling (2 engines)	24,800 ft
Service ceiling (1 engine)	8,800 ft
Takeoff run (short field)	725 ft
Takeoff to 50 ft (short field)	1185 ft
Landing run (short field)	670 ft
Landing from 50 ft (short field)	1235 ft

Payload/range, normal tanks, 45
min reserve
200 miles — 8600 lb
600 miles — 7200 lb
1100 miles — 5417 lb

Internal Dimensions

Cabin length	28 ft 9 in
Maximum width	7 ft 3 in
Maximum height	6 ft 3 in
Floor area	176 sq ft
Volume	1150 cu ft
Cabin doors (L&R)	4 ft 7 in x 2 ft 6 in
(Rear)	6 ft 3 in x 6 ft 1½ in

DHC-5D BUFFALO

Engine 2 x GE CT64-820-4
(turboprop)
Shaft horsepower 3133
Propellers Hamilton Standard
63E60-25, 3-bladed, feathering
and reverse.

External Dimensions

Wing span	96 ft 0 in
Length overall	79 ft 0 in
Height over tail	28 ft 8 in
Tailplane span	32 ft 0 in
Wheel track	30 ft 6 in
Wheel base	27 ft 10 in
Wing area (total)	945 sq ft
Aileron area (total)	39 sq ft
Flap area (inc. ailerons)	280 sq ft
Fin area	92 sq ft
Rudder area	60 sq ft
Tailplane area	151.5 sq ft
Elevator area	81.5 sq ft

Weight (Transport)

Basic (3 crew)	25,000 lb
Maximum takeoff	49,200 lb
Maximum landing	46,900 lb
Zero fuel weight	43,500 lb
Maximum wing loading	52 lb/sq ft
Maximum power loading	7.85 lb/shp

Performance (Transport)

Maximum cruise speed (10,000 ft)	227 mph
Maximum permissible dive	334 mph
Economical cruise speed (10,000 ft)	208 mph
Stalling speed	84 mph
Rate of climb S/L (2 engines)	1780 ft/min
Rate of climb S/L (1 engine)	310 ft/min
Service ceiling (2 engines)	27,000 ft
Service ceiling (1 engine)	7900 ft
Takeoff run	2300 ft
Takeoff to 50 ft	2875 ft
Landing run	850 ft
Landing from 50 ft	2010 ft

Payload/range, normal tanks, 45
min reserve
690 miles — 18,000 lb
1150 miles — 15,000 lb
2000 miles — 12,000 lb

Internal Dimensions

Cabin length	31 ft 5 in
Maximum width	8 ft 9 in
Maximum height	6 ft 10 in
Floor area	242 sq ft
Volume	1580 cu ft
Cabin doors (L)	5 ft 6 in x 2 ft 9 in
(Rear)	20 ft 9 in x 7 ft 8 in

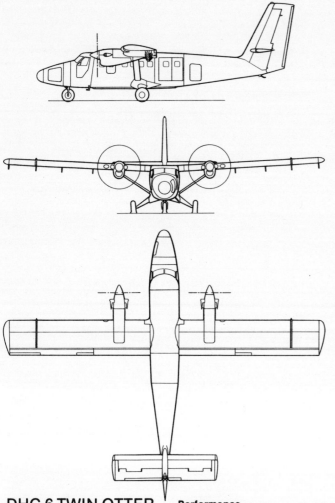

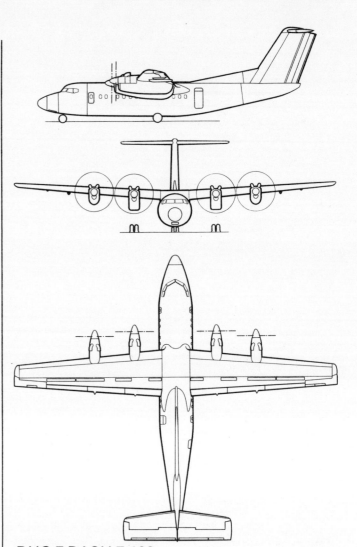

DHC-6 TWIN OTTER (Series 300 Landplane)

Engine 2 x P&W PT6A-27 (turboprop)
Shaft horsepower 620
Propellers Hartzell, 3-bladed, full-feathering reverse.

External Dimensions

Wing span	65 ft 0 in
Length overall	51 ft 9 in
Height over tail	19 ft 6 in
Tailplane span	20 ft 8 in
Wheel track	12 ft 2 in
Wheel base	14 ft 10½ in
Wing area (total)	420 sq ft
Aileron area (total)	33.2 sq ft
Flap area	112.2 sq ft
Fin area	48.0 sq ft
Rudder area (inc. tabs)	34.0 sq ft
Tailplane area	100.0 sq ft
Elevator area (inc. tabs)	35.0 sq ft

Weight

Basic operational	7407 lb
Maximum takeoff	12,500 lb
Maximum landing	12,300 lb
Maximum wing loading	29.8 lb/sq ft
Maximum power loading	10 lb/shp

Performance

Maximum speed S/L	196 mph
Maximum permissible dive	227 mph
Maximum cruise (10,000 ft)	210 mph
Stalling speed	67 mph
Rate of climb (2 engines)	1600 ft/min
Rate of climb (1 engine)	340 ft/min
Service ceiling (2 engines)	26,700 ft
Service ceiling (1 engine)	11,600 ft
Takeoff run	860 ft
Takeoff distance to 50 ft (SFAR 23)	1500 ft
Landing run	950 ft
Landing run from 50 ft (SFAR 23)	1500 ft
Accelerate-stop (SFAR 23)	2280 ft
Range, maximum payload	830 miles

Internal Dimensions

Cabin length	18 ft 6 in
Maximum width	5 ft 3¼ in
Maximum height	4 ft 11 in
Floor area	80.2 sq ft
Volume	384 cu ft
Cabin doors (L)	4 ft 2 in x 4 ft 8 in
(R)	3 ft 9½ in x 2 ft 6¼ in
Total baggage area	126 cu ft
Passengers	20

DHC-7 DASH 7-100

Power plant 4 x P&W PT6A-50 (turboprop)
Snaft horsepower 1120
Propellers 4 x Hamilton Standard, 4-bladed, full feathering, reverse

External Dimensions

Wing span	93 ft 0 in
Length overall	80 ft 7.7 in
Height over tail	26 ft 2 in
Tailplane span	31 ft 0 in
Wheel track	23 ft 6 in
Wheel base	27 ft 6 in
Wing area	860 sq ft
Aileron area	23.22 sq ft
Flap area	294.2 sq ft
Vertical tail surfaces	170.0 sq ft
Horizontal tail surfaces	217.0 sq ft

Weight

Basic operational	27,600 lb
Maximum takeoff	44,000 lb
Maximum landing	42,000 lb
Zero fuel weight	39,000 lb
Maximum wing loading	51.2 lb/sq ft
Maximum power loading	9.37 lb/shp

Performance

Maximum cruise (15,000 ft)	264 mph
Stalling speed	76 mph
Rate of climb (4 engines)	1200 ft/min
Rate of climb (3 engines)	720 ft/min
Service ceiling (4 engines)	20,900 ft
Service ceiling (3 engines)	15,100 ft
Takeoff field length (FAR 25)	2260 ft
Landing field length (FAR 25)	1950 ft

Payload/range (15,000 ft), 115 mile diversion, 45 min reserve

400 miles	11,400 lb
800 miles	9400 lb
1335 miles	6400 lb

Internal Dimensions

Cabin length	39 ft 6 in
Maximum width	8 ft 6 in
Maximum height	6 ft 4½ in
Floor area	246.7 sq ft
Volume	1910 cu ft
Cabin doors — Passenger	5 ft 9 in x 2 ft 6 in
Baggage	3 ft 4 in x 2 ft 9 in
Total baggage volume	240 cu ft
Passengers	50

Appendices

The DHC Logo

The DHC Canada logo provides a link with the past and has a history of its own that goes back to 1927. The original was designed by Leonard Bridgeman, who was at the time the editor of *Janes' All the World's Aircraft*. He prepared the original DH logo based on the lettering style and aircraft profile of the day. It saw much use in company advertising from then on and Bridgeman is reputed to have received a gold watch for his efforts.

It was the original of the decals that graced every DH aircraft from the Cirrus Moth to Canada's postwar Fox Moths. A variation of the original even went on the early Chipmunks and Beavers. During the war the Mosquito profile was used under a slightly modified DH and seen on letterhead from all the de Havilland branches. The Canadian symbol changed to its present form in the late '40s and is a stylized profile resembling the Mosquito. At one time the word TORONTO was used under the DH but the present use of CANADA adds the finishing touch to a bit of company history.

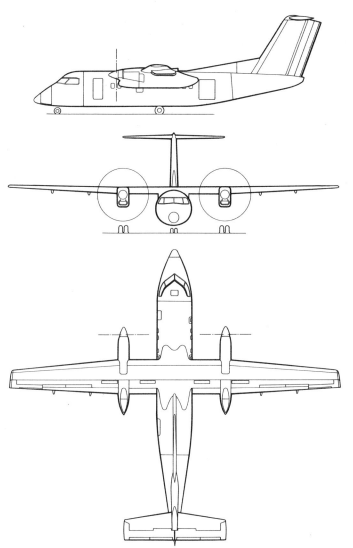

DHC-8 DASH 8-100

Enginges 2 x P&W PW120
(turboprop)
Shaft horsepower 2000
Propellers Hamilton Standard,
4-bladed, full feathering and
reverse.

External Dimensions

Wing span	84 ft 0 in
Length overall	73 ft 0 in
Height over tail	25 ft 0 in
Tailplane span	26 ft 0 in
Wheel track	25 ft 10 in
Wheel base	26 ft 1 in
Wing area	585 sq ft
Horizontal tail surfaces	150 sq ft
Vertical tail surfaces	152 sq ft

Weight

Basic operational	20,176 lb
Maximum takeoff	30,500 lb
Maximum landing	30,000 lb
Zero fuel weight	28,000 lb
Maximum wing loading	52.1 lb/sq ft
Maximum power loading	8.1 lb/shp

Performance ISA (Gross Weight)

Maximum speed S/L	276 mph
Maximum cruise (15,000 ft)	310 mph
Stalling speed	83 mph
Rate of climb S/L (2 engines)	2070 ft/min
Rate of climb S/L (1 engine)	530 ft/min
Service ceiling (2 engines)	25,000 ft
Service ceiling (1 engine)	16,000 ft
Takeoff field length (FAR 25)	2710 ft
Landing field length (FAR 25)	1980 ft
Payload/range (15,000 ft), 115 mile diversion, 45 min reserve	
400 miles — 7824 lb	
800 miles — 5900 lb	
1230 miles — 4500 lb	

Internal Dimensions

Cabin length	30 ft 2 in
Maximum width	8 ft 2 in
Maximum height	6 ft 2 in
Floor area	203.5 sq ft
Cabin volume	1300 cu ft
Baggage volume	300 cu ft
Cabin doors — Passenger	5 ft 0 in x 2 ft 6 in
Baggage	5 ft 0 in x 4 ft 2 in
Passengers	36

The original design by Leonard Bridgeman which also formed a decal that was placed on the Moth interplane struts.

Another combination of the familiar DH seen most often on the wheel hub covers of the early Moth series.

The original Moth logo was combined with a maple leaf to provide a distinctive Canadian decal for all new and over-hauled DH types to emerge from the prewar shops at Downsview.

The wartime logo using a Mosquito as the aircraft symbol which received worldwide use.

The present de Havilland Canada logo combines a graceful wing profile with the distinctive Mosquito tail design and maintains a tradition as old as the company itself.

The DH Moth Variants

Any aircraft with the interchangeability of the D.H.60 Moth developed variations over the years that are bound to confuse historians. The aircraft became tagged with an unofficial prefix of the engine fitted, hence the terms Cirrus Moth, Gipsy Moth and Genet Moth. The first model '60 had a plywood box fuselage, fabric-covered wings and a straight-axle undercarriage. The '60X denoted the change to a split-axle undercarriage, while a '60G had both the split axle and the de Havilland-manufactured Gipsy engine. A '60M indicated a "G" type configuration but with a welded tubular metal fuselage. None of the other variants, the Moth Majors or the Moth Trainers, came to Canada, although one pre-production Tiger Moth was sent from England as a demonstrator.

Another point of confusion for the researcher was the practice of calling the later models "Moths." The Giant Moth, the Hawk Moth, the Puss Moth, the Fox Moth and the Hornet Moth all have their own designating D.H. Number as shown in the following table.

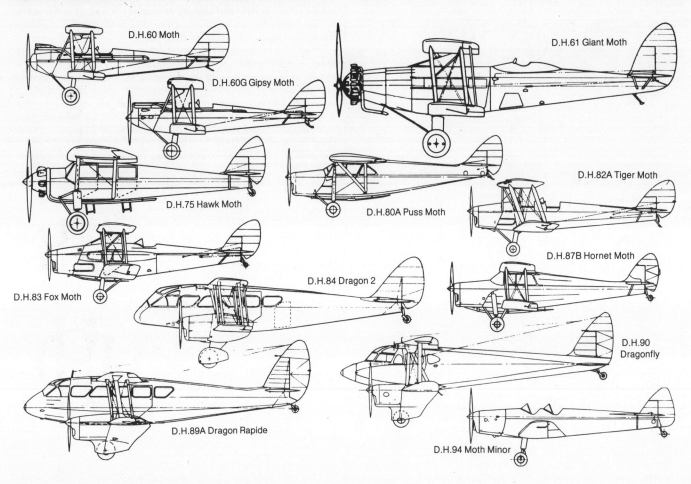

DH England Designs Imported to Canada before World War 2

Designation	Name	First Imported	Engine	BHP	Gross Wt. Lb.	Total
D.H.4	D.H.Four	1917	R-R Eagle VIII	325	3500	12
D.H.9A	D.H.NineA	1920	Liberty 12	400	5000	12
D.H.60&60X	Cirrus Moth	1926	ADC Cirrus I, II & III	85 & 90	1550	100
D.H.60	Genet Moth	1928	A-S Genet	75	1550	2
D.H.60G	Gipsy Moth	1928	D.H. Gipsy I	100	1750	15
D.H.60M	Gipsy Moth	1934	D.H. Gipsy I & II	100 & 120	1750	202
D.H.60T (spl)	Tiger Moth	1931	D.H. Gipsy III	120	1750	1
D.H.61	Giant Moth	1928	Bristol Jupiter	465	7000	3
D.H.75	Hawk Moth	1930	A-S Lynx	247	3500	3
D.H.80A	Puss Moth	1930	D.H. Gipsy III	120	2050	34
D.H.82A	Tiger Moth	1935	D.H. Gipsy Major	130	1825	5
D.H.83	Fox Moth	1933	D.H. Gipsy Major	130	2100	8
D.H.84	Dragon	1933	D.H. Gipsy Major	130x2	4500	3
D.H.87A	Hornet Moth	1935	D.H. Gipsy Major	130	1950	2
D.H.87B	Hornet Moth	1936	D.H. Gipsy Major	130	1950	8
D.H.89	Dragon Rapide	1935	D.H. Gipsy Six2	205x2	5550	16
D.H.90	Dragonfly	1936	D.H. Gipsy Major	130x2	4000	8
D.H.94	Moth Minor	1939	D.H. Gipsy Minor	90	1550	1

Aircraft Produced by DH Canada under Licence

Designation	Name	Engine	Horsepower	Years	Production Military	Production Civil	Production Total
D.H.82A (Can)	Tiger Moth	Gipsy Major I	130bhp	1938-39	25	3	28
D.H.82C 1&3	Tiger Moth	Gipsy Major IC*	142bhp	1940-42	1384	—	1384
D.H.82C 2&4	Menasco Moth	Pirate D4	125bhp	1940-41	136	—	136
D.H.83C	Fox Moth	Gipsy Major IC	142bhp	1945-47	—	53	53
D.H.98	Mosquito	Packard Merlin 67	2x1705bhp	1942-45	1133	—	1133
Avro 652	Anson II	Jacobs L6MB	2x330bhp	1941-43	375	—	375
Grumman CS2F-1&2	Tracker	Wright R1820-82	2x1525bhp	1955-57	100	—	100

*The Gipsy Major, series I, developing 130 hp at 2350 rpm (with a 5.25:1 compression ratio), was improved for the D.H.82C Tigers in Canada and called the IC. It was approved for the use of leaded fuel, had aluminum cylinder heads and dome forged pistons. It had a 6:1 compression ratio and developed 142 hp at 2350 rpm. The Major IC was used in the postwar Fox Moth and early Chipmunk before changing to the Gipsy Major 10 of 145 bhp at 2550 rpm.

DH Canada Designs Manufactured in Canada to January 1, 1983

Designation	Name	Engine	Horsepower	Years	Production Military	Production Civil	Production Total
DHC-1	Chipmunk	Gipsy Major 1C & 10	142 & 145bhp	1946-56	153	64	217*
DHC-2 Mk.I	Beaver	P&W R-985	450bhp	1947-67	1098	533	1631
Mk.II	Leonides Beaver	Alvis Leonides 502/4	570bhp	1953	—	1	1
Mk.III	Turbo Beaver	P&W PT6A-6	550shp	1963-68	—	60	60
DHC-3	Otter	P&W R-1340 (geared)	600bhp	1951-67	335	131	466
DHC-4	Caribou	P&W R-2000-7M2	2x1450bhp	1958-73	293	14	307
DHC-5	Buffalo	GE T-64	2x3133shp	1964-	121	—	121**
DHC-6 (100)	Twin Otter	P&W PT6A-20	2x 579shp	1965-68	15	99	114
(200)	Twin Otter	P&W PT6A-20	2x 579shp	1968-69	10	105	115
(300)	Twin Otter	P&W PT6A-27	2x 620shp	1969-	38	535	573**
DHC-7 (100)	Dash 7	P&W PT6A-50	4x1020shp	1975-	2	86	88**

*1000 manufactured in England and 60 manufactured in Portugal.
**Production to January 1983.

Some Aircraft Selling Prices

These are approximate prices in Canadian funds that applied when the aircraft were first offered on the market.

D.H.60M Moth	$4450
D.H.80A Puss Moth	$6850
D.H.82A Tiger Moth	$6000
D.H.83 Fox Moth	$5350
D.H.84 Dragon	$15,400

(CM&S traded in a Dragon on a Rapide in 1937 for $11,500)

D.H.87B Hornet Moth	$4500
D.H.89 Rapide	$23,000
D.H.90 Dragonfly	$13,500
D.H.94 Moth Minor	$3200
D.H.83C Fox Moth	$10,500
DHC-1 Chipmunk	$10,500
DHC-2 Beaver	$21,000
DHC-3 Otter	$80,000
DHC-4 Caribou	$425,000
DHC-5 Buffalo	$1,550,000
DHC-6 Twin Otter	$248,000
DHC-7 Dash 7	$1,700,000
DHC-8 Dash 8	$4,350,000

Cartoon by Wren from the *Aeroplane*, April 17, 1953.

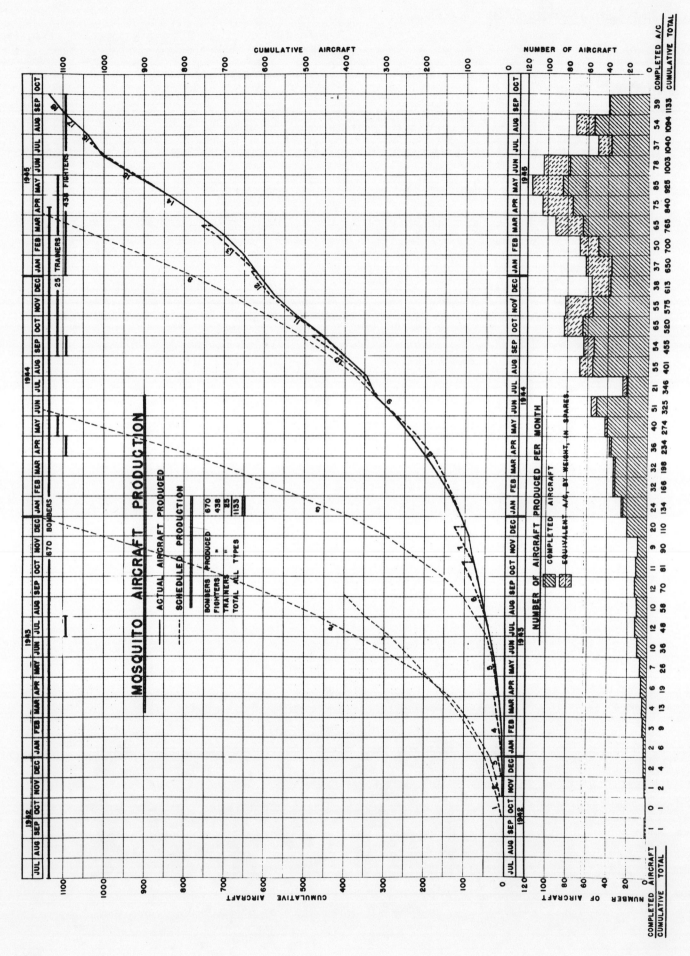

MOSQUITO AIRCRAFT PRODUCTION

——— ACTUAL AIRCRAFT PRODUCED

- - - SCHEDULED PRODUCTION

BOMBERS PRODUCED   670
FIGHTERS   "   438
TRAINERS   "   25
TOTAL ALL TYPES   1133

NUMBER OF AIRCRAFT PRODUCED PER MONTH

COMPLETED AIRCRAFT

EQUIVALENT A/C. BY WEIGHT, IN SPARES.

670 BOMBERS

438 FIGHTERS

25 TRAINERS

CUMULATIVE AIRCRAFT

NUMBER OF AIRCRAFT

COMPLETED A/C
CUMULATIVE TOTAL

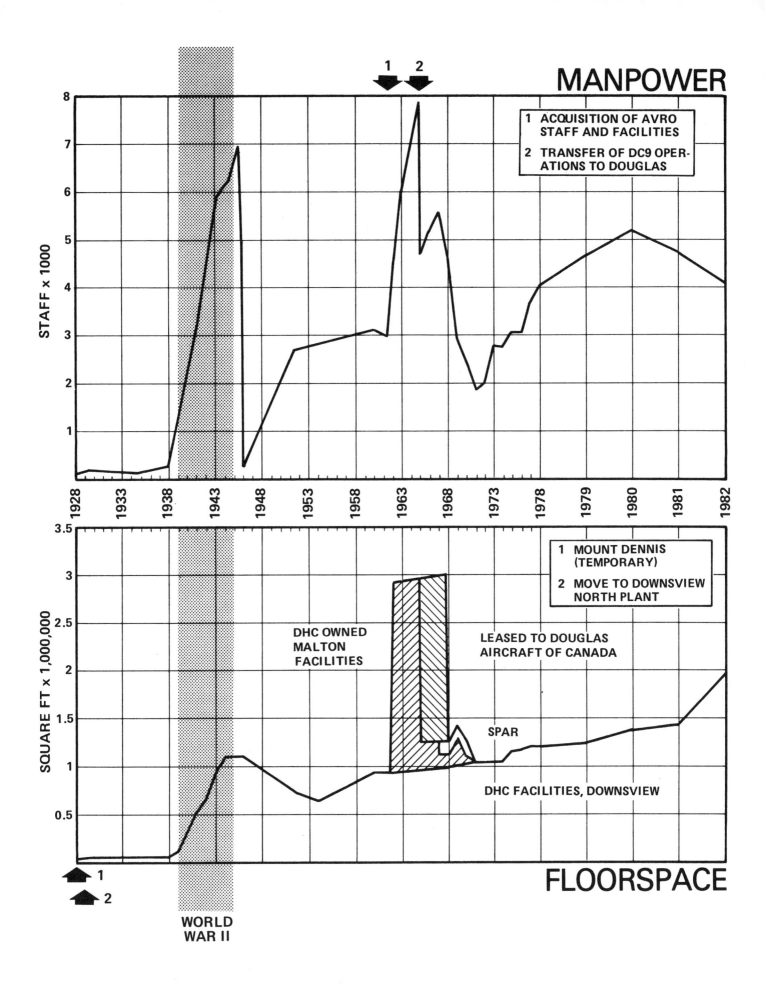

MANPOWER

STAFF x 1000

8
7
6
5
4
3
2
1

1 ACQUISITION OF AVRO
   STAFF AND FACILITIES

2 TRANSFER OF DC9 OPER-
   ATIONS TO DOUGLAS

1928 1933 1938 1943 1948 1953 1958 1963 1968 1973 1978 1979 1980 1981 1982

SQUARE FT x 1,000,000

3.5
3
2.5
2
1.5
1
0.5

1 MOUNT DENNIS
   (TEMPORARY)

2 MOVE TO DOWNSVIEW
   NORTH PLANT

DHC OWNED
MALTON
FACILITIES

LEASED TO DOUGLAS
AIRCRAFT OF CANADA

SPAR

DHC FACILITIES, DOWNSVIEW

1

2

FLOORSPACE

WORLD
WAR II

245

In the span of 54 years, de Havilland Canada has progressed from the small shop on Sheppard Avenue shown above to the extensive complex seen below. In 1929 the selection of a plant site in the open fields of Downsview with a railway siding proved ideal for the expansion that followed during the war. The present south plant was enlarged during 1981-82 to a total of 1,814,715 square feet. (DHC)

De Havilland Canada Directors

The company was incorporated under section 118 of the Ontario Companies Act March 13, 1929. Authorized share capital included 25,000 Class "A" and 5000 Class "B" shares plus 5000 cumulative redeemable preference shares at $100 per share. The parent company maintained control with 700 preference, along with 12,996 Class "A" and 5000 Class "B" shares. Other holders of Class "A" were: W.R.P. Parker, 2699; R.A. Loader, 449; V.S. Bennett, 200; J.H. Black, 499; and W. Zimmerman, 8149. A brokerage company, K.F. McLaren and Company Limited, took 2300 of the preference shares on the first day they were offered. There were minority shareholders until the Canadian government took over the company in 1974.

Name	Elected	Retired
Provisional Directors Elected March 13, 1929		
A.J. Thompson		
R.A. Loader		
L.E. Blackwell		
K.D. Haywood		
W. Zimmerman		
G.J. Mickleborough		
Electa Coates		
Gertrude V. Lyons		
W.R.P. Parker	Mar. 13, 1929	Jan. 13, 1934
J.H. Black	Mar. 13, 1929	Jan. 19, 1934
Sir G. de Havilland	Mar. 27, 1929	May 20, 1965
F.E.N. St. Barbe	Mar. 27, 1929	May 03, 1966
C.C. Walker	Mar. 27, 1929	Jan. 09, 1936
F.L. Trethewey	Jan. 4, 1930	Oct. 18, 1939
L.E. Blackwell	Jan. 4, 1930	Feb. 06, 1933
A.S. Butler	Mar. 27, 1930	Jun. 29, 1950
L.C.L. Murray	Dec. 01, 1933	Feb. 10, 1937
A.H.K. Russell	Jan. 29, 1934	Feb. 10, 1937
W.M. Archibald	Jan. 29, 1934	Nov. 11, 1949
R.A. Laidlaw	Jan. 29, 1934	Feb. 14, 1945
G.S. O'Brian	Feb. 07, 1935	Oct. 18, 1939
G.J. Mickleborough	Jan. 09, 1936	Dec. 23, 1940
P.C. Garratt	July 01, 1936	Apr. 06, 1971
C.W.F. Burns	Feb. 10, 1937	Aug. 21, 1941
J. Grant Glassco	Feb. 02, 1940	May 06, 1940
C.C. Walker	Feb. 02, 1940	Apr. 04, 1952
Bethune L. Smith	Nov. 15, 1940	Feb. 14, 1945
J.D. Woods	Dec. 23, 1940	Feb. 23, 1945
L.C.L. Murray	Jan. 26, 1942	Jan. 30, 1945
G.J. Mickleborough	Sep. 27, 1945	Jul. 29, 1965
W.D. Hunter	Jun. 13, 1945	Feb. 02, 1961
H.R. Smyth	Jun. 13, 1946	Jun. 30, 1949
C.H. Dickins	Jun. 12, 1947	May 09, 1967
W.E. Nixon	Jan. 27, 1950	Jun. 30, 1959
R.E. Bishop	Jan. 27, 1950	Nov. 30, 1950
R. Bannock	Jul. 11, 1950	Jan. 31, 1968
W.W. Parry	Dec. 18, 1950	May 03, 1966
D.G. Simpson	Apr. 04, 1952	Jan. 21, 1954

Name	Elected	Retired
A.S. Kennedy	Jan. 21, 1954	May 27, 1964
Sir A.F. Burke	Jun. 30, 1959	May 02, 1963
F.A. Stanley	Feb. 06, 1961	Dec. 04, 1970
T.J. Emmert	Aug. 16, 1962	Feb. 01, 1968
N.E. Rowe	Aug. 16, 1962	Dec. 31, 1966
Dr. O.M. Solandt	May 02, 1963	Dec. 31, 1966
Sir Arnold Hall	May 27, 1964	May 03, 1966
W.B. Boggs	Jul. 29, 1965	Apr. 29, 1970
D.B. Annan	Jul. 29, 1965	Nov. 26, 1976
Sir Roy Dobson	May 03, 1966	Sept. 26, 1967
A.A. Bailie	May 03, 1966	Feb. 01, 1968
A.J. MacIntosh, QC	May 03, 1966	Jun. 26, 1974
A.S. Kennedy	Feb. 01, 1968	Jun. 26, 1974
Sir H. Broadhurst	Feb. 01, 1968	Jun. 26, 1974
B.B. Bundesman	Apr. 29, 1970	Jan. 10, 1976
D.N. Kendall	Sep. 20, 1970	
D.L. Buchanan	May 14, 1970	Jul. 11, 1975
W.T. Heaslip	May 14, 1970	Nov. 26, 1976
S.B. Kerr	May 27, 1971	Nov. 26, 1976
F.A. Johnson	Mar. 01, 1974	Jul. 10, 1976
R.M. Barford	Jun. 26, 1974	May 01, 1976
J.F. Grandy	Jun. 26, 1974	Sep. 19, 1975
Dr. J.H. Smith	Jun. 26, 1974	Mar. 31, 1978
R. Bannock	Jul. 11, 1975	Jul. 14, 1978
O.G. Stoner	Sep. 17, 1975	Dec. 14, 1976
T.M. Burns	Mar. 19, 1976	Dec. 30, 1977
J.A. Timmins	May 14, 1976	Nov. 26, 1976
D.G.A. McLean	Nov. 26, 1976	Dec. 31, 1980
P. Genest	Nov. 26, 1976	
J.W. McLoughlan	Nov. 26, 1976	
G.F. Osbaldeston	Feb. 18, 1977	Nov. 12, 1979
A.M. Guérin	Feb. 24, 1978	Sep. 10, 1981
J.W. Sandford	Jul. 14, 1978	
R.M. Barford	Dec. 08, 1980	
J.E. Carstairs	Nov. 10, 1980	
B.J. Danson	Nov. 02, 1981	
S.N. Filer	Nov. 10, 1980	
R. Garneau	Nov. 10, 1980	
J.I. Bell	Feb. 07, 1983	

Recognition at de Havilland Canada

Trans Canada (McKee) Trophy	P.C. Garratt	1951 & 1965	**J.A.D. McCurdy Award**	R.D. Hiscocks	1954
	R.H. Fowler	1974		F.H. Buller	1971
	D.C. Fairbanks	1975		D.C. Whittley	1973
	D.H. Rogers	1982		J.P. Uffen	1982
Prior McKee winners with DHC	C.H. Dickins	1928	**Officer, Order of Canada**	P.C. Garratt	1967
	W.M. Archibald	1935		C.H. Dickins	1968
	R.T. Heaslip	1956		R.H. Fowler	1975
Canada's Aviation Hall of Fame	P.C. Garratt	1973			
	C.H. Dickins	1973			
	W.M. Archibald	1973			
	R.T. Heaslip	1973			
	R.H. Fowler	1979			
	R. Bannock	1983			

DH Canada Production Highlights to January 1983

Type	Test Flight (Canadian)	Crew	First Delivery	Total Production	Chief Customer	Remarks
DH.82 A&C Tiger Moth	Dec. 21, 1937	P.C. Garratt	Jan. 18, 1938	1548*	RCAF	136 with Menasco D4 engine
Avro Anson Mk.II	Sept. 21, 1941	R. Spradbrow	Oct. 24, 1941	375	RCAF	Jacobs L-6MB engine
D.H.98 Mosquito	Sept. 23, 1942	R. Spradbrow F. Burrell	Dec. 30, 1942	1133	RAF-RCAF	9 variants in Canada
D.H.83C Fox Moth	Dec. 9, 1945	G. Turner	Jan. 12, 1946	53	36 Canadian sales. 16 world sales	One assembled by Leavens Bros. from spares
DHC-1 Chipmunk	May 22, 1946	P. Fillingham	Jan. 23, 1947	217 Canada**	RCAF	First DHC design manufactured under licence
DHC-2 Mk.I Beaver	Aug. 16, 1947	R. Bannock	Apr. 26, 1948	1631	U.S. Army & Air Force	Civil orders to 62 countries
DHC-3 Otter	Dec. 12, 1951	G. Neal	Nov. 6, 1952	466	200 to U.S. Army & Navy	Used as test bed for 2 PT6A Engines
DHC-2Mk.II Beaver	Mar. 10, 1953	G. Neal	June 13. 1953	1	DH England	Alvis Leonides engine. No further production.
Grumman CS2F-1 Tracker	May 31, 1956	G. Neal A. Verrico	Oct. 12, 1956	100	RCN	Last delivery Oct. 27, 1960
DHC-4 Caribou	July 30, 1958	G. Neal D. Fairbanks H. Brinkman	Sept. 5, 1959	307	165 to U.S. Army	Test bed for GE T64 engine
DHC-2 Mk.III Turbo Beaver	Dec. 31, 1963	R. Fowler J. Aitken	Jan. 25, 1965	60	Ont. Min. of Natural Resources	Production ended June 1968
DHC-5 Buffalo	Apr. 9, 1964	R. Fowler A. Saunders R. Dingle	Apr. 22, 1965	121	Brazil Air Force	In production
DHC-6 Twin Otter	May 20, 1965	R. Fowler A. Saunders B. Hubbard	July 18, 1966	802	Short-haul airlines	In production
DHC-7 Dash 7	Mar. 27, 1975	R. Fowler A. Saunders R. Dingle J. Aitken	Nov. 21, 1977	88	Short-haul airlines	In production
DHC-8 Dash 8	June 20, 1983	R. Fowler A. Saunders D. Band C. Pyne				

* + 200 fuselages for DH England
**Manufactured under licence   1000 — England, 60 — Portugal

Cartoon by Wren from the *Aeroplane*, April 17, 1953.

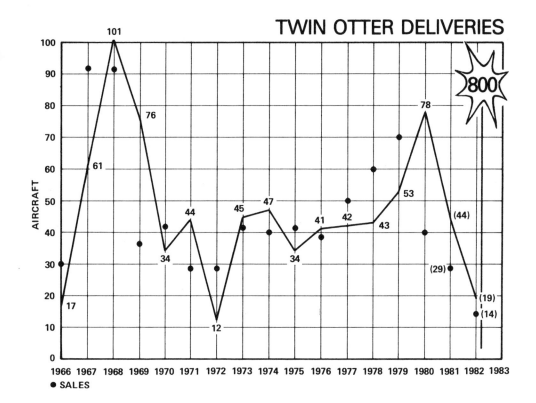

TWIN OTTER DELIVERIES

AIRCRAFT

101 · 800 · 78 · 76 · 70 · 61 · 60 · 53 · 47 · 45 · 44 · 43 · 42 · 41 · 34 · 34 · 30 · 29 · 17 · 14 · 19 · 12

1966 1967 1968 1969 1970 1971 1972 1973 1974 1975 1976 1977 1978 1979 1980 1981 1982 1983

● SALES

Bibliography

Books

Bishop, Edward: *The Wooden Wonder, The Story of the de Havilland Mosquito.* Max Parrish, London, 1959.

Clarkson, R.M.: *The First de Havilland Memorial Lecture.* Royal Aeronautical Society, February 1967.

De Havilland, Sir Geoffrey: *Sky Fever.* Hamish Hamilton, London, 1961.

Ellis, John R.: *The Canadian Civil Aircraft Register, 1920-1945.* Canadian Aviation Historical Society.

Fuller, G.A., Griffin, J. & Molson, K.M.: *125 Years of Canadian Aeronautics — A Chronology — 1840-1965.* Canadian Aviation Historical Society, 1983.

Griffin, J.A.: *Canadian Military Aircraft, Serials & Photographs, 1920-68.* Queen's Printer, Ottawa, 1969.

Hall, H. Duncan: *History of the Second World War — North American Supply.* H.M. Stationery Office, London, 1955.

Hayes, Karl E.: *De Havilland Canada — DHC-3 Otter.* Irish Air Letter, Dublin, 1982.

Holliday, Joe: *Mosquito.* Doubleday, Toronto, 1970.

Jackson, A.J.: *De Havilland Aircraft since 1909.* Putnam, London, 1978.

Milberry, Larry: *The Avro CF-100.* Canav Books, Toronto, 1981.

Molson, K.M.: *Pioneering in Canadian Air Transport.* D.W. Friesen, Altona, Man., 1974.

Molson, K.M. & Taylor, H.A.: *Canadian Aircraft since 1909.* Putnam, London, 1982.

Sharp, C. Martin & Bowyer, J.F.: *Mosquito.* Faber and Faber, London, 1967, 1971.

Sharp, C. Martin: *D.H. An Outline of de Havilland History.* Faber and Faber, London, 1960.

Sutherland, Alice Gibson: *Canada's Aviation Pioneers.* McGraw-Hill Ryerson, Toronto, 1978.

West, Bruce: *The Firebirds.* Ontario Ministry of Natural Resources, 1974.

Periodicals and Miscellaneous Sources

Bakke, Oscar: "STOL Operation in the City Centre." Federal Aviation Agency, 1965.

Bell, Dana: "American Mosquitos." *Flight Plan,* Vol. 3, No. 2, International Plastic Modelers Society.

Long, C.D.: "The de Havilland DH90 Dragonfly." *Canadian Aviation Historical Society Journal,* Summer 1969.

Long, C.D.: "The Tiger Moth in Canada, 1931-1969." *Canadian Aviation Historical Society Journal,* Winter 1969.

McIntyre, M.L.: "CAF Mosquito Register." *Canadian Aviation Historical Society Journal,* Vol. 17, No. 2, Summer 1979.

Postan, M.M., Hay, D. & Scott, J.D.: "Design and Development of Weapons." H.M. Stationery Office, London, 1964.

Sandford, John W.: "De Havilland — The Changes Ahead." DH Canada, 1979.

Sharp, C. Martin: "A Brief Review of de Havilland Military Aeroplanes." *Aerospace,* June/July, 1977

Stewart, George: "Mosquitos Over the Yangtse." *Canadian Aviation Historical Journal,* Vol. 17, No. 2, Summer 1979.

Whittley, Donald C.: "The Augmentor Wing — Powered-Lift STOL, A Proven Concept." *Interavia,* Vol. XXIX, No. 2, February 1974.

"40 Year Bulletin." Association of Polish Engineers in Canada, 1981.

"Canadian Aircraft Production WW II." Department of Reconstruction & Supply, Quarterly Reports.

Airborne
Aircraft & Airport
Air Pictorial
The Canadian Aircraft Operator
Canadian Air Review
Canadian Aviation
The de Havilland Gazette

Index

250